PLATE V.

THE TREASURY CLOSE TO THE LIONS' GATE. Excavated by Mrs. SCHLIEMANN. *Frontispiece.*

MYCENÆ;

A NARRATIVE OF RESEARCHES AND DISCOVERIES
AT MYCENÆ AND TIRYNS.

By DR. HENRY SCHLIEMANN,

CITIZEN OF THE UNITED STATES OF AMERICA :

AUTHOR OF 'TROY AND ITS REMAINS,' 'ITHAQUE, LE PÉLOPONNÈSE ET TROIE,'
AND 'LA CHINE ET LE JAPON.'

THE PREFACE

By THE RIGHT HON. W. E. GLADSTONE, M.P.

MAPS, PLANS, AND MORE THAN 700 OTHER ILLUSTRATIONS.

A NEW EDITION, WITH IMPORTANT ADDITIONS AND NEW PLATES.

Benjamin Blom
New York

First Published 1880
Reissued 1967 by Benjamin Blom, Inc. New York 10452
Library of Congress Catalog Card No. 66-49424

45,839

Printed in U.S.A. by
NOBLE OFFSET PRINTERS, INC.
NEW YORK 3, N. Y.

𝔇𝔢𝔡𝔦𝔠𝔞𝔱𝔢𝔡

TO

HIS MAJESTY DOM PEDRO II..

EMPEROR OF BRAZIL,

WITH THE PROFOUND RESPECT OF

THE AUTHOR.

’Επὶ δ’ ἐγδούπησαν ’Αθηναίη τε καὶ ῞Ηρη
Τιμῶσαι βασιλῆα πολυχρύσοιο Μυκήνης.
Hom. Il. XI. 45, 46.

Πρὸς ἡμῶν
κάππεσεν, κάτθανε, ἡμεῖς καὶ καταθάψομεν
οὐχ ὑπὸ κλαυθμῶν τῶν ἐξ οἴκων.
Æsch. Agam. 1552-1554,

῍Ω τοῦ στρατηγήσαντος ἐν Τροίᾳ ποτὲ
’Αγαμέμνονος παῖ, νῦν ἐκεῖν’ ἔξεστί σοι
παρόντι λεύσσειν. ὧν πρόθυμος ἦσθ’ ἀεί.
Τὸ γὰρ παλαιὸν ῎Αργος οὑπόθεις τόδε,
τῆς οἰστροπλῆγος ἄλσος ’Ινάχου κόρης·
αὕτη δ’, ’Ορέστα, τοῦ λυκοκτόνου θεοῦ
’Αγορὰ Λύκειος· οὑξ ἀριστερᾶς δ’ ὅδε
῞Ηρας ὁ κλεινὸς ναός· οἷ δ’ ἱκάνομεν,
φάσκειν Μυκήνας τὰς πολυχρύσους ὁρᾶν·
πολύφθορόν τε δῶμα Πελοπιδῶν τόδε.
Sophocles, Electra, 1-10.

PREFACE.

It has been with much reluctance that, at the persevering request of Dr. Schliemann, I have undertaken to write a Preface to his Mycenean volume. I have managed perhaps, though with long intermissions of the pleasant labour, to maintain a tolerable acquaintance with the text of Homer; and the due establishment of the points of contact between that text and the remains from Mycenæ is without question one of the essential aims, to which comment on this work requires to be addressed. But I have a horror of all specialism which travels beyond its proper province; and in this matter I am at best no more than a specialist, probably, too, not one of very high pretensions. I have not that practised skill, that comprehensive outlook over the whole field of Hellenic, and other than Hellenic archæology, which has conferred upon Mr. Newton his well-earned fame. The just conclusion from these premises appears to be, that I ought to have declined a charge *quod ferre recusent humeri.** But there was, in ancient poetry, a Destiny stronger than the will of gods. To me, on this occasion, Dr. Schliemann is the vicegerent and organ of that Destiny. In view of the splendid services which he has conferred upon classical science, a power, that thrusts argument out of court, brings me to perceive, that I cannot but accede to his desire. I have however given the reader fair warning where and why he should be on his guard:

* Hor. *A. P.* 39

and I shall make all the use I can of the landmarks laid
down in the report which Mr. Newton, after an ocular
inspection of these remains, published in the *Times* of
April 20, 1877; and of the valuable papers of Mr.
Gardner in the *Academy* (April 21 and 28). I believe that
the interest, excited by Dr. Schliemann's discoveries, has
been by no means confined to classical scholars. I shall
therefore endeavour to be as little technical as possible, and
to write, so far as may be, for a circle wider than that of
the persons among us who are acquainted with the Greek
tongue.

When the disclosures at Tiryns and Mycenæ were an-
nounced in England, my own first impression was that of a
strangely bewildered admiration, combined with a prepon-
derance of sceptical against believing tendencies, in regard
to the capital and dominating subject of the Tombs in the
Agora. I am bound to say, that reflection and a fuller knowledge have nearly turned the scales the other way. There
are indeed, not only gaps to be supplied, but difficulties to be
confronted, and to be explained; or to be left over for future
explanation. Yet the balance, I will not say of evidence,
but of rational presumption, seems as though it might
ultimately lean towards the belief that this eminent
explorer has exposed to the light of day, after 3000 years,
the memorials and remains of Agamemnon and his companions in the Return from Troy. But let us endeavour
to feel our way by degrees up to this question, gradually
and with care, as a good general makes his approaches to a
formidable fortress.

I find, upon perusing the volume of Dr. Schliemann,
that the items of evidence, which connect his discoveries
generally with the Homeric Poems, are more numerous, than I had surmised from the brief outline, with
which he favoured us upon his visit to England in the
spring.

1. He presents to us the rude figures of cows; and

upon a signet ring (No. 531) and elsewhere, cow-heads not to be mistaken. He then points to the traditional worship, from the first, of Hera in Argolis; and he asks us to connect these facts with the use of *Boöpis* (cow-eyed) as a staple epithet of this goddess in the Poems; and he might add, with her special guardianship of Agamemnon in his interests and his personal safety (*Il.* I. 194–222).

This appears to me a reasonable demand. We know that upon some of the Egyptian monuments the goddess Isis, mated with Osiris, is represented in human figure with the cow's head. This was a mode of exhibiting deity congenial to the spirit of an Egyptian immigration,* such as might, compatibly with the text of Homer, have taken place some generations before the *Troïca*. But it was also a mode against which the whole spirit of Hellenism, according to the authentic type of that spirit supplied in the Poems, utterly revolted. We find there a Hera, who wore, so to speak, the mantle of Isis, besides carrying the spoils of one or more personages enrolled in the Golden Book of the old Pelasgian dynasties. Nothing could be more natural than a decapitation of the Egyptian Isis, not penally but for her honour She might consequently appear with the human head; but, not to break sharply with the traditions of the people, the cow-head, and even the cow figure, might nevertheless be retained as symbols of religion. And the great Poet, who invariably keeps these symbols so to speak at arms' length, in order that he may prevent their disparaging the creed of which he was the great doctor, might nevertheless select from the bovine features that one which was suited to his purpose, and give to his Hera, who was never a very intellectual

---

* Since this Preface was put in type, the fragments of an ostrich egg, originally mistaken for an alabaster vase, have been tested and verified. This object seems to afford a new indication of prehistoric relations between Mycenæ and Egypt.

deity, the large tranquil eye of the cow. The use of the epithet for Hera in Homer is not, indeed, exclusive, and I admit that he may have inherited that use. But, though not exclusive, it is very special, and this speciality is enough to give a sensible support to the doctrine of our famous explorer.

2. The buildings improperly called Cyclopean, and still more improperly endowed with the alternative name of Pelasgian, have long been known, more or less, to exist in Argolis; but Dr. Schliemann has thrown some light on what I may perhaps be allowed to call their diversity of style. He admits three forms found in this kind of building   I have objected to the current names, the first because it does not inform : the second because it misleads, for these buildings have no true connection with the Pelasgian tribes. What they indicate is the handiwork of the great constructing race or races, made up of several elements, who migrated into Greece, and elsewhere on the Mediterranean, from the south and east, and who exhibit an usual, though perhaps not an invariable connection with the Poseidon-worship, a worship, with which the Cyclopean name is, through the Odyssey, perceptibly associated, and which is one of the main keys, as I have long been persuaded, wherewith in time to unlock, for Hellenic and Homeric regions, the secrets of antiquity. The walls of Troy were built by Poseidon; that is, by a race who practised the worship of the god   How far those walls conform to any of the minuter points of the descriptions of 'Cyclopean' architecture by Dr. Schliemann, (pp. 42, 123), I cannot say. But if he is right, as seems probable, in placing Troy at Hissarlık, it is important to notice that this work of Poseidon had a solidity, which bore it unharmed through the rage of fire, and kept it well together amidst all the changes which have buried it in a hill of rubbish and promiscuous remains. And of course the modes, used by the very same race in the

business of building, could not but vary much with the circumstances of each case, and especially with the material at hand. I am tempted, at least until a better name can be found, to call this manner of building Posejdonian ; at any rate, whatever it be called, to note it as a point of correspondence between the Poems and the discoveries, admitting at the same time that the matter is not sufficiently developed to warrant me in laying upon it any considerable stress.

3. The beehive-like building, which is rather loosely called the Treasury of Atreus, presents to us over the doorway (p. 43) two enormous slabs, one of them supposed to weigh from 130 to 135 tons. I only refer to them for the sake of reminding the reader that, as I think, we must be prepared, in this and other matters, freely to recognise the hand of the foreigner at work ; who brought with him into Greece attainments, not to be despised, of material civilisation. More pointedly I wish to observe that in the interior of the Treasury, from the fourth course upwards, there are visible (p. 44) in each stone two bored holes, and in many of them the remains of ' bronze ' nails still existing. Similar holes, it appears, are found (p. 45) in the Treasury of Minyas at Orchomenos. The purpose of these nails, says our author, could only be to attach to the wall what in one place he calls the bronze, and in another the brazen plates, with which the whole interior was once decorated. On the secondary question, what was the exact material employed, let me here observe that of brass those ages knew nothing, and that bronze, particularly in that stage of material development, was wholly unsuited for sheeting. But, as to the structural point, we have here a remarkable point of contact with the Homeric text. For in the palace of Alkinoös, king of the Phaiakes, a splendour as of sun or moon dazzled the eye, for the walls were of *chalkos* (*Od.* VII. 86, cited p. 44), which I hope

I may now boldly translate copper: a metal unlike bronze
(a) in being readily malleable, (b) in being throughout the
Poems most usually lustrous, a character I do not suppose
we should assign to bronze. On the other hand, the
comparative softness of copper was not well suited for the
nails, so bronze might very well be employed. Nor does
this conjunction of the two metals, pure and mixed, in
the same work, carry us away from the text of Homer:
for his wall-sheets of copper in Scheriè were crowned with
a cornice of his dark *kuanos*, which I take to be bronze.
This copper sheeting is a feature of the supreme Olympian Palace (*Il.* I. 426, *Od.* VIII. 321), built by Hephaistos
of the skilful mind. I think I could show that it also
adorned the palaces of Menelaos and Odysseus, and could
point out, moreover, why all this is in accordance with the
distinctly foreign and eastern character of the embellish-
ment: but an exhibition of the evidence would lead me
into too great length; and I note only for the present
purpose the remarkable correspondence of the archæology
with the Poems.

4. Passing from architectural to moveable objects, I
observe that Dr. Schliemann found both knives and keys
of iron in Mycenæ, but that from their form he assigns
them to a later and strictly historic period. Old Mycenæ,
therefore, in accordance with Hissarlik, has afforded us, up
to the present time, no remains of this metal. In the
Poems it is freely mentioned, but as a rare and valuable
substance, used where great hardness was required, and for
objects comparatively small and portable; except, indeed,
in the case of the Gates of Tartaros (*Il.* VIII 15), where
the Poet could dispose of as much material as he pleased.
The aggregate quantity, then, was small; and the instruments were likely to be carried away on the abandonment or
destruction of a city. Its absence may therefore be
accounted for, in part by its value, but also, and more

especially, because it so readily corrodes.* Therefore, although we cannot here establish a positive correspondence, neither have we any occasion to admit a discrepancy.

5. Neither need we, I think, suppose any variance between the chariot, as our author found it on the second tombstone of the Acropolis (p. 84), and the Homeric picture. True, he finds a wheel of four spokes, and the Olympian car of Hera had eight (*Il.* V. 723); but this diversity of structure is probably introduced, like the diversity of material, by way of divine distinction, and to show the superior elaboration and strength of the vehicle.*

6. We have at Mycenæ the *Agora*, or place of Assembly, in full agreement with the Poems on the two points, first of its circular form (pp. 338, 339), and secondly of the smoothed horizontal slabs, bounding the circle, on which the Elders sate. I do not dilate upon these, as they are fully noticed in the text: but I shall return to the subject, in connection with the situation chosen for the tombs, and the inferences which are to be drawn from this important circumstance.

I will now hazard, before proceeding further with my list, one or two general remarks on the works of art and ornament, referring again to the reports of Mr. Newton and Mr. Gardner, as the most trustworthy comment on the text of our author concerning them.

First, I have to offer some reflections on the general

---

* In the remarkable Museum of the Royal Academy of Ireland are two swords referred to the Danish period, which were taken out of a bed of mud. After a repose of perhaps a thousand years, they do not exhibit corrosion to the common eye. But the case is considered exceptional, and probably due to some peculiar ingredient in the moisture.

† I do not think it proved that, as Schliemann seems to convey (p. 84), the chariot-box was removed and fastened on each occasion of using it. The passages in *Il.* XXIV. 190 and 267 refer to the *peirins* of the waggon. In *Od.* XV. 131, it is simply mentioned as a portion of the carriage, with no reference to detaching it.

character of the discoveries, and on its relation to the state
of Art exhibited in the Poems. It seems reasonable
to believe, especially after what has been shown by
Mr. Gardner respecting the four tombstones, that they
constituted the contemporary seal of a great deposit. It
results, I think, from the evidence before us that it is
impossible to reduce to one school or style or stage of
art the whole of the objects exhumed. But on this I
would observe first that, although they were simultaneously deposited in honour of the dead, they might have
been the productions of more than one generation :
secondly, that not only are we not required, but, in so
far as we draw light from the Homeric Poems, we are
hardly permitted, to refer them collectively to a domestic
origin.

I gather from Mr. Gardner's report that the Art
exhibited on the Pottery is more uniformly backward,
than that exhibited by the works of metal. But this
pottery, which was, whether wheel made or hand-made, of
an early stage in the manufacture, was far more likely to be
domestic ; while the works in the precious metals might be
imported. Or they might be the productions of foreign
artists, attracted to the Court of Agamemnon ; in the
same manner as we find that Daidalos, whose name, however mythical, represents a foreign influence, executed in
Crete, for Ariadne, the representation of a dance in
metal.

The discovery, or the inspection, of the works must
without doubt in the first instance suggest a reference of
them to a local school of goldsmiths. But, considering
the numerous points of contact between the discoveries
and the Homeric Poems, it is important to know whether,
and how far, they really favour such a supposition. This is
not the place for an examination in detail of all the works
of Art mentioned by Homer. I believe there is no one
of them, of which the purely Greek origin can be esta-

blished by proof from the text, while the manufacture
abroad and importation are frequently mentioned.   At the
same time, there are some considerations which tend to
show that, if there were local workmen in Greece capable
of producing objects such as those now exhumed, it is at
Mycenæ that we should expect to find them.   First, on
account of the wealth of the city, and of its position as the
capital of the country.   Secondly, on account of the
wealth of Agamemnon personally, and his acquisitiveness
if not his avarice, which made him eager to spoil those
whom his spear had slain, and which is the subject of
varied allusions in the *Iliad*.   It must be remembered that
in those days works of art were not merely ornamental,
but were a favourite form, as their name (*keimelia*) shows,
of stored wealth: and of these, even in Troas, Agamemnon possessed many (*Il*. IX. 330).   Thirdly, an indication, perhaps, more significant, may be drawn from the
remarkable passage in the Eleventh Book (15–46), which
describes the arming of Agamemnon for the field.   The
first portion of the armour, that attracts observation, is an
elaborately wrought breast-plate, which had come from
Cyprus, a seat of Phœnician settlement.   We next come
to the sword, which I shall presently describe.   This is
followed by the shield, adorned with many bosses of
metal, but also carrying a representation of the Gorgon
with the heads or figures of Fear and Panic.   This shield
must be considered as a work of art; and the same may
be said of its band or strap, which carried the figure of a
three-headed snake.   There is nothing said to connect
these works with foreign manufacture.   The family of
Agamemnon was of a foreign origin comparatively recent;
but it may remain an open question, whether these arms
are presumptively referable, or not, to a domestic manufacture.

The deposits appear, again, to differ extremely in point of
merit.   I set aside the objects directly symbolical, because,

where religion, or idolatry, is in question, excellence in
workmanship becomes secondary, or even ceases to be
desired.   Among the other objects, I gather that none
exhibit a very high order of technical qualities.   But, if
we may rely upon photographic representation, they surely
exhibit lively and forcible movement, as well as many
of the elements of nobleness, beauty, and fertility of
invention ; particularly in ornamentation, as distinguished
from the representation of life, either animal or vegetable.
Some of this diversity may be due to difference of date ;
some, perhaps much, to the superiority of the immigrant
hand, or of imported works.   That there were foreigners
resident in Greece at the time of the *Troïca*, we have every
reason to infer from one conspicuous case, that of Eche-
polos, a son of Anchises, who was allowed to present the
mare Aithè to Agamemnon, as the price of his exemption
(*Il.* XXIII. 296) from service against Troy.   If there be
anywhere in the Poems an account of a work of art produced
in Greece or by a Greek, it is the bedstead of Odysseus,*
wrought by himself (*Od.* XXIII. 190-201) ; and to him,
after a good deal of consideration, I am inclined to ascribe
a close connection with the immigrant or Phœnician stock ;
though this representation might also be due to his unequalled versatility and universality of accomplishment.
There was indeed a *Chrusochoös* or gold-plater at the Court
of Nestor (*Od.* III. 425) ; but the very same man goes by
the name of *Chalkeus* or coppersmith (*Ibid.* III. 432). And it
would even seem that working in metals cannot have been
a principal or prominent employment in an Achaian community, for no such person is named in the remarkable

---

* Ikmalios is mentioned in *Od.* XIX. 57 as the maker of a chair
inlaid with ivory and silver.   I cannot doubt that this was foreign, since
it is marked as the work of a former age : ἥν ποτε τέκτων ποίησ᾽ Ἰκμάλιος,
" which erewhile Ikmalion with cunning hand had made " (Norgate).
' Erewhile ' will not be found in Todd or Latham : but it is in Shakespeare, and the Dictionary of Worcester and Webster contains it.

passage of the Odyssey (XVII. 384) which supplies a sort of list, and where the wood-worker, or carpenter, appears.

The list of these objects, and of their ornaments, is on the whole richer and more diversified than the Poems, with the exception of the famous Shield of Achilles, would have led us to expect. Possibly a knowledge of the Mycenean treasures may have prompted or aided a vigorous imagination, in that wonderful anticipation of excellences which had not been realized in practice. The most remarkable feature, I think, of all Homer's delineations of art is the force and reality with which he confers animation on things inanimate. And perhaps the eye may be struck, in examining Schliemann's illustrations, with the vigour of life and motion which asserts itself in many of the Mycenean works, where the delineation is technically most imperfect. But we cannot compare the text with these remains alone; we are bound also to avail ourselves of such light as can be had from Hissarlik, what ever its effect upon our prepossessions or our arguments. Now I, for one, am struck with the wealth of Mycenæ, and the comparative poverty of what is probably Troy. I do not mean merely as to the small number of valuable remains, for this may be due to chance; though, indeed, fortune, for once renouncing her caprice, seems in both cases to have obeyed the dictates of archæological justice, and to have treated Dr. and Mrs. Schliemann as her favourite children. But I mean that there is far less of *luxe* in the ornamentation of the works at Hissarlik; I might, perhaps, say no representation at all of life, except in the rudest and most barbarous form. There seem to be very good forms in the gold and silver objects of Hissarlik, but always associated with plain work; no animal or even vegetable representation calling for notice from the present point of view, none of the *repoussé* work, nothing resembling the (apparently) beautiful cylinder (p. 287), or the elaborate rings photographed in this volume How are we to account for this?

And does an argument hence arise, that the Hissarlik remains belong to a period different from, and anterior to, that which produced the works at Mycenæ? That the adverse case may be made as strong as possible, let it be borne in mind that while Homer indicates Orchomenos, and above all Egyptian Thebes, as the wealthiest cities of his little world, he seems designedly to assign the very same stage of opulence to Troy, which he gives to Mycenæ; for he describes by one and the same epithet, *poluchrusos*, which means gold-abounding, these two cities and these two alone. Troy has it in *Il.* XVIII. 289. For Mycenæ it was almost a formula; see *Il.* VII. 180, XI. 46; *Od.* III. 305.

We have now before us, as is not improbable, the choicest samples of what the two cities had to boast of; and the question is, can we account for the difference in opulence, and stage of art, between them? I conceive that we can, at least in a considerable degree; but it is only by that acknowledgment, which some are still indisposed to make, of the broad vein of historic reality, that runs through the delineations of the *Iliad* and *Odyssey*.

Three passages of the *Iliad*, in particular, convey to us that the city of Troy was suffering great impoverishment by the War. Indeed, if there be a grain of fact in the tale, it could not be otherwise. For the means of resisting the truly national attack of the Achaians, she was dependent neither on a good cause, nor on a soldiery commensurate with theirs. She had to seek strength from without; first from the grudging support of Dardania, secondly from the neighbouring tribes both of Europe and of Asia. It might even be inferred from the text that nine-tenths of the fighting power (*Il.* II. 123–33) were other than strictly domestic. But this support from without could only be got by paying for it. Accordingly Hector, in the Seventeenth Book speaks with the authority (220–32) of a general addressing allies, who are duly compensated for their services. So also we know that the great Eurupulos and his Keteians,* or Hittites (*Od.* XI. 520), fall in numbers on the plains of Troy, "serving for gifts." "I wear out the Trojans," says Hector, "with presents and with victualling for you." Again in the Twenty-fourth Book, Achilles, compassionately addressing Priam, says, "We hear that you once were prosperous, and exceeded in wealth, as well as in the number of your sons, all the neighbouring countries" (543–6). The inference is obvious; that at the time, though the city had not been captured, it was becoming comparatively poor. But the most express testimony is that of *Il.* XVIII. 288–92, when Hector stimulates his countrymen to sally out, by reminding them that they are already well-nigh ruined. Once, he says, all men were wont to celebrate the wealth of Troy; "but now the fine valuables have utterly disappeared from our mansions."

νῦν δὲ δὴ ἐξαπόλωλε δόμων κειμήλια καλά·

And, under the wrath of Zeus, multitudes of their possessions had been sent in exchange to Phrygia and Mæonia; in exchange, that is, as I presume, for necessaries. But the great Mycenean deposit, if Schliemann be right in his view, was made before the time of any sack or depopulation of the city. Upon such an issue of life and death, as that offered to the Trojans, the best objects would naturally be parted with, as the most effective for their purpose (see *Il.* XXIV. 234–7); and accordingly, if we are comparing Troy and Mycenæ at all, we are comparing Troy in its exhaustion with Mycenæ in its prosperity.

We have among the remains in the precious metals from Hissarlik, I believe, no representation of an animal, either chased or in the round. But the Poems give us several examples of such works in the possession of Greeks;

---

* 'Homeric Synchronism,' pp. 171 *seq.* I do not here enter on the curious question what is the precise meaning of γυναῖα δῶρα.

though commonly under presumptions of foreign produc
tion, as it would not be difficult to show.

It is true, indeed, that Troy, in immediate contact with
the large fertile districts of Asia Minor, had means of
material growth by land-trade, which Greece, split by
her mountain chains into comparatively narrow tracts of
cultivable soil, did not possess. But it seems likely that
even in those days the maritime commerce, stimulated by
Phœnician ships and settlements, may have compensated,
or more than compensated, for this disadvantage. Of the
trade in metals and in corn, carried on by their race, we
have distinct information in the Poems (*Od.* I. 183–4,
XIV. 333–5). They had, in all likelihood, already been
followed by the Greeks. The voyage of the ship Argo
seems to have been of a mixed character. The ships of
the armament against Troy could hardly have been supplied
by a people, who had not made a substantial beginning
in maritime trade. The navigation of the coasts, without
reference to purposes of war, is evidently a familiar idea in
the *Odyssey.* But, in the *Iliad,* the construction of the
ships of Paris is noted as the remarkable work of a remarkable man (*Il.* V. 59–64) ; nor do we, except in this one
ill-omened case, ever hear of Trojan navigation.

Once more. We are given to understand * that signs
of the art of writing have been discovered at Hissarlik ;
whereas the new volume supplies us with nothing of the
kind for Mycenæ. But nothing, I apprehend, can be
affirmed of its existence either in Greece or Troas during
the Homeric age, except as the secret of a few ; in Greece
it was manifestly exotic, and perhaps it may have been
the same in Troas. As long as the evidence remains in
this state, we cannot infer from it with confidence any
important proposition as to comparative advancement.

I now resume the list of points of contact between the

---

* 'Troy and its Remains,' pp. 369, 371.

Mycenean discoveries and the Poems, by noticing such of them as are found in movables.

1. As the first of these I take the free use of copper for large utensils (pp. 274–277). We have also the analysis supplied by Dr. Percy of a sword and a vase-handle of bronze (pp. 372–5). In my judgment, we have no sign whatever from the Poems of the fusion of metals together as a domestic practice; while we have abundant proof of the importation and foreign production of works of art and implements in bronze. This vase, then, may probably have been foreign. The same is likely with respect to the sword. We know that swords were exported and imported between different countries. Thrace was a seat of manufacture both for fine works of art (*Il.* XXIV. 234) and for weapons (*Il.* XXIII. 808): and we find a sword, "beautiful and long," from Thrace, in the possession of the Trojan Prince Helenos (*Il.* XIII. 577). Moreover, copper was an abundant metal, tin a rare one. Bronze weapons, therefore, must have been expensive. And the swords of bronze found in the tombs, in conjunction with all other costly objects, are just where we should have expected them. Even so at Hissarlik, two battle-axes found in the Treasure, and presumably belonging therefore to distinguished persons, were of bronze.* But axes made of pure copper may be seen in the Museum of the Irish Academy; and the great layer of copper-scoriæ at Hissarlik, without any tin, seems effectually to show that copper was the staple metal of the heroic period, and that our archæologists will have to insert a copper age in their lists, between their age of stone and their age of bronze. If weapons of copper were to be discovered in the tombs at Mycenæ, no circumstance could more enhance the proofs afforded by the Poems of the general use of copper;

---

* 'Troy and its Remains,' p. 361. One of these had only about four per cent. of tin. Could this have been a native admixture?

because the weapons in the tombs are weapons of the persons most likely to be able to command the use of bronze. I hope that the analysis, already begun, will be applied to a much larger number of objects. In the meantime, as to large utensils, I find the discoveries already in close correspondence with the Poems.

2. The most remarkable, perhaps, in themselves, of all the objects discovered at Hissarlik, were the two elaborate head-dresses of gold, which for the first time enabled us to construe, with reasonable confidence, the entire passage in the Iliad (XXII. 468–72), which describes the head-dress cast away by Andromachè in the agony of her grief. The print will not have been forgotten, which exhibits the *plektè anadesmè*.* It was a series of gold plaits, hanging down, over the forehead and the ears, from the broad band (*ampūx*) which ran round the head, and which constituted as it were the base of the ornament. With these objects, and with the Poems, Schliemann associates, incontestably as it would appear, the ornament No. 357 (p. 248); a band or frontlet adorned " with rosettes and crosses. It has two perforations in the rim, a little way from either end, from one of which is still hanging the fragment of a very fine chain." The only variation in the fashion of the thing seems to be, that the plaits have not been continued over the forehead.

3. Hissarlik did nothing for us towards explaining the *kredemnon;* an article of head-dress worn by many or some women of the heroic age, who could not add to it the splendid decorations then reserved for princesses. But the definitions of this commodity are supplied for us by the Poems, piecemeal indeed, yet with adequate clearness. In the first place, it crowned the head like the battlements of a walled city; for the destruction of the walls of Troy is described as the ruin of its sacred *kredemna* (*Il.* XVI. 100).

---

* 'Troy and its Remains,' p. 335.

It was not, however, a metallic or solid object; for the
deified Ino, to save Odysseus from the fury of the storm,
throws to him her own *kredemnon* and bids him bind it
round his chest (*Od.* V 346). It used to be made of
delicate and glossy material (*Od.* I. 334), and was worthy
even to be a marriage gift from Aphroditè to the bride of
Hector (*Il.* XXII. 470). But finally, it had a long wing,
tail, or lappet (I am not skilled or confident in this voca-
bulary), descending from behind, perhaps more than one.
This is shown indirectly, but I think conclusively, by the
information given us in *Od.* VI. 100, that the handmaidens
of Nausicaä, when about to play at ball, first put away their
kredemna, evidently lest the free movement of their arms
should be embarrassed by the long lappets. Again, it is
evident that Penelope, when she used her *kredemna* to
cover her face, brought the lappets round and employed
them as a veil; on any other ground the use of the plural
can hardly be explained (*Od.* I. 334). And now this part
of the prehistoric lady's toilette is as complete as I can
make it from the Poems.

I turn, then, to Dr. Schliemann's volume, and call
attention to the signet ring at p. 354, which, though
apparently not of a high order in art, combines so many
objects of interest. On the extreme left of the picture
stands a child, or small woman, who is picking fruit from
a tree. Behind her head appear to descend long tresses of
hair. What if these should prove on further examination
to be lappets from a head-dress which the head seems to
carry? Passing to the right of the tree, first comes a tall
seated woman in a turban, which carries in front, says our
author, a diadem and behind a "tress of hair" from the
point into which the turban runs. I cannot but suppose
this "tress" to be a lappet of the *kredemnon*. She offers
poppies to another tall woman, again dressed in a turban
running out into a point (p. 356), "from which a long
ornament hangs down on the back," a third time, in all

likelihood, the lappet of the *kredemnon*.   Below her outstretched right arm we have another small figure, probably
of a child, again in a turban, and with " a long tress of
hair, or some ornament, hanging down its back : " yet once
more, I conjecture, the lappet indicated by Homer.   There
is also a fifth : we have still the figure to the right of the
picture (p. 357) ; and she, too, wears a turban terminating in
a point " from which a long band-like ornament hangs
down on her back."   Now let us go aloft ; and we find a
small figure, towards the right of the picture.   This figure
(p. 357) is described by Schliemann as female, from his
observing breasts upon it: and again, " from the back
project the long bands."   Thus, in all the six cases, we
appear to have the same remarkable form described for the
main article of female head-dress, which is also given us by
Homer.

It may, however, be said that the female figures on
this ring are foreign, rather than Hellenic, in their
character and habiliments.   But it happens that the
evidence of the Poems more copiously establishes the use
of the *kredemnon* among foreigners, than in Greece.   We
hear indeed of the *kredemna* of Penelopè ; and Hera,
when about to inveigle Zeus, assumes the *kredemnon*
(*Il.* XIV. 184).   But it is worn, as we have seen, by
Andromachè in Troy ; by Ino, a deity of Phœnician
extraction ; and by the maidens attendant on Nausicaä in
Scherìè.

4. In the upper region, or what we might call the sky
of the picture, are presented to us, apparently in very
rough outline, the sun and a thinly horned moon.*   Below

---

* I wish here to call attention to the fact that, as always (I believe)
in the Egyptian and Assyrian monuments, the moon is on this ring also
distinguished from the sun, not by its size, but by its being a crescent
moon.   In truth, the distinction of size, to the common eye, is variable ;
and is sometimes against the sun.   Two full-formed globes of equal
diameter would have presented a picture alike defective in composition

them is an uneven band, forming rudely an arc of a circle. This, I am led to suppose, is an indication of mother-earth, with its uneven surface of land and its rippling sea, in the proper place, beneath the sun and moon. If this be so, it greatly confirms the conjecture of Mr. Newton respecting the six objects on the rim of the picture to the right. He asks whether these can be the *teirea* (*Il.* XVIII. 485), the stars of heaven, which are described by Homer as placed upon the Shield of Achilles, together with the sun, moon, sky, earth, and sea. Schliemann assigns to this *sestetto* heads and eyes: Mr. Newton says they are thought to be heads of lions. That they should be things animate is not, I imagine, in conflict with the conjecture that they may be stars. The spirit of Hellenism transmuted the older Nature-worship by impersonations, of which we have an Homeric example in the astral Orion (*Il.* XVIII. 486, *Od.* XI. 572). Should these conjectures be confirmed, the matter will be of peculiar interest: for we shall then have before us, in actual collocation, the very objects, which people the first compartment of the god-wrought Shield of Achilles: the earth (of land and sea), sun, moon, and all the stars of heaven. The *ouranos* or heaven itself, which the Poet also includes, is here in all likelihood represented by the curvature of the picture.

5. The goblet (No. 346 of the volume) has on each of its two handles, we are told, the carved figure of a dove in gold. Schliemann observes on the correspondence with the goblet of Nestor (*Il.* XI. 632–635). We are not indeed

---

and in meaning: and ancient art, not content with this, seized, more poetically as I think, upon the distinction of character in the two bodies respectively. Homer, as I contend, has exactly followed this form of representation in his σελήνην τε πλήθουσάν: and I venture to hope that the sense of growing, filling, waxing, or crescent moon will now be allowed to prevail over the more customary rendering of 'full' moon (*Il.* XVIII. 434).

told that this was of gold; probably a different material is
to be supposed from the mention of gold as the material of
these parts or appendages. But it had four handles, and
on each handle were two doves. We are also told that he
did not get it in Troy, which may remind us of the argument already presented, but brought it from home. It
was probably a foreign work; for the Phœnician associations of Nestor are attested by his descent from Poseidon
(*Od.* XI. 254). This is fairly to be noted for an instance
of equable development in art, as between the discoveries
and the Poems.

6. We frequently hear in the Poems of the golden
studs or buttons which were used as ornamental adjuncts.
In many passages we have the silver-studded sword, *xiphos*
or *phasganon arguroëlon* (*Il.* II. 45, III. 334 *et al.*) This,
I say, is common. We have also studs, or bosses, of gold
upon the staff or sceptre of Achilles (*Il.* I. 246), upon the
cup of Nestor XI. 632–635 : and upon a sword, only once
it is true, but then that sword is the sword of Agamemnon,
king of gold-abounding Mycenæ (*Il.* XI. 29). On this
sword, says the Poet, there were gilt, or golden, bosses ; and
the expression he uses about them (*pamphainon*) is worthy
of note. It is not easy to represent by any one English
word. It means not merely shining brightly, but shining
all over; that is to say, apparently, all over the sheath to
which they were attached, so as to make it seem a shining
mass. Is not this precisely what must have been the effect
of the line of bosses found lying by the sword in p. 303,
which lie closely together, are broader than the blade,
and probably covered the whole available space along the
sheath of wood, now mouldered away ? And is it not now
startling, to descend into the tombs with Dr. Schliemann,
and to find there lying silently in rows these gold studs or
bosses, when the wooden sheaths they were attached to have
for the most part mouldered away, but by the very sides
of the very swords which they adorned like binding on a

book, and of the slight remains of warriors by whom, there
need be little doubt, those swords were wielded?

> "Expende Annibalem; quot libras in duce summo
> Invenies?"*

They also appear on the sword-handle knobs. The *helos*
of Homer is commonly rendered a nail or stud, which
has a head of small size; but the word probably includes
the larger buttons or bosses, which lie in lines along some
of the swords. (See on this point pp. 281, 2; 303, 5, 6.)
I will not attempt to pursue further an enumeration
which, growing more and more minute, would be wearisome.
If porcelain and glass have been found, I should at once
assign them to foreign importation. The art of casting
and tooling in the precious metals, of which the examples
would appear, both from our author and from Mr. Newton,
to be few, are probably to be referred to a like source.
The hammer and the pincers are the only instruments for
metallic manipulation, of which Homer appears to be
aware (*Il.* XVIII. 477, *Od.* III 434-5). As regards the
pottery mentioned by our author, if some of the goblets
were of light green (p. 285), we have a colour developed
in their manufacture of which Homer had certainly no
distinct conception, though it may still be true that, as in
nature, so in human art, objects bearing that colour may
have met his eye. Of the scales in the third sepulchre there
seems no reason to doubt that we may find the interpretation,
by referring them to the Egyptian scheme of doctrine with
regard to a future life (pp. 197, 8). In the Books of the
Dead, we have an elaborate representation of the judgment-
hall, to which the departed soul is summoned. Here the
scales form a very prominent object;† and it seems very
possible that the Poet, who was Greek and not Egyptian in

---

* Juvenal, *Sat.* X. 147.
† See, *e.g.*, the print in Manning's 'Land of the Pharaohs,' p. 129.

his ideas of the future state, may have borrowed and trans-
posed, from this quarter, the image of the balances displayed
on high, which he employs with such fine effect in some
critical passages of the *Iliad*. As regards the emblem of the
double-headed or full-formed axe, I venture to dispense with
the cautious reserve of Schliemann. As the usual form of
a weapon familiar to the age, it seems to require no special
explanation (p. 252). But where we find it conjoined with
the ox-head (p. 218), or on the great signet ring in conjunction with a figure evidently representing Deity, I cannot hesitate to regard it as a sacrificial symbol. We have
only to remember the passage in the third Odyssey, where
the apparatus of sacrifice is detailed, and Thrasumedes, who
was to strike the blow, brought the axe (III. 442): —

πέλεκυν δὲ μενεπτόλεμος Θρασυμήδης
ὀξὺν ἔχων ἐν χερσὶ παρίστατο, βοῦν ἐπικόψων.

The boar's teeth (p. 273) supply a minor, perhaps, but
a clear and significant point of correspondence to be added
to our list (*Il.* X. 263–264). Another is to be noticed in
the manner of attaching, by wire, lids and covers. On
these subjects, I refer to the text of the volume.

By the foregoing detail I have sought to show that there
is no preliminary bar to our entertaining the capital question
whether the tombs now unearthed, and the remains exposed
to view, under masks for the faces, and plates of gold covering
one or more of the trunks, are the tombs and remains of
the great Agamemnon and his compeers, who have enjoyed,
through the agency of Homer, such a protracted longevity
of renown. For the general character of the Mycenean
treasures, I take my stand provisionally on the declaration
of Mr. Newton (supported by Mr. Gardner), that, in his
judgment, they belong to the prehistoric or heroic age, the
age antecedent to his Greco-Phœnician period; and in important outlines of detail I have endeavoured to show that
they have many points of contact with the Homeric Poems,

and with the discoveries at Hissarlik. But this Preface makes no pretension whatever to exhibit a complete catalogue of the objects, or to supply for each of them its interpretation. We encounter, indeed, a certain number of puzzling phenomena, such as the appearance of something like visors, for which I could desire some other explanation, but which Schliemann cites as auxiliaries to the masks of the tombs, and even thinks to prove that such articles were used by the living, as well as for the dead (p. 359).

Undoubtedly, in my view, these masks constitute a great difficulty, when we come to handle the question who were the occupants of the now opened sepulchres? It may be, that as Mr. Newton says, we must in the main rest content with the "reasonable presumption" that the four tombs contained Royal personages, and must leave in abeyance the further question, whether they are the tombs indicated to Pausanias by the local tradition; at any rate, until the ruins of Mycenæ shall have been further explored, according to the intention which the government of Greece is said to have conceived.

At the same time this is a case where the question before us, if hazardous to prosecute, is not easy to let alone.

It is obviously difficult to find any simple, clear, consistent interpretation of the extraordinary inhumation disclosed to us by these researches. Such an interpretation may be found hereafter: it does not seem to be forthcoming at the present moment. But the way towards it can only be opened up by a painstaking exhibition of the facts, and by instituting a cautious comparison between them and any indications, drawn from other times or places, which may appear to throw light upon them. For my own part, having approached the question with no predisposition to believe, I need not scruple to say I am brought or driven by the evidence to certain conclusions; and also led on to certain conjectures suggested by those conclusions. The first conclusion is that we cannot refer the five entombments in the Agora at Mycenæ to any period within the historic age. The second is that they are entombments of great, and almost certainly in part of royal, personages. The third, that they bear indisputable marks of having been effected, not normally throughout, but in connection with circumstances, which impressed upon them an irregular and unusual character. The conjecture is. that these may very well be the tombs of Agamemnon and his company. It is supported in part by a number of presumptions, but in great part also by the difficulty, not to say the impossibility, of offering any other suggestion which could be deemed so much as colourable.

The principal facts which we have to notice appear to be as follows :—

1. The situation chosen for the interments.

2. The numbers of persons simultaneously interred.

3. The dimensions and character of the graves.

4. The partial application of fire to the remains.

5. The use of masks, and likewise of metallic plates, to adorn or shelter them, or both.

6. The copious deposit both of characteristic and of valuable objects in conjunction with the bodies.

1. Upon 'the situation chosen for the interments, Dr. Schliemann opines that they were not originally within the Agora, but that it was subsequently constructed around the tombs (p. 340). His reasons are that the supporting wall, on which rest, in double line, the upright slabs, formerly, and in six cases still, covered by horizontal slabs as seats for the elders, is careless in execution, and inferior to the circuit wall of the Acropolis. But, if it was built as a mere stay, was there any reason for spending labour to raise it to the point of strength necessary for a work of military defence? Further, he finds between the lines of slabs, where they are uncovered, broken pottery of the prehistoric period more recent than that of the tombs. But

such pottery would never have been placed there at the time of the construction ; with other rubbish, it would only have weakened and not strengthened the fabric of the inclosure. Nor can we readily see how it could have come there, until the work was dilapidated by the disappearance of the upper slabs. If so, it would of course be later in date than the slabs were.

It appears to me that the argument of improbability tells powerfully against the supposition that the *Agora* was constructed round the tombs, having previously been else-where. The space within the Acropolis appears to be very limited : close round the inclosures are 'Cyclopean' houses and cisterns. When works of this kind are once con-structed, their removal would be a work of great difficulty : and this is a case, where the earliest builders were followed by men who aimed not at greater, but at less, solidity. Besides which, the *Agora* was connected with the religion of the place, and was, as will be shown, in the immediate neighbourhood of the palace. In addition to these material attractions, every kind of moral association would grow up around it.

It can be clearly shown that the ancient Agora was bound down to its site by manifold ties, other than those of mere solidity in its construction. It stands in Mycenæ, says our author (p. 341), on the most imposing and most beautiful spot of the city, from whence the whole was over-looked. It was on these high places that the men of the prehistoric ages erected the simple structures, in many cases perhaps uncovered, that, with the altars, served for the worship of the gods. In Scheriè, it was built round the temple, so to call it, of Poseidon (*Od* VI. 266). In the Greek camp before Troy the *Agora* was in the centre of the line of ships (*Il.* XI. 5-9, 806-8). There justice was administered, and there " had been constructed the altars of the gods." Further, it is clear, from a number of passages in Homer, that the place of Assembly was always close to

the royal palace.   In the case of Troy we are told expressly
that it was held by the doors of Priam (*Il.* II. 788, VII.
345, 6)   In Scheriè, the palace of Alkinoös was close to
the grove of Athenè (*Od.* VI. 291–3); and we can hardly
doubt that this grove was in the immediate vicinity of
the Posideïon, which was itself within the *Agora.*   In
Ithaca (*Od.* XXIV. 415 *seqq.*), the people gathered before
the Palace of Odysseus, and then went in a mass into the
Agora.   While it was thus materially associated with
those points of the city which most possessed the character
of fixtures, it is not too much to say, considering the
politics of early Greece, that it must, in the natural course,
have become a centre around which would cling the fondest
moral and historical associations of the people.   Into the
minor question whether the encircling slabs are the remains
of an original portion of the work or not, I do not think
it needful for me to enter.

But, while I believe that the *Agora* is where it was, the
honour paid to the dead by the presence of their tombs
within it is not affected by either alternative; but only the
time of paying it.   If this be the old *Agora,* they were
honoured by being laid in it; if it is of later date, they
were honoured by its being removed in order to be built
around them; if at least this was done knowingly, and
how could it be otherwise, when we observe that the five
tombs occupy more than a moiety of the whole available
space? We know, from the evidence of the historic period,
that to be buried in the Agora was a note of public honour;
we cannot reasonably doubt, with the five graves before us,
that it was such likewise in the historic age.

It was a note of public honour, then, if these bodies
were originally buried in the *Agora.*   If we adopt the less
probable supposition that the Agora was afterwards constructed around them by reason of their being there, the
honour may seem even greater still.

2. Next, the number of persons simultaneously interred,

when taken in conjunction with the other features of the transaction, offers a new problem for consideration. An argument in p. 337, to show that the burials were simultaneous, seems quite conclusive. They embraced (*ibid.*) sixteen or seventeen persons. Among the bodies one appears to be marked out by probable evidence as that of the leading personage. Lying in the tomb marked as No. 1, it has two companions. Now Agamemnon had two marshals or heralds (*Il.* I. 320), whose office partook of a sacred character. There might, therefore, be nothing strange in their being laid, if so it were, by their lord. The most marked of the bodies lay to the north of the two others, all three having the feet to the westward. It was distinguished by better preservation, which may, at least not improbably, have been due to some preservative process at the time of interment. It carried, besides a golden mask (p. 296), a large golden breastplate (15⅔ by 9½ in.), and other leaves of gold at various points; also a golden belt across the loins, 4 ft. long and 1¾ in. broad. By the side of the figure lay two swords, stated by Dr. Schliemann to be of bronze (p. 302), the ornamentation of one of them particularly in striking accordance with the description in the *Iliad* of the sword of Agamemnon (*Il.* XI. 29-31). Within a foot of the body, to the right, lay eleven other swords (p. 304), but this is not a distinctive mark, as the body on the south side has fifteen, ten lying at the feet, and a great heap of swords were found at the west end, between this and the middle body.

The entire number of bodies in the five tombs (p. 337), which is stated at sixteen or seventeen, seems to have included three women and two or three children. The local tradition recorded by Pausanias (*inf.* p. 59) takes notice of a company of men with Agamemnon, and of Cassandra, with two children whom she was reported to have borne. This is only significant as testifying to the ancient belief that children were buried in the tombs ·

for Cassandra could only be taken captive at the time
when the city of Troy was sacked, and the assassination
immediately followed the arrival in Greece. But it is
likely enough that these children may have been the
offspring of another concubine, who may have taken the
place Briseis was meant to fill. This is of course mere
speculation ; but the meaning is that there is nothing in
these indications to impair the force of any presumptions,
which the discoveries may in other respects legitimately
raise.

3. Like the site in the Agora, so the character of the
tombstones, which is in strict correspondence with the
style of many of the ornaments,* and the depth of the
tombs, appear with one voice to signify honour to the
dead. As I understand the Plans, they show a maximum
depth of 25 feet (see, *e.g.*, p. 155) below the surface, hollowed for the most part out of the solid rock. But then
we are met with the staggering fact that the bodies of full-
grown, and apparently (p. 295) tall, men have been forced
into a space of only five feet six inches in length, so as to
require that sort of compression which amounts almost to
mutilation.

We seem thus to stand in the face of circumstances that
contradict one another. The place, the depth, the coverings
of the tombs, appear to lead us in one direction ; the forcing
and squeezing of the bodies in another. But further, and
stranger still, there seems to have been no necessity for
placing the bodies under this unbecoming, nay revolting,
pressure. The original dimensions of the tomb (p. 294)
were 21 ft. 6 in. by 11 ft. 6 in. These are reduced all round,
first by an inner wall two feet thick, and secondly by a
slanting projection one foot thick (at the bottom) to 5 ft.
6 in. and 15 ft. 6 in. Why, then, were the bodies not laid
along, instead of across, it ? Was not the act needless as

---

* Mr. Percy Gardner, in the *Academy*, April 21, 1877.

well as barbarous? And to what motive is a piece of needless barbarism, apparently so unequivocal, to be referred? I hardly dare to mention, much less, so scanty is the evidence, to dwell upon the fact that their bodies lie towards the west, and that the Egyptian receptacle for the dead lay in that quarter.* The conflict of appearances, at which we have now arrived, appears to point to a double motive in the original entombment; or to an incomplete and incoherent proceeding, which some attempt was subsequently made to correct; or to both. But let us pay a brief attention to the remaining particulars of the disclosures.

4. We have next to observe (*a*) that fire was applied to these remains; (*b*) that the application of it was only partial; (*c*) that the metallic deposits are said to show marks † of the action of it (pp. 158, 165, 188, 198, 201, 208, 215, 218, 260, 266, 321, 330) : so do the pebbles (p. 294). We see, therefore, that the deposition of the precious objects took place either at the same moment with the fire, or, and more probably I suppose, before it had entirely burned out.

The partial nature of the burning requires a more detailed consideration. In the Homeric burials, burning is universal. It must be regarded, according to the Poems, as the established Achaian custom of the day, wherever inhumation was normally conducted. And for burial there was a distinct reason, namely, that without it the Shade of the departed was not allowed to join the company of the other Shades, so that the unburied Elpenor is the first to meet Odysseus (*Od.* XI. 51) on his entrance into the Underworld; and the shade of Patroclos entreats Achilles to bury him as rapidly as may be, that he may pass the gates of Aïdes (*Il.* XXIII. 71). I think the proof of the universal use of fire in regular burials at this period is con-

---

* 'Homeric Synchronism,' p. 240.
† These marks, I now learn from Dr. S., are universal.

clusive. Not only do we find it in the great burials of the
Seventh Book (429–32), and in the funerals of Patroclos
(XXIII. 177) and Hector (XXIV. 785–800), but we have
it in the case of Elpenor (*Od.* XII. 11–13), whom at first
his companions had left uninterred, and for whom therefore
we must suppose they only did what was needful under established custom. Perhaps a yet clearer proof is to be found
in a simile. Achilles, we are told, wept while the funeral
pile he had erected was burning, all night long, the bones
of Patroclos, " as a father weeps when he burns the bones
of his youthful son " (XXIII. 222–5). This testifies to a
general practice.

In the case of notable persons, the combustion was not
complete. For not the ashes only, but the bones, were
carefully gathered. In the case of Patroclos, they are
wrapped in fat, and put in an open cup or bowl (*phialè*)
for temporary custody (XXIII. 239–44) until the funeral
of Achilles, when with those of Achilles himself, similarly
wrapped, and soaked in wine, they are deposited in a golden
urn (*Od.* XXIV. 73–7). In the case of Hector, the bones
are in like manner gathered and lodged in a golden box,
which is then placed in a trench and built over with a mass
of stones (*Il.* XXIV. 793–8). Incomplete combustion,
then, is common to the Homeric and the Mycenean
instances. But in the case of the first tomb at Mycenæ,
not only was there no collection of the bones for deposit in
an urn, but they had not been touched; except in the
instance of the middle body, where they had simply been
disturbed, and the valuables perhaps removed, as hardly
anything of the kind was found with it. In the case of the
body on the north side, the flesh of the face remained
unconsumed.

But though the use of fire was universal in honourable
burial, burial itself was not allowed to all. Enemies, as a
rule, were not buried. Hence the opening passage of the
Iliad tells us that many heroes became a prey to dogs and

birds (*Il.* I. 4). Such says Priam, before the conflict with Hector, he would make Achilles if he could (XXII. 42); and he anticipates a like distressing fate (66 *seqq.*) for himself. In the Odyssey, the bodies of the Suitors are left to be removed by their friends (XXII. 448; XXIV. 417). Achilles, indeed, buried Eëtion, king of Asiatic Thebes, with his arms, in the regular manner. "He did not simply spoil him, for he had a scruple in his mind" (*Il.* VI. 417); and no wonder; for Eëtion, king of the Kilikes, was not an enemy: that people does not appear among the allies of Troy in the Catalogue. Thus there was a variance of use; and there may have been cases of irregular intermediate treatment between the two extremes of honourable burial and casting out to the dogs.

5. With regard to the use of masks of gold for the dead, I hope that the Mycenean discoveries will lead to a full collection of the evidence upon this rare and curious practice. For the present, I limit myself to the following observations:

(1.) If not less than seven of these golden masks have been discovered at Mycenæ by Dr. Schliemann, then the use of them, on the occasion of these entombments, was not limited to royal persons, of whom it is impossible to make out so large a number.

(2.) I am not aware of any proof at present before us that the use of such masks for the dead of any rank or class was a custom prevalent, or even known, in Greece. There is much information, from Homer downwards, supplied to us by the literature of that country concerning burials; and yet, in a course of more than 1200 years, there is not a single allusion to the custom of using masks for the dead. It seems to be agreed that the passage in the works of Lucian, who is reckoned to have flourished in the second half of the second century, does not refer to the use of such masks. This might lead us to the conjecture that, where the practice has appeared, it was a remainder of foreign usage, a survival from immigration.

(3.) Masks have been found in tombs, not in Greece, but in the Crimea, Campania, and Mesopotamia. Our latest information on the subject is, I believe, the account mentioned in Dr Schliemann's last report from Athens (pp xlvii, xlviii), of a gold mask found on the Phœnician coast over against Aradus, which is of the size suited for an infant only. It is to be remembered that heroic Greece is full of the marks of what I may term Phœnicianism, most of which passed into the usages of the country, and contributed to form the base of Hellenic life. Nor does it seem improbable, that this use of the metallic mask may have been a Phœnician adaptation from the Egyptian custom of printing the likeness of the dead on the mummy case. And, again, we are to bear in mind that Mycenæ had been the seat of repeated foreign immigrations.

(4.) We have not to deal in this case *only* with masks, but with the case of a breastplate in gold, which, however, could not have been intended for use in war; together with other leaves or plates of gold, found on, or apparently intended for, other portions of the person.

6. Lastly, with regard to the deposit of objects which, besides being characteristic, have unchangeable value, the only point on which I have here to remark is, their extraordinary amount. It is such, I conceive, as to give to these objects, and particularly to those of the First Tomb, an exceptional place among the sepulchral deposits of antiquity. I understand that their weight is about one hundred pounds troy, or nearly that of five thousand British sovereigns It is difficult to suppose that this deposit could have been usual, even with the remains of a King; and it is at this point that I, for one, am

compelled to break finally and altogether with the supposition, that this great entombment, in the condition
in which Dr. Schliemann found it, was simply an entombment of Agamemnon and his company effected by
Ægisthus and Clytemnestra, their murderers.

So far, with little argument, I have endeavoured fairly
to set out the facts.   Let me now endeavour to draw to a
point the several threads of the subject, in order to deal
with the main question. namely, whether these half-wasted,
half-burned remains are the ashes of Agamemnon and his
company?   And truly this is a case, where it may be said
to the inquirer, in figure as well as in fact,

> " et incedis per ignes
> Suppositos cineri doloso." *

Let us place clearly before our eyes the account given
by the Shade of Agamemnon, in the Eleventh Odyssey
(405–434), of the manner of his death.   No darker picture
could be drawn.   It combined every circumstance of
cruelty with every circumstance of fraud.   At the hospi-
table board, amid the flowing wine-cups, he was slain like
an ox at the stall, and his comrades like so many hogs for
a rich man's banquet; with deaths more piteous than he
had ever known in single combat, or in the rush of armies.
Most piteous of all was the death of Cassandra, whom the
cruel Clytemnestra despatched with her own hand while
clinging to Agamemnon; nor did she vouchsafe to her
husband the last office of mercy and compassion, by
closing his mouth and eyes in death.   Singularly enough,
Dr. Schliemann assures me that the right eye, which alone
could be seen with tolerable clearness, was not entirely
shut (see the engraving at p. 297); while the teeth of the
upper jawbone (see the same engraving) did not quite
join those of the lower.   This condition, he thinks, may

Hor. *Od.* II. i. 8.

be due to the superincumbent weight. But if the weight had opened the jaw, would not the opening, in all likelihood, have been much wider?

Now, as we are told that Ægisthus reigned until Orestes reached his manhood, we must assume that the massacre was in all respects triumphant. Yet there could hardly fail to be a party among the people favourable to the returning King, who had covered his country with unequalled glory. There might thus be found in the circumstances a certain dualism, a ground for compromise, such as may go far to account for the discrepancies of intention, which we seem to find in the entombments. There was this division of sentiment among the people, in the only case where we know the return of the prince from Troy to have been accompanied with a crisis or conflict, I mean the case of Ithaca.

The assassins proceeded in such a way, that the only consistent accomplishment of their design would have been found in casting forth the bodies of the slain like the bodies of enemies. But this may have been forbidden by policy. In the Julius Cæsar of Shakespeare, Brutus says (III. 1.)—

> "We are contented Cæsar shall
> Have all due rites and lawful ceremonies.
> It shall advantage more than do us wrong."

Ægisthus was not Brutus. Even fury was apparent in the incidents of the slaughter. Yet there might be a desire to keep up appearances afterwards, and to allow some semblance of an honourable burial. There is one special circumstance that favours the idea of a double process, namely, that we readily find the agents for both parts of it; the murderers for the first, with necessity and policy controlling hatred; Orestes on his return for the second, with the double motive of piety and revenge.

We are now on the road not of history, but of reasonable conjecture. I try to account for a burial, which according to all reasonable presumption is of the heroic age, and of royal and famous personages, but which presents conflicting features of honour and of shame. That there is no conflicting hypothesis, is not a good reason for precipitate assent to the hypothesis which we may term Agamemnonian. Conjecture, to be admissible, ought to be consistent with itself, to meet the main demands of the known facts, and to present no trait at actual variance with any of them. In this view I present the hypothesis of a double procedure, and a double agency : and I submit, that there is nothing irrational in the following chain of suppositions for the First Tomb, while the others are probably included in the argument. That the usurping assassins, from the same policy, granted the honour of burial in the *Agora ;* hewed the sepulchre deep and large in the rock; and built the encircling wall within it. That honour stopped with the preparation of the tomb, and the rest, less visible to the public eye, was left to spite or haste. That the bodies were consequently placed in the seemingly strange and indecent fashion, which the tomb has disclosed. That, as they were protected by the rock, and by the depth from the surface, their decomposition was slow. That Orestes, on his return, could not but be aware of the circumstances, and, in the fulfilment of his divinely ordered mission, determined upon reparation to the dead. That he opened the tombs and arranged the means of cremation. That, owing to the depth, it was imperfect from want of ventilation ; we may remember that in the case of Patroclos the winds were specially summoned to expedite the process (*Il.* XXIII. 192-218). In calling it imperfect, I mean that it stopped short of the point at which the bones could be gathered ; and they remained *in situ.* That the masks, breastplate, and other leaves of gold were used, perhaps, in part with reference to custom ; in part, especially as regards all beside the masks, to replace in the wasted bodies the seemliness and majesty of nature, and to shelter its dilapidation. That the profuse deposits of arms and valuables were due to filial piety. That the same sentiment carried the work through even to the careful sculpturing of the four tomb-stones (others have been found (p. 100), but without sculpture); and sought, by their means, to indicate for renown and reverence, and to secure from greedy violation, the resting-place of the dead.

A complex solution, perhaps; but one applicable to very complex facts, and one of which the ground at least is laid in those facts; one also, which I offer as a contribution to a most interesting scrutiny, but with no claim or pretension to uphold it against any other, that may seem better entitled to fill the vacant place.

W. E. G.

HAWARDEN, *November*, 1877.

DR. SCHLIEMANN'S ACCOUNT OF A TOMB
AT SPATA, IN ATTICA.

Athens, 1st Oct., 1877.

FOR some months past it has repeatedly been asserted in the Press by travellers that there exists a very great similarity between the Mycenean antiquities and those recently discovered in a tomb at Spata. Having now visited the latter, in company with my esteemed friend Professor E. Castorches, of the University of Athens, and his daughter Helen, and having carefully examined the objects found in it, I think it in the interest of science to offer the following remarks on the subject. The village of Spata, which is exclusively inhabited by Albanians, lies about nine miles to the east of Athens, on the further side of Mount Hymettus, on the road to Marathon. Close to that village is a small mount, whose circular summit has evidently been artificially levelled; it is covered to a depth of about three feet with *débris*, in which we see now and then fragments of archaic vases with painted parallel horizontal bands. The villagers assert that until very recently the summit was surrounded by the ruins of fortress walls, which have now altogether disappeared, the stones having been used for the building of the new village. The name of the settlement which existed here in antiquity is altogether uncertain. Colonel Leake* recognises in the present name, Spata, a corruption of the ancient *demos* of

* 'Demi of Attica,' p. 125.

Sphettus (Σφῆττος or Σφηττός), which is mentioned by Aristophanes,[*] Strabo,[†] Pausanias,[‡] Stephanus Byzantinus,[§] and others.

In the south-west side of the mount, which slopes at an angle of 52 degrees, there occurred last winter in one place a sudden breaking down of the ground, and in the hollow thus formed there was discovered a sepulchre cut out in the sandstone rock. The Archæological Society had the place explored, and it was found that an inclined road, cut in the rock, 74 feet long, led into the tomb. The road is 8¼ feet broad up to the entrance, which is 10 feet long and 3⅓ feet broad. The sepulchre consists of three quadrangular chambers, which are united by two passages 6½ feet long and 3⅓ feet broad; and the ceilings of these chambers are cut out in the rock in the form of roofs with two slanting sides. The primitive architect had evidently intended to give to each of these three chambers exactly the shape of a house, because the slanting sides of the roof-like ceiling do not converge directly from the vertical walls, but hang over by 8 inches like the eaves of a house. The height of the first chamber is 16½ feet, its breadth 15, and its length 20 feet; the two other chambers are 12½ feet high, 12 feet long, and 11½ feet broad. Of the existence of wooden doors there are no traces, except in the passage from the first to the second chamber. Seen from the extremity of the "dromos" this tomb reminds us of the Egyptian sepulchres.[||]

In each of the three chambers was found a human skeleton, with a quantity of ashes and charcoal, which seems to prove that each body had been burnt on the pyre in the very spot where it lay, but so superficially that the bones were preserved. In this respect, as well regarding the burning of the bodies in the tombs, we find a resemblance to the

---

[*] *Plutus*, 720.   [†] IX., p. 397.   [‡] II., 30, 8.   [§] P. 627.
[||] " Si parva licet componere magnis."

mode of burial of the bodies in the five royal sepulchres at Mycenæ. But here the bones crumbled away on being exposed to the air. This tomb had evidently been already rifled in ancient times, for but a few objects were found with the bodies; nearly all of them lay dispersed in the *débris*, in and before the entrance. They consisted of bone or ivory, glass, bronze, stone, and terra-cotta. Only a few flowers of very thin gold-leaf having been found, whose aggregate weight cannot exceed the eighth part of a pound, it appears that the tomb-robbers only aimed at the golden ornaments, and that they threw away all the rest.

The few terra-cotta vessels found here are all wheel-made; among the number there is one which perfectly resembles the vase represented under No. 25, p. 64; it is ornamented with red and black circular bands, and is in the shape of a globe with a flat foot; it terminates above in a very pretty narrow neck, without an opening, the top of which is joined on each side by a beautifully shaped handle to the upper part of the body. The real mouth of the vase is in the shape of a funnel, and near to the closed neck. There was also found the upper part of a similar vase. I remind the reader that forty-three vases of exactly the same form were found in a sepulchre at Ialysus in Rhodes, and are now in the British Museum; that they sometimes, though but seldom, occur in Attica, and that some specimens of them have also been found in the Egyptian tombs and in Cyprus.

Another vase found in the tomb of Spata is ornamented with black spirals.

I also mention among the findings at Spata the large quantity of small ornaments which Professor Landerer's analysis has proved to consist of glass alloyed with much protoxide of lead, the latter having the property of breaking the rays of light; these ornaments present a silvery mirror-like glimmer. Landerer observes that it is soda-glass (in German, *Natrum-Glas*), and that it has the

property of dividing into small leaves or splinters. It is
very remarkable that all these ornaments of glass have
evidently been cast in moulds, and that many of them
resemble more or less the types which we see in the
Mycenean moulds represented under No. 162 and No.
163, p. 107 and p. 109. On the reverse side of most of
these objects are one, two, or three small holes, or tubular
rings, for fastening them on other objects, probably on
clothes. A most frequent object here is that which we
recognise in the type on the lower side of the mould, No.
162, p. 107. There also occur small cones of a much
weather-beaten glass, which have the very greatest similarity to the type which we see in that side of the mould,
No. 163, which is represented on page 109 in the upper
row to the right of the spectator ; it also resembles very
much the small cone, No. 164, p. 109, of which a large
number were found at Mycenæ; the only difference is
that the cones of Spata have an impressed spiral line,
whereas the cones of Mycenæ show impressed concentric
circles. However, it deserves attention that the mould,
No. 163, represents the type of such a cone with a spiral
line. But then, again, there is the greatest difference in
the substance, for whilst at Spata all these small ornaments are of glass, the Mycenean cones and other objects,
such as Nos. 164, 165, 166 and 167, are of a hard-baked
clay, which has been varnished with a lead glaze; no trace
of glass having been found at Mycenæ except some small
glass beads, the small object, No. 177, and the almost
microscopical tubes of cobalt glass described at pages 157
and 158. As, on the other hand, there have been found a
large quantity of small ornaments of hard-baked clay
varnished with a lead-glaze, we cannot reasonably doubt
that the manufacture of glass at Mycenæ was only in its
first beginning, that until the capture of the city (468 B.C.)
it made no progress there, and that all the types contained
in the Mycenean moulds served merely for the casting of

similar ornaments of baked clay varnished with a lead-glaze.

But there also occur in the tomb at Spata objects of blue cobalt glass, some of which are identical in shape with the object of stone represented under No. 172, p. 111.

All these objects of glass lead us to the conclusion that the sepulchre of Spata belongs to a much later time than the royal tombs of Mycenæ. But we find a much stronger proof of this in the carved works discovered in the Spata sepulchre, which are generally thought to consist of ivory, but which by the investigation of Professor Landerer are proved to consist of common bone. All these carved works appear to belong to a late period of Assyrian art; perhaps the most remarkable object among them is a beardless man's head covered with a very high Assyrian mitre, the lower part of which is ornamented all round with a diadem, whilst the upper part is divided by three double bands into four compartments. As usual in the Assyrian hair-dress, the hair hangs down on the neck in three tresses, lying the one on the other. I also mention a comb 5·8 in. long, 3·4 in. broad, the upper part of which is divided by narrow borders into two horizontal compartments; the upper one containing in the midst a flower and on either side a female sphinx; the lower one containing three female sphinxes. There are also two bone plates with female sphinxes. All these sphinxes have very large and broad wings and exhibit a most excellent Assyrian style of art. In comparison with them the golden sphinxes of the Mycenean tombs, of which I have represented one under No. 277, on p. 183, show a most ancient and very primitive style of art.

Among the carved works found in the tomb at Spata particular attention is due to a plate of bone, on which is represented a lion devouring an ox; the whole body of the former is represented as hovering in the air, and his long outstretched hind-legs vividly remind us of the representation of the lions on the Mycenean goblets and plates of gold. On the other hand the lion's head and the ox which he devours most decidedly show an Assyrian style of art.

I repeat here that no trace of Assyrian art was found at Mycenæ.

Another of the carved works from Spata which deserves attention is a disk of bone of 4·6 in. in diameter, with a border formed by two double lines, the whole interior space being in the form of a net, divided by treble wavelike lines into small triangles.

Professor Landerer asserts that these large plates and disks of bone prove beyond any doubt that the art of softening bone in water, and pressing it, and thus preparing very large pieces of bone, was known in Attica at a remote antiquity.

I still call attention, among the objects found at Spata, to the small disks of stone, which have on one side in the centre a small tube, and may have been used as ornaments on the house doors. They are mostly similar to objects which I found at Mycenæ ; * but they were also found in the sepulchre at Ialysus, and may be seen in the British Museum.

Of bronze arrow-heads several specimens were found in the sepulchre at Spata, but no trace of them occurred in the Mycenean tombs. On the other hand there were found in one of the latter the thirty-five arrow-heads of obsidian represented under No. 435, p. 272, and arrow-heads of the same stone also occurred in the *débris* above the tombs; it was only in the upper layers of *débris* at Mycenæ that I found some arrow-heads of bronze.†

Among the objects found at Spata I further mention the fragment of a vase of black granite, with two holes for

---

* See No. 126, in the upper row to the right and left, p. 76.
Pages 76, 123.

suspension; fragments of similar vases occurred also at Mycenæ.

Close to this tomb was discovered another, consisting of but one small chamber, approached by a *dromos* which has but half the length of that which leads to the large tomb. In the small tomb was found the skeleton of a man which had evidently likewise been burned on a pyre on the very spot where it lay; there was also found the skeleton of a stag, but nothing more.

Colonel Leake is in all probability right in proclaiming the identity of Spata with the ancient *demos* of Sphettus (Σφῆττος or Σφηττός), and as, according to Plutarch,* the fifty Pallantides, sons of Pallas, the brother of Ægeus, marched from Sphettus against Athens; and as Colonel Leake, guided by an inscription published by Finlay, identifies the site of the *demos* of Pallenæ, which the Pallantides inhabited, with a spur of mount Hymettus, which bars the road to Probalinthus and Marathon, and is thus in the immediate neighbourhood of Sphettus —for all these reasons it has been supposed that the tombs of Spata might possibly belong to the Pallantides killed by Theseus. But this opinion is contradicted by the objects discovered, which make it impossible for us to attribute the large tomb to an earlier period than the eighth century, B.C., whilst the royalty at Athens belongs to a very remote antiquity, and must be contemporaneous with royalty at Mycenæ.

The use of masks in antiquity being a question very important for Archaeology, I cannot conclude without mentioning that my esteemed friend Professor A. Rhousopoulos, of the University of Athens, reminds me of a very small golden mask found last spring in a sepulchre on the coast of ancient Phoenicia, just opposite to the island of Aradus. It had been bought there by a trader in antiqui-

---

* *Theseus*, 13.

ties, who brought it first to Athens, and showed it to me at Boulogne-sur-Mer, on his way to London, where he intended to sell it. It is of thin gold plate, and so small that it could apparently only fit on the face of a new-born child. It represents a human face with shut eyes, in very rude *repoussé* work.

THE FALL OF MYCENÆ AS DESCRIBED
BY DIODORUS SICULUS.

I give, at my worthy friend Professor F. A. Paley's suggestion, a literal translation of the account which Diodorus Siculus (xi. 65) gives us of Mycenæ's tragic end :

"In the seventy-eighth Olympiad (B.C. 468) a war was set on foot between the Argives and the people of Mycenæ, on the following grounds. The Myceneans, proud of the high renown which their own country had formerly enjoyed, refused to obey the Argives as the other cities in that territory had done, but took up an independent position and paid no regard to the Argives. They had disputes with them also about the worship of the goddess Hera, and put in a claim to have the sole conduct and management of the Nemean games. And still further they were at variance with them because, when the Argives had passed a resolution not to aid the Spartans at Thermopylae, unless they should be allowed a share in the command, the Myceneans alone of all the inhabitants of Argolis joined the ranks of the Lacedæmonians. The Argives had besides a general suspicion that some day their rivals might become too powerful and dispute with them the sovereignty, from the former greatness of their city. Such being the motives for hostility, they had long been watching an opportunity to raze Mycenæ to the ground ;

and they thought the fitting time had now arrived, as they saw the Lacedæmonians had been defeated and were unable to bring any aid to the Myceneans. Accordingly they collected a strong force from Argos and the other states in alliance, and led them to the attack. The Myceneans were beaten, driven into the walls of their city, and besieged. For some time they defended themselves with spirit against the besieging hosts; but at length, partly because they had been worsted in the war, partly because the Lacedæmonians were unable to aid them, from having wars of their own on hand, as well as through the disastrous effects of the earthquakes, and having no one now to help them, through mere deficiency of aid from without they were taken by assault. The Myceneans were thus made slaves by the Argives, a tithe of their property was consecrated to the service of religion, and their city was razed to the ground. Thus a state that had been great and wealthy in times of old, had numbered many illustrious men and performed many glorious actions, met with its final overthrow, and it has remained desolate up to our times" (*i.e.*, to the time of Augustus).

TABLE OF CONTENTS.

—•◇•—

CHAPTER I.

EXCAVATIONS AT TIRYNS.

Situation of the City — Description by Pausanias — Cyclopean Walls :
meaning of the epithet — The Quarry — The rock of Tiryns and its
bordering Wall — Galleries, Gate, and Tower — Walls and Terraces of
the Acropolis — Mythical traditions and History of Tiryns — Its destruction
by the Argives — Its connection with the myth of Hercules — Morasses in
the Plain of Argos — The Walls of Tiryns the most ancient monument in
Greece — Pottery a test of antiquity — Beginning of the Excavations —
Cyclopean house-walls and conduits — Objects discovered — Terra-cotta
cows, and female idols with cow's-horns — Both represent the goddess
HERA BoÖPIS — A bird-headed idol — A bronze figure, the only piece of
metal at Tiryns, except lead — No stone implements found — Pottery —
Hellenic remains outside the citadel, which was the primitive city —
Proofs of different periods of habitation — The later city of Tiryns — The
archaic pottery of Tiryns like that of Mycenæ — Its forms and decoration
denote higher civilisation than the rude walls would lead us to expect —
Older pottery on the virgin soil, but no cows or idols — Probable date of
the second nation at Tiryns, about 1000 to 800 B.C. ; of the Cyclopean
walls, about 1800 to 1600 B.C. — No resemblance to any of the pottery in
the strata of Hissarlik, except the goblets — A human skeleton found —
Whorls — Estimate of soil to be moved at Tiryns — Greater importance
of MYCENÆ .. .. *Page* 1

CHAPTER II.

TOPOGRAPHY OF MYCENÆ.

GATE OF THE LIONS AND TREASURY OF ATREUS.

The road from Argos to Mycenæ — The Plain of Argos : its rivers and hills,
horses and vegetation — Myth regarding its arid nature — Swamps in the
southern part ; and fable of the Lernæan hydra — Early social develop-

CHAPTER III.

History of Mycenæ and the Family of Pelops.

THE SEPULCHRES OF AGAMEMNON AND HIS COMPANIONS.

CHAPTER IV.

Excavations in the Citadel of. Mycenæ—*continued.*

CHAPTER V.

EXCAVATIONS IN AND NEAR THE ACROPOLIS—*continued.*

THE LIONS' GATE AND THE AGORA.

CHAPTER VI.

THE SECOND GREAT TREASURY ; ACROPOLIS ; AND CYCLOPEAN REMAINS IN THE NEIGHBOURHOOD OF MYCENÆ.

CHAPTER VII.

THE FIRST, SECOND, AND THIRD TOMBS IN THE ACROPOLIS.

CHAPTER VIII.

THE FOURTH TOMB IN THE ACROPOLIS OF MYCENÆ.

CHAPTER IX.

THE FIFTH SEPULCHRE, AND THE FIRST AGAIN.

At length again a guard and watchfire on the Acropolis of Mycenæ — Exploration of the *Fifth Tomb* — Its sepulchral *stêlæ* — The tomb described ; containing only one body — Golden diadem and other objects found in the tomb — Hand-made vases of terra-cotta ; one with female breasts, like the prehistoric vases at Santorin and Troy — Wheel-made pottery — Excavation of the *First Tomb* completed — Its position and construction. Three bodies in it : the middle one has been disturbed and rifled of its ornaments — Large size of the bodies — Golden mask and state of the first — Wonderful preservation of the third — Its ponderous gold mask, face, and teeth — Description of the body — its remarkable compression — Golden breast-plate, and leaves of gold on the forehead, eyes, and breast — Excitement caused by the discovery — Measures taken to preserve and remove the body — Its shoulder belt and bronze sword

CHAPTER X.

Connection of the Five Tombs with the Royal House of Pelops ; and Date of the Agora.

CHAPTER XI.

Treasure of the Tomb South of the Agora.

Note to Page 145.

With reference to the visit paid to the excavations at Mycenæ by the Emperor of Brazil, I feel bound to mention the renewed mark of his Majesty's interest in the discoveries, when he did me the signal honour of visiting my lodgings in London on June 22. 1877. His Majesty spent two hours in examining with great attention my large Album of Mycenean photographs, and repeatedly congratulated me on the results of my excavations.

H. S.

COMPARATIVE TABLE OF FRENCH AND ENGLISH MEASURES, EXACT AND APPROXIMATE.

Metric.	Inches.	Ft.	Inch.	Approximate.
Millimètre .	0·0393708	,,	·03937	·04 or $\frac{1}{25}$ of inch.
Centimètre.	0·393708	,,	·39371	4 ,, $\frac{2}{5}$,,
Décimètre .	3·93708	,,	3·9371	4 inches.
Mètre . .	39·3708	3	3·3708	$3\frac{1}{3}$ feet.
2	78·7416	6	6·7416	$6\frac{2}{3}$,,
3	118·1124	9	10·1124	10 ,,
4	157·4832	13	1·4832	13 ,,
5	196·8540	16	4·8540	$16\frac{1}{3}$,,
6	236·2248	19	8·2248	$19\frac{2}{3}$,,
7	275·5956	22	11·5956	23 ,,
8	314·9664	26	2·9664	$26\frac{1}{4}$,,
9	354·3372	29	6·3372	$29\frac{1}{2}$,,
10	393·7089	32	9·7080	33 ,,
11	433·0788	36	1·0788	36 (12 yds.)
12	472·4496	39	4·4496	$39\frac{1}{3}$ feet.
13	511·8204	42	7·8204	$42\frac{2}{3}$,,
14	551·1912	45	11·1912	46 ,,
15	590·5620	49	2·5620	$49\frac{1}{4}$,,
16	620·9328	52	5·9328	$52\frac{1}{2}$,,
17	669·3036	55	9·3036	$55\frac{3}{4}$,,
18	708·6744	59	0·6744	59 ,,
19	748·0452	62	4·0452	$62\frac{1}{3}$,,
20	787·416	65	7·4160	$65\frac{2}{3}$,,
30	1181·124	98	5·124	$98\frac{1}{2}$,,
40	1574·832	131	2·832	$131\frac{1}{4}$,,
50	1968·54	164	0·54	164 ,,
100	3937·08	328	1·08	328 (109 yds.)

N.B.—The following is a convenient approximate rule :—" To turn *Metres* into *Yards*, add 1-11th to the number of Metres."

LIST OF ILLUSTRATIONS.

CHAPTER I.—TIRYNS.

CHAPTER II.—MYCENÆ.

Chapter IV.—Mycenæ.

* All the objects figured in the Illustrations to this Chapter, from and after No. 239, belong to the *Third Sepulchre.*

CHAPTER VIII.—SEPULCHRE IV.

PAGE

CHAPTER IX.—SEPULCHRE I.*

---

* No. 453 only belongs to Sepulchre V.

CHAPTER X.—THE ROYAL TOMBS.

CHAPTER XI.—TOMB SOUTH OF THE AGORA.*

---

* Only Nos. 539–541 are not from this Tomb.

APPENDIX.

ANALYSIS OF METALS. FROM SEPULCHRE IV.

PLATES OF TERRA-COTTA FIGURES.

(*To follow Index.*)

PLANS.

(*At End of Volume.*)

PLATE I.

THE ACROPOLIS OF TIRYNS.

To face page 1.

No. 1. Map of Argolis.

CHAPTER I.

EXCAVATIONS AT TIRYNS.

Situation of the City—Description by Pausanias—Cyclopean Walls:
meaning of the epithet—The Quarry—The rock of Tiryns and its
bordering Wall—Galleries, Gate, and Tower—Walls and Terraces of
the Acropolis—Mythical traditions and History of Tiryns—Its
destruction by the Argives—Its connection with the myth of
Hercules—Morasses in the Plain of Argos—The Walls of Tiryns
the most ancient monument in Greece—Pottery a test of antiquity
—Beginning of the Excavations—Cyclopean house-walls and conduits—Objects discovered—Terra-cotta cows, and female idols
with cow's-horns—Both represent the goddess HERA BOÖPIS—
A bird-headed idol—A bronze figure, the only piece of metal at
Tiryns, except lead—No stone implements found—Pottery—
Hellenic remains outside the citadel, which was the primitive
city—Proofs of different periods of habitation—The later city of
Tiryns—The archaic pottery of Tiryns like that of Mycenæ—Its
forms and decoration denote higher civilisation than the rude walls

would lead us to expect—Older pottery on the virgin soil, but no cows or idols—Probable date of the second nation at Tiryns, about 1000 to 800 B.C. ; of the Cyclopean walls, about 1800 to 1600 B.C.— No resemblance to any of the pottery in the strata of Hissarlik, except the goblets—A human skeleton found –Whorls—Estimate of soil to be moved at Tiryns—Greater importance of MYCENÆ.

Tiryns, August 6, 1876.

In the south-east corner of the Plain of Argos, on the lowest and flattest of a group of rocky hills, which rise like islands out of the marshy lowlands, only eight stadia or one mile from the Gulf of Argos, was situated the ancient citadel of Tiryns, now called *Palæocastron.** It was celebrated as the birthplace of Hercules and was famous for its gigantic Cyclopean walls, of which Pausanias says, " The circuit wall, which is the only remaining ruin (of Tiryns) was built by the Cyclopes. It is composed of unwrought stones, each of which is so large that a team of mules

---

* See Plan A. and Plate I. The etymology of the name Tiryns (probably a Pelasgic word) is difficult to explain. It is very probable that the city was originally called Licymnia, for Strabo (VIII. p. 373) says that a citadel with that name is twelve stadia from Nauplia, and this distance perfectly agrees with that of Tiryns from the latter city. He does not distinctly say that he alludes to Tiryns ; but this is very probable, because Pindar says (*Olymp.* 7, v. 47) :

καὶ γὰρ ᾿Αλκμήνας κασίγνητον νόθον σκάπτῳ θένων,
σκληρᾶς ἐλαίας ἔκταν᾿ ἐν Τί-
ρυνθι Λικύμνιον, ἐλθόντ᾿ ἐκ θαλάμου Μιδέας,
τᾶς δέ ποτε χθονὸς οἰκιστὴρ χολωθείς.

' Because he (Tlepolemus) killed in wrath with a stick of the hard olive-tree Alcmena's bastard brother Licymnius, who descended from Midea's nuptial chamber and was the builder of the city.' Apollodorus (II. 8, 2) confirms this, but says that he killed him accidentally : Τληπόλεμος οὖν, κτείνας οὐχ ἑκὼν Λικύμνιον τῇ βακτηρίᾳ γὰρ αὐτοῦ θεραπεύοντα πλήσσοντος ὑπέδραμε, ' Tlepolemus involuntarily killed Licymnios, who approached him when he was chastising his servant with a stick.'

Eustathius (*ad loc.*) says that the first name of Tiryns was Haliis or Haleis, fishermen having been the first settlers on the rock ; this is also confirmed by Stephanus Byzantinus (*s.v.* Τίρυνς). Pausanias (II. 25, 8) says that the city received its name from the hero Tiryns, a son of Argos.

cannot even shake the smallest one : small stones have been interposed in order to consolidate the large blocks."*

The usual size of the stones is 7 feet long and 3 feet thick, but I measured several which were 10 feet long and 4 feet thick. Judging by the masses of fallen stones, I think it probable that the walls, when entire, were not less than 60 feet high. Had the circuit wall consisted of wrought stones it would doubtless have disappeared ages ago, because its stones would have been used for the buildings in the neighbouring cities of Nauplia and Argos. But the wall was preserved on account of the enormous size of the blocks, for the later builders found it much more easy and convenient to cut the material they needed at the foot of the rocks than to destroy the wall and break up the blocks.

I may here mention that the name " Cyclopean walls " is founded on an error, being derived from the mythic legend that the Cyclopes were distinguished architects. According to Strabo (VIII. 6), the Cyclopes, seven in number, came from Lycia and erected in the Argolid walls and other buildings, which were known under the denomination " Cyclopean walls." According to Apollodorus (II. 2, 1) and Pausanias (II. 16, 4) they built the walls of Tiryns and Mycenæ. Probably in consequence of this the whole of Argolis is called " Cyclopean land."†
There is of course no historical foundation for calling walls of huge blocks " Cyclopean," after the mythical giant race of the Cyclopes. But as the word has come into general use, I cannot avoid employing it.

It must be distinctly understood that not every wall built of stones, without any binding material, may be called

---

* Paus. II. 25, 8. Τὸ δὴ τεῖχος, ὃ δὴ μόνον τῶν ἐρειπίων λείπεται, κυκλώπων μέν ἐστιν ἔργον, πεποίηται δὲ ἀργῶν λίθων, μέγεθος ἔχων ἕκαστος λίθος ὡς ἀπ' αὐτῶν μηδ' ἂν ἀρχὴν κινηθῆναι τὸν μικρότατον ὑπὸ ζεύγους ἡμιόνων· λίθια δὲ ἐνήρμοσται πάλαι ὡς μάλιστα αὐτῶν ἕκαστον ἁρμονίαν τοῖς μεγάλοις λίθοις εἶναι.

† γᾶ κυκλωπία (Euripides, Orestes, 965).

" Cyclopean ;" and that under that denomination are only comprised, firstly, the walls of large unwrought blocks, the interstices of which are filled in with smaller stones; secondly, the walls composed of large polvgonal stones well fitted together; and, thirdly, the very ancient walls (such as we see in the Lions' Gate at Mycenæ) where immense quadrangular blocks, rudely wrought, are roughly put together in horizontal layers, but the joints not being quite straight, there remain small interstices between the stones. House or fortress walls of well-cut quadrangular slabs, which are closely joined without mortar, can never be called " Cyclopean ;" and thus, even the large subterranean Treasuries at Mycenæ and Orchomenus can in no way claim this denomination, though they may belong to the remotest antiquity.*

The quarry from which these walls were built can easily be distinguished at the foot of a rock one mile distant, which is crowned by a chapel of the prophet Elias. But this quarry does not form a pit, such as we see at Syracuse, Baalbec, or Corinth. At Tiryns, as at Mycenæ, the Cyclopean builders have contented themselves with cutting away the blocks from the rocky surface.

The flat rock of Tiryns, which is 900 feet long, from 200 to 250 feet broad, and from 30 to 50 feet high, extends in a straight line from north to south, and its margin is lined by the aforesaid Cyclopean circuit wall, which is from 25 to 50 feet thick, and in a pretty good state of preservation; but it is not always massive, being

---

* Cf. Ch. II. p. 28. It should also be observed that these forms of construction do not invariably denote successive steps of antiquity and the art of building. Unhewn boulders, rough quarried stones, and those which had a polygonal cleavage due to their nature, were often used for convenience by builders who were quite able to work quadrangular blocks, as is proved by walls in which the former kinds are placed *above* the last. See Mr. E. H. Bunbury's " Cyclopean Remains in Central Italy," in the ' Classical Museum,' 1845, vol. ii. pp. 147, *seqq.*, and the article MURUS in Dr. Smith's ' Dictionary of Greek and Roman Antiquities.'

traversed by interior passages or galleries with ogival vaults, of which four can easily be discerned. One of these galleries, which is 90 feet long and 7 feet 10 inches broad and high and free from *débris*, has in its external wall six gate-like recesses or window openings, which reach down to the bottom. Their pointed arches are formed like the angle in the passage, merely by over-lapping the ends of the courses of the masonry.*

These niches were most probably intended for archers, whilst the galleries themselves must have served for covered communications leading to armouries, guard-chambers, or towers. Of the other three galleries, two are in the south-eastern corner and run parallel to each other; the third, which traverses the western wall, seems to have served as a sally-port, and was probably concealed in some way or other.†

On the eastern side is the only gate, which is 15 feet broad. It is approached by a ramp 20 feet wide, which is supported by a wall of Cyclopean masonry.‡ The right flank of the gate is defended by a tower 43 feet high and 33 feet broad, which may have procured for the Tirynthians the credit of having been the first to build towers.§ In this place the walls are better preserved than anywhere else, and they rise considerably

---

* See the margin of Plan A.

† Dodwell (' A Classical and Topographical Tour through Greece ') and Prof. Ernst Curtius (*Peloponnes*) consider this gallery to be a second gate, which I think impossible, as it leads straight out into the plain.

‡ Colonel Leake states (' Travels in the Morea,' Vol. II. p. 351) that the principal entrance of Tiryns is on the south side, adjacent to the south-east angle. He is right if he speaks of the present day, for there has indeed been made at that point in modern times a zigzag roadway, leading up the steep slope ; but there was most decidedly no gate or entrance whatever here in ancient times.

§ Aristotle and Theophrastus, *ap.* Plin. *H. N.* VII. 56. Pliny says that the former of these authors attributes the building of towers to the Cyclopes, the latter to the Tirynthians.

above the flat summit of the mount within the Acropolis
or citadel.

This citadel consists of an upper enclosure on the
south, and a lower one on the north side; both are of
about equal size, and are divided by an abrupt slope, 14
feet high, which was fortified by a Cyclopean wall of minor
proportions. In this wall I perceive some stones shaped
by art, and some even rectangular, which leads me to
think that it belongs to a later time than the Cyclopean
circuit walls. In the upper enclosure are a number of
terraces supported by Cyclopean walls.

Through all antiquity the Greeks themselves looked
upon the walls of Tiryns as a work of the demons.
Pausanias * regards them as a structure more stupendous
than the Pyramids of Egypt; and Homer manifests
his admiration of them by the epithet "τειχιόεσσα,"
which he applies to Tiryns.†

According to ancient tradition, Tiryns was founded
(about 1400 B.C.) by Prœtus, who was its first king, and
whose son Megapenthes ceded the town to Perseus, the
builder of Mycenæ. Perseus gave it to Electryon, whose
daughter Alcmena, the mother of Hercules, married
Amphitryon, who was expelled by Sthenelus, the king of
Mycenæ and Argos. Hercules conquered Tiryns and inhabited it for a long time, in consequence of which he is
often called the Tirynthian.‡ On the return of the
Heraclidæ (80 years after the Trojan war) Mycenæ itself,
as well as Tiryns, Hysiæ, Mideia, and other cities, were
forced to increase the power of Argos, and were reduced
to the condition of dependent towns. Tiryns remained
nevertheless in the hands of its Achæan population, and,
together with Mycenæ, took part in the battle of Platææ

---

* Paus. IX. 36.
† *Iliad*, II. 559 :—Οἳ δ' Ἄργος τ' εἶχον Τίρυνθά τε τειχιόεσσαν. •
‡ Pind. *Ol.* XI. 40; Ovid, *Met.* VII. 410 ; Virgil, *Æn.* VII. 662.

with 400 men.* In consequence of this event the name
of Tiryns was engraved, among those of the other Greek
cities which had fought there, on the bronze column with
the golden tripod-stand, which the Spartans dedicated as the
tithe of the booty to the Pythian Apollo at Delphi. The
glory which Tiryns thus acquired excited the envy of the
Argives, who had taken no part in the Persian war, and
who also began to consider that city as a very dangerous
neighbour; particularly when it had fallen into the hands
of their insurgent slaves (Γυμνήσιοι), who maintained themselves for a long time behind its Cyclopean walls and
dominated the country.† The insurgents were finally subdued, but soon afterwards (Ol. 78, 1 ; 468 B.C.) the Argives
destroyed the city, demolished part of its Cyclopean walls,
and forced the Tirynthians to emigrate to Argos.‡ But
according to Strabo § they fled to Epidaurus. Pausa-
nias || mentions that between Tiryns and the gulf are the
" θάλαμοι " of the insane daughters of Prœtus, of which
no vestige is to be seen now; they cannot have been
underground buildings on account of the morass. Theo-
phrastus¶ speaks of the laughing propensities of the Tirynthians, which rendered them incapable of serious work.**

The myth of the birth of Hercules at Tiryns and the
twelve labours he performed for Eurystheus, the king of

---

* Herodot. IX. 28.   † Herodot. VI. 83.
‡ Paus. II. 17, 5 ; VIII. 27, 1.   § VIII. p. 373.
|| II. 15, 9.   ¶ *Apud* Athenæum, VI. 261.
** Theophrastus adds that, desirous to get rid of their propensity
to laugh, the Tirynthians consulted the oracle at Delphi, and got the
god's answer that, if they could sacrifice an ox to Poseidon and throw
it into the sea, without laughing, the evil would at once cease. The
Tirynthians, who feared to fail in the .execution of the god's command,
forbad the children to be present at the sacrifice. But one of them
having heard this, and having mixed in the crowd, they cried out at
him to drive him away, on which he exclaimed, " How, are you afraid
that I shall upset your sacrifice ?" This excited universal laughter, and
they became convinced that the god intended to show them by ex-
perience that an inveterate evil custom cannot be remedied.

the neighbouring Mycenæ, may, I think, be easily explained by his double nature as hero and as sun-god.* As the most powerful of all heroes, it is but natural that he should be fabled to have been born within the most powerful walls in the world, which were considered as the work of supernatural giants. As sun-god he must have had numerous sanctuaries in the plain of Argos and a celebrated cultus at Tiryns, because the marshy lowlands by which it is surrounded, and which even at present are nearly unproductive from want of drainage, were in remote antiquity nothing but deep swamps and morasses, which extending far up the plain engendered pestilential fevers, and could only be made to disappear gradually by incessant human labour and by the beneficent influence of the sun.

For the existence of the immense morasses in the plain of Argos we have no less an authority than Aristotle, who says,† " At the time of the Trojan war, the land of Argos being swampy, it could only feed a scanty population, whilst the land of Mycenæ was good and was therefore highly prized. But now the contrary is the case, for the latter has become too dry and lies untilled, whilst the land of Argos, which was a morass and therefore lay untilled, has now become good arable land." Thus it will appear but natural that Hercules, as sun-god, should be fabled to have performed for Eurystheus, the king of Mycenæ, who possessed the whole plain of Argos, the twelve labours which have been long known to mean nothing else than the twelve signs of the zodiac, through which the sun appears to pass in the annual revolution of our globe.

The topography of the plain south of Tiryns appears not to have changed since the time of Aristotle, for the northern shore of the gulf consists of deep swamps, which even now extend for nearly a mile inland.

---

* Max Müller, ' Essays,' II. 79.   † Aristot. *Meteorol.* I. 14.

I perfectly agree with the common opinion that the Cyclopean walls of Tiryns are the most ancient monument in Greece; but, having the conviction that no city or fortress wall can be more ancient than the most ancient pottery of the site it surrounds, I was very anxious to investigate the chronology of the Tirynthian walls by systematic excavations. I therefore proceeded to Tiryns on the 31st ultimo, in company with Mrs. Schliemann and my esteemed friends, Castorches, Phendikles and Pappadakes, Professors of Archæology in the University of Athens.

There I engaged fifty-one workmen, and dug a long broad and deep trench in the highest part of the citadel, and sank besides this thirteen shafts 6 feet in diameter.* I further sank three shafts in the lower part of the fortress, and four more at a distance of 100 feet outside the walls. In the higher citadel I struck the natural rock at a depth of from $11\frac{1}{2}$ to $16\frac{1}{2}$ feet; in the lower citadel, at from 5 to 8 feet; and outside the citadel I reached the virgin soil at from 3 to 4 feet.

In seven or eight of the shafts sunk in the upper citadel I brought to light Cyclopean house-walls built on the natural rock, and in three shafts I found Cyclopean water-conduits of a primitive sort, being composed of unwrought stones, laid without any binding material. Though these water-conduits rest on the rock, yet I cannot conceive how water can ever have run along them without getting lost through the interstices between the stones.

Neither in the long trench nor in the deep twelve or thirteen shafts did I find any stones at all. I conclude from this that the majority of the houses consisted of unburnt bricks, which still form the building material of most of the villages in the Argolid. The houses can hardly have been of wood, for, if so, I should have found large quan-

---

* The exact depths are indicated by the proportional numbers appended to the sectional plans of the excavations in the margin of Plan A.

tities of ashes. All my excavations in Tiryns remain of
course open, and visitors are invited to inspect them.

Among the objects discovered I must first mention the
small terra-cotta cows, of which I collected eleven,* for they

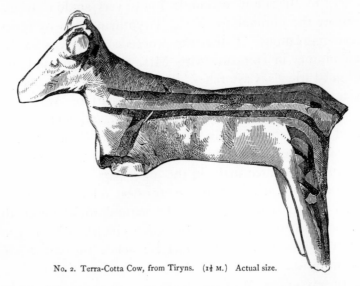

No. 2. Terra-Cotta Cow, from Tiryns. (1¼ M.) Actual size.

seem to solve a great problem, and are, at all events, of
capital importance to science. Nearly all of them are
covered with painted ornaments of red colour; one only
has a black ornamentation.

At the same time I found nine female idols, seven of
which are painted with red and two with black or dark
yellow ornaments.† They have a very compressed face,
no mouth, and a "polos" on the head; of the idol No. 8
the head is missing, and the idol, No. 10, has a broader
face and an uncovered head. The breasts of all these
idols are in high relief, and below them on each side
protrudes a long horn, in such a way that both horns
together must either be intended to represent the moon's
crescent or the two horns of the cow, or both the one
and the other at the same time. I found cows and idols

---

* See Nos. 2–7, and the coloured Plate A, figs. a, b.
† See Nos. 8–11 on p. 12, and the coloured Plate A, fig. d.

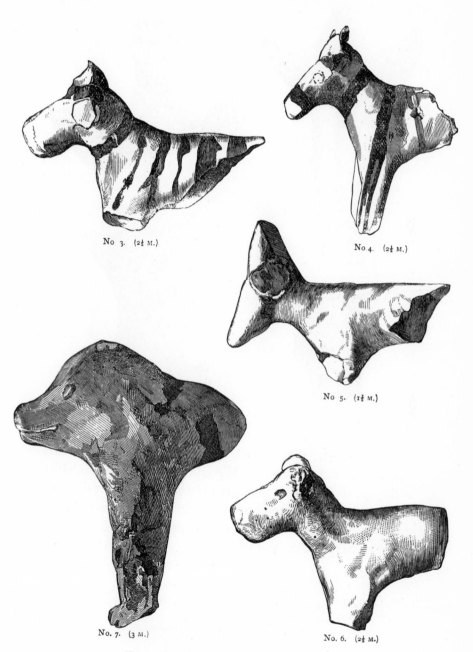

No 3. (2½ M.)

No 4. (2½ M.)

No 5. (1½ M.)

No. 7. (3 M.)

No. 6. (2½ M.)

Nos. 3-7. Terra-Cotta Cows, from Tiryns. Actual size.

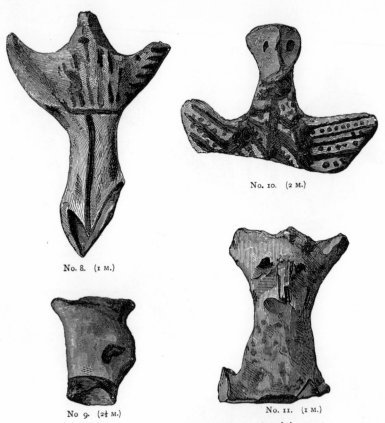

No. 8.   (1 M.)

No. 10.   (2 M.)

No 9.   (2¼ M.)

No. 11.   (1 M.)

Nos. 8–11. Terra-Cotta Idols from Tiryns. Actual size.

perfectly similar, three years ago, in the thirty-four shafts
I sank in the Acropolis of Mycenæ, which city was close
to the great Heræum and was celebrated for its cultus of
Hera, whose cow-character and identity with the Pelasgic
moon and cow-goddess Io, with the Bœotian goddess
Demeter Mycalessia, and with the Egyptian moon-goddess
Isis,* I have already sufficiently proved.† My opinion is

---

* To these may be added the Syrian and Phœnician Ashtoreth.

  "Astarte, *queen of heaven, with crescent horns,*
  To whose bright image nightly, *by the moon,*
  Phœnician virgins paid their vows and songs."—
      Milton, *Par. Lost*, Bk. I. vv. 439–441.

† See note A.—" Hera Boöpis," at the end of this chapter.

also shared by the high authority of the Right Honourable W. E. Gladstone, who says in his celebrated work, 'Homeric Synchronism,' p. 249: "The goddess Isis, mated with Osiris, is represented with the cow's head on some of the Egyptian monuments.* She is identified by Herodotus with Demeter: but Demeter and Herè are very near, and Herè seems in Homer to be the Hellenic form which had in a great degree extruded Demeter from many of her traditions, and relegated her into the insignificance which belongs to her in the poems. The epithet Boöpis seems therefore possibly to indicate a mode of representing Herè which had been derived from Egypt, and which Hellenism refined.

"It must, however, be borne in mind that the Egyptian representation was not with the eyes, but with the full countenance and head, of the ox or cow; and further, that the Homeric epithet is not confined to Herè, but is applied to Klumené, one of the attendants of Helen,† and to Philomedousa, wife of Areithoos.‡ It is likewise given to Halié, one of the Nereid Nymphs.§ The inference, probable though not demonstrative, would seem to be that in Homer's time the epithet had come to bear its later and generalised sense, and that the recollection of the cow had worn away."

I therefore do not hesitate to declare that both the cows and the horned female figures found at Mycenæ and Tiryns must needs be idols of Hera, who was the tutelar deity of both cities.

All the above idols, in the form of a cow and of a horned female, were found at a depth of from 3 to 11½ feet below the surface, and none at a greater depth.

Several terra-cotta idols of a different form were found; one of them at a depth of 8 feet.‖ This also seems to be a

---

* See Bunsen's 'Egypt,' Vol. I. p. 420 (Transl.).
† *Il.* III. 144.   ‡ *Il.* VII. 10.   § *Il.* XVIII. 40.
‖ See the coloured Plate A, fig. c.

female idol; its two hands are joined on the breast, as if
in the attitude of prayer; the head, which is uncovered,
exactly resembles a bird's head, and at the first glance
one is involuntarily struck by the resemblance of this idol
to those on one of the many painted figures of the Attic
vases with geometrical patterns which are preserved in the
small collection of antiquities in the Ministry of Public

Instruction at Athens,* and which have been
until now considered to be the most ancient
pottery in Greece. But I hope to prove in
the subsequent pages that this is a great
mistake, and that they must belong to a
later period.

Of the idol No. 11 there remain only
the neck and the head, which very much
resembles an owl's head.

Except lead, the only piece of metal
found was a beautiful archaic male figure of
bronze, wearing a Phrygian cap, and seemingly in the attitude of throwing a lance
(see No. 12). But copper or bronze at
least, if not iron, must have been extensively
used at Tiryns, for I did not find there a
single implement of stone.

The surface of the citadel is scantily
strewn with potsherds of the Middle Ages,
and probably of the time of the Frank

No. 12. Bronze figure,
from Tiryns. (3 M.) dominion, for that period seems to be indi-
Actual size.
cated by the chalk floors of a villa and its
dependencies. These potsherds, as well as entire vases of the
same fabric, are sometimes found as far down as 3 feet, but
immediately below them follow archaic potsherds, which are
usually met with at as little as a few inches under the surface;

---

* Published by Dr. G. Hirschfeld ('Vasi Arcaici Ateniesi, estratto
dagli Annali dell' Instituto di Corr. Archeol.,' 1872. Roma).

and thus it is evident that the site of the citadel of Tiryns was never inhabited from the time of the capture of the city by the Argives (468 B.C.) to about 1200 A.D.

But in the four shafts which I sank outside the citadel I found nothing but remains of Hellenic household vessels, which, judging by the potsherds, I am inclined to attribute to the 2nd, 3rd, and 4th centuries B.C. I am confirmed in this conjecture by quite a treasure of small Tirynthian copper coins, discovered some years ago at the foot of the citadel, and evidently of the Macedonian time. These medals, which are of splendid workmanship, show on one side the head of Apollo with a diadem, on the other a palm-tree with the legend ΤΙΡΤΝΣ. Thus there can be no doubt that the most ancient city of Tiryns was confined to the small space within the walls of the citadel, and that a new city, with the same name, was built outside of it some time after the capture by the Argives, and probably in the beginning of the 4th century B.C. This city seems to have extended especially to the east and still more to the north side of the citadel, where a number of its house-walls may be seen on the road to Mycenæ. From the absence of pottery of a later period I conclude that the new town was already abandoned before the Roman rule in Greece. It seems to have been quite insignificant, for it is not mentioned by any ancient author.

The Tirynthian archaic pottery is of precisely the same fabric, and has the same painted ornamentation, as the pottery of Mycenæ. There are the same tripods, with from one to five perforations in each foot; the same large vases, with perforated handles and holes in the rim of the bottom for suspension by a string; the same fantastically-shaped small vases, jugs, pots, dishes, and cups—all made on the potter's wheel, and usually presenting, on a light red dead ground, the most varied painted ornamentation of a lively red colour, which seems to be quite indestructible; for the thousands of potsherds with which the site of Mycenæ is covered have lost nothing of their freshness of colour,

though they have been exposed for more than 2300 years
to the sun and rain.

I dug up at Tiryns a large quantity of fragments of
terra-cotta goblets, which, like those found at Mycenæ,
are of white clay, and without any painted ornaments; *
but they are not found beyond a depth of 8 feet below
the surface. At a depth of from 8 to 10 feet I found only
goblets of a greenish or dark red colour. All of them
have the form of the large modern Bordeaux wine-glasses.

All this splendid pottery denotes a high civilisation, such
as the men who built the Cyclopean city walls can hardly
have reached. Hence, all this beautiful pottery was either
imported, or (and this appears more likely) it has been
manufactured by the nation which succeeded the Cyclopean
wall-builders, and to these latter must belong all the hand-
made monochromatic pottery which I found in Tiryns on
and near the virgin soil. The colour of this pottery is that
of the clay itself, which on the vast majority of the smaller
vases has been wrought by hand-polishing to a lustrous
surface; nearly all the black vases have been hand-polished
both on the inside and outside, and are very pretty. All
the larger jars are bulky, as well as many of the other large
vases; and many of them have on each side a very short
handle placed horizontally, with a broad hole, which may
have been used for suspension by a string. In this stratum
I found neither cows nor female idols. Of this hand made
pottery I have been fortunate enough to take out, besides
hundreds of fragments, two entire vases, of which I give
the drawings annexed (Nos. 13 and 14).†

With regard to the chronology of the Tirynthian pottery,

---

* Such as the goblet represented on p. 70, No. 83.

† *To each object is attached a number denoting the exact depth in meters
at which it was found; so e.g.* 3½ *M. means* 3½ *meters; each meter has
about* 3⅓ *feet. I call particular attention to this.* In order to retain the
precision of these numbers, and to avoid the labour and chance of
error in converting them into feet and inches, a comparative table of
French and English measures is prefixed to the book.

if the date of about 1400–1200 B.C., generally attributed to the most ancient Attic vases, were correct, we might

No. 13.   Terra-Cotta Vessel, from Tiryns.   (3 M.)   About half-size.

perhaps assign a like date to the establishment in Tiryns of the second nation; for to the same period must be ascribed the bird-headed idol described above,* and a quantity of

No. 14.   Terra-Cotta Vessel, from Tiryns.   (3¼ M.)   Size 2 : 3 about.

fragments of very ancient painted vases with similar patterns. But for several reasons, which will hereafter be explained,

---

See p. 13, and the coloured Plate A, fig. c.

I am unable to attribute these vases to a remoter age than from 1000 to 800 B.C., and I cannot therefore admit the settlement of the second nation at Tiryns to have taken place at an earlier epoch. It will probably for ever remain mere guesswork to what date belongs the stratum of hand-made pottery on and near the virgin soil; but if we suppose that the most ancient examples of this pottery are older, by 800 years, than the most ancient painted vases of the second nation, and that, consequently, the building of the Cyclopean walls of Tiryns was from 1800 to 1600 B.C., I think we shall be very near the right date. I have vainly endeavoured to recognise an affinity between the primitive Tirynthian pottery and that of any one of the four prehistoric cities of Troy. After mature consideration, I find that there is no resemblance whatever, except in the goblets whose form is also found in the oldest prehistoric city on Mount Hissarlik.

Not the least interesting object I discovered at Tiryns was the skeleton of a man at a depth of 16½ feet. The bones are partly petrified, but I attribute this merely to the nature of the soil in which the skeleton has been imbedded. Some of the bones had swollen considerably owing to the damp, and this may also be the case with the lower jaw-bone, which is enormously thick. Unfortunately I have been able to save only part of the skull.

I have still to mention that in all the prehistoric strata I found very small knives of obsidian; but, as before stated, no weapon or implement of stone. Many small conical whorls of blue or green stone* were found in the strata

---

* These are exactly like the whorls found at Mycenæ. See No. 15.

No. 15.   Stone Whorl, found at Mycenæ.   (5 M.)   Actual size.

of the nation second in succession, but only two very rude
ones of baked clay.

Taking the average depth of the virgin soil in the upper
and lower citadels, as ascertained by my shafts, to be 11·66
feet, I find by accurate calculation, that the quantity of
débris to be removed at Tiryns does not fall short of
36,000 cubic metres. From this, however, are to be deducted
the cubic contents of the Cyclopean house-walls, of the
curious water-conduits and of a couple of cisterns (only one
of which, however, I have been able to find), on the south
side. I hope to accomplish this work some day, but first
of all I must finish the much more important excavation
in the Acropolis of Mycenæ, and of the Treasury close to
the Lions' Gate, which I intend to commence forthwith. I
know that, after Troy, I could not possibly render a greater
service to science than by excavating at Mycenæ ; because
if, as is probable, the Cyclopean walls of its Acropolis
belong to the same remote antiquity as the walls of Tiryns,
the architecture of its Treasuries is at all events more
modern, and there can be no doubt whatever that such
was in general use in the time of Homer, who describes
it by the phrase θάλαμοι ξεστοῖο λίθοιο ("chambers of
polished stone ").

My esteemed friends, Professors Castorches, Phendikles,
and Pappadakes return to-day to Athens.

NOTE A.—" HERA BOÖPIS."

I extract the following from my Paper on Troy, read on the 24th of
June 1875, before the Society of Antiquaries in London.

It has been said by a great scholar,[1] that, whatever else the
Homeric epithet γλαυκῶπις may mean, it cannot mean owl-headed,
unless we suppose that Ἥρη βοῶπις was represented as a cow-headed
monster. I found in my excavations at Troy three splendid cow-
heads with long horns of terra-cotta,[2] and I believe them to be derived
from Hera idols, but I cannot prove it. But it is not difficult to

---

[1] Professor Max Müller, in the ' Academy,' January 10, 1874.
[2] See ' Troy and its Remains,' p. 294.

prove that this goddess had originally a cow's face, from which her Homeric epithet βοῶπις was derived.   When in the battle between the gods and the giants, the former took the shape of animals, Hera took the form of a white cow, "nivea Saturnia vacca." [1]   We find a cow's head on the coins of the island of Samos, which had the most ancient temple of Hera, and was celebrated for its worship of this goddess.[2] We further find the cow's head on the coins of Messene, a Samian colony in Sicily.[3]   The relation of Hera to the cow is further proved by the name Εὔβοια, which was at once her epithet,[4] the name of one of her nurses,[5] the name of the island in which she was brought up,[6] and the name of the mountain at the foot of which her most celebrated temple (the Heræon) was situated.[7]   But in the name Εὔβοια is contained the word βοῦς.   Hera had in Corinth the epithet βουναία,[8] in which the word βοῦς is likewise contained.   White cows were sacrificed to Hera.[9]   The priestess rode in a car drawn by white bulls to the temple of the Argive Hera.[10]   Iö, the daughter of Inachus, the first king of Argos, was changed by Hera into a cow.[11]   Iö was priestess of Hera,[12] and she is represented as the cow-goddess Hera.[13]   Iö's cow-form is further confirmed by Æschylus.[14]   The Egyptian goddess Isis was born in Argos, and was identified with the cow-shaped Iö.[15]   Isis was represented in Egypt as a female with cow-horns, like Iö in Greece.[16]

The cow-shaped Iö was guarded in Hera's sacred grove at Mycenæ by the hundred-eyed Argus, who was killed by Hermes, by order of Zeus ; and Hera next persecuted Iö by a gad fly, which forced her to wander from place to place.[17]   Thus Prometheus says : " How should I not hear the daughter of Inachus, who is chased around by the gad fly?"   But the wandering of Iö is nothing else than the symbol of the moon, which restlessly moves in its orbit.   This is also shown by the very name of Iö ('Ιώ), which is derived from the root I (in εἶμι, I go).   Even in classical antiquity Iö was still frequently represented as a cow ; as at Amyclæ.[18] Iö continued to be the old name of the moon in the religious mysteries

[1] Ovid. Metam. V. 330.   [2] Mionnet, 'Descr. des Méd. Ant.' pl. lxi. 6.
[3] Millingen, 'Anc. Coins of Greek Cities,' tab. ii. 12.
[4] Pausanias, II. 22, 1, 2.
[5] Plut. Quæst. Conviv. III. 9, 2 ; Etym. Mag. 388, 56.
[6] Plut. Fr. Dædal. 3.   [7] Paus. II. 17, 1.   [8] Paus. II. 4, 7.
[9] Paus. IX. 3, 4 ; Hesych. s. v. ἄγαν χαλκεῖος.   [10] Herod. I. 31.
[11] Lucian, Θεῶν Διάλ. 3 ; Diod. Sic. I. 24, 25 ; Herod. II. 41.
[12] Æsch. Suppl. 299 ; Apollod. II. 1, 3—

Κληδοῦχον Ἥρας φασὶ δωμάτων ποτὲ
'Ιὼ γενέσθαι τῇδ ἔν 'Αργείᾳ χθονί,— .

[13] Creuzer, 'Symbolik,' II. 576.
[14] Prom. 573, seq. and Hygin. Fab. 145.
[15] Diod. Sic. I. 24, 25 ; Apollod. II. 1, 3 ; Hygin. 145.   [16] Herod. II. 41.
[17] Apollod. II. 1, 3 ; Æschyl. Prom., 585 : πῶς δ'οὐ κλύω τῆς οἰστροδινήτου κόρης τῆς 'Ιναχείας.   [18] Paus. III. 18, 13.

at Argos.[1] Apis, king of the Argive realm, was the son of Phoroneus, and thus the grandson of Inachus, and the nephew of Iö. From Apis, the Peloponnesus and also Argos were called *Apia;* after his death he was worshipped under the name Serapis.[2] According to another tradition, Apis ceded his dominion in Greece to his brother, and became king of Egypt,[3] where, as Serapis, he was worshipped in the shape of a bull. Æschylus makes the wanderings of Iö end in Egypt, where Jove restores her to her shape, and she bears Epaphus, another name for the bull-god Apis. The cow-horns of the Pelasgian moon-goddess Iö, who became later the Argive Hera and is perfectly identical with her, as well as the cow-horns of Isis, were derived from the symbolic horns of the crescent representing the moon.[4] No doubt Iö, the later Hera, had at an earlier age, besides her cow-horns, a cow's face. Hera, under her old moon-name Iö, had a celebrated temple on the site of Byzantium, which city was said to have been founded by her daughter Keroëssa—i.e., "the horned." [5] The crescent, which was in all antiquity and throughout the Middle Ages the symbol of Byzantium, and which is now the symbol of the Turkish empire, is a direct inheritance from Byzantium's mythical foundress, Keroëssa, the daughter of the moon-goddess Iö (Hera); for it is certain that the Turks did not bring it with them from Asia, but found it already an emblem of Byzantium. Hera, Iö, and Isis, must at all events be identical also with Demeter Mycalessia, who derived her epithet " the lowing," from her cow-shape, and had her temple at Mycalessus in Bœotia. She had as door keeper Hercules, whose office it was to shut her sanctuary in the evening, and to open it again in the morning.[6] Thus his service is identical with that of Argus, who in the morning unfastens the cow-shaped Iö, and fastens her again in the evening to the olive tree,[7] which was in the sacred grove of Mycenæ, close to the Ἡραῖον.[8] The Argive Hera had, as the symbol of fertility, a pomegranate, which, as well as the flowers with which her crown was ornamented, gave her a telluric character.[9]

---

[1] Eustath. *ap.* Dionys. Perieg. 92, 94, Ἰὼ γὰρ ἡ σελήνη κατὰ τὴν τῶν Ἀργείων διάλεκτον, on which Heyne, *ad* Apollod. p. 100, says : "fuisse suspicor nomen hoc caputque feminæ cornutum symbolum Lunæ apud Argivos antiquissimum." See also Jablonsky, *Panth.* II. p. 4 ff.

[2] Apollod. II. 1, 1; Schol. Lykophr. 177; Schol. Apoll. Rhod. IV. 263; Steph. Byz.

[3] Euseb. *Chron.* Pars I. pp. 96, 127, 130, ed. Aucher; Augustin. *de Civit. Dei,* XVIII. 5.

[4] Diod. Sic. I. 11; Plut. *de Is. et Os.* 52, compare c. 39; Macrob. *Sat.* I. 19; Ælian, *Hist. Anim.* X. 27.

[5] O. Müller, *Dorier,* I. 121; Steph. Byz. *s.v.* Βυζάντιον.

[6] Paus. IX. 19, 4.   [7] Ovid. *Metam.* I. 630.   [8] Apollod. II. 1, 3.

[9] Panofka, 'Argos Panoptes,' tab. ii. 4; Cadalvène, 'Recueil de Méd. Gr.' Pl. III. 1; Müller, 'Denkmäler,' XXX. 132; Duc de Luynes, 'Études Numismat.' pp. 22-25.

In the same way that in Bœotia the epithet Mycalessia, "the lowing," a derivation from μυκᾶσθαι, was given to Demeter, on account of her cow-form, so in the plain of Argos the name of Μυκῆναι, a derivative from the same verb, was given to the city most celebrated for the cultus of Hera, and this can only be explained by her cow-form. I may here mention that Μυκάλη was the name of the mount and promontory directly opposite to and in the immediate neighbourhood of the island of Samos, which was celebrated for the worship of Hera.

In consideration of this long series of proofs, certainly no one will for a moment doubt that Hera's Homeric epithet βοῶπις shows her to have been at one time represented with a cow's face, in the same way as Athena's Homeric epithet γλαυκῶπις shows this goddess to have once been represented with an owl's face. But in the history of these two epithets there are evidently three stages, in which they had different significations. In the first stage the ideal conception and the naming of the goddesses took place, and in that naming, as my esteemed friend Professor Max Müller rightly observed to me, the epithets were figurative or ideal, that is, natural. Hera (Iö), as deity of the moon, would receive her epithet βοῶπις from the symbolic horns of the crescent moon and its dark spots, which resemble a face with large eyes ; whilst Athena, as goddess of the dawn, doubtless received the epithet γλαυκῶπις to indicate the light of the opening day.

In the second stage of these epithets the deities were represented by idols, in which the former figurative intention was forgotten, and the epithets were materialised into a cow-face for Hera, and into an owl-face for Athena ; and I make bold to assert that it is not possible to describe such cow-faced or owl-faced female figures by any other epithets than by βοῶπις and γλαυκῶπις. The word πρόσωπον for 'face,' which is so often used in Homer, and is probably thousands of years older than the poet, is never found in compounds, whilst words with the suffix -ειδης refer to expression or likeness in general. Thus, if Hera had had the epithet of βοοειδής, and Athena that of γλαυκοειδής, we should have understood nothing else but that the former had the shape and form of a cow, and the latter that of an owl.

To this second stage belong all the prehistoric ruins at Hissarlik, Tiryns, and Mycenæ.

The third stage in the history of the two epithets is when, after Hera and Athena had lost their cow and owl faces, and received the faces of women, and after the cow and the owl had become the attributes of these deities, and had, as such, been placed at their side, βοῶπις and γλαυκῶπις continued to be used as epithets consecrated by the use of ages, and probably with the meaning "large-eyed," and " owl-eyed." To this third stage belong the Homeric rhapsodies.

THE WEST SIDE OF T

In the background is the principal summit of Mount Euboea, 2

PLATE II.

OPOLIS OF MYCENÆ.
et high, crowned with an open Chapel of the Prophet Elias.

No. 16. Ruins of the Cyclopean Bridge at Mycenæ.*

CHAPTER II.

TOPOGRAPHY OF MYCENÆ.

GATE OF THE LIONS AND TREASURY OF ATREUS.

The road from Argos to Mycenæ—The Plain of Argos : its rivers and
hills, horses and vegetation—Myth regarding its arid nature—Swamps
in the southern part ; and fable of the Lernæan hydra—Early social
development here—Legend of Phoroneus—The Pelasgian Argos—
The Achæan states of Argos and Mycenæ—Situation of Mycenæ—
The *Citadel* and its Cyclopean walls—The term defined—" Gate of
the Lions "—The postern gate—Cisterns—Poetical confusion of
Argos and Mycenæ.

The *Lower City :* its house-walls, bridge, treasuries, and pottery—Its
partially enclosing wall—The undefended suburb, and its large

---

* In the background is the second peak of Mount Eubœa, 2000
feet high, which rises immediately south of the Acropolis of Mycenæ.

buildings—Its extent—The only two wells in Mycenæ—Three
Treasuries in the suburb—Treasuries in the Lower City—Description
of the " Treasury of Atreus "—Dodwell's Argument for regarding the
building as a Treasury—Uniqueness of these structures—Excavation
of the Treasury by Veli Pasha.

Mycenæ, August 19, 1876.

I ARRIVED here on the 7th inst. by the same road which
Pausanias * describes. The distance from Argos is only
50 *stadia*, or 5·8 English miles. Pausanias saw, on that
side of Argos which looked toward Mycenæ, the temple of
Lucina (Εἰλείθυια), and next an altar of the Sun, which
appears to have been on the bank of the Inachus. After
having passed this river he saw, to his right, the temple
of the Mysian Demeter, and further on to his left the
mausoleum of Thyestes, the brother of Atreus and uncle
of Agamemnon. This monument was crowned with a ram
of stone, in commemoration of the adultery of Thyestes
with his brother's wife. Still further on he saw, to his right,
the temple (ἡρῷον) of Perseus, the founder of Mycenæ.
But of all these monuments not a vestige now remains.

The first river I passed, in coming from Argos. was the
ancient Χαράδρος, now called *Rema*, an affluent of the
Inachus, on the banks of which, as Thucydides † informs
us, the Argives were in the habit of holding a military
court on the return of their armies from abroad, before
allowing them to enter the city. Soon afterwards I passed
the very wide bed of the famous river Inachus, now called
Bonitza, which traverses the plain of Argos in its entire
length. The beds of both these rivers are dry except when
heavy rain falls in the mountains ; and this appears to have
been the case also in the time of Pausanias, who says ‡
that he found the sources of the Inachus on Mount Artemisium, but that the quantity of water was very insignificant and it only ran for a short distance. This seems to

---

* II. 18. See the Sketch Map on p. 1.
† V. 60.   ‡ II. 25, 3.

prove beyond any doubt that the Arcadian mountains were then already as bare of trees as they are now.

But as the Inachus plays so important a part in the mythic legends of the Argolid, which make him the husband of Meleia and father of Phoroneus, the first king of Argos, and of the moon-goddess Iö (the later Hera), there can be no doubt that in prehistoric times the Inachus was a river of some consequence. This, however, seems to be only possible if we suppose the Arcadian mountains to have been at that time overgrown with forests. That the Inachus was once, and for ages, an abundant river, is proved also by the fact that the whole plain of Argos has been formed by the alluvia of its rivers, but principally by those of the Inachus.

Further upon the road from Argos to Mycenæ I passed another smaller river-bed, which seems to be the Cephisus mentioned by Pausanias.* In speaking of the rivers of the plain of Argos, I must further mention the two streams Eleutherion and Asterion, between which was situated the celebrated Heræum on the lower slope of Mount Eubœa. Both are now dry and have no water except in heavy and long-continued rains, but they seem still in classical antiquity to have had an abundance of water all the year round, for the Eleutherion was the sacred water used in the religious ceremonies at the temple, whilst the water of the Asterion fed the asterion-plant (a kind of aster), sacred to Hera, from the leaves of which wreaths and festoons were made for the goddess. The very name also of Mount Eubœa seems to indicate that it was once a rich pasture ground, whilst now it is as completely barren of all vegetation as are the beds and banks of the two rivers.

The plain of Argos is enclosed on the west and north

---

* Κηφισός. II. 15, 5; the lesser streams are not shown on the Sketch Map, p. 1.

by the highlands of Artemisium, on the east by those of Arachnæon. From the former several parallel ridges of hills advance for some distance into the plain; the most northerly of them is Mount Lycone, which terminates in Mount Larissa, 900 feet high, with the Acropolis of Argos, the city itself being situated at the foot of the mount, in the plain. The second ridge is the Chaon, at the foot of which the river Erasinus issues in a copious stream and falls into the Argolic Gulf, turning many mills. This river was in all antiquity considered to be identical with the Stymphalus, which disappears by two subterranean channels under Mount Apelauron in Arcadia. The third parallel ridge is the Pontinus. On the east side much smaller and more detached hills slope gently into the plain. To the north the mountains are very rough and abrupt. On the north and south-east of the Acropolis of Mycenæ are the two highest peaks of Mount Euboea;* the northern one, which is crowned with an open chapel of the prophet Elias, is 2500 feet high.

In all antiquity the plain of Argos was celebrated for the breeding of horses, and Homer,† seven times in the Iliad, praises its splendid horse-pasture grounds by the epithet "ἱππόβοτος."

Owing to the great dryness of the land, wine and cotton can now be grown only in the fertile lower plain, and a little corn and tobacco is all that can be produced in the highlands. Even as late as the Greek war of independence (1821) there must have been much more moisture here, because at that time the whole plain, and even a large portion of the highlands, were thickly planted with mul-

---

* The accuracy of this name is confirmed by Pausanias, II. 17, § 2.
† *Il.* II. 287, III. 75 and 258, VI. 152, IX. 246, XV. 30, and XIX. 329. Comp. Horat. *Carm.* I. 7, 8, 9 :—

" Plurimus in Junonis honorem
Aptum dicet equis Argos, ditesque Mycenas."

berry, orange, and olive trees, which have now altogether disappeared.

The epithet πολυδίψιον, " very thirsty," which Homer gives to the plain of Argos, agrees perfectly with its present condition, and also with the myth told by Pausanias : * " Poseidon and Hera disputed about the possession of the land (the plain of Argos), and Phoroneus, son of the river Inachus, Cephisus, Asterion, and Inachus himself, had to decide ; they adjudged the plain to Hera, whereupon Poseidon made the waters disappear. Hence neither Inachus nor any other of the aforesaid rivers have any water, except when Jove sends rain (Ζεὺς ὕει) ; in summer all the rivers are dry except the (springs of) Lerna." The epithet πολυδίψιον, however, does not agree with the passage already cited from Aristotle,† which asserts that at the time of the war of Troy the land of Argos was swampy, whilst that of Mycenæ was good.

The most southern part of the plain of Argos has at all times had a great abundance of water, but with little or no profit to agriculture ; for the sea-shore is lined with vast and almost impassable swamps, and the river Erasinus, which pours down from Mount Chaon, soon empties itself into the Gulf of Nauplia. Further, the springs at the foot of Mount Pontinus form the famous swamps of Lerna, where Hercules is fabled to have killed the Hydra. Probably this myth is the symbolic account of an attempt once made to drain the swamps and to convert them into arable land.

Owing to its exuberant fertility and exceptional situation on the splendid gulf, this plain has been the natural centre and the point of departure for the whole political and social development of the country, and for this reason it deserves the appellation "ancient Argos." ‡ Here Phoroneus, son of the river Inachus and the nymph Meleia,

---

* II. 15.   † *Meteorol.* i. 14.   ‡ Soph. *Electra*, 4.

was said, with his wife Niobe, to have first united the inhabitants, who till then had lived dispersed, into one
community, and to have founded a city which he called
Ἄστυ φορωνικόν,* which was renamed by his grandson
Argos, and became the centre of a powerful Pelasgic state.†
Indisputable proofs of this Pelasgic settlement are found in
both the names Argos and Larissa, which are Pelasgic,
the former meaning "plain," the latter "fortress"; further,
in the myth of the ancient Pelasgic moon and cow-goddess
Iö, who, as has been said above, was fabled to have been
born here, her father being the river Inachus.   The
Pelasgic state comes afterwards under the dominion of the
Pelopids, under whom the country is divided into two
states, as we find it still in the Iliad; the northern part,
with the capital Mycenæ, being under the sceptre of
Agamemnon; the southern, with Argos as its capital,
under the dominion of Diomedes, who was, however, only
a vassal of the former.   At all events, at the time of the
invasion of the Peloponnesus by the Dorians, Argos was
the mightiest state in the peninsula, and thus tradition
allots it to the Heraclid Temenus, the firstborn son of
Aristomachus.

The situation of Mycenæ is beautifully described by
Homer,‡ "In the depth of the horse-feeding Argos,"
because it lies in the north corner of the plain of Argos,
in a recess between the two majestic peaks of Mount
Eubœa, whence it commanded the upper part of the great
plain and the important narrow pass, by which the roads
lead to Phlius, Cleonæ, and Corinth.   The Acropolis
occupied a strong rocky height, which projects from the
foot of the mountain behind it in the form of an irregular
triangle sloping to the west.§   This cliff overhangs a

---

* Paus. II. 15, 5 ; comp. Plato, *Timæus.*
† Comp. Æschyl. *Suppl.* 250.
‡ *Od.* III. 263 :—" μυχῷ Ἄργεος ἱπποβότοιο."
§ See the large Plate II. and Plan B of the Acropolis.

deep gorge, which protects the whole south flank of the citadel. Through the abyss below winds the bed of a torrent usually almost dry, because it has no other water than that of the copious fountain Perseia, which is about half a mile to the north-east of the fortress. This gorge extends first from east to west, and afterwards in a south-westerly direction. The cliff also falls off precipitously on the north side into a glen, which stretches in a straight line from east to west. Between these two gorges extended the lower city. The cliff of the citadel is also more or less steep on the east and west side, where it forms six natural or artificial terraces.

The Acropolis is surrounded by Cyclopean walls, from 13 to 35 feet high, and on an average 16 feet thick. Their entire circuit still exists, but they have evidently been much higher. They are of beautiful hard breccia, with which the neighbouring mountains abound. They follow the sinuosities of the rock, and show three different kinds of architecture. By far the greater portion of them is built exactly like the walls of Tiryns, although not so massively; and as this kind of architecture is generally thought to be the most ancient, I have marked it on the adjoining cut (No. 17)

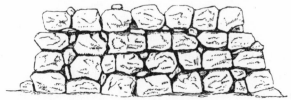

No. 17. Walls of the First Period.

with the words, "Walls of the first period." A large piece of the western wall I have marked on the accompanying cut (No. 18) as "Walls of the second period," because it consists of polygons, fitted together with great art, so that, in spite of the infinite variety of the joints, they formed as it were one solidly united and neat wall, as if of rock; and this sort of building, which can be seen in so many places in

Greece and Southern Italy, is universally acknowledged to
be generally of a later period than the former.   I have

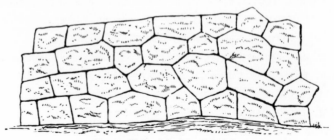

No. 18.   Walls of the Second Period.

marked here (No. 19) as "Walls of the third period" those
walls to the right and left of the great gate, which consist
of almost quadrangular blocks arranged in horizontal layers;
but their joints are not always vertical and they present
lines more or less oblique.

No. 19.   Walls of the Third Period.

I have made this division into three periods merely to
point out the different architecture of the walls, and with
no intention of maintaining that the one must be more
ancient than the other.   On the contrary, after mature
consideration, I cannot think that the one kind of wall
should be considered older than the other, for, after the
circuit walls had once been built of rough stones of enormous size, it is hardly possible that in after times part of
them should have been destroyed in order to replace them
by walls of another type.   Or if part of the primitive walls
had been razed by an enemy, there could have been no
reason why they should not be restored in the same style,

which was quite as solid as the other, and was besides much cheaper and easier, because only the wall could have been destroyed, but not the stones, which lay ready to be put up again. It appears also to have been the custom of the primitive builders to pay a little more attention to symmetry and regularity in the more monumental portions of their work. I conclude, therefore, that the three kinds of architecture existed simultaneously in that remote age of antiquity when the walls of Mycenæ were built, but that in later times the style of architecture marked as of the " first period" went out of fashion, and the two other modes of building alone remained in use. Walls of polygonal blocks continued in use in Greece until the time of the Macedonian dominion ; a proof of which is seen, for instance, in the masonry of the sepulchres at the Hagia Trias in Athens, as well as the fortifications on the island of Salamis, of which we know with certainty that they were erected in the fourth or fifth century, B.C.* Within the last sixteen years walls of polygonal blocks have come extensively into use in Sweden and Norway, particularly for the substructions of railway bridges.

The first western terrace is bordered on its east side, for a distance of 166 feet, by a Cyclopean wall 30 feet high, which is crowned by the ruins of a tower, and runs parallel with the great circuit wall ; it is no doubt part of a second enclosure.† Remnants of other enclosures are visible a little higher up the mount to the left, as well as on the eastern side. A second interior tower appears to have stood at the south-western corner of the summit.

Near the north-western corner the circuit wall is traversed by an ogive-like passage 16½ feet long, like those of Tiryns (see No. 20). Traces of Cyclopean house-walls

---

* See Émile Burnouf, ' La Ville et l'Acropole d'Athènes.'

† A good view of this wonderful wall is seen in the background of Plate VI., which represents the Ichnography of the tombs discovered in the Acropolis. (See Chap. V.)

and foundations can be seen on all but the first eastern and western terraces.

No. 20.   Entrance to the ogive-like Gallery in the
Walls of the Citadel of Mycenæ.

Notwithstanding the remote antiquity of Mycenæ, its ruins are in a far better state of preservation than those of any of the Greek cities which Pausanias saw in a flourishing condition, and whose sumptuous monuments he describes (about 170 A.D.); and, owing to its distant and secluded position, and to the rudeness, magnitude, and solidity of the ruins, it is hardly possible to think that any change can have taken place in the general aspect of Mycenæ since it was seen by Pausanias.

No. 21.   Gate of the Lions.

In the north-western corner of the circuit-wall is the great "Lions' Gate," of beautiful hard breccia.*   The opening, which widens from the top downwards, is 10 ft. 8 in.

* See Plan B., Plate III., and Nos. 21, 22 (p. 34)

PLATE III.

To face page 32.

GATE OF THE LIONS. The Principal Entrance to the Acropolis of Mycenæ.

high, and its width is 9 ft. 6 in. at the top, and 10 ft.
3 in. below. In the lintel (15 feet long and 8 feet broad)
are round holes, 6 inches deep, for the hinges, and in the
two uprights, which it roofs over, are four quadrangular
holes for the bolts. Over the lintel of the gate is a triangular gap in the masonry of the wall, formed by an oblique
approximation of the side courses of stone. The object of
this was to keep off the pressure of the superincumbent
wall from the flat lintel.

This niche is filled up by a triangular slab of the same
beautiful breccia of which the gateway and the walls consist: it is 10 feet high, 12 feet long at the base, and 2 feet
thick. On the face of the slab are represented in relief two
lions, standing opposite to each other on their long outstretched hind-legs, and resting with their fore-paws on
either side of the top of an altar, on the midst of which
stands a column with a capital formed of four circles
enclosed between two horizontal fillets. The general belief
that the heads of the lions are *broken off* is wrong, for
on close examination I find that they were *not* cut out
of the same stone together with the animals, but that
they were made separately and fastened on the bodies
with bolts. The straight cuts and the borings in the
necks of the animals can leave no doubt as to this fact.
Owing to the narrowness of the space, the heads could
only have been very small, and they must have been
protruding and facing the spectator. I feel inclined to
believe that they were of bronze and gilded. The tails
of the lions are not broad and bushy, but narrow, like
those which are seen in the most ancient sculptures of
Egypt.

It is universally believed that this sculpture represents
some symbol, but many different conjectures have been made
as to its meaning. One thinks that the column alludes to
the solar worship of the Persians; another believes that it is
the symbol of the holy fire, and a *pyratheion* or fire altar, of

which the lions are the guardians; a third conjectures that
it represents Apollo Agyieus, that is, the "guardian of the
gateway." I am of this last opinion, and firmly believe
that it is this very same symbol of that god which Sophocles makes Orestes and Electra invoke when they enter
their father's house.* As to the two lions, the explanation is still more simple. Pelops, son of the Phrygian
king Tantalus,† migrated hither from Phrygia, where the
mother of the gods, Rhea, whose sacred animal is the lion,
had a celebrated worship. Most probably, therefore, Pelops

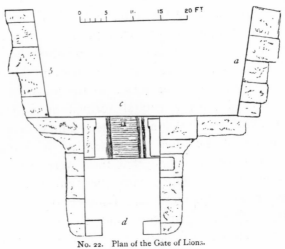

No. 22.   Plan of the Gate of Lions.

(a) Wall of Acropolis on E. side.   (b) Face of projecting masonry on W. side.
(c) Gateway and Cill.   (d) Inner Gateway.

brought with him the cultus of the patron deity of his
mother-country, and made her sacred animal the symbol of
the Pelopids. Æschylus compares Agamemnon himself
to a lion;‡ he also compares Agamemnon with Ægisthus
as a lion with a wolf.§ Thus here above the gate the two
lions, either as the sacred animals of Rhea or as the symbol

---

* Soph. *Electra*, 1374.
† Schol. Eurip. *Orest.* 5 ; Apollod. iii. 5, 6; Soph. *Antig.* 818.
‡ *Agam.* 1259 : λέοντος εὐγενοῦς ἀπουσίᾳ.   § *Agam.* 1258.

of the powerful dynasty of the Pelopids, have been united to the symbol of Apollo Agyieus, the guardian of the gate-way. To the left of the sculpture of the lions is a large quadrangular window in the wall.

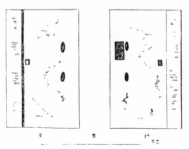

No. 22a. The Right and Left Door Posts of the Gate of Lions.

The great gate stands at right angles to the adjoining wall of the citadel, and is approached by a passage, 50 feet long and 30 feet wide, formed by that wall and by another exterior wall, which runs nearly parallel to it, and which forms part of a large quadrangular tower erected for the defence of the entrance.* Within these walls the enemy could advance only with a small front of perhaps seven men, exposed on three sides to the arrows and stones of the defenders. A zigzag road on immense Cyclopean substructions, now covered with large blocks which have fallen from the wall, led up to the entrance of the gateway. Leake rightly says that the early citadel builders bestowed greater labour than their successors on the ap-proaches to the gates, and de-vised various modes of protract-ing the defence of the interior by numerous enclosures and by intricacy of communication.

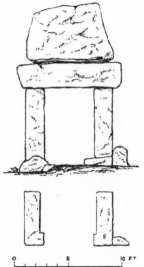

No. 23. Elevation and Plan of the Postern Gate.

The postern-gate† consists likewise of three large slabs,

---

* For an account of the discovery of the ground plan of the Lions' Gate and its enormous threshold, see Chapter V.

† See Plan C, and the cut No. 23.

namely, two uprights and the lintel by which these are
roofed.   The opening of this gateway likewise widens from
the top downward; at the top it is 5 ft. 4 in. wide and
5 ft. 11 in. at the bottom.   On the lintel stands a triangular
slab, inclusive of which the gate is 14 feet high.   The
grooves for the bolts in the jambs of the door are square
and of large dimensions.   The situation of this gate is not
very favourable, because the enemies who attacked it would
have their left arm, which was guarded by the shield, on
the side of the Acropolis.   On the slope on the west side
are several subterranean cisterns.

According to Plutarch, the first name of the mount of
the citadel was Argion.*   It is significant that it is never mentioned by ancient authors under the appellation of "acropolis." Sophocles (*Electra*) calls it δῶμα Πελοπιδῶν or 'residence of the Pelopids,' also οὐράνια τείχη, 'heavenly walls'
Euripides † also calls it, "stone Cyclopean heavenly walls,"
and further ‡ "Cyclopean heavenly walls," and this must
refer to the hugeness of the walls and towers.   Strabo §
justly observes that, on account of the close vicinity
of Argos and Mycenæ, the tragic poets have made a
confusion regarding their names, continually substituting
the one for the other. But this is to be excused, because
in antiquity travelling was both difficult and very unsafe.
Besides, people were not archæologists, and though every
one took the very deepest interest in the ancient history of
Greece, no one cared to submit to the trouble and hardship,
or to incur the danger, of visiting even the places which
had been the scene of his country's most glorious actions.
This could not possibly be better proved than by the fact
that no ancient author mentions the reconstruction of
Mycenæ after its capture and destruction in 468 B.C.

---

* Τὸ Ἄργιον ὄρος. *De Fluv.* 18, 7.
† *Troad.* 1088, τείχη λάϊνα κυκλώπια οὐράνια.
‡ *Electra*, 1158, κυκλώπεια οὐράνια τείχη.   § VIII. p. 377.

Homer himself is seemingly guilty of making a confusion regarding the names of Argos and Mycenæ, because he puts into the mouth of Agamemnon the words concerning Chryseis:

> " Her I release not, till her youth be fled ;
> Within my walls, in Argos, far from home,
> Her lot is cast, domestic cares to ply,
> And share a master's bed   .   .   ."—LORD DERBY.*

But by the name Argos Homer understands here the Argolid territory and perhaps the whole Peloponnesus; a sense of which another passage can leave no doubt: †

> " O'er all the Argive coast and neighbouring isles to reign."

The same may be the case, more or less, with the later tragic poets, and at all events it must be so with Euripides, because he knew Mycenæ too well to mistake it for Argos. Thus he calls Mycenæ‡ " the altars of the Cyclopes;" " the Cyclopean Mycenæ";§ and " the handiwork of the Cyclopes":—‖

> " Do you call the city of Perseus the handiwork of the Cyclopes ? "

In other passages he says, " O Cyclopean houses, O my country, O my dear Mycenæ!"¶ Again, " Standing

---

* *Iliad*, I. 29-31 :
> τὴν δ᾽ ἐγὼ οὐ λύσω πρίν μιν καὶ γῆρας ἔπεισιν
> ἡμετέρῳ ἐνὶ οἴκῳ, ἐν Ἄργει, τηλόθι πάτρης,
> ἱστὸν ἐποιχομένην καὶ ἐμὸν λέχος ἀντιόωσαν.

† *Iliad*, II. 108 : πολλῇσιν νήσοισι καὶ Ἄργεϊ παντὶ ἀνάσσειν.

‡ *Iphigenia in Aulide*, 152 : κυκλώπων θυμέλαι.

§ *Ibid.* 265 : Μυκῆναι κυκλωπίαι.

‖ *Ibid.* 1500-1501 :
> καλεῖς πόλισμα Περσέως,
> Κυκλωπίων πόνον χερῶν ;

¶ *Iphig. Taur.* 845 :
> κυκλωπίδες ἑστίαι, ὦ πάτρις,
> Μυκήνα φίλα.

on (or *at*) the stone steps, the herald calls aloud ' *To the Agora, to the Agora,* ye people of Mycenæ, to see the portents and the terrific signs of the blessed kings.'"*
Again, " O mother-country, O Pelasgia, O my home, Mycenæ."† Again, " Dear ladies of Mycenæ, first in rank in the Pelasgic settlement of the Argives."‡ Again, " I will go to Mycenæ ; crow-bars and pickaxes will I take to destroy with twisted-iron the town, the foundations of the Cyclopes, which are well fitted together with the chisel and the purple rule."§

This description can only refer to Cyclopean walls composed of well-fitted polygons, such as we see in the western part of the great circuit walls.‖ Besides Euripides knew accurately that the Agora, with the Royal sepulchres, was in the Acropolis; and thus it appears certain that Euripides visited Mycenæ, and that the grand Cyclopean walls of the Acropolis, as well as the sacred enclosure of the circular Agora, with the mysterious tombs of the most glorious heroes of antiquity, made a profound impression upon him, for otherwise we cannot explain his so often

---

* *Electra,* 710 :
  πετρίνοις τ' ἐπιστὰς
  κάρυξ ἰάχει βάθροις,
  ἀγοράν, ἀγοράν, Μυκηναῖοι
  στείχετε, μακαρίων ὀψόμενοι τυράννων
  φάσματα, δείματα.

† *Iphigenia in Aulide,* 1498–1499 :
  ἰὼ γᾶ μᾶτερ ὦ Πελασγία,
  Μυκηναῖαί τ' ἐμαί θεράπναι.

‡ *Orestes,* 1246–1247 :
  Μυκηνίδες ὦ φίλαι,
  τὰ πρῶτα κατὰ Πελα-
  σγὸν ἕδος 'Αργείων.

§ *Hercules Furens,* 974–944 :
  πρὸς τὰς Μυκήνας εἶμι λάζυσθαι χρεὼν
  μοχλοὺς δικέλλας θ', ὡς τὰ κυκλώπων βάθρα
  φοίνικι κανόνι καὶ τύκοις ἡρμοσμένα
  στρεπτῷ σιδήρῳ συντριαινώσω πόλιν.

‖ See Plate II.

speaking of the gigantic Cyclopean walls, describing also their structure and mentioning even the Agora situated in the Acropolis (see Chapter V.).

Seneca says of the walls of Mycenæ :

> "majus mihi
> Bellum Mycenis restat, ut cyclopea
> Eversa manibus saxa nostra concidant.

and again—

> "cerno Cyclopum sacras
> Turres, labore majus humano decus."

and in another passage *

> "Ulixes ad Ithacæ suæ saxa sic properat, quemadmodum
> Agamemnon ad Mycenarum nobiles muros."

Over the space of about a square mile to the west-south-west and south of this Acropolis, and exactly between the aforesaid deep ravines, extended the Lower City,† the site of which is distinctly marked by the remnants of numerous Cyclopean substructions of houses, by a Cyclopean bridge, by five Treasuries, and finally by the fragments of beautifully painted archaic pottery with which the ground is strewn. The site of the lower town is traversed in its whole length by a ridge, which to the right falls off gradually into the plain, and to the left more steeply into the deep ravine, which issues from between the south end of the citadel-cliff and the second peak of Mount Eubœa. The summit of this ridge has evidently been artificially levelled for two purposes; firstly, for the principal street of the town, which commenced at the Lions' Gate and ended at the Cyclopean bridge, an engraving of which forms the vignette to this chapter ;‡ and secondly, for the city wall, which ran to the right of the street as far as the same bridge, and undoubtedly united it with the Acropolis at its north-west corner, near the Lions' Gate.

---

* *Epistul Mor.* 66, 26.　　† See Plan D.　　‡ See No. 16, p. 23.

Another branch of this wall extended all along the western bank of the torrent which the bridge spanned, and doubtless connected the latter with the south-western corner of the Acropolis. Of both branches of this wall very numerous traces remain, though with difficulty perceptible. Thus a part of the lower town, but scarcely one-third of it, was enclosed by a circuit wall. This was very insignificant, because its thickness on the ridge is only 6 feet, and it is still less on the bank of the torrent; so that it cannot have been high, and it was probably intended only to impart greater strength to the great Cyclopean walls of the Acropolis, and to prevent the Lions' Gate leading directly into the open country. After carefully examining the remnants of this city wall in numerous places, I see, in consideration of its weakness, no reasonable ground to object to regarding it as of later date than the walls of the citadel.

The remaining part of the town has been, as the remnants of the house-walls show, a vast and well-built suburb, whence, when attacked by the enemy against whom their own means of defence were insufficient, the inhabitants could retire into the fortified part of the city and into the citadel. Some of the buildings of this suburb are very large, and show a most splendid Cyclopean masonry. I call particular attention to the vast building on the very bank of the deep glen in a westerly direction from the Lions' Gate, of which all the four walls are still visible. It is 93 feet long and 60 feet broad, and may have been a temple. I call attention also to the foundations of a large Cyclopean building, perhaps a temple, on the crest of a hill S.S.W. of the Acropolis and north of the village of Charvati. This hill appears to have been at the extremity of the suburb in this direction, for the Mycenean potsherds cease beyond it. I found there two well-polished axes of diorite.

In two glens in the immediate vicinity of this hill are

the only two wells of Mycenæ. The ruins of Cyclopean
buildings close to them, and the Mycenean potsherds which
extend beyond them, can leave no doubt that both wells
were within the suburb. Strange to say, Professor E.
Curtius has thought the ancient quarry of Charvati to be
ruins of the city wall, and he has therefore put this village
on his map still within the site of Mycenæ; but this is a
great mistake; the city never extended so far.

But not all the Cyclopean walls in the suburb are
house-walls, for many of them are only intended for the
support of the terraces.

Much more interesting than all the other buildings in
the suburb are the "Treasuries," which, owing to their
great resemblance to ovens, are now called φοῦρνοι by the
country people. One of them is just without the line of
the town wall, on the slope of the hill near the Gate of the
Lions. The doorway is visible, but it is nearly buried; the
entrance is roofed with three large thick slabs; and the
length of the passage is 18 feet, its width 7 ft. 9 in. Only
a small part of the lower circular wall of the dome-shaped
building can now be seen, the upper part having fallen in,
probably ages ago.*

Descending the slope in a south-westerly direction, we
come to a smaller Treasury, the entrance passage of which
is 15½ feet long, and likewise roofed with three large
slabs. The width of the door is 7½ feet; part of the lower
circular wall of the dome-like building is here also above
ground, and shows at the height of the top of the entrance
a diameter of 25 feet; so that the diameter on the ground
floor may be 32 feet. Turning thence to the south, and
ascending the slope, we come, near the crest of the ridge,
to a third Treasury, of which only the entrance passage
remains. This is 20 feet long, and only 5 ft. 3 in. broad;
and is roofed by five large slabs.

---

* All these Treasuries are indicated on Plan D.

The whole site of the vast suburb being on slopes, and having been but scantily inhabited, on account of its vast extent, the accumulation of *débris* is everywhere small, and seldom exceeds a foot and a half in depth. A much greater accumulation is found only on the terraces immediately to the west and north-west of the Lions' Gate.

Though the site of the enclosed city is also on slopes, yet, as it is but small and must at all times have been more densely inhabited, the accumulation of *débris* is in general more considerable there, and particularly on the western and south-western side of the Acropolis. But at points more distant from the Acropolis, and particularly on the steeper slopes whence the remains of houses have been washed away by the rains, the accumulation does not exceed the quantity general in the suburb. It deserves particular attention that, except close to the western circuit-wall of the citadel, the site of the enclosed city shows far less of Cyclopean substructions or remnants of house-walls than the suburb; but immediately beyond the Cyclopean bridge on the opposite bank of the ravine are the ruins of two vast buildings which may have been forts and may have served for the defence of the bridge. I may here mention that traces of the ancient Cyclopean highway from Mycenæ to Tiryns are still visible for some distance beyond the bridge.

On the site of the enclosed city are the two largest Treasuries. One of these is the famous Treasury which tradition attributes to Atreus. The other, which is close to the Lions' Gate, appears to have been entirely under ground, and was therefore unknown in historical times; the upper part of its dome has fallen in, but I have not been able to ascertain whether, as some of the inhabitants of the Argolid affirm, this has occurred accidentally, or whether, as others maintain, it is the sacrilegious work of Veli Pasha, the son of the notorious Ali Pasha, who towards the end of 1820 attempted to force an entrance this way, but was pre-

PLATE IV.

THE TREASURY OF ATREUS.

To face page 43

vented by the outbreak of the Greek revolution from proceeding much further.

The "Treasury of Atreus," which is about 400 yards
further south, was entirely subterranean, being constructed
under the eastern slope of the ridge which traverses the
city, and towards the ravine of the same torrent which
passes the south side of the cliff of the citadel. On the
slope below the Treasury is a large platform of Cyclopean
masonry, from which the *dromos*, or approach—20 ft. 7 in.
broad, and lined with walls of wrought stones—leads to the
doorway of the building, which is 8 ft. 6 in. wide at the
top and 9 ft. 2 in. at the bottom. Its height is 18 feet; it
is roofed by two enormous slabs, beautifully cut and polished,
of which the inner one measures 3 ft. 9 in. in thickness, and
27½ feet in length on its lower and 29 feet on its upper
surface; its breadth is 17 feet, and it is computed that it
weighs approximately 300,000 English pounds.*

The great chamber, which resembles a dome or a vast
bee-hive, is 50 feet high and 50 feet in diameter. It is
built of well-wrought blocks of hard breccia, placed in
regular layers, and joined with the greatest precision without
any binding material. The stones, which on the inside are
smooth and well-fitted, are on the outside very irregular,
and, contrary to the general belief, they are not immediately
covered with earth, but with enormous masses of stone, which,
by their ponderous weight, keep all the stones of the circular
layers of masonry in their position. Thus the principle of
this construction is, as Colonel Leake justly remarks, that
of an arch-shaped wall resisting a great superincumbent
weight, and deriving its strength and coherence from the
weight itself. The same idea, which suggested the circular
shape to the Cyclopean architect, induced him also to curve
the sides vertically, as they derived from that form an additional power of resistance to the lateral pressure.

----

* See Plate IV., "Treasury of Atreus."

The blocks of the lower courses are 1 ft. 10 in. high
and from 4 to 7 ft. long; but towards the top of the dome
the courses become gradually narrower. The floor of the
vast chamber, which is entirely excavated, is the natural
rock. A number of large stones, which have remained in
the Treasury, make on travellers the erroneous impression
that there is still a great deal of *débris* left.

From the fourth course of stones upwards there are
visible in each stone two bored holes, and in many of these
can still be seen remnants of bronze nails which, according
to Sir W. Gell ("Argolis"), contain 88 per cent. of copper
and 12 per cent. of tin. These nails, of which several have
been found entire, had broad flat heads, and they can have
had no other purpose than to retain the bronze plates,
with which the whole interior was once decorated. We
know by the testimony of the ancient authors that the
Greeks in a remote antiquity ornamented their buildings
in this manner, because in no other way can we explain
the bronze houses and chambers which they mention.*

---

* Thus we read in Homer (*Od.* VII. 84–87):

"Ὥστε γὰρ ἠελίου αἴγλη πέλεν ἠὲ σελήνης,
Δῶμα καθ' ὑψερεφὲς μεγαλήτορος Ἀλκινόοιο,
Χάλκεοι μὲν γὰρ τοῖχοι ἐρηρέδατ' ἔνθα καὶ ἔνθα,
Ἐς μυχὸν ἐξ οὐδοῦ· περὶ δὲ θριγκὸς κυάνοιο.

"Like the sun or the moon beam in bright splendour, so beamed the high palace of
the magnanimous Alcinoüs; for the brazen walls extended from the threshold of the
gate to the innermost part of the building; their entablature was of blue steel."

Further the palaces of the immortal gods on Olympus must have
been thought to be also ornamented with brazen plates, because Homer
says (*Iliad*, I. 426): Διὸς ποτὶ χαλκοβατὲς δῶ, "To the brazen house
of Jove."

We also read in Pausanias (II. 23):

Ἀλλὰ δέ ἐστιν Ἀργείοις θέας ἄξια· κατάγαιον οἰκοδόμημα, ἐπ' αὐτὸ δὲ ἦν ὁ χαλκοῦς
θάλαμος, ὃν Ἀκρίσιός ποτε φρουρὰν τῆς θυγατρὸς ἐποίησεν. Περίλαος δὲ καθεῖλεν αὐτὸν
τυραννήσας· τοῦτό τε οὖν τὸ οἰκοδόμημά ἐστι. "In Argos there are still other
remarkable objects: a subterranean vault, over which was the brazen chamber which
Acrisius made for his daughter (Danaë's) prison; it was destroyed under the
dominion of Perilaüs, but the building still exists."

The only other example extant of walls which had once this kind of decoration is presented by the Treasury of Minyas in Orchomenus, which is built of beautiful white marble, but shows in other respects the very greatest resemblance to the Treasury of Atreus. It is constructed on the same principle, and appears to be of the same age and to have been erected for the same purpose. Each stone of this treasury likewise shows two or more holes, with frequent remnants of the bronze nails which once retained the brazen plates that decorated the inner walls of the edifice.* Thus it is certain that in a remote antiquity, before sculpture or painting came into use for wall

---

Further in Horace (*Carm.* III. 16):

> " Inclusam Danaën turris ahenea
> Robustæque fores et vigilum canum
> Tristes excubiæ munierant satis
> Nocturnis ab adulteris."

"A bronze tower, solid doors, and the severe watch of the dogs, had been for the imprisoned Danaë a sufficiently strong protection against nocturnal lovers."

Another case is the temple of *Athena Chalciœcus* at Sparta, where King Pausanias was put to death. The name of this sanctuary can of course refer to nothing else than to the brazen plates with which the walls were decorated.

My esteemed friend, Mr. Chas. T. Newton, of the British Museum, calls my attention to Colonel Mure's article in the *Rheinisches Museum*, VIII. 272, in which the author states that General Gordon told him he had in his collection in Scotland fragments not only of the bronze nails, but also of the brazen plates of the Treasury of Atreus. At the same time Colonel Mure quotes the passage of Sophocles (*Antigone,* 944–947):

> ἔτλα καὶ Δανάας οὐράνιον φῶς
> ἀλλάξαι δέμας ἐν χαλκοδέτοις αὐλαῖς ·
> κρυπτομένα δ' ἐν τυμβήρει θαλάμῳ κατεζεύχθη.

("The body also of Danaë endured to exchange the heavenly light against the darkness in the halls covered with brazen plates; hidden in a sepulchral chamber, she was fettered").

* Pausanias (ix. 38) says of this Treasury: "The Treasury of Minyas is the most wonderful edifice in Greece, and is second to no work of art abroad; it is built in the following manner: it consists of stone and has a circular form; the summit is not very pointed; it is said that the topmost stone holds together the whole building."

decoration, polished metal plates were employed to give both splendour and dignity to the houses of the rich.

In the Treasury of Atreus, the exterior of the door-lintel is decorated with two parallel mouldings, which are also carried down the jambs of the door. Above the lintel numerous holes can be discerned, to which bronze ornaments must have been attached. There are more such holes in the flat wall above the entrance, and all testify to the elaborate exterior ornamentation of the edifice. Above the entrance is an equilateral triangular niche, each side of which measures 10 feet. It is constructed like the triangular niche over the Lions' Gate ; namely, the courses of masonry are shaped to the form of the niche, and it can have had no other purpose than to bear up the weight which would otherwise have pressed on the lintel.

On the outside, before each door-post, there stood formerly a semi-column, having a base and capital with fantastical sculptures in the Persepolitan style. In the middle of the doorway can be seen the holes for the bolts and hinges of the doors, and in the same line are a number of round holes, 2 inches in diameter and half an inch deep ; in these are two small holes for bronze nails, of which fragments still exist, to fasten on ornaments of a circular form.

To the right of the great circular hall, a doorway, 9½ ft. high and 4 ft. 7 in. broad, leads to a second dark chamber, which is nearly square, being 27 feet long and broad, and 19 feet high. It is entirely cut out in the rock. Over the door is a triangular niche, which is likewise intended to bear up the weight of the masonry from the lintel. In this chamber is an accumulation of rubbish, from 3½ to 4 feet deep, mostly consisting of the detritus of bats' dung. By means of the two trenches, which I dug three years ago in this chamber, I found in the centre a circular depression, in the form of a large wash-bowl, 1 ft. 9 in. deep, and 3 ft. 4 in. in diameter. Near this I found some large wrought calcareous stones, which seem to indicate that some monument once existed in this chamber, for otherwise their presence is inexplicable.

This Treasury is the most important and the only complete monument of prehistoric times in Greece, and the interest attached to it is so much the greater, as tradition assigns it to Atreus, the father of Agamemnon, king of men.

Dodwell,* in speaking of this treasury and the smaller ones, says:—"There is moreover complete evidence that these structures were called θησαυροί, and belong to ages prior to the origin of that architecture of which the Doric temple in Europe and the Ionic in Asia are the crowning invention. As this latter architecture advanced, temples served for treasuries, or, when buildings were erected solely for treasuries, they had the ordinary forms of that later style of architecture, as we learn from the description which Pausanias has given of the treasuries at Olympia and Delphi.† Nevertheless subterranean buildings, similar in construction to the treasuries of the heroic ages, continued to serve for containing oil or corn or water, and when attached to private houses might often be employed for depositing property of any kind. These are very numerous in Greece, but in no instance are they entered at the side. The largest I know of is in the Acropolis of Pharsala. But the strongest reason for designating the constructions at Mycenæ as treasuries is the evidence of Pausanias,‡ unless it be denied that he intended those buildings by the words ὑπόγαια οἰκοδομήματα, which can hardly be alleged, as the ruins agree too well with his words to render such a supposition reasonable. Seventeen hundred years ago, therefore, those buildings were believed to be the Treasuries of Atreus and his sons. Nothing had then occurred to

---

* 'A Classical and Topographical Tour through Greece.'
† Paus. VI. 19, 1 ; X. 11, 1.
‡ II. 16, 6. See the passage fully quoted in the next chapter, p. 59

interfere with the course of the mythology or history of Greece, as transmitted to the Greeks by their ancestors: and although on many occasions the reports received by Pausanias from the ἐξηγηταί may have been inventions of a date comparatively recent, no such suspicion can well attach to the principal traditions of Mycenæ, which accord with all that has reached us concerning that city in poetry or prose. The extant edifice was the largest of the treasuries, and bears proofs of having been a costly building, highly decorated at the entrance and lined within with metallic plates. To Atreus himself, therefore, the most opulent and powerful of the kings of the πολύχρυσος Μυκήνη, and not to either of his sons, this greatest of extant treasuries may, with a high degree of probability, be attributed. Agamemnon dissipated the wealth of Atreus in the expedition to Asia, passed the greater part of his reign abroad, and returned home poor and powerless, leaving Μυκῆναι to be, after his time, no more than a secondary town of Argolis. Nor is it likely, under these circumstances, that the sepulchre of Agamemnon was a monument of any great magnificence. Pausanias, who saw it, does not mention it as such, but gives us clearly to understand that the Treasury and the Gate of the Citadel were the most remarkable antiquities at Mycenæ."

I think that nothing could better prove the remote antiquity of this majestic underground Treasury and its companions, than their very singularity and dissimilarity to other ancient buildings in Greece and Asia Minor; besides, the barbarian method of securing treasures by burying them argues a very early state of society.

As a further proof of these underground buildings having been used as treasuries, I may mention that Mycenæ and Orchomenus are the only cities which can boast of such edifices, and also the only cities to which Homer gives the epithet πολύχρυσος, or to which he attributes great wealth.

The Professor of Medicine in Athens, Johannes P. Pyrlas, has kindly called my attention to an article he published in the Tripolis newspaper, "Βελτίωσις," of the 19th November, 1857, on the first excavation of the Treasury of Atreus (commonly called in the Argolid the "Tomb of Agamemnon"), of which I give here the translation with all reserve.

"The Tomb of Agamemnon in Mycenæ.

"In 1808, as old people relate, in the month of April, a Mahomedan of Nauplia presented himself before Veli Pasha, who was at that time governor of the Peloponnesus, and told him that he knew there were several statues hidden in the 'Tomb of Agamemnon.' Veli Pasha, who was energetic and ambitious, at once began to excavate the space in front of the tomb with forced labour. When he had dug down to a depth of three fathoms, the workmen descended by means of a ladder into the interior of the dome, and found there a great many ancient tombs, and having opened these they found in them bones covered with gold, which was no doubt derived from the gold embroidered drapery. They found there also other gold- and silver- ornaments, also precious stones in the form of those called 'antiques' (gems), but without any incised work. Outside of the tombs they found about twenty-five colossal statues and a marble table, all of which Veli Pasha transported to the Lake of Lerna (the Mills), and having got them washed and cleaned and wrapped up in mats, he sent them on to Tripolis, where he sold them to travellers and obtained for them about 80,000 gros (then worth about 20,000 francs). Having gathered the bones and all the *débris* contained in the tombs, he got these also transported to Tripolis, and entrusted them there to the most notable goldsmiths, D. Contonicolacos and P. Scouras, who, after having cleaned the *débris* and scraped off the gold from the bones, collected about 4 okes (4800

grammes) of gold and silver. The stones in form of antiques as well as the bones were thrown away. I had this
account from the mouth of the two goldsmiths when
they were still alive, and from my own father, who saw
the statues at the Mills."

Now not to speak of the improbability that statues of
the heroic age should have been found, the above account
is in no way confirmed by the old men of Charvati, the
village nearest to the site of Mycenæ, nor by those of the
other villages of the plain of Argos, all of whom agree
that the excavation took place in 1810, and that the sole
objects found in the Treasury were some half-columns
and friezes, a marble table, and a long bronze chain suspended from the top of the dome, at the end of which was
hanging a bronze candelabrum.* I have heard this account
repeated so many hundred times by the old people of the
Argolid that I believe it to be perfectly correct, except, of
course, as to the candelabrum; because, not to speak of
candles, even lamps were totally unknown to Homer, and
I never found them either at Troy, or at Tiryns or
Mycenæ, in the strata of prehistoric house remains. Nay,
lamps appear not to have existed at Tiryns or Mycenæ
before their capture by the Argives in 468 B.C., because I
only found them in the latter place in the *débris* of the
more modern city, and none were found at Tiryns. Thus
the object which the villagers had regarded as a candelabrum must necessarily have been something else.

Moreover, this whole story of the excavations by Veli
Pasha seems to relate to a spoliation of the treasury which
took place at a much more remote period; for Dodwell,
who began his journeys in Greece in 1801, and ended them
at all events not later than 1806, gives a description and
plans of both the exterior and interior of the great chamber.
Gell (*Argolis*), who visited Mycenæ about 1805, also gives

---

* The reader is warned not to confound this with Veli Pasha's
attempt to rifle the other Treasury, mentioned on p. 42.

exact drawings of the exterior and interior of the Treasury. Clarke (*Travels*), who visited Mycenæ at the same period, says of the treasury of Atreus (vi. 492): " This chamber has evidently been opened since its construction, and its interior thus revealed; but absolutely nothing certain is known as to the time when this may have occurred.   To judge by the present appearance of the edifice, it must have been at a very remote epoch."   Dodwell, Colonel Leake, and Ernst Curtius speak also of excavations made by Lord Elgin in the treasury of Atreus.   But in the collection of Lord Elgin's drawings preserved in the British Museum, nothing is found which relates to this treasury.

According to Professor E. Curtius

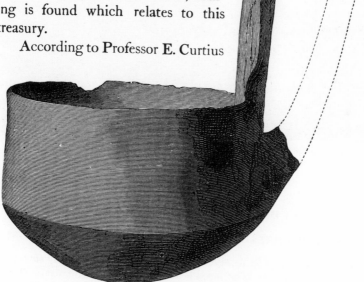

No. 23*a*.   A Terra-cotta Vase.   (3 M.)   Actual size.

(' Peloponnes,' II. p. 408), the following fragments of ancient ornaments were found before the entrance of the Treasury:—

" The basis of a semi-column of greenish marble with wreathed stripes in relief ; further, the fragment of a half round column with a zigzag decoration ; stone tables, the one of greenish, the other of lustrous red colour, a third of white marble, all with a relief ornamentation in the form of muscles, fans or spiral lines, which are distinguished by sharply and neatly chiselled outlines; finally, a red marble slab, which Gell found in a neighbouring chapel."

No. 24. The first of the Tombstones found above the Sepulchres in the Acropolis. Size 8 : 100.

CHAPTER III.

HISTORY OF MYCENÆ AND THE FAMILY OF PELOPS.

THE SEPULCHRES OF AGAMEMNON AND HIS COMPANIONS.

Traditional foundation of Mycenæ by Perseus — His dynasty succeeded by the Pelopids — The legend of their crimes unknown to Homer and Hesiod — The Homeric story of Agamemnon's murder by Ægisthus and Clytemnestra, avenged by Orestes — Cycle of crimes devised by the later bards — Dominion of Agamemnon — End of the dynasty at Mycenæ with Ægisthus — Orestes and his sons — The Dorian invasion — Part taken by Mycenæ in the Persian wars — The Argives besiege and take Mycenæ — The walls of the citadel preserved from religious reverence — Homeric epithets of Mycenæ — Its "abundance of gold" confirmed by Thucydides — The Treasuries of the Pelopids mentioned by Pausanias — Treasury at the

Heræum, near Mycenæ — Probable existence of another Treasury at Mycenæ.

The *Royal Sepulchres* described by Pausanias — General misinterpretation of the passage — Experimental shafts sunk there in February 1874 — Excavations begun, August 7, 1876 — Porter's lodge at the Lions' Gate — The later habitation of the city after 468 B.C. — No coins of Mycenæ known — Remains below this first stratum — Painted archaic vases, like those at Tiryns — The vases almost all made on the potter's wheel — Female idols and cows of terra-cotta — Other idols and animals — Iron knives and curious keys of a later period — Bronze knives and arrowheads — Stone implements and other objects — A little gold and much lead found — Fragments of a lyre and flute — Plates of ornamented terra-cotta for lining walls — Cyclopean house-walls — A remarkable water-conduit — Twelve tomblike reservoirs — Two tombstones with bas-reliefs, probably of the same epoch as that over the Lions' Gate.

Mycenæ, August 19, 1876.

TRADITION attributes the foundation of Mycenæ to Perseus, son of Danaë and Jove, who had by Andromeda a son Sthenelus, to whom he left the kingdom. Sthenelus married Nicippé, the daughter of Pelops, by whom he had a son Eurystheus, who succeeded him. The dynasty of Perseus ended with Eurystheus, who was succeeded by his uncle Atreus, the son of Pelops. The latter left the kingdom to his brother Thyestes, who left it to his nephew Agamemnon, son of Atreus.

According to tradition, Atreus and his brother Thyestes contended for the dominion of Mycenæ. Atreus was married to Aëropé, who was seduced by his brother Thyestes. Atreus, in revengeful fury at this, butchered the two (or three) sons of Thyestes, and served them up at a banquet to their father. When Thyestes learnt the fact, in his horror he overturned the table, vomited the dreadful meal, and ran off, cursing the whole race of the Pelopids.* Aëropé is thrown into the sea. Thyestes consults the oracle how he can revenge himself on his brother, and

---

* Horace, *Epod.* V. 86.

gets the answer that, if he begets a son by his own daughter, Pelopia, this son will avenge him. To avoid the incest, he intended to leave for Lydia; but when he was sacrificing in the night to Athena at Sicyon, his daughter joined him there, and unwittingly he begat by her the future avenger, Ægisthus, who, exposed by his mother immediately after his birth, was found by shepherds, and was nursed by a goat, whence his name.* He was afterwards sought for by Atreus, who brought him up as his son, for Atreus had married Pelopia in the very beginning of her pregnancy and thought the child belonged to him. But Ægisthus killed Atreus when he was sacrificing on the seashore, because Atreus, thinking him to be his own son, had ordered him to kill his brother Thyestes. Ægisthus then, with Thyestes, took possession of the realm.

But Homer knows nothing at all of the bloody brawl in the house of the Pelopids, for according to him † Jove sent the royal sceptre to Pelops, by Hermes, as a symbol of dominion; Pelops gave it to Atreus, who dying left it to Thyestes; Thyestes left it to Agamemnon, and there is not even an allusion to dispute or violence. Hesiod speaks of the proverbial wealth and the royal majesty of the Atridæ, but he knows nothing of their crimes. Homer knows only the outrage of Ægisthus and Clytemnestra. During Agamemnon's absence in Troy, Ægisthus had succeeded in seducing Clytemnestra, and he was insolent enough to make thank-offerings to the gods for having succeeded.‡ To avoid being taken unawares by Agamemnon, he stationed a watchman on the shore, and when at length he heard of the king's arrival, he invited him to a meal and, in concert with Clytemnestra, killed him at table.§ Ægisthus then reigned seven years over

---

* From αἴξ (root αἰγ), a *goat*.   † *Il.* II. 101.
‡ Homer, *Od.* III. 263–275.
§ *Od.* IV. 524–535 ; compare I. 35 ; III. 234 ; IV. 91 ; IX. 387 ; XXIV. 20, 97.

Mycenæ, until in the eighth, as the gods had foretold to him,* Orestes appeared and avenged his father by killing Ægisthus and his own mother Clytemnestra.†

The later Homeric bards, who were followed by the tragic poets, seem to have formed the myths of the horrid deeds of Atreus and Thyestes by carrying back the outrages in the house of Agamemnon into the former generation; and, by the help of other traditions, and particularly from the history of the kings of Thebes, they devised a concatenation of crimes and mischief, which had its first origin in the murder of Myrtilus or in that of Chrysippus.‡

It appears from Homer § that Agamemnon had brought under his sceptre nearly all the Peloponnesus. But according to another passage ‖ it would appear that he reigned only over its whole northern part. The dynasty of the Pelopids appears to have ceased in Mycenæ with the death of Ægisthus, for tradition says that Agamemnon's son Orestes reigned in Arcadia and Sparta, but not that he succeeded his father. According to Strabo,¶ he died in Arcadia. Pausanias ** states that his tomb was at first on the roadside between Sparta and Tegea; at a later time his bones were buried in Sparta.†† Neither of the two sons of Orestes, Penthilus and Tisamenus, seems to have reigned at Mycenæ. Strabo ‡‡ says that they remained in the Æolian colonies in Asia Minor, which had been founded by their father. According to Pausanias,§§ the invasion of the Dorians had already occurred in the time of Orestes; according to Thucydides,‖‖ it took place eighty years after the Trojan war.

Pausanias seems probably to be in the right, because

---

* *Od.* I. 36.
† *Od.* III. 305–310.
‡ Welcker, *Gr. Trag.* I. s. 358.
§ *Il.* IX. 149–154.
‖ *Il.* II. 569.
¶ XIII. p. 582.
** III. 3, 6.
†† Paus. III. 11, 10.
‡‡ IX. p. 401.
§§ VIII. 5, 1.
‖‖ I. 12.

only a fearful political revolution and catastrophe can have
prevented Orestes from becoming king in Mycenæ, which
was the richest and most powerful state of Greece, and
which belonged to him as only son to the glorious and
universally lamented Agamemnon.

Strabo* confirms the statement that the decline of
Mycenæ began with the death of Agamemnon and particularly from the return of the Heracleidæ.   But, though the
city had decayed in power and population and had sunk to
the rank of a small provincial town, yet it kept up a certain
independence; and, inspired by the reminiscences of its
glorious past, it equipped eighty men as its contingent at
Thermopylæ,† and a year later, in conjunction with Tiryns,
it sent 400 men to Platææ.‡   The name of Mycenæ was
engraved, together with those of the other cities which had
participated in this glorious campaign, on the brazen
column representing three serpents sustaining a golden
tripod, which the Spartans dedicated to the Delphian Apollo
as a tithe of the booty taken from the Persians.   This
brazen column stands now on the old hippodrome (the
present Maidan) in Constantinople, whither it was probably brought by Constantine the Great.   The Argives,
who had remained neutral, envied the Myceneans the
honour of having participated in these battles, and they
feared besides, considering the city's ancient glory, that
Mycenæ might usurp the dominion of the whole Argolid.

For these reasons, in league with the Cleoneans and
the Tegeatans, they besieged Mycenæ in Ol. LXXVIII.
(468 B.C.).   The powerful walls of the citadel, behind
which the inhabitants had retired, withstood all assaults of
the enemy, but at last the Myceneans were forced to surrender for want of food.   It appears that, in consideration
of the past glory of the city, the victors treated the Myceneans with clemency, for they allowed them to emigrate

* VIII. p. 372.   † Herod. VII. 202.   ‡ Herod. IX. 28.

whither they pleased; and they settled partly at Cleonæ, partly in Cerynia in Achæa, but principally in Macedonia.* But this account is not quite confirmed by Diodorus Siculus,† who says that on the surrender of Mycenæ the Argives enslaved all the inhabitants. If this is correct, then it is to be supposed that the Argives forced the Myceneans to settle at Argos, because it was very material to them at that time to increase the population of their city. At all events, as Dodwell says, a religious fear seems to have prevented the Argives from destroying the huge Cyclopean walls of the citadels of Mycenæ and Tiryns, because these were considered as sacred enclosures, and were revered as sanctuaries of Hera, who was worshipped with equal adoration by all the inhabitants of the Argolid. The Argives therefore contented themselves with dismantling only a very small part of the walls of the citadel, whilst they razed those of the lower city completely to the ground.

Homer gives to Mycenæ the epithets of the "well-built city," ‡ "with broad streets," § and "rich in gold." ‖ The second of these epithets can only apply to the wide street which led from the Lions' Gate, along the ridge, through the enclosed town, to the bridge over the torrent of the ravine; for all the remaining part of the town as well as the suburb being on slopes, the other streets must have been more or less steep, and cannot have been alluded to by the epithet εὐρυάγυια. Regarding the third epithet πολύχρυσος, we have the great authority of Thucydides ¶ that Mycenæ had immense wealth under the dominion of the Pelopids, for he says: "Pelops, having brought from Asia large treasures to the indigent people (of the peninsula), soon acquired great power, and, though a foreigner,

---

* Paus. VII. 25, 6. † XI. 65.
‡ *Il.* II. 569 : ἐϋκτίμενον πτολίεθρον.
§ *Il.* IV. 52 : εὐρυάγυια Μυκήνη.
‖ *Il.* VII. 180 : *Od.* III. 305 : πολυχρύσοιο Μυκήνης.
¶ I. 9.

he nevertheless gave his name to the country, and his descendants (the Pelopids, Atreus and Agamemnon) became
still much more powerful." Thucydides adds that it appears
to him "that the other Greeks joined Agamemnon's
expedition to Troy less out of good will than from fear
of his power; for not only did he himself bring the greatest
contingent of ships, but he also gave ships to the Arcadians,
as Homer says, if he can be considered a trustworthy wit-
ness. But in speaking of Agamemnon's inheritance of the
sceptre, he says that he (Agamemnon) reigned over many
islands and over the whole Argolid (πολλῆσιν νήσοισι καὶ
'Αργεϊ παντὶ ἀνάσσειν); but as he lived on the continent, he
could not have reigned over islands, except those in the
immediate neighbourhood (but of these there could not be
many) if he had not had a fleet. From this expedition (to
Troy) we must therefore form an opinion of the nature of
those which preceded it. If Mycenæ was small, and if
several other cities of that age do not appear to us now to
be considerable, we could not cite this as a valid reason
to doubt that the expedition was as great as the poets
have represented it and as tradition confirms it to have
been."

The port of Mycenæ was not Nauplia, but Eïones
('Ηϊόνες), which was likewise situated on the Gulf of Argos,
to the south-east of Nauplia. It seems to have been destroyed as far back as the Dorian invasion. Strabo * mentions that it was entirely destroyed, and was no longer a
port in his time. According to Homer,† 'Ηϊόνες took part
in the Trojan war, and belonged to Diomedes, the king of
Argos and vassal of Agamemnon.

Of the power and riches of the Pelopids we see
the most substantial and unmistakable proofs in the many
vast subterranean buildings which Pausanias,‡ following
the tradition, calls their Treasuries, and which cannot have

---

* VIII. p. 373.   † *Il.* II. 561.   ‡ II. 16, 6.

served for any other purpose than to hoard up the royal wealth.

I must here mention that, besides the Treasuries before described in Mycenæ proper and in its suburb, there is still another Treasury close to the great Heræum, which is, according to Strabo,* 10 stadia, but according to Pausanias,† 15 stadia from Mycenæ. Besides, the conformation of the slopes between the Treasury of Atreus and the Lions' Gate leads me to think that there is still one more large treasury hidden about halfway between these two points.

Pausanias ‡ writes: "Amongst other remains of the wall is the gate, on which stand lions. They (the walls and the gate) are said to be the work of the Cyclopes, who built the wall for Proteus at Tiryns. In the ruins of Mycenæ is the fountain called Perseia and the subterranean buildings of Atreus and his children, in which they stored their treasures. There is the sepulchre of Atreus, and the tombs of the companions of Agamemnon, who on their return from Ilium were killed at a banquet by Ægisthus. The identity of the tomb of Cassandra is called in question by the Lacedæmonians of Amyclæ. There is the tomb of Agamemnon and that of his charioteer Eurymedon, and of Electra. Teledamus and Pelops were buried in the same sepulchre, for it is said that Cassandra bore these twins, and that, while as yet infants, they were slaughtered by Ægisthus together

---

* VIII. p. 368.   ‖ II. 17.

† II. 16, 6 : Λείπεται δὲ ὅμως ἔτι καὶ ἄλλα τοῦ περιβόλου καὶ ἡ πύλη · λέοντες δὲ ἐφεστήκασιν αὐτῇ · κυκλώπων δὲ καὶ ταῦτα ἔργα εἶναι λέγουσιν, οἳ Προίτῳ τὸ τεῖχος ἐποίησαν ἐν Τίρυνθι. Μυκηνῶν δὲ ἐν τοῖς ἐρειπίοις κρήνη τέ ἐστι καλουμένη Περσεία καὶ Ἀτρέως καὶ τῶν παίδων ὑπόγαια οἰκοδομήματα, ἔνθα οἱ θησαυροί σφισι τῶν χρημάτων ἦσαν. Τάφος δέ ἐστι μὲν Ἀτρέως · εἰσὶ δὲ καὶ ὅσους σὺν Ἀγαμέμνονι ἐπανήκοντας ἐξ Ἰλίου δειπνίσας κατεφόνευσεν Αἴγισθος. Τοῦ μὲν δὴ Κασσάνδρας μνήματος ἀμφισβη- τοῦσι Λακεδαιμονίων οἱ περὶ Ἀμύκλας οἰκοῦντες · ἕτερον δέ ἐστιν Ἀγαμέμνονος, τὸ δὲ Εὐρυμέδοντος τοῦ ἡνιόχου καὶ Τελεδάμου τὸ αὐτὸ καὶ Πέλοπος, τούτους γὰρ τεκεῖν διδύμους Κασσάνδραν φασι, νηπίους δὲ ἔτι ὄντας ἐπικατέσφαξε τοῖς γονεῦσιν Αἴγισθος, καὶ Ἠλέκτρας · Πυλάδῃ γὰρ συνῴκησεν Ὀρέστου δόντος. Ἑλλάνικος δὲ καὶ τάδε ἔγραψε, Μέδοντα καὶ Στρόφιον γενέσθαι Πυλάδῃ παῖδας ἐξ Ἠλέκτρας. Κλυταιμνήστρα δὲ ἐτάφη καὶ Αἴγισθος ὀλίγον ἀπωτέρω τοῦ τείχους ἐντὸς δὲ ἀπηξιώθησαν, ἔνθα Ἀγαμέμνων τε αὐτὸς ἔκειτο καὶ οἱ σὺν ἐκείνῳ φονευθέντες.

with their parents. Hellanicus (495–411 B.C.) writes that
Pylades, who was married to Electra with the consent of
Orestes, had by her two sons, Medon and Strophius.
Clytemnestra and Ægisthus were buried at a little distance
from the wall, because they were thought unworthy to
have their tombs inside of it, where Agamemnon reposed
and those who were killed together with him."

Strange to say, Colonel Leake,[*] Dodwell,[†] Prokesch,[‡]
Ernest Curtius,[§] and all others who have written on the
Peloponnesus, have interpreted this passage of Pausanias
erroneously; for they thought that, in speaking of the wall,
he meant the wall of the city, and not the great wall of the
Acropolis; and they therefore understood that he fixed the
site of the five sepulchres in the *lower* city, and the site of
the tombs of Clytemnestra and Ægisthus outside of it.
But that such was not his intention, and that he had solely
in view the walls of the citadel, he shows by saying that in the
wall is the Lions' Gate. It is true that he afterwards speaks
of the ruins of Mycenæ, in which he saw the fountain
Perseia and the treasuries of Atreus and his sons, by which
latter he can only mean the large treasury described above,
which is indeed in the lower city, and perhaps some of the
smaller treasuries in the suburb. But as he again says
further on that the graves of Clytemnestra and Ægisthus
are at a little distance outside the wall, because they were
thought unworthy to be buried inside of it, where Agamemnon and his companions reposed, there cannot be any
doubt that he had solely in view the huge Cyclopean walls
of the citadel. Besides, Pausanias could only speak of such
walls as he *saw*, and not of those which he did *not see*. He
saw the huge walls of the citadel, because they were at his

---

* 'Peloponnesiaca,' vol. ii. p. 365.

† 'A Classical and Topographical Tour through Greece,' vol. ii.
p. 236.

‡ 'Denkwürdigkeiten und Erinnerungen,' vol. ii. p. 276.

§ 'Peloponnes,' vol. ii. pp. 411–413.

time exactly as they are now ; but he could not see the
wall of the lower city, because it had been originally only
very thin, and it had been demolished 638 years before his
time; nor was he an archæologist, to search for its traces
or still less to make excavations to find them.

The site of Mycenæ presented in the time of Pausanias
just the same bare wilderness of rugged pasture land, interspersed with slopes and precipitous cliffs, as at the present
day. No change can have taken place there, and the
remnants of the lower city wall were undoubtedly in his
time as trifling as they are now. Nay, such is their insignificance, that only the traces of the wall on the ridge
seem to have been remarked by travellers, and nobody
before me appears to have ever noticed the traces of
the wall on the opposite side, which runs along the bank
of the ravine torrent.

For these decisive reasons, I have always interpreted
the famous passage in Pausanias in the sense that the five
tombs were in the Acropolis. I proved this in my work
' Ithaque, le Péloponnèse et Troie,' which I published
in the beginning of 1869, page 97. In February, 1874,
therefore, I sank there thirty-four shafts in different places, in
order to sound the ground and to find out the place where I
should have to dig for them. The six shafts which I sank
on the first western and south-western terrace gave very
encouraging results, and particularly the two which I dug
within 100 yards south of the Lions' Gate ; for not only did
I strike two Cyclopean house-walls, but I also found an
unsculptured slab resembling a tombstone, and a number
of female idols and small cows of terra-cotta. I therefore
resolved at once on making extensive excavations at this
spot, but I was prevented by various circumstances which
I need not explain here, and it is only now that I have
found it possible to carry out my plan.

I began the great work on the 7th August, 1876, with

sixty-three workmen, whom I divided into three parties.   I
put twelve men at the Lions' Gate, to open the passage
into the Acropolis ; I set forty-three to dig, at a distance
of 40 feet from that gate, a trench 113 feet long and 113
feet broad; and the remaining eight men I ordered to dig a
trench on the south side of the Treasury in the lower city,
near the Lions' Gate, in search of the entrance.   But the
soil at the Treasury was as hard as stone, and so full of
large blocks, that it took me two weeks to dig only as far
down as the upper part of the open triangular space above
the door, from which I could calculate that the threshold
would be 33 feet lower.

I had also very hard work at the Lions' Gate, owing to
the huge blocks by which the passage was obstructed, and
which seem to have been hurled from the adjoining walls
at the assailants, when the Acropolis was captured by the
Argives in 468 B.C.   The obstruction of the entrance must
date from that time, for the *débris* in which the boulders
are imbedded has not been formed by a series of successive
habitations, but it has evidently been gradually washed
down by the rain water from the upper terraces.

Immediately to the left, on entering the gate, I brought
to light a small chamber, undoubtedly the ancient door-
keeper's habitation, the ceiling of which is formed by
one huge slab.   The chamber is only 4½ feet high, and it
would not be to the taste of our present doorkeepers ; but
in the heroic age comfort was unknown, particularly to
slaves, and being unknown it was unmissed.

No ancient writer mentions the fact that Mycenæ was
reinhabited after its capture by the Argives and the expul-
sion of its inhabitants.   On the contrary, Diodorus Siculus,
who lived at the time of Julius Cæsar and Augustus, after
having described the tragic fate of Mycenæ, adds: " This
city, which was in ancient times blessed with wealth and
power, which produced such great men and accomplished

such important actions, was thus destroyed and *remained
uninhabited till the present time."* That Mycenæ was
uninhabited at the time of Strabo (that is, under Augustus),
we must conclude from his remark, " So that *of the city of
the Myceneans not even a vestige can now be found."†* It
was certainly also uninhabited at the time of Pausanias
(A.D. 170), who describes its ruins.

But I have brought to light most positive proofs that
it had been again inhabited, and that the new town must
have existed for a long period, probably for more than two
centuries; because there is at the surface of the Acropolis
a layer of *débris* of the Hellenic time, which goes to an
average depth of three feet. Though I cannot fix by the
fragments of pottery the precise period of the reoccupation of
the town, yet as painted pottery of the best Hellenic period
is missing, and as the numerous terra-cotta figures and
fluted vases which I find are evidently of the Macedonian
age down to the second century B.C., I presume that the
new colony may have been founded in the beginning of the
fourth, and may have been abandoned in the beginning of
the second century B.C. These two limits seem to be
confirmed by the bronze medals found, nearly all of which
show on one side a Hera head with a crown, on the other a
column, having to its left a helmet and to its right a ⊟.
This character is generally thought to be a ⊖, and thus
the coin is attributed to the Argolic city of Thyrea. But,
in the opinion of my worthy friends A. Postolaccas and P.
Lampros, which I accept, the ⊟ is the *spiritus asper*, and
belongs to the still unknown word which records the value
of the coin. This coin belongs to the city of Argos, and
is of the Macedonian age, which makes it utterly impossible
that the sign should be a ⊖, the ⊟ with this meaning
having only come into use at the time of the Roman con-

---

* XI. 65 : καὶ διέμεινεν ἀοίκητος μέχρι τῶν καθ' ἡμᾶς χρόνων.
† Strabo, VIII. p. 372 : ὥστε νῦν μηδ' ἴχνος εὑρίσκεσθαι τῆς Μυκηναίων
πόλεως.

quest. There was an entire absence of Roman or Byzan-
tine coins. I may here remark that Mycenæ proper appears
to have struck no coins ; at least none has ever been found.

Below the comparatively modern Hellenic city I find
by thousands the fragments of those splendidly-painted
archaic vases, which I have already mentioned when speak-

No. 25.   Terra-cotta Vase.   (3 M.)   Size, 3 : 4. about.

ing of Tiryns. The type of vase which I most frequently
find here is in the shape of a globe with a flat foot, and
terminating above in a very pretty narrow neck, without an
opening, the top of which is joined on each side by a beau-
tifully-shaped handle to the upper part of the body. The
real mouth of the vase is in the shape of a funnel, and
always near to the closed neck.* These vases always show

---

* In the engraving, No. 25, the spout is partly hidden by one of the
handles.

the most variegated painted ornamentation of horizontal circular bands, spiral lines, or other fanciful decorations, which vary on each vase.   In the centre of the flat top of the closed neck is usually a white point, surrounded by three, four, six or more red circles; but sometimes there is a cross painted in the middle of the circles.

Vases of the same form sometimes occur in Attica; some specimens of them have also been found in Cyprus

No. 26.   Terra-Cotta Jug.   Ground yellow : lines black.   (3 M.)   Size, 7 : 9, about.

as well as in Egyptian tombs.   Mr. Charles T. Newton has called my attention to forty-three vases of exactly the same form, which have been found in a tomb at Ialysus on the island of Rhodes, together with other objects which also occur in Mycenæ; but in the same tomb was also found an Egyptian *scarabæus* with the cartouche of

Amunoph III., who is thought by Egyptologists to have reigned not later than B.C. 1400.

As there are almost as many varieties of painted ornamentation as there are vases, and as in most instances this ornamentation is most complicated and has never been found before, it would be a vain attempt on my part to describe it, and I therefore simply refer to the engravings.* But generally speaking, I may remark that the decoration with spiral lines prevails; that fragments like the so-called Attic vases with geometrical patterns are

No. 27.   Vase of Yellow Ware, with black and yellow lines.   (3 M.)   Actual size.

numerous; that flowers, branches, and leaves occasionally occur; and that bands of wedge-shaped signs, resembling fish-spines, are frequent, as well as zigzag lines and circular bands. The cross with the marks of four nails may often be seen; as well as the ⊐⊔, which is usually also represented with four points indicating the

---

* See the Plates of Mycenean Pottery, Nos. 30–78. A Vase (No. 23a) is placed, for the sake of convenience, as a tail-piece to Chapter II. p. 51.

No. 28.   A Vase of Black and Yellow Ware.   (6 M.)   Size 4 : 5, about.

four nails, thus 卐. These signs cannot but represent
the *suastika*, formed by two pieces of wood, which were
laid across and fixed with four nails, and in the joint of

No. 29.   A Terra-Cotta Vase.   The bands yellow and reddish, the lines black.   (1·15 M.)   Actual size.

which the holy fire was produced by friction by a third piece of wood.*   But both the cross and the ⊓⊔ occur for the most part only on the vases with geometrical patterns.

Representations of birds and quadrupeds sometimes occur on vases; all are very archaic, particularly the quadrupeds, of which it is sometimes difficult to find out what the artist intended to represent.† Thus there often occur animals with very long legs, a body resembling that of a horse and the head like the beak of a stork, but with two horns like those of a gazelle.‡ Usually these animals have a uniform red colour; but sometimes they have an ornamentation of spiral lines.   In a few

No. 80.   Painted Vase.   Ground yellow,
lines black, shields reddish.
(2 M.).   Actual size.

instances animals are represented which perfectly resemble gazelles or he-goats.§   The bird, in the representation of which the Mycenean artist has succeeded best is the swan.‖ Of the other birds the species is difficult to discern.¶   In the representation of men also the artist may be said to have succeeded; but the vases are broken into so many fragments that there are but few entire painted human figures.   The small vase (No. 80) shows warriors with large round shields; and on a fragment (No. 47) is represented a man with a helmet on his head, leading with his right hand a horse, and holding in his left a lance.   On other fragments are only the bodies of men without heads.   No. 81 is the mouth-piece of a jug, on which

---

* See 'Troy and its Remains,' chap. vi. pp. 103–4.
† See Nos. 31, 35, 41, 46, 50 and 52.   § See Nos. 41 and 48.
‡ See Nos. 31, 35, 50 and 52.   ‖ See Nos. 33, 40, 42, 45.
¶ See Nos. 30, 43, 44.

a human head is modelled.   There is also a human head
painted on a fragment of pottery (No. 82); it has a very
large eye, and a head-dress in the form of a Phrygian
cap.   All these representations are very archaic.

No. 81.   Human Head on the mouth of a jug.   No. 82.   Human Head on a potsherd.
(5 M.)   Actual size.   (6 M.)   Half size.

The greater number of the vases with a large opening
are painted both outside and inside; and in many instances
the internal paintings by far exceed those on the outside
in originality and profusion of colours.   Thus, for example,
I found the fragment of a vase decorated outside with
representations of deer, and inside with those of men and
women.

I often find fragments of tripods of terra-cotta with
two large handles, of which the three feet as well as the
handles have two, three, four, or even five perforations,
which can only have served for suspension with a string.
On many vases without feet, the rim of the base is perforated on either side as many times as the handles.

No perforated lids were found, but I have no doubt that
they existed, and that, as with nearly all those found in
Troy, the perforations in the vases served not only for
hanging them up, but also for fastening the lids, so as to
secure the contents.

All the painted vases hitherto found have been made
on the potter's wheel, except the very small ones, which are
evidently hand-made.   It is true that I found two fragments
of coarse hand-made pottery, which can only be compared

to the rudest pottery of the Danish " kitchen-middens" (*Kjökkenmöddinge*); but they had evidently been transported hither from another place.

As at Tiryns, the goblets are for the most part of white clay, and in the shape of large Bordeaux wine-glasses; nearly all have one handle (see No. 83). But there are a great many other goblets of the same form which have a uniform bright red colour, and others which, on a light red dead ground, have an ornamentation of numerous parallel dark red circular bands (see Nos. 84, 88).

No. 83. A Goblet of Terra-cotta. (3 M.) Size 5 : 8, about.

It deserves very particular attention that goblets of perfectly the same form were found by me in Troy at a depth of 50 feet (see my 'Atlas des Antiquités Troyennes,' Plate 105, No. 2311); further, that fourteen goblets of exactly the same form were found in the tomb at Ialysus in Rhodes, already mentioned, and are now in the British Museum. Only the painted ornamentation of these latter goblets is different, for it represents mostly the cuttlefish (sepia), but also spirals, or that curious sea-animal which so frequently occurs on the pottery of Mycenæ (see No. 213, *a, b,* p. 138), but never on the Mycenean goblets.

Since the 7th inst. I have been able to gather here more than 200 terra-cotta idols of Hera, more or less broken, in the form of a woman or in that of a cow.* Most of the

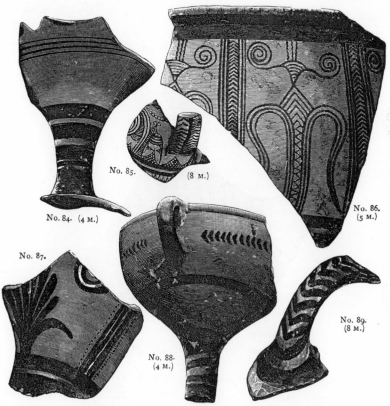

No. 85. (8 M.)

No. 84. (4 M.)

No. 86. (5 M.)

No. 87.

No. 89. (8 M.)

No. 88. (4 M.)

Nos. 84-89. Fragments of Painted Pottery. Half-size.

former have ornaments painted in bright red on a dead ground of light red, two breasts in relief, below which protrudes on each side a long horn, so that both horns together form a half-circle; and, as I have said regarding the idols in

---

* See the coloured and plain Plates of Idols; the latter containing the figures Nos. 90-110.

Tiryns, they must either be intended to represent cow-horns, or the symbolic horns of the crescent moon, or both at once. The head of those idols is of a very compressed shape, and usually covered by a large " polos." The lower part is in the form of a gradually widening tube. It deserves particular attention that a terra-cotta idol of exactly the same form was found in the aforesaid tomb in Ialysus, and is now in the British Museum.

But there were also found idols of this sort with a very

No. 111.   Terra–cotta Idol.   (4 M.)   Actual size.

low *polos* (No. 111), and perhaps a dozen idols without any horns ; the whole upper part of the body, as far as the neck, being in the form of a disk (Nos. 90, 91, 92, 93, 112*) ; the head is uncovered, and the hair is often indicated by a long tress on the back. There have also been found some idols with a bird's head, covered or uncovered, large eyes, no horns, but two well-indicated hands joined on the breast (Nos. 99, 100, 101 †). I also

---

* See also the coloured Plate C, fig. m.
† See also the coloured Plate C, fig. l.

found the terra-cotta figure (six inches high) of an old
and ugly woman, probably a priestess (No. 113); the
features are certainly neither Assyrian nor Egyptian; the
hands are broken off, but they have evidently been protruding; the figure has a very rude ornamentation of
black lines on a dead ground of strong red; the waist is
ornamented with a number of zigzag lines, which may

No. 112. Terra-cotta Idol.   No. 113. Terra-cotta Figure.
        Actual size.   (1 M.) Size 5 : 6.

possibly represent fire.   The fragment (No. 110) seems,
from its attitude, to have represented a rider on horseback.
    Of idols in the form of a cow hundreds were found, but
all are more or less broken.   It is very remarkable that in
the sepulchre at Ialysus there were also found two such
cow-idols, which are now in the British Museum; they are

very well preserved, and have the same painted ornamentation as the cow-idols from Mycenæ.

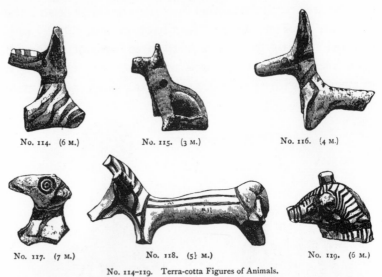

No. 114. (6 M.)   No. 115. (3 M.)   No. 116. (4 M.)

No. 117. (7 M.)   No. 118. (5½ M.)   No. 119. (6 M.)

No. 114–119.   Terra-cotta Figures of Animals.

Iron was already known to the Myccneans, for I found some knives of this metal ; also some curious keys, one of

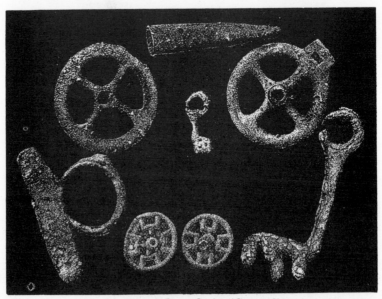

No. 120.   Objects in Bronze, Lead, and Iron.   Size, 1 : 3.

which is very thick, is 5·6 inches long, has four teeth, each 1·6 inch long, and has a ring at the other end (see No. 120). But judging by the form of these knives and keys, I make bold to express the opinion that they belong to a late period in the history of Mycenæ,

No. 121.   No. 122.   No. 123.   No. 124.   No. 125.
(4 M.)   (3 M.)   (3¼ M.)   (7 M.)

Nos. 121–125.   Bronze Knives.   Actual size.

and that they date even from the beginning of the 5th century B.C.

I also found a large number of button-like objects which seem to have served as ornaments in the house-doors or elsewhere.* They have a lustrous blackish colour, and according to the analysis of my esteemed friend Mr. Xavier Landerer, Professor of Chemistry at Athens, they consist of a strongly-burnt clay varnished with a lead glazing. Of bronze I discovered several well-preserved knives, one of which (No. 125) still has part of its bone handle; further, two arrow-heads of a pyramidal form without barbs (γλωχῖνες), like the Carthaginian arrow-heads, which I gathered last year in my excavations at Motyë, in Sicily.

No. 126.   Arrow-heads, hatchets, and other objects of stone.   (3 M.)   Actual size.

Of stone implements, I found two beautifully-polished hatchets of serpentine (see No. 126, in the lower row);

* They are like those figured under Nos. 137, 139, p. 79, and No. 165, p. 109.

further, a number of weights of diorite and a number of hand millstones of trachyte, 8 inches long and 5¼ inches broad, in the form of an egg which has been cut lengthwise. The grain was bruised between the flat sides of two of these millstones; but only a kind of groats can have been produced in this way, not flour; the bruised grain could not have been used for making bread. In Homer,* we find it used for porridge, and also for strewing on the roasted meat.† Of gold only a small particle has been found; of silver none as yet; of lead a large quantity.

I also found a small and thick terra-cotta disk, with a furrow all round for suspension by a string; on one side, which is well polished, and seems to have been covered with wax, are engraved a number of ⊓⌐'s, the sign which occurs so frequently in the ruins of Troy. Whorls are found here by hundreds; nearly all are of a beautiful blue stone without any ornaments (see No. 15, p. 17). Whorls of exactly the same kind were also found in the tomb at Ialysus. As yet only five whorls of terra-cotta have been found, and without any ornaments.

The Myceneans seem to have been musicians, for I found the beautifully ornamented fragments of a lyre of bone (No. 127), and a flute, of which we have the three pieces (Nos. 128, 129, 130), which were found at the same place, though at different depths, and evidently belong to

---

* *Il.* XVIII. 558–560 :—

κήρυκες δ' ἀπάνευθεν ὑπὸ δρυῒ δαῖτα πένοντο,
βοῦν δ' ἱερεύσαντες μέγαν ἄμφεπον, αἱ δὲ γυναῖκες
δεῖπνον ἐρίθοισιν, λεύκ' ἄλφιτα πολλὰ πάλυνον.

' A little way removed, the heralds slew
A sturdy ox, and now beneath an oak
Prepared the feast ; while women mixed, hard by,
White barley porridge for the labourers' meal."
                                        LORD DERBY.

† *Od.* XIV. 76–77 :—

ὀπτήσας δ' ἄρα πάντα φέρων παρέθηκ' 'Οδυσσῆϊ
θερμ' αὐτοῖς ὀβελοῖσιν · ὁ δ' ἄλφιτα λευκὰ πάλυνεν.

And when he had roasted all, he brought it and put it before Ulysses, still warm
on the spits, strewn over with white flour.

the very same instrument. No. 129, which is the upper
piece of the flute, consists, according to Professor Landerer,
of bone; No. 128, which is the lower piece, consists of
very hard-baked clay: both have a very symmetrical intaglio

No. 127.   Fragment of a Lyre of Bone.   (3¼ M.)   Size, 7 : 8, about.

ornamentation.   The fragment of the tube of the flute
(No. 130*a*) consists of potstone, the *lapis ollaris* of Pliny,
and we therefore have here a marvellous Mycenean flute
consisting of bone, baked clay, and stone.   But potstone

Nos. 128, 129.   Lower and Upper Ends of a Flute.   Actual size.

seems to have been frequently used for flutes in antiquity,
for I myself possess a flute of *lapis ollaris* found in a
tomb in Ithaca: it bears the inscription ἱερῶθ,* and seems
to belong to the 6th or 7th
century B.C.   Also a fragment of a crystal vase was
found; and a comb (No. 130), which, by the analysis of
Professor Landerer, consists of very hard white baked clay.

H ϟ Λ Ϸ Ϙ M

---

* See my 'Ithaque, le Péloponnèse, Troie.'

It was found at a depth of 12 feet; it has in the middle a
hole for suspension with a string. I frequently find here flat

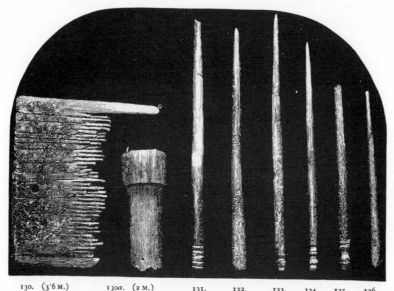

130. (3'6 M.)   130a. (2 M.)   131.   132.   133.   134.   135.   136.
                                            (4 M.)   (3 M.)   (7 M.) (3 M.) (5 M.) (3 M.)

Nos. 130–136. Comb and Needles of Terra-cotta. Size 5 : 8.

NOTE.—No. 130a is part of the Flute to which Nos. 128 and 129 also belong.

pieces of terra-cotta with painted or impressed ornaments,
which must have served for coating the interior walls of the
houses (Nos. 137 and 139). At a depth of from 10 to

No. 137. (5 M.)   No. 138.   No. 139. (3 M.)

Nos. 137, 139. Terra-cotta Ornaments. Actual size.   No. 138 is a Gold Button.

11 feet, and sometimes of only 6½ feet, below the surface, I
am bringing to light Cyclopean house-walls, built of un-

wrought stones, joined without clay or cement, and founded on the natural rock, from 20 to 24 feet below the surface. The corner-stones of these mansions are remarkable for their massiveness.

At the north end of my trench I have brought to light part of a Cyclopean water-conduit, which is still more remarkable than those of Tiryns, for there at least the water-conduit rests on the natural rock, while here it is imbedded in the *débris*, and, as the uncut stones are joined without any binding material, it is really wonderful how a current of water could have passed along them without being lost through the interstices. Close to the Cyclopean water-conduit are twelve recesses, consisting of large slabs of calcareous stone and covered by smaller ones; in my opinion they cannot possibly be anything else than small cisterns. A few yards south of these reservoirs I have brought to light two tombstones, which stand in a direct line from north to south, and are ornamented with bas-reliefs of the highest interest. Unfortunately the tombstone to the north consists of a soft calcareous stone, in consequence of which it is broken in several places, and its upper part has not been preserved. It is 6 inches thick, 4 feet high, 4 ft. 2 in. broad below, and 3 ft. 8½ in. above; it shows one undivided picture, encompassed below as well as on both sides by a broad border, which is formed in the simplest way into rows, and it represents a hunting scene.* On a chariot, drawn by one horse, stands the hunter, who holds in his left hand the reins, in his right a long broad sword. Owing to fractures in the stone the upper part of the chariot is not distinctly visible, but the wheel can be well seen, with its four spokes forming a cross. The outstretched fore and hind legs of the horse appear to indicate his great speed. Below to the left is a tolerably well-formed

---

* See the Vignette to this Chapter, No. 24, p. 52.

dog, with a curved tail, chasing a flying deer, probably a roe, whose tail however is by far too long.   Just above

No. 140.   The Second Tombstone, found above the Sepulchres in the Acropolis   (4 M.)
About one-twelfth of the actual size.

the roe's back, and between the horse's feet, lies an object
which cannot be recognised; it may equally well represent a man lying prostrate, or a cart with two wheels.
On either side, in the broad border formed by two vertical
parallel fillets, are three ovals or *cartouches*, containing a
very curious ornamentation, which at first sight seems to
have a symbolic signification; but on close examination
one finds that it is nothing more than a beautiful ornamentation of spiral lines.   At the base are three horizontal
fillets.   Behind the chariot is a row of signs resembling
letters, but this also is probably nothing more than ornamentation.

At a distance of one foot from this sepulchral *stêlê*
and in the same line with it is the other (No. 140), which
is of much harder calcareous stone, and has been therefore
much better preserved.   It is only damaged at the top,
where a piece 6 to 8 inches high may be missing; its
breadth at bottom is 3 ft. 10 in., and at top 3 ft. 7 in.; its
height is 6 feet.   It is divided into an upper and a lower
compartment, which are separated by a horizontal fillet,
and enclosed on three sides by two parallel bands.   The
upper compartment shows four horizontal parallel rows,
each of six spirals, two complete and two imperfect; making
in all twenty-four spirals united with each other and representing a band in relief, which covers the whole field
with a network, and which, as my friend the well-known
archæologist, Dr. Fr. Schlie, rightly observes, is in principle
the same as the filling up with straight lines, horizontally
and vertically combined, into what is called a fret or key-
pattern (see p. 83).

The lower part of the sculpture represents a warrior
in a chariot, rather in a sitting than in a standing posture,
for the lower part of his body is not visible; and whilst,
in a very primitive manner, his head is represented in
profile, the front side of his breast is given almost without
any perspective diminution.   He holds in his left hand

a sword which is still in the sheath, its handle ending in a large knob. In his right he holds a long object, which ends at the horse's mouth, and which, being at first thick and becoming gradually thinner, resembles much more a lance than the reins; and it is difficult to say which of the two the artist intended to represent. The chariot is drawn by a stallion, whose outstretched legs seem to indicate that he is running at great speed.* The tail of the animal stands upright, and its end only forms a curve. The legs and the tail are so thick in

No. 140a. Pattern of straight and spiral Frets.

proportion to the body that, were it not for the head, one would think that the sculptor intended to represent a lion; the stallion's ears also appear more like horns than like real horse-ears. Just before the horse is standing a warrior, apparently naked, who grasps the animal's head with his right hand, and holds in his uplifted left hand a

---

* As we never hear of heroic chariots with one horse, this may be an imperfect representation of two. The same remark applies to the next tombstone. See p. 86.

double-edged sword; he seems to be full of anguish; his head is represented in profile, while the rest of his body is shown without the slightest perspective reduction.

To fill up the vacant space, there is represented below this figure and below the horse a pattern of volutes, whose second, third, and fourth spirals are much larger, in proportion to the space, than the other five spirals. Mr. Postolaccas calls to my notice that the curious relief-band above the horse resembles the *pelta lunata* of the Amazons on the ancient vases; this relief-band consists of two horizontal spirals opposite to each other. The chariot gives us a unique and most precious specimen of the Homeric chariot, of which we had before but a confused idea. The body of the chariot (πείρινς) does not form a semicircle, as we were wont to imagine from the sculptures of classical antiquity and from the ancient chariot preserved in the museum at Munich, but it is quadrangular; according to the Iliad,* the chariot-box was fastened on the chariot every time it was used. We see on three sides of the chariot-box a band or fillet, which is what Homer† doubtless means by the word ἄντυξ, translated by the Earl of Derby 'rail.'

Unlike Homer's chariot of the gods, the wheels of which (κύκλα) had eight spokes, the wheels of the chariot before us have only four spokes, which form a cross around the axle (ἄξονι ἀμφίς).‡ Just behind the warrior in the chariot

------

* XXIV. 190 and 267. Homer also uses πείρινθα (the word only occurs in the accusative) for the wicker-basket which held the load fastened on to a cart (ἄμαξα); and this, its original sense, may be a guide to its form in the chariot also (comp. *Od.* xv. 131).

† *Il.* V. 727-728 :—

δίφρος δὲ χρυσέοισι καὶ ἀργυρέοισιν ἱμᾶσιν
ἐντέταται· δοιαὶ δὲ περίδρομοι ἄντυγές εἰσιν.

" The chariot-board on gold and silver bands
    Was hung, and round it ran a double rail."

‡ My friend, Mr. W. S. W. Vaux, calls my attention to the fact that this four-spoked chariot wheel, seen also in the cut No. 120 (p. 74) and on the Mycenean intaglios hereinafter described, is characteristic of the

there is a very curious sign, the lower part of which forms a long hook, the upper part a spiral line. M. Postolaccas reminds me that this same sign very frequently occurs on the medals of Roman families, as, for example, on those of Julius Cæsar, Marcus Antonius, and so forth, and in his opinion it is nothing else than the augur-staff, in Latin " *lituus*."

On carefully examining the sculpture of the tombstones, I find such a marvellous accuracy and symmetry in all the spiral ornamentation, that I feel almost tempted to think such work can only have been produced by a school of sculptors which had worked for ages in a similar style. On the other hand, the men and the animals are made as rudely and in as puerile a manner as if they were the primitive artist's first essay to represent living beings. But still there is a great resemblance between the bodies of the animals and those of the two lions on the gate ; there is the same style of art, and much of the coarseness in the animals on the tombstones may be due to the inferiority of the calcareous stone; probably the primitive sculptor who chiselled them would have produced something better if he had had to work on the beautiful hard *breccia* of which the sculpture above the Lions' Gate consists. I have therefore not the slightest objection to admit that the sculptured sepulchral slabs may be of nearly the same epoch as the lions over the gate.

---

earliest Greek coins. The early Egyptian and Ethiopian and Assyrian wheels have six spokes. The Persian Achæmenid sculptures show chariots with eight-spoked wheels.

No. 141. The Third Tombstone, found above the Sepulchres in the Acropolis. (4 M)
About one-tenth of the actual size.

CHAPTER IV.

EXCAVATIONS IN THE CITADEL OF MYCENÆ—*continued.*

Wages and worth of labour at Mycenæ — The double circle of slabs—
Two more sculptured *stêlæ* — Unsculptured *stêlæ* — Ashes and bones,
probably of sacrifices — Fragments of other sculptured tombstones—
The style of these *stêlæ* unique — Their probable age about 1500
B.C. — A Cyclopean house filled with ashes, bones, &c. — Objects
found there and in the twelve reservoirs — Great significance
of the tombstones found in the Acropolis — They mark the Royal

Tombs, mentioned by Pausanias from tradition only — Excavation of the Treasury close to the Lions Gate: about as large as that of Atreus — Antiquity of the covering-up proved by the ancient vases, idols, &c. in the *débris* above — Hera-idols, and others, found in the *dromos*, and in the Acropolis — Their vast abundance — Cow-heads on handles of vases, as at Troy — Moulds for earrings and other ornaments of gold and silver, and curious clay cones — Other ornaments of glazed clay, potstone, &c. — Numerous objects of bronze — Curious wheels — Necklace beads of various stones, with intaglios of animals, and similar objects of other shapes — Two-handled goblets ; the δέπας ἀμφικύπελλον of Homer — Depth of the *débris* — Breach in the great Cyclopean wall, repaired by an ancient wall of small stones — The quarry of Mycenæ.

Mycenæ, Sept. 9, 1876.

Since the 19th of August I have continued the excavations with an average number of 125 workmen and 4 horse-carts, and have made good progress. As it may interest the reader to know what wages are paid here, I mention that the daily wages of a common labourer are 2½ drachmas,* the wages of my overseers 5 to 6 drachmas, and the cost of each cart 8 drachmas, but the labourers here work much better and are much more honest than those in the Troad.

In the trench close to the Lions' Gate I have been obliged to stop the work for a time, the Archæological Society of Athens having promised to send an engineer to repair the Cyclopean wall above and beside the gate, and to fasten the sculpture of the two lions with cramp-irons, so as to secure it against the shock of an earthquake.

In the large second trench I have brought to light a second wall of smaller stones, 12 feet high, which runs parallel with the great circuit wall, and thus forms a curve of about the third part of a circle. It enters the adjoining field, which is now being excavated, and its direction parallel with the great circuit wall seems to have been unintentional. It is not, however, vertical, but its western face slopes at an

---

* The Greek drachma is worth about 8½*d.* English.

angle of 75 degrees with the horizon, like the great tower of Ilium. It deserves attention that here and there we see in this wall wrought flat slabs, which give the impression that the wall belongs to a later period than the Cyclopean circuit wall. On this wall are two parallel rows of large, closely-joined slabs of a calcareous stone, which show the same inclination as the wall, and appear to form, with the part in the adjoining field, a full circle. If so, the wall, on which these rows of slabs stand, can only have been built for the purpose of supporting them in this lower part of the Acropolis, and of raising them to the level of their prolongation on the much higher neighbouring ground. It deserves particular attention that on the inner side of the supposed circle, namely, on the side towards which the parallel rows of slabs incline, the vacant space has evidently been filled up with *débris* to the very top of the wall immediately after its completion.*

I frequently found here, at a depth of from three to four feet, ashes of burnt animal matter, also masses of bones of animals, but no bones which I can identify as human, for no skull has turned up. The space between the two slanting parallel rows of slabs was filled with *débris*, mixed with innumerable fragments of beautiful archaic pottery, and a great many Hera-idols, but no bones were found there. Within the curve, and very near to the two parallel rows of slabs, I brought to light two more sculptured tombstones of a hard calcareous stone (see Nos. 141, 142), one of which is in the same line with the two sculptured slabs which I have already described, and only 1 ft. 5 in. south of them. It is 3 ft. 8¾ in. broad at the base, and 3 ft. 7½ in. at top; 6 in. thick, and 4 ft. 2 in. long; and thus the line of the three tombstones together is 13 ft. 8 in. long. This newly discovered third tombstone (No. 141)

---

* This most curious enclosure will be more fully described, and the important question of its use discussed, in the following Chapter.

shows, like the two others, on its western side, a sculpture in bas-relief, which is divided by a horizontal fillet into two compartments, and is encompassed on all sides by two parallel fillets. Of the upper part of the stone a piece, apparently about one foot high, is missing. In the upper compartment is represented a warrior, whose head and neck are not now visible on account of the breaking of the stone. He is represented standing on a chariot drawn apparently by only one horse*, the outstretched hind and fore legs and the uplifted tail of which seem to indicate that he is running with great velocity, just as on the two tomb-stones already described; the fore and hind legs of the horse are not separated, but appear as one broad leg. In this case the reins with which the warrior guides the horse are well indicated by one broad band; also the horse's tail is less bushy and better proportioned, but the rest of the animal's body is a perfect copy of that of the horse on the preceding bas-relief. The chariot-box is here exceedingly low, and very small when compared with that of the chariot on the other tombstone, but it is not less remarkable, because it is surrounded by a band or fillet ($\overset{\text{\textasciibreve}}{\alpha}\nu\tau\upsilon\xi$), which is double on the lower part. Just behind this chariot-box is repre-sented an enormously broad two-edged knife, the handle of which terminates in a very thick knob. As such a knife can never have existed, I presume that the artist intended to represent here a two-edged sword with a thick knob at the end of the handle, but that for want of space he made it very short, without however diminishing its breadth, for which there was room enough. The one wheel which is visible is much like that of the chariots on the other tombstones, for it has also only four spokes, forming a cross round the axle. The adversary on foot, who is visible on the right side, and whose upper part is likewise missing owing to the breaking of the stone, does

---

* See note on p. 83.

not stand on the same level as the horse and the chariot, but he appears às if hovering in the air, on a level with the warrior in the chariot. He assaults the latter with a long lance, on which can be seen an object of a peculiar form, which much resembles one of the plain Trojan idols,* and must have served to attach the lance to the shoulder.

In the lower compartment we see two large circles, forming a figure of eight, lying horizontally, and in each of the two circles six spirals, of which the adjacent parts are linked together alternately, on the inside and outside, by curved bands in relief. Below the sculpture at the foot of the tombstone we see two spiral ornaments imperfectly scratched in the stone, as if the artist had made a trial sketch of what he was going to carve on the tablet. Our present artists make their sketches on paper, but the early Mycenean sculptor had neither paper and pencil nor pen and ink at his disposal, and so he made his trial sketch on the stone itself, but on its lower part, which was to be sunk into the ground and was therefore hidden from the eye.

At a distance of only 10 feet south of the sculptured tombstone last described, and almost in a straight line with the three slabs, is the fourth tombstone (No. 142), carved with a bas-relief which likewise faces the west. This *stêlé* is also a trapezium, 6 in. thick, 6 ft. high, 4 ft. broad at the lower end, and 3 ft. 10½ in. at the upper end. Of the upper end a piece, probably about a foot long, is missing. That side of the *stêlé* which faces the west has a broad border to the right and left, and the remaining space is divided into three vertical compartments of equal breadth, which reach down to more than half the height of the stone. With the exception of two vertical lines, which form a border to the right and left, the middle compartment is left unsculptured, and was

---

* See 'Troy and its Remains,' p. 36, fig. 30.

No. 142.   The Fourth Tombstone, found above the Sepulchres in the Acropolis.   (4 M.)
About one-ninth of the actual size.

probably intended to represent a column. The two side compartments contain a broad wave-pattern, which represents the coils of a serpent, and descends vertically from the top to the bottom, following the direction of the fillets. Though it is only in low-relief, it appears to be vigorously carved. If, as Dr. Fr. Schlie observes to me, we had to show this pattern (*a*) by broken straight lines, we should do it in the manner shown by the pattern (*b*).

Immediately to the south of this tombstone, in the same line with it, and separated from it by only one foot, is another tombstone, unsculptured. Two more unsculptured sepulchral slabs stand close to each other, 23 feet to the east of the first three sculptured tombstones; and at a distance of 40 feet directly to the south of the former, stand two more unsculptured tombstones, 4 feet apart. All the unsculptured slabs likewise stand vertically and face the west.

No. 143.
Piece of a Tombstone. (4 M.)   Size 1 : 5, about.

At the foot of the sculptured tombstone first described I found a handful of black ashes, and among them a large button of wood, covered with a thick leaf of gold, on which is engraved a circle, and within it a triangle containing the representations of three long broad knives, the handles of

which are formed by beautiful spiral lines. I also found
at the feet of most of the tombstones grey ashes of burnt
animal matter, which I at first thought was from human
bodies ; but as I found together with them bones which on
closer investigation turn out to be those of animals, I
now think the ashes must be from sacrifices.   There

No. 144.   Piece of a Tombstone.   (4 M.)   Size 1 : 7, about.

certainly appear to have been some more sculptured tombstones here, for I find in this and in the adjoining field,
at a depth of 10 to 13 feet below the surface, a number
of fragments of sepulchral *stêlæ*.

Of these the most interesting (No. 143) consists of
hard calcareous stone, and is 15 in. long, 11 in. broad, and
6½ in. thick. It represents a boy, apparently naked, who

had no doubt been made standing on a chariot, for he holds in his left hand the reins, indicated by a broad band: his right hand is also stretched out, but not holding anything: his head-dress is indicated by two curved lines on the head: the two vertical lines to the left were part of the border of the *stêlê*. A second fragment is 22 in. long,

No. 145. Piece of a Tombstone. (3¾ M.) Size 1 : 5, about.

17 in. broad, and 6 in. thick, and consists of a soft calcareous stone, in consequence of which the sculpture is much defaced and quite indistinct.

The third fragment (No. 144), 2 ft. 6 in. long, 2 ft. broad, and 6 in. thick, is evidently the upper right-hand part of a *stêlê*. This also consists of a soft calcareous stone, and the sculpture is consequently much defaced. It

is divided by broad fillets into three compartments, of
which the upper one as well as that to the right contain
spirals, whilst we see the fore-part of two horses in that
to the left below.

Another fragment (No. 145) is apparently the left
upper part of a *stêlé:* it is 1 ft. 8 in. broad, 2 ft. 2 in.

Nos. 146, 147, 148. Three pieces of Tombstones. (3·4 M.) Size 1 : 6, about.

high, and 4 in. thick, and likewise consists of a soft
calcareous stone. It has to the left a border of two
fillets, at the top the slight remnant of one fillet, and is
divided by a horizontal fillet into two compartments, of
which the upper one has beautiful spirals, forming the same
pattern as on No. 140, whilst of the lower compartment

only a small part remains, the sculpture of which is effaced.

I also show three fragments of tombstones, all of a harder calcareous stone, and therefore better preserved. The· upper one (No. 146), which is 1 ft. high, 10¾ in. broad, and 4¾ in. thick, has a border of two broad and three narrower bands, above which only the foot of a horse is visible. The two lower fragments (Nos. 147, 148) show spirals; the former is 10¾ in. long and broad, and 4¾ in. thick; the latter is 10¾ in. long, 10 in. broad, and 4¾ in. thick. Of two more fragments of *stêlæ* of a soft calca-

Nos. 149, 150. Fragments of Tombstones. (3-4 M.) Size 1 : 12, about.

reous stone (Nos. 149, 150), the first represents to the left spirals, to the right a horse; the second, which has only spirals, is 1 ft. 6 in. high, 16 in. broad, and 4 in. thick.

I have also been fortunate enough to discover, only 3 ft. below the surface, a piece of a quadrangular column of red porphyry, 12⅔ in. long, 10⅔ in. broad, and 8 in. thick, ornamented with a splendid low relief of palmettos lying horizontally (No. 151). Two of these stand opposite to each other, and are united by a rectangular middle piece, which, within an upper and a lower horizontal border, is divided on both sides, to the right and left, by three vertical band-like cuts into seven upright rectangular fields, of which the middle one is as broad as the three on either side. This middle piece reminds one of the Doric triglyphs. To the right and left of the palmettos we see the fragments of other ornaments of a similar kind, and it seems that the whole column has been decorated in this way. Above the palmettos there is a row of denticles, and there has no doubt been a similar row below. The two middle palmettos resemble a saloon furnished with seats all round. I further found at a depth of about 11 ft. 6 in. the fragment of another column or frieze of red porphyry, 8¾ in. long, 10 in.

No. 151.   Piece of a quadrangular Column of Red Porphyry.   (1 M.)   Size 1 : 4, about.

broad, and 4¼ in. thick, carved with a beautiful spiral (see No. 152).

Although, as Dr. Fr. Schlie thinks, the technical treatment of the low-relief of all these stêlæ may not be vastly different from a whole series of archaic reliefs of ancient Greek art, yet such figures and such an ornamentation have never been found yet on Greek sculptures. The stêlæ of Mycenæ are, therefore, unique in their kind. It is true that the manner of filling up with manifold beautiful spiral ornaments the space not covered by the forms of men and animals reminds us of the principles of the painting on the so-called orientalizing vases.

But nowhere do we see on the sculptures of Mycenæ the ornamentation of plants, which is so characteristic of this class of ancient Greek representations.   The whole style is rather a linear ornamentation with forms in powerful low-relief, and herein we obtain an interesting guide to that epoch in the development of Greek art, which preceded the so-called Græco-Phenician period, that is the time when

Nos. 152, 153, 154.   Fragments of Friezes.   Size 1 : 5, about.*

its course was determined by oriental influences.   The beginning of this latter period Mr. Newton fixes with certainty not later than B.C. 800.   But these Mycenean representations, which are decorated exclusively with linear ornamentation in relief, are again remarkable because we see in them living beings such as man, the horse, the dog,

----

* The frieze, No. 153, is described, and its broad face shown on p. 140, No. 216 ; the fragment No. 154 is described on p. 121.

and the deer, which are not reduced to a more or less linear design, such as those on the Trojan whorls,* but which are given, though rudely, and in a puerile way, in full bodily form, precisely as the nature of the relief requires.

These reflections lead us to the conviction that the Mycenean reliefs must be brought into relation with the ancient architecture of Mycenæ. Let us compare with them only the preserved remnants of the ornamentation of the gateway of the "Treasury of Atreus" and its semi-column, as restored by Professor Donaldson.† Therefore it cannot appear an unfounded assumption, if we claim for these ancient monuments the middle of the second millen-nium B.C., and if we insert them for the future as an important link into the history of art. As Mr. A. S. Murray, of the British Museum, justly observed to me, the spiral ornamentation is no proof whatever of an orien-talizing influence, because every wire must have given to the early artist the idea of the spiral ornamentation; nay, we find the spiral ornamentation even on the ancient Mexican and Peruvian monuments.

Close to the twelve small reservoirs on the north side of my second trench, is a Cyclopean house without a roof, which even now is on its south side 24 ft. high. It contains only one chamber, 17 ft. long and 9½ ft. broad; its east wall is 3 ft. 4 in., and its west wall 3 ft., thick. On the south side it has two walls, the inner one 3 ft. 4 in., the outer one 3 ft. 8 in., thick; against its north wall, which is 3 ft. thick, leans another, 6½ ft. thick; and thus the passage of the door, which is on this side, is not less than 9½ ft. long. I excavated in this house, and found it filled with ashes both of wood and of animal matter, intermixed with bones, particularly of swine, and with

---

* See ' Troy and its Remains,' Plates xxvii–xxxi.
† See supplementary volume to Stuart's ' Athens.'

millions of fragments of painted archaic vases. But I found
nothing worth mentioning, except a certain quantity of
baked wheat and vetches, a weight of jasper with a perforated handle for suspension (No. 155), some well-preserved
archaic vases, the fragment (No. 156) of a vase with sieve-
like perforations, and a certain number of whorls of blue
stone. One of these vases is particularly interesting for its
painted ornamentation, showing two swans, which hold
their heads together, much like the two eagles in the
Russian arms.

No. 155.   A Jasper Weight, with a hole for suspension.   (5¼ M.)   Actual size.

I have not been more lucky with the twelve small
reservoirs formed of four large slabs, for they contain
nothing else than the remnants of household utensils, and
particularly fragments of archaic vases.

The four sculptured and five unsculptured sepulchral
slabs undoubtedly mark the sites of tombs cut deep in the
rock, the exploration of which, however, I must needs delay
until I have terminated all my excavations in the northern
part of the Acropolis.

The presence of these numerous sepulchres near the

Lions' Gate, and thus in the most prominent part of the citadel, in a place where one would have expected to find the king's palace, is very significant; the more so, as the slabs of the two parallel rows perfectly resemble the five unsculptured tombstones and the slabs of the twelve small reservoirs, and all these monuments appear to have been erected simultaneously.

I know of no example in history of an acropolis having ever served as a burial place, except the small building of the Caryatides in the Acropolis of Athens, which was called

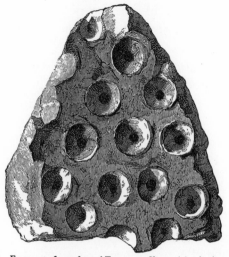

No. 156.   Fragment of a perforated Terra-cotta Vase.   (2¼ M.)   Actual size.

the Sepulchre of Cecrops, the first king of Athens.   But we now know with certainty that Cecrops is nothing else than Kacyapa or Cacyapa, who was a sun-god, and thus the story of Cecrops having been buried in the Acropolis is a pure myth.   But here in the Acropolis of Mycenæ the tombs are no myth, they are a tangible reality.   But who have the great personages been, and what immense services did they render to Mycenæ, to have received the signal honour of such a burial place?

I do not for a moment hesitate to proclaim that I have

found here the sepulchres which Pausanias, following the tradition, attributes to Atreus, to the "king of men" Aga- memnon, to his charioteer Eurymedon, to Cassandra, and to their companions.   But it is utterly impossible that Pausanias should have seen these tombstones, because, when he visited Mycenæ, about 170 A.D., all the sepulchral monuments had for ages been covered by a layer of pre-historic *débris*, from 8 to 10 ft. thick, on which an Hellenic city had been built and had again been abandoned about four centuries before his time, after having added a layer of Hellenic ruins, 3 ft. thick, to the deep stratum of prehistoric remains.   Thus he could only have known of the existence of these sepulchres by tradition.

In the Treasury close to the Lions' Gate the work ad- vances but very slowly, the soil being as hard as stone, and only to-day has my trench reached a sufficient depth to enable me to begin the excavation of the triangular space above the door.   My supposition that this Treasury would turn out to be nearly of the same size as the Treasury of Atreus seems to be confirmed by the width of the approach ("dromos"), which is in the latter 20 ft. 7 in., in the former 19 ft. 8 in., broad.

These conical buildings, 50 ft. high, were constructed under the slope of a hill, and were destined to remain subter- ranean: for, as before stated, the outside surface of the stones is quite irregular, and the whole building is covered all round with a thick layer of stones, the weight of which holds the masonry fast together.   I feel certain that the tradition is correct which says that these mysterious build- ings served as the store-houses of the wealth of the early kings; but there can be no doubt that as long as they served as treasuries the "dromos" and the entrance gate were unobstructed, and the great question, therefore, arises, why and when were the "dromos" and the gate hidden under the tremendous masses of *débris?*

It has been asserted that they were buried at the time of the Dorian invasion; but did the excavation of the Treasury of Atreus in 1810 by Veli Pasha, the son of Ali Pasha,

produce anything else than a stone table, a few sculptured slabs, and fragments of brazen plates? and was it worth while to bury empty treasuries? But it is a fact that they were buried, and, as to the chronology of the event, the pottery in the layer of *débris*, which covers the "dromos" of each, gives us fortunately some clue, for I find there continually very ancient painted pottery

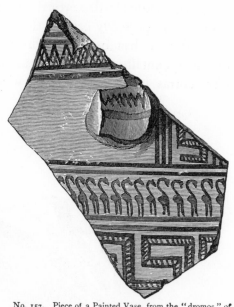

No. 157. Piece of a Painted Vase, from the "dromos" of the Treasury near the Lions' Gate. (2¼ M.) Half-size.

with geometrical patterns, resembling the Attic vases which until now have been considered as the most ancient terra-cottas in Greece; as well as very rude terra-cotta idols of Hera in the female and cow forms. The style of the pottery is seen in the annexed piece (No. 157), which shows to the right of the handle a ⊐⊏ of which only part is visible, and then follows a row of the frequently recurring animal in form of a crane, but which

No. 158. Fragment of the same Pottery from the "dromos." (5 M.) Half-size.

may have been intended to represent a horse, and after that follows a beautiful band of key-patterns. On another fragment (No. 158) is only a row of the same birds or horses between two bands, each of three parallel circular lines; also a small can, ornamented with vertical lines, was found there. Of course it is perfectly certain that the *débris* which covers the entrance has been brought there from other places, but as it contains solely fragments of very ancient painted terra-cottas nearly all of them with geometrical patterns,

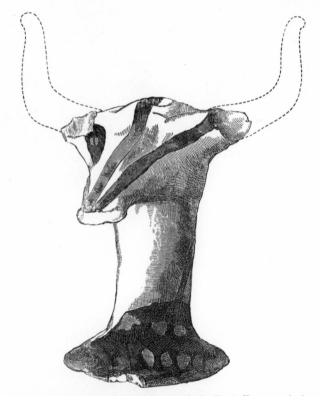

No. 159. Idol of Terra-cotta, with a Cow's head, on the handle of a Vase. (4 M.) Actual size.

the filling-up of the entrance must have been already effected in a remote antiquity, and the Treasury itself is doubtless more ancient than the Treasury of Atreus.

Of the idols found in the " dromos " before the Treasury now in question the most ancient Hera-idols, in the shape of a woman, are very rudely made, sometimes without painted ornaments, and they have a head either oblong or round, with or without a diadem, and large eyes. Some are with breasts, others without; the hands are either protruding or folded on the breast. To the same epoch no doubt belong the female idols with a very compressed bare head, large eyes, out-stretched hands, and no breasts; or with two breasts, below which a horn protrudes on each side, so that both horns together form a semicircle;* also the male idol, with its head orna- mented in front with a diadem, bearing a star, a long aquiline nose, large eyes, and a long protrud- ing beard ;† and some very archaic cow idols, with painted red or black ornamentation (see No. 118, p. 74); also the fragment of a vase of granite, and a small female figure in silver with long hair.

No. 160.   Idol of Terra-cotta with a Cow's head.
(2 M.)   Actual size.

In the Acropolis the most common idols are those of Hera as a woman with horns or in the shape of a cow. In fact, they are so abundant that up to this time I have been able to gather more than (say) 700 of them, but all are more or less mutilated. Among the forms of the idols found abundantly in the Acropolis I must further mention

---

* See No. 94.   † See No. 106.

that with a round uncovered bird's head,* and that with a very compressed head, with large eyes, and a *polos* in the form of a bowl, on which is often painted a cross; both these idols hold their hands on the breasts, and have no characteristic of the cow.† I may further mention the very frequently occurring idol, the whole middle part of which is in the form, or nearly so, of a disk,‡ and which

No. 161. Cow-headed Idols of Hera. (1·5 M.) Half-size.

may have been intended primitively to represent the full moon, because Hera was originally the moon-goddess, and her cow-horns, and subsequently her whole cow-character, cannot but be derived from the symbolic horns of the crescent moon. Lastly, I have to mention the less frequent female idol with a perfectly modelled cow-head; but

* See No. 100.   † See No. 101.   ‡ See Nos. 90–93.

this type is only found on the handles of vases, and the body of the woman is always incomplete, never reaching further down than the breast, and frequently finishing

No. 162.　The two faces of a Granite Mould for casting various Ornaments. (4 M.)　Actual size.

with the neck, on which the necklace is never forgotten.*
By a strange coincidence the three or four terra-cotta

---

* See Nos. 159, 160, and the coloured Plate D, figs. n, o, p.

cow-heads found in Troy were likewise on the handles of
vases.*   One headless Hera-idol was found, with two well
preserved horns and two breasts.   The head is not broken
off, for it was never intended to have a head.   I may also
mention that many perfectly flat idols were found, showing
on each side a head with a long muzzle and large eyes in
profile, but no indication of horns.   (See No. 161.†)

Except the button with a gold plate, already mentioned,
no objects of gold or silver have been found yet; but that
these metals were in extensive use cannot be doubted.   I
found a mould consisting, according to Professor Xavier
Landerer, of very fine dark red granite; it shows on both
sides together fourteen different fanciful types of earrings
and other ornaments, all of which were probably cast in
gold or silver (see No. 162).   I found also a smaller
mould, which consists, according to the same Professor, of
basalt, and is in form of a cube (see No. 163): it has on
all the six sides moulds for casting ornaments, of which
the types may be seen in the engravings; amongst others,
it has a type for casting small cones with parallel horizontal
circles, of which I find here a large number.   (See No. 164.)
They consist of a lustrous blackish mass, which Professor
Landerer has analysed and found to consist of a hard-
baked clay which has been varnished with. a lead glaze.
Mr. Newton also kindly showed me, among the objects
found in the tomb at Ialysus, very small cones with parallel
horizontal circles of the very same composition as these
Mycenean cones.   I also very frequently find here small
disks of the same composition, with impressed flowers or
other ornamentation, which must have served as ornaments

---

* See 'Troy and its Remains,' p. 294.
† I call particular attention to the Egyptian sepulchral paintings
published by Mr. G. A. Hoskins in his 'Travels in Ethiopia and Upper
Egypt,' where we see among the offerings some vases from which
similar heads look out.

on the doors or elsewhere (No. 165), and these also figure
in the British Museum among the objects from the tomb

No. 163.   Four faces of a six-sided Mould of Basalt.   (5 M.)   Actual size.

of Ialysus.   The quadrangular piece (No. 166), on which
may be seen a very well-represented cuttle-fish between two

Nos. 164, 165, 166.   Ornaments of Glazed Clay.   (3-4 M.)   Actual size.

vertical borders with teeth-like cuts, has four perforations
for attaching it with pins.   As I have already mentioned,

the object No. 167, which has the form of a mushroom, but a perforation in its whole length, is of the same material; this also must have served as an ornament, while the whole tube-like lower part was sunk into the object which was to be ornamented, so that the head alone protruded, and may have served to put in a flower or something else. Of the same baked clay with a varnished lead glaze there was further found a large perforated bead (No. 168).

Nos. 167, 168, 169. Ornaments of Glazed Clay. (3-4 M.) Actual size.

I also very often find small objects in the form of a cone or with points more obtuse, and in this case perforated; they are turned from a mineral, which, according to Professor Landerer, is the Siphnian stone (*lapis ollaris*), commonly called potstone. The same scholar calls my attention to a passage of Pliny, who says: "On the island of Siphnos there is a stone which is hollowed out and turned for vases; these latter are very useful for cooking victuals or for the preservation of eatables, which, as we know, is the case with the *Comnes stone* in Italy. The Siphnian stone has the peculiarity that, being heated, it becomes black by the contact of oil and much harder, it being naturally soft. It can be turned and used for ornaments." The small cones of this stone have in the lower border two small holes on either side, which must have been made for the pins by which the object was fastened. A likeness of such a cone is No. 172; of another object of the same material, No. 169. The curious object, No. 171, which has almost the form of a Trojan idol, is of decomposed glass, but its use is inexplicable to me; it has on its lower side a tubular

hole for fastening it to something else, and may have
served as an ornament. The little ball, No. 170, on which

Nos. 170, 171, 172. Ornaments of Glazed Clay, &c. (3-4 M.) Actual size.

we see curious incised drawings, is of very hard baked
clay. I also find very frequently button-like objects, like
those already shown under No. 126,* which, according
to Professor Landerer, have been turned out of a stone
called "lapis serpentinus." I cannot explain the use of
them otherwise than that they have served as ornaments
in the doors and on the walls, like No. 167. There was
also found a large perforated bead of white glass, and
further a large block of diorite, with circular moulds for
casting various objects.

A treasure of bronze objects was found at a depth of
13 feet. It consists of five knives (like Nos. 121–125),†
two small wheels and an inexplicable object with a ring,‡
two lances, two double-edged hatchets (No. 173), hair-

No. 173. A double-edged Hatchet of Bronze. (3 M.) Half-size.

---

* See p. 76.   + See p. 75.   ‡ See under No. 120, p. 74.

pins, two vases, and remnants of four others, and a tripod.
It is incomprehensible to me for what purpose the wheels
may have served; they can never have been intended for
rotation, for, as may be seen by the engraving,* there is
attached to them a quadrangular handle, which proves that
they can never have been turned round. From one of the
wheels† this handle is broken off; as for the rest, the
wheels perfectly resemble those represented on the chariots
in the sculptures, for there are four spokes, which form a
cross round the axle. Also two very small and exceedingly
curious wheels of lead were found, the one at the depth of
11 ft. 8 in., the other at 16½ ft.‡

There were also found a certain number of lentoid gems
of steatite, onyx, or agate, polished, nearly round, and

Nos. 174–181.   Lentoid Gems.   (4–7 M.)   Actual size.

somewhat convex, with intaglios of animals, which are very
archaic, but show in several instances an advanced art; all
of these have evidently belonged to necklaces. No. 176
is of steatite (*lapis ollaris*); it gives us a very rude and
primitive representation of an animal with a very long tail,

---

* See under No. 120, p. 74.   † *Ibid.*

‡ Also engraved under No. 120. I here again call particular attention to the fact, *that the depth in which each object has been found is
always marked in metres below each object in the engravings.*

long legs, and a pointed head, which is turned backward, and on which we see a horn standing vertically: probably we must understand that this horn covers the second horn: the body of the animal resembles the body of a horse, the head that of an antelope. No. 178 is of red agate, and this also gives a rude representation of an animal with its head turned backward; above its hinder part is a trident, and it is difficult to distinguish whether the primitive artist intended to represent by this the animal's uplifted tail or some-thing else. The most beautiful of all the intaglios is of red onyx (No. 174), showing an antelope perfectly true to nature. Both horns are well represented, and the head and body are beautiful; the animal seems to kneel on its two fore-legs; the tail is lifted sideways

No. 182–185. Lentoid Gems and a bead. (3–6 M.) Size 3 : 4.

above the back. I call particular attention to the object above the back of this animal; it looks like an overturned flower-pot, with a long plant lying horizontally. The object on the lentoid gem (No. 183) cannot be recognised; this gem consists of serpentine. On No. 184, which is of black agate, we again see a very rudely-engraved animal with the head turned back, but without horns. No. 185 is a bead.

Nos. 186–189. Lentoid Gem, cylinder and beads. (3–6 M.) Size 3 : 4.

Another beautiful intaglio (No. 186), on black serpen-tine, represents an animal with the head turned back and very large eyes; it seems to run with great speed. The object No. 189 is also of black serpentine, and has no intaglio. Similar lentoid gems, with rudely-incised animals, found in the Greek islands, are in the gold room of the British Museum, and I call particular attention to them, as well as to the lentoid gem of rock crystal, representing in intaglio a goat, which turns her head. This gem, again, was found in the repeatedly-mentioned sepulchre of Ialysus, and is also in the British Museum. Very pretty is the small parallelopiped (No. 182), likewise of serpentine, ornamented on two sides with fourteen lines which cross each other, and on the other two sides with two incised squares, in each of which we see a small circle with a point in the centre. No. 187 represents a light green cylinder of opal, on which a human head is rudely carved, with closed eyes, a very broad nose, a large mouth, and a necklace, and very much in the ancient Egyptian style of art. It is cylindrical, and has no hole, and it seems therefore not to have served as a stick-handle. No. 188 is a bead of white glass; No. 180 is an object of blue glass cast in the form of a long but narrow mussel-shell, surrounded by horizontal parallel cuts; it is coloured with cobalt; No. 179 is a small bead of blue glass twice perforated. There is also a well-polished brown onyx, without any intaglio, and it deserves attention that a similar one was found in the tomb of Ialysus. No. 181 is of an artificial glass paste. I repeat that, with the exception of Nos. 175, 180, 187, all these objects are perforated and are beads or lentoid gems of necklaces.

Of combinations of signs resembling inscriptions, I have hitherto only found three or four; one of them is on both sides of a mutilated Hera-idol in the form of a woman (see No. 102); another inscription is on a mutilated cow-idol *; and a third is on a disk (No. 190). Of all of them I have sent copies to Professor Max Müller, who considers

---

* See the Coloured Plate B, fig. g.

them too indistinct and fragmentary to warrant any expression of opinion for the present.

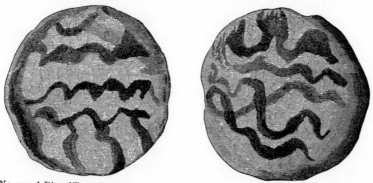

No. 190. A Disc of Terra-Cotta, with an uncertain appearance of an Inscription. (5 M.) Actual size.

I found at a depth of 6 feet a short Greek inscription:

$$T^oBER^{oo}\}EM$$

for which, however, I cannot claim a higher antiquity than the 6th century B.C.; in fact, the fragment of a vase on which it is scratched is of the usual black Hellenic pottery, which is so widely different from the archaic pottery of Mycenæ that I could not venture to attribute it to a remoter epoch than the 5th century, were it not for the archaic characters which are decidedly of the 6th century. But this fragment of black pottery again gives us an idea of the age of the ancient Mycenean pottery. I suppose that the first O stands for OY, the second O for Ω, and that the sign] is merely a comma. I read it thus: τοῦ ἥρωός εἰμ(ι), "I belong to the heros."

Besides the goblets already mentioned in the form of large Bordeaux wine-glasses with one handle,* which continue to be found in enormous quantities, there are also frequently found goblets of the same form with two handles. Although these goblets have not the slightest resemblance to the

---

* See Nos. 83, 84, 88, pp. 70, 71.

splendid Trojan goblets,* yet, like the latter, those with two
handles can fully claim to represent the Homeric δέπας
ἀμφικύπελλον.   I think Aristotle † is wrong in his theory
that the ἀμφικύπελλον had the shape of a bee's cell.   The
best judge, nay, the highest authority, for the form of the
Homeric δέπας ἀμφικύπελλον must necessarily be Homer
himself; and according to him the δέπας ἀμφικύπελλον is
always synonymous with ἄλεισον ἄμφωτον,‡ which latter
cannot possibly mean anything else than a simple goblet
with a large handle on each side.   In speaking of the shape
of the Homeric δέπας ἀμφικύπελλον, Athenæus § does not
even mention the opinion of Aristotle, but he cites the
opinion of Asclepiades of Myrlea, who says that ἀμφικύπελλον does not mean anything else than that the goblet
is ἀμφίκυρτον.   But the following phrase leaves no doubt
that the latter word signifies "with two handles," and this is
confirmed by Passow's Greek Lexicon (ed. Rost and Palm).

As far as my excavations have proceeded, I nowhere find
an accumulation of *débris* exceeding 26 ft.; and even this
depth is only found near the great circuit wall.   Thence
the rock rises rapidly, and further on the depth of the
débris is not more than from 13 to 20 ft.   On the west
side the Cyclopean wall has been nearly demolished for
a distance of 46 ft., and on its interior side a wall of
small stones joined with earth has been built to sustain its
ruins.   It must remain mere guesswork when the Cyclopean wall was destroyed and the small wall built, but at all
events this must have occurred long before the capture of
Mycenæ by the Argives in 468 B.C., because the small wall
was buried deep in the prehistoric *débris*.

The great quarry, whence all the stones for the Cyclopean walls, the Treasuries, and other buildings, were cut, is
on the site of and around the village of Charvati, a little

* See 'Troy and its Remains,' p. 158.
† *Hist. Animal.* IX. 40.
‡ See *Od.* III. 41, 46, 50 and 63, and XXII. 9, 10, 86.
§ Δειπνοσοφισταί, 783.

over a mile from this place; but the rock has in no instance been cut away deeper than the surface. I give a view of this village, in which the greater part of the ancient quarry is visible.* The name Charvati is no doubt derived from the Arabic word خراب (ruins), which has passed over into the Turkish language.

Mrs. Schliemann and I superintend the excavations from morning till dusk, and we suffer severely from the scorching sun and incessant tempest, which blows the dust into the eyes and inflames them; but in spite of these annoyances, nothing more interesting can be imagined than the excavation of a prehistoric city of immortal glory, where nearly every object, even to the fragments of pottery, reveals a new page of history.

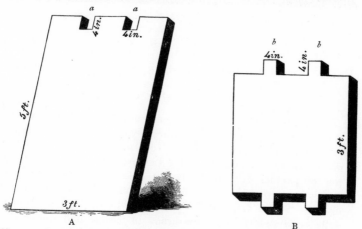

No. 190?. Pattern of the Slabs, forming the Double Paralle¹ Circle enclosing the Agora.

A. One of the vertical inner and outer slabs, both being inclined *inwards*, towards the enclosed space of the Agora, at an angle of 75°.

B. One of the cross slabs, with the tenons, *b, b,* to drop into the notches *a, a.*

N.B.—The slabs are not all of the dimensions here shown, but vary in size in different parts of the circle. (See p. 124.)

The slabs of the double circle, which serves both as the enclosure of the Agora and for its benches, are in a slanting position from the entrance on the north side all along the east side until a few yards before the point on the south side where the double circle passes from the rock on to the wall which supports it in the lower part of the Acropolis. At this point the slabs have the maximum size, which seems to have been maintained by all the slabs which stood on the supporting wall, and which have now nearly all fallen; but their inclination can be recognized by observing those still standing on the north-west side of the circle. On the north, on both sides of the entrance, where the Agora is bordered by those tomb-like recesses in which we have recognized small reservoirs, the slabs of these recesses are of necessity all perpendicular, because, had they been slanting, they would not have sustained the pressure of the water.

---

* See Vignette to Chapter V. p. 118.

No. 191.   The Village of Charvati with the ancient Quarry of Mycenæ.

CHAPTER V.

EXCAVATIONS IN AND NEAR THE ACROPOLIS—*continued.*

THE LIONS' GATE AND THE AGORA.

The Treasury excavated by Mrs. Schliemann—Older and less sumptuous than that of Atreus — The entrance, its ornaments — Archaic pottery found in the passage — Necklace beads — Fragment of a marble frieze — Threshold of the Lions' Gate — The great double row of parallel slabs, probably not of a remote antiquity — The Acropolis only partly accessible to chariots — The gateway double, like the Scæan Gate at Troy — Corridors of Cyclopean house-walls — Hera-idols and arrow-heads of bronze and iron — Door-keeper's lodge — Retaining walls — Tower of the Acropolis resting on a massive wall—The double circle of slabs formed the enclosure of the royal tombs and the Agora—Arguments in proof of this view —Objects of interest found there—A vast Cyclopean house with cisterns and water conduit, probably the ancient Royal Palace—The spring Perseia—No windows in the house—Objects of art and luxury found there—An onyx seal-ring—Vase-paintings of mail-clad warriors—Hand-made pottery in the Acropolis.

Mycenæ, Sept. 30, 1876.

SINCE the 9th inst. I have continued the excavations with the greatest energy, employing constantly 125 workmen and five horse-carts, and the weather being beautiful I have made excellent progress. In the Treasury, in which Mrs. Schliemann is excavating, we work with thirty labourers and two horse-carts, and find the very greatest difficulty in removing the hundreds of huge wrought stones which have fallen from the vault.

The interior walls of this Treasury have never been covered with brazen plates like the Treasury of Atreus here and the Treasury of Minyas in Orchomenus; at least, I see nowhere in the stones the holes of the bronze nails by which the metal plates were fastened; but I cannot avoid mentioning that on the inner east side of the Treasury, there protrudes from between the stones the fragment of a bronze plate, which sticks so fast that it cannot be drawn out; I therefore suppose that it was fastened there when the Treasury was built. It appears hardly possible that this could have happened merely by accident, but on the other hand I find it difficult to believe that this bronze plate could be a remnant of an ancient wall-coating of bronze plates, which were not fastened to the stones with nails but were attached in the joints between them, because in this case, I presume, we ought to find remnants of those plates in many places.

This Treasury is less sumptuous, and appears to be more ancient, than the Treasury of Atreus here, or the Treasury of Minyas at Orchomenus.

The entrance, which is 13 ft. long and 8 ft. broad, is roofed with four slabs 18½ ft. in length; the holes for the upper door-hinges are 5 in. deep. From certain traces in the walls it appears that the entrance has been ornamented on the right and left with two semi-columns, which we hope to find by digging deeper. A remnant of an ornamentation with semicircles is visible on the slab above the entrance, and the same can easily be distinguished in the engraving of the Treasury.* After having been buried for ages in

---

* See the Frontispiece, Plate V.

the damp *débris*, the large wrought stones of the walls of the approach (*dromos*) and of the façade of this Treasury have contracted by exposure to the sun, and, as may be seen from the engraving, a great number of them have crevices.

As in the Treasury of Atreus and in the Lions' Gate, the triangular space above the entrance is formed by an oblique approximation of the ends of the courses of stone. On all three sides of this triangle can be seen cuttings, which make it highly probable that it has once been filled up by a triangular piece of sculpture similar to that above the Lions' Gate.*

Among the archaic pottery found in the "dromos" before the Treasury, the very rudely modelled men on horseback holding the horse's neck with both hands, of which also several were found in the tomb at Ialysus, deserve particular attention; further, the fragments of large painted vases profusely covered with an ornamentation of key patterns, zigzag lines, stripes of ornaments like fish-spines, bands with very primitive representations of cranes or swans, or circles with flowers, and occasionally with the sign ⌐⌐.† Vases with such geometrical patterns are sometimes found in Athens, and have hitherto been universally considered to be the most ancient pottery of Attica, but I perfectly share my learned friend Mr. Chas. T. Newton's opinion, that the vases with geometrical patterns are later than all the different sorts of terra-cottas found in the five Royal tombs, and hereafter to be described. Of vases with other patterns I have found but very few fragments. Together with these fragments of pottery there was found part of a necklace with a large bead of white glass (No. 205), two beads of fluor-spar of a transparent bluish, and three of a red-bluish colour, all perforated and strung on a thin copper wire (Nos. 206,

---

* See Plan E, which shows the Plan and Sections of this Treasury.
† See the examples grouped on the two Plates, Nos. 192–204.

207, 208, 209); also the fragment of a white marble frieze with an ornamentation.* Just above the lower part of

Nos. 205–209. Beads of Glass and Fluor-spar. (4 M.) Actual size.

the "dromos" are the foundations of an Hellenic house, apparently of the Macedonian period.

The Archæological Society in Athens has not yet sent an engineer to consolidate the sculpture above the Lions' Gate, and to repair the Cyclopean wall close to it; but they intend still to do so. Meanwhile they have allowed me to continue the excavations at the Lions' Gate on the condition that I leave to the right and left of it a considerable portion of the _débris in situ_ in order to facilitate the raising of the blocks which are necessary for the repairs. Therefore I have been able to resume the excavations at the Lions' Gate, and I have brought to light its enormous threshold.

No. 210. Threshold of the Gate of Lions.

Two exact drawings of this are appended. It consists of a very hard block of breccia

---

* See No. 154, p. 98.

15 ft. long and 8 ft. broad. The ruts caused by the chariot-wheels, of which all guide books speak, exist only in the imagination of enthusiastic travellers, but not in reality. The immense double parallel row of closely joined slabs, which I have brought to light in close proximity to the Lions' Gate, would now altogether bar the access of chariots to the Acropolis. But as I cannot ascribe a very remote antiquity to the wall which sustains the double row of slabs in the lower part of the Acropolis, so neither can I claim a high antiquity for the circle of slabs itself, and before its erection chariots could certainly have had access to the Acropolis. But on account of the precipitous slopes of the cliff, it is impossible that chariots should ever have penetrated further than the first or lowest of the six natural or artificial terraces. Thus it is obvious that chariots were but little in use here, and that beasts of burden, horses, mules, or asses, were employed in their stead. No doubt the fifteen small straight parallel furrows, which are cut all along the surface of the threshold to prevent the beasts of burden from slipping, might have been mistaken for ruts of chariot-wheels. But again, the threshold having been deeply buried in the *débris* for ages, and at all events since the capture of the Acropolis by the Argives (468 B.C.), no mortal eye can have seen it for more than 2300 years.

There is a quadrangular hole, 1 ft. 3 in. long and 1 ft. broad, in the middle of the threshold, where the two doors of the gate met. The threshold further shows on its east side a straight furrow, artistically cut, 1 ft. broad, and on its west side another which forms a curve. Both these seem to have served as channels for rain water, the rush of which must have been great, the threshold being lower than the natural rock forming the floor of the passage, which rises gradually. In the side of the threshold which faces the north is a long artificial hole of a peculiar form, which must have been connected with the gate in some way or other, for a cutting of exactly the same form exists in the large flat stone in the middle of the gate at Troy. At a distance of 11½ ft. from the threshold on either side of the passage there is, as at Troy,* a quadrangular mass of Cyclopean masonry, 2 ft. broad and high, and 3 ft. long, which marks the site of a second gate of wood.

Further on to the right I have brought to light, below the foundations of an Hellenic house, quite a labyrinth of Cyclopean house-walls, forming a number of parallel corridors from 4 ft. to 6½ ft. broad, filled with stones and *débris*, which I am now clearing out. One of the corridors leads straight into the Cyclopean house already described.† In several places the walls retain traces of their clay-coating. I found here many Hera-idols, also three arrow-heads, all of bronze; two have barbs (γλωχῖνες); the third has the form of a pyramid, like the Carthaginian arrows which I found last year in my excavations in Motyë in Sicily.

To the left of the entrance is, first, the small chamber of the door-keeper, and then follows a wall of huge stones, intended merely to sustain the masses of *débris* (24 ft. to 26 ft. high) which have been washed down from the mount in the course of ages. Further on, in the same line, is a Cyclopean wall (166 ft. long and 30 ft. high) of enormous stones joined together with small ones, which, as already mentioned, is crowned by the ruins of a tower, and gives the Acropolis a peculiarly grand aspect.‡ This wall was imbedded from 10 ft. to 12 ft. deep in the *débris*, and has now been brought to light down to the rock on which it is founded.

My supposition that the double parallel row of large slabs would be found to form a complete circle has been proved correct. One-half of it rests on the wall which was

---

* See the Plan of the Lions' Gate, No. 22, p. 34. Comp. 'Troy and its Remains,' pp. 303, 321.

† Chapter IV. p. 99.   ‡ See Plates VI. and VII.

intended to support it in the lower part of the Acropolis, the other half is founded on the higher flat rock, and touches the foot of the Cyclopean wall before mentioned; the entrance to it is from the north side.*

At first I thought that the space between the two rows might have served for libations or for offerings of flowers in honour of the illustrious dead. But I now find this to be impossible, because the double row of slabs was originally covered with cross-slabs, of which six are still *in situ* ; they are firmly fitted in and consolidated by means of notches, 1¼ to 3⅓ in. deep, and 4 in. broad, in the upper edges of the aslant standing slabs of the two parallel rows, which received similar projections on the cross stones, forming a mortice and tenon joint.† As these latter exist on all the slabs, there can be no doubt that the whole circle was originally covered in the same way. The vertical slabs are from 4 ft. 2 in. to 8 ft. 2 in. long and 1 ft. 8 in. to 4 ft. broad, and the largest are in the two places where the double row descends from the rock to the supporting wall. Inside, there is first a layer of stones 1 ft. 4 in. thick, for the purpose of holding the slabs in their place; the remaining space is filled up with pure earth mixed with long thin cockle shells in the places where the original covering remains in its position, or with household remains, mixed with innumerable fragments of archaic pottery wherever the covering is missing. This circumstance can leave no doubt that the cross slabs were only removed after the city had been captured and deserted, because all the fragments of archaic pottery must necessarily have been washed down by the rain from the five natural or artificial upper terraces of the Acropolis, and this can of course only have taken place after Mycenæ had been abandoned by its inhabitants.

It must be particularly observed that the whole arrange-

* See Plan C and Plates VI., VII.   † See the cut No. 190*a*, p. 117.

ICHNOGRAPHY OF THE ROYAL TOM

PLATE VI.

WITHIN THE CIRCLE OF THE AGORA.

ment of slabs slopes *inwards* at an angle of 75°; so that, the ground within the circle being raised, as just described, the horizontal slabs formed a
continuous bench, on which
people could sit, looking towards the enclosure, the inclination leaving convenient
room for the feet, as is the
case also with the stone seats
for the priests in the theatre
of Dionysus at Athens.

My esteemed friend, Pro-
fessor F. A. Paley, has been
the first to advance the

No. 210 a.   Bench of the Agora.

opinion, accepted by Mr. Charles T. Newton and by myself, that the double parallel circle of slabs, having been in the most solid way covered with cross slabs, must necessarily have served as a bench to sit upon and as the enclosure of the Agora of Mycenæ. He thinks that the first idea for the form of an Agora was given by the circular-dances (κύκλιοι χοροί) and the recitation of the dithyrambs.* The assembled people sat in a circle, and the orator stood in the centre, as we see in Homer,† and in Sophocles ‡; and just in the centre of this enclosure at Mycenæ I found a rock forming a slight elevation, which might well have

---

* The Dithyramb was an ancient Bacchanalian performance, as early at least as Archilochus, who says "he knows how to lead off the dithyramb, the beautiful song of Dionysus, when his mind is inflamed with wine" (Frag. *ap.* Athen. XIV. p. 628). It seems to have been a hymn sung by one or more members of a κῶμος, or irregular band of revellers, to the music of the flute. Arion, at Corinth, first gave a regular choral or antistrophic form to the dithyramb (Herodot. I. 24; Pindar, *Olymp.* XIII. 18–25). The choruses, which ordinarily consisted of fifty men or youths, danced in a ring round the altar of Dionysus. Hence they were termed *cyclic choruses* (κύκλιοι χοροί), and dithyrambic poets were understood by the term κυκλιοδιδάσκαλοι.

† *Il.* I. 58, 68, 101; II. 53, 96, 99.

‡ *Oed. Tyr.* 161: Ἄρτεμιν ἃ κυκλόεντ' ἀγορᾶς θρόνον εὐκλέα θάσσει.
"Artemis who sits on the Agora's glorious circular seat."

served as the platform (βῆμα), from which the speakers addressed those sitting on the circular bench.*

We therefore know with certainty, in the first place, that the Agora was round, and, secondly, that people used to sit there. The circular form of the Agora is also proved by Euripides,† who speaks of the "circle of the Agora" (ἀγορᾶς κύκλον). Professor Paley infers from the passage of Euripides already cited (*Electra*, 710), that the poet had known this Agora in the Acropolis of Mycenæ from personal inspection, and that by πέτρινα βάθρα he means the enormous circular stone bench by which the Agora is enclosed, and that consequently on this bench he makes the herald stand, when in a loud voice he calls the people of Mycenæ to the Agora; he also believes that Euripides had perhaps in mind the βῆμα in the Athenian Pnyx. I should not hesitate to accept Professor Paley's opinion, had I not found the Agora deeply buried in the pre-historic *débris*. But it may very well be that at the time of Euripides the Agora was not yet entirely covered, and that the greater part of the prehistoric *débris*, with which I found it covered, was only after his time washed down by the heavy winter rains from the five upper natural or artificial terraces of the Acropolis. At all events it appears from the pottery of the later Hellenic city that the latter was not built till after the time of Euripides. ‡

Mr. Charles T. Newton calls my attention to the passage in Thucydides, who says of Corcyra, "the houses which lie in a circle around the Agora." § Also to the following passages in Pausanias, which prove that the heroic tombs were in the Agora of Megara. "Here they built the place for council in order that they might have the tomb of the heroes within the place for council;" ** for there can

---

* This rock has now partially fallen, in consequence of the excavation of the third and fourth tombs, which it overhangs.

† *Orest.* 919.   ‡ See Appendix A.   § Thucyd. III. 74 : τὰς οἰκίας τὰς ἐν κύκλῳ τῆς ἀγορᾶς.

** Paus. I. 43, § 4 : βουλευτήριον ἐνταῦθα ᾠκοδόμησαν, ἵνα σφίσιν ὁ τάφος τῶν ἡρώων ἐντὸς τοῦ βουλευτηρίου γένηται.

be no doubt that this βουλευτήριον was in the Agora. (It must be borne in mind that this was done at Megara by the advice of the Delphic oracle.) Further: " also the tomb of Coroebus is in the Agóra of the Megarians."*

Another esteemed friend also calls my attention to the passage in Pausanias: " Here is the tomb of Opheltes, with an enclosure of stones and altars in the walls ; (here) is also the tumulus, the sepulchre of Lycurgus, the father of Opheltes."† But Opheltes was a son of the Nemean King Lycurgus and Eurydice, and he was killed by a serpent whilst his nurse, Hypsipyle, showed a spring to the seven heroes when on their expedition to Thebes. Owing to this event the people of Nemea founded in his honour the Nemean games, and he, as well as his father, was interred in the sacred grove of the Nemean Jove, where their tombs were seen by Pausanias, who mentions nothing of an Agora.‡

Professor Paley reminds me of Pindar's Pythian Ode (V. 69–98), in which we read:§ " (Apollo) caused the valorous descendants of Hercules and Aegimius to dwell in Lacedaemon, and at Argos, and at sacred Pylos. Now they say that from Sparta came my own much cherished race. Sprung from thence the heroes called Aegidae came to Thera, even my ancestors,—not indeed without the guidance of the god, but a certain destiny brought thither a festive rite attended with much sacrificing ; and from thence receiving thy Carnea, Apollo, we honour at the banquet the grandly built city of Cyrene, possessed as it is by the brass-loving strangers, Trojan descendants of Antenor. For they came thither with

---

* Paus. I. 43, § 8 : Κοροίβῳ δέ ἐστι τάφος ἐν τῇ Μεγαρέων ἀγορᾷ.

† Paus. II. 15, § 4 : ἐνταῦθά ἐστι μὲν 'Οφέλτου τάφος, περὶ δὲ αὐτὸν θρίγκος λίθων, καὶ ἐντὸς τοῦ περιβόλου βωμοί · ἔστι δὲ χῶμα γῆς Λυκούργου μνῆμα τοῦ 'Οφέλτου πατρός.

‡ Paus. II. 15, § 2 ; Apollod. I. 9, § 14 ; III. 6, § 4 ; Hyg. Fab. 74 ; Stat. Theb. V. 296.

§ Translation of the Odes of Pindar by F. A. Paley, M.A.

Helen, after they had seen their native city become a
smoking ruin in the war.   And the horse-driving race is
religiously received with sacrifices, and propitiated by
offerings (at their tombs), by the men whom Aristoteles
(Battas) brought, when he opened the deep highway of the
sea for his swift vessels.   He founded also larger groves of
the gods, and laid down a paved road, cut straight through
the plain, to be smitten with the feet of horses in processions
to Apollo for averting evil from mortals; and there he lies
in death, apart from the rest, at the furthermost end of the
Agora.   Happy did he live while among men, and afterwards he was blessed as a hero worshipped by the people.
And away from him, in front of their palaces [but of
course also in the Agora], lie other consecrated kings that
have their lot with Hades."

From this passage in Pindar we see that Battas, also
called Aristoteles, the founder of Cyrene, 640 B.C., and its
first king, descended from Hercules, and that his ancestors,
the Heracleids or Dorians, had emigrated from Sparta to
Thera.   As Pindar saw his tomb, as well as those of other
consecrated kings (probably the successors of Battas), in
the Agora of Cyrene, Professor Paley thinks that it was an
ancient Doric and not an Achæan custom to bury the
kings in the Agora.   But this is in contradiction with the
above statement of Pausanias (I. 43, §§ 4, 8), that the
Megarians had the sepulchres of Coroebus and other
heroes in their Agora, because Coroebus was an Elian
Olympic victor in the stadium (Ol. I.), and, according to
tradition, he killed Ποινή, sent by Apollo to the Argives.*
Besides the Megarians had nothing whatever to do with
Doric customs.

In like manner as at Megara and Cyrene, so in the
Acropolis of Mycenæ, in honour of the illustrious personages who lie buried here, the Agora was erected in a circle

---

* Paus. V. 8, § 3 ; VIII. 26, § 2 ; Strabo, VIII. 355.

around their tombs. Had the circle of slabs served only as
an enclosure for the five royal tombs there would have
been no necessity either to make it double and slanting and
to cover it horizontally, or to build a huge wall for the
sole purpose of sustaining it in the lower part of the Acropolis, and of raising it to the level of that part which rested
on the rock in the higher part of the Acropolis; nay, one
single circular enclosure, following the sinuosities of the
rock, would in my opinion have done just as much honour
to the five royal sepulchres as the artificially levelled and
covered double row.

It deserves particular notice that between and on both
sides of the double circular row of slabs, there were found
many objects of interest, such
as a fish of wood (No. 211),
and a large number of Hera-
idols of the various forms already
described; also some in the
shape of a standing or a sitting

No. 211.   A Fish of Wood. (3¼ M.)
Actual size.

cow without horns, but with a female head-dress,* or
with the neck perforated for suspension with a string,†
which seems to indicate that they were worn
as amulets. Also a female idol having two feet
instead of a tube as usual; it has an uncovered
bird's head, no mouth, very large eyes, protruding hands, and a necklace; the hair is
well represented on the back; the dress is
marked with a red colour.‡ There was also
found an unpainted male figure of clay, with
large eyes, an aquiline nose, and no mouth;
the head is covered with a cap in form of a
turban. I doubt if this is an idol. There was also found
a very primitive idol, with an uncovered bird's head and

No. 212.
A curious Idol.
(4 M.) Actual size.

---

* See the coloured Plate C, fig. k.
† See No. 115.   ‡ See No. 107.

two ears ; the hands are on the breast, but not joined; the
head is turned towards heaven (No. 212). I here call
attention to the large number of idols of Aphrodite in
the British Museum, which are represented touching both
breasts with the hands, probably as symbols of fecundity.

There were also found two knives of lever-opal and
three arrows of obsidian,* which are of rare occurrence
here ; further, a number of small perforated glass necklace
beads, and three whorls of terra-cotta.

I frequently find here, in the prehistoric *débris*, fragments of a wall-coating of chalk with painted archaic ornamentations of red, blue, green, or yellow spiral lines. As
no trace of chalk is found in any of the Cyclopean houses,
I cannot claim for these wall-coatings a remote antiquity ;
and I fancy they are derived from frame houses of the last
century before the capture of the city by the Argives.

To the south of the circular double row of slabs my
excavations have brought to light a vast Cyclopean
house, which, so far as it has been uncovered, contains
seven chambers intersected by four corridors of four feet
in breadth (see Plans B and C). Here and there the walls
still retain their clay coating, which, however, nowhere
shows a trace of painting. The walls are from 2 to 4½ ft.
thick, and the same wall is in some places 6 to 8 in.
thicker than in others. The largest room is 18½ ft. long
by 13½ ft. broad, and its east side is cut out in the rock
to a depth of 16 in.

Below this and the adjoining room is a deep cistern cut
out in the rock. Into it runs a Cyclopean water-conduit,
which comes down the hill, and probably brought water
from the spring *Perseia*, half a mile east of the Acropolis,
which has a well-deserved celebrity in the plain of Argos for
its purity and its salubrious properties. Pausanias (II. 16)
saw this spring in the ruins of Mycenæ ; but the city never

---

* See No. 126, p. 76.

extended so far east. I suppose, therefore, that what he saw of the water of the Perseia was nothing but the discharge of an artificial conduit from the natural source above the citadel. This would also perfectly agree with the word κρήνη, which he constantly employs with that meaning, in opposition to πηγή, a natural spring.

Although there are no windows in the Cyclopean house—and although the scanty daylight through the doors must have been still further diminished by the Cyclopean circuit-wall, which is only separated from the west side of the house by a corridor 4 ft. broad—yet there can be no doubt that it served as a dwelling-house, and further as the dwelling house of the most prominent family of Mycenæ, for it is only such a house that we can imagine close to the Agora in the most imposing part of the Acropolis, within which the space was very scanty and therefore precious. Professor Paley thinks that the passage so often cited from Euripides (*Electra*, 710) proves beyond any doubt that it must be the Royal Palace, because the people of Mycenæ are there called to *the Agora to see the wonderful lamb with the golden fleece.* But this lamb (which was a portent symbolical of the monarchy) had been conveyed *to the palace* by Aëropé, wife of Atreus. Thyestes then and there told the people that he *had it in his house* (ἔχειν κατὰ δῶμα), consequently the palace was close to the Agora.

If at the time of Euripides the Agora was still partly visible above the *débris*, such must have been still much more the case with the ruins of that Cyclopean house, and it is more than probable that tradition pointed to it as the Palace of the Atridæ, in which Agamemnon and his companions had been murdered, and that it was shown under this denomination to Euripides. The objects discovered in this house prove that its inmates had pretensions even to luxury; for in one of the chambers, at a depth of 20 feet below the surface, was found a finger-ring cut out of a splendid

white onyx, with a seal, on which are represented in intaglio
two animals without horns. At first sight they certainly
appear to be hinds, but on attentive examination we see that
the artist's intention has been to represent cows ; both have
their heads turned round looking at their calves, which
suck the milk from their udders.* Though in a very
archaic style, the intaglio is nevertheless well wrought ; the
anatomy of the animal is tolerably observed, and one feels
astonished how it could have been possible to do the work
without a magnifying glass. On seeing this intaglio, and
reflecting that it belongs to an antiquity preceding Homer
by centuries, we are ready to believe that all the works of
art mentioned by Homer, such as the wonderful shield of
Achilles,† the dog and the deer in the mantle-brooch of
Ulysses,‡ Nestor's goblet,§ and others, all existed in his
time, and that he merely describes what he saw with his
own eyes. Mr. Achilles Postolaccas calls my attention to
the most ancient didrachms of Corcyra, of the 7th century
B C., on which a cow is giving milk to her calf, this representation being similar in style to the cows and calves on
the onyx ring.

There were further found in the Cyclopean house some
beautiful axes of diorite or serpentine,‖ and many whorls
of blue stone, and a great many painted terra-cottas, among
which the fragments of a large vase, with two or three
handles, the ends of which have been modelled into the
shape of cowheads, deserve particular attention. Some of
the fragments which I have been able to readjust represent
six full-armed warriors, painted with a dark red colour on
a light yellow dead ground ; they are evidently setting out
on a military expedition, and all wear coats of mail which
reach from the neck down to below the hips. (See

---

* See No. 175, p. 112.   † *Iliad*, XVIII. 478–608.
‡ *Od.* XIX. 224–231.   § *Il.* XI. 632–635.
‖ Like those shown under No. 126, p. 76.

No. 213). These coats of mail consist of two distinct
parts, which are fastened round the waist by a girdle,

No. 213. Fragments of a painted Vase, representing armed Warriors. (5 M.) Size 1 : 3. about.

and their lower edge is fringed with long tassels. Each
warrior's back is covered with a large round shield, which
seems to be fastened on the left shoulder, for, though
the shield protrudes far on both sides, it does so much
more on the left than on the right. Its lower end is cut
out in the form of a crescent. In their right hands the
warriors hold long lances, to each of which is attached that
curious object resembling a Trojan idol, which I have
already mentioned in describing one of the bas-reliefs.*
Though it certainly appears to us that this curious object
can have served for no other purpose than for fixing the
lances on the right shoulder, yet it deserves particular
attention that the primitive Mycenean artist has taken care
to represent it a little above the shoulder, in order that it
might be seen separately, for had he represented it leaning
on the shoulder, it would have been confounded with, and
partly covered by, the shield, and it would have been impossible to recognise its shape. For the rest, the shape of
the lances is such as we were led to expect from the Homeric
" δολιχόσκιον ἔγχος,"† for they are very long. We further
see that the spear-head has a tube in which the shaft is
fixed, and this appears also to have been the case with the
Homeric lances.‡

Very peculiar are the greaves (κημῖδες) which appear
to be of cloth, and reach from a little above the knee down
nearly as far as the ankles; their upper end is attached by
means of a string, which is turned three times round the
lower part of the thigh. In my opinion this string is in
itself a proof that the greaves are of cloth. All the warriors
wear sandals fastened on by straps reaching as far up as
the greaves. Of the highest interest are the helmets, dotted
all over with a large number of points, which may be

---

* See Appendix B, for an ingenious suggestion as to the nature of
these objects.

† Literally, 'a spear casting a very long shadow.'

‡ See for example, *Il.* XVII. 297 :—

ἐγκέφαλος δὲ παρ' αὐλὸν ἀνέδραμεν ἐξ ὠτειλῆς.

" And the brain ran out from the wound on the tube of the lance."

intended to represent the lustre of the bronze. The lower part of the helmets is nearly in the form of a crescent, and protrudes both in front and behind ; the upper part of the helmet is no doubt the Homeric φάλος.* On the top of this φάλος was the λόφος or tube, in which the horse-tail crest (ἵππουρις) was fastened.† But unfortunately no space was left for this λόφος, and thus the artist has been obliged to leave it out and to represent the crest as fastened on the φάλος itself. What this crest consists of is not clear, but as it is here shewn in the form of a long leaf, it is highly probable that the artist meant to represent it as a horsetail.

From the fore part of the helmet rises a long and very curious object, which forms a curve, and is much like a horn. It is altogether inexplicable to me what it can have been used for, and there is no word in Homer which might be interpreted so as to indicate its existence on the Homeric helmet.

Now, with regard to the physiognomy of the six war-riors, it is most decidedly not Assyrian or Egyptian. All have exactly the same type—very long noses, large eyes, small ears, and a long well-dressed beard, which ends in a

---

* *Il.* III. 361–362 :—

> Ἀτρείδης δὲ ἐρυσσάμενος ξίφος ἀργυρόηλον,
> πλῆξεν ἀνασχόμενος κόρυθος φάλον.

" Drawing his silver-studded sword and lifting up his arm, Atreides struck the φάλος off the helmet."

† The following passage of the *Iliad*, XIX. 379–383, can leave no doubt on this point :—

> ὣς ἀπ' Ἀχιλλῆος σάκεος σέλας αἰθέρ' ἵκανε
> καλοῦ, δαιδαλέου· περὶ δὲ τρυφάλειαν ἀείρας
> κρατὶ θέτο βριαρήν· ἡ δ', ἀστὴρ ὣς, ἀπέλαμπεν
> ἵππουρις τρυφάλεια· περισσείοντο δ' ἔθειραι
> χρύσεαι, ἃς Ἥφαιστος ἵει λόφον ἀμφὶ θαμειάς.

" So shone up to the sky the glance of the beautiful artistic shield of Achilles. Lifting then up the powerful helmet, he put it on his head, and the plumed helmet glanced like a star, and the hairs of gold waved, which Hephæstus had thickly set round the cone (λόφον)."

See the description of these parts of the Homeric helmets in ' Troy and its Remains,' pp. 279–281, and 334.

point. Thus, except the beard, there is nothing Asiatic about them. Five of the warriors are followed by a woman, seemingly a priestess, who is dressed in a long gown fastened at the waist by a girdle ; her forehead is ornamented with a diadem, and she seems to wear some kind of a head-dress. Only her right arm remains, which is uplifted, and by the curve it forms it appears that the woman has lifted her joined hands and is praying to the gods to be propitious to the departing warriors, and to grant them a safe return. This custom of lifting both hands when praying is continually found in Homer.*

On other fragments of the same vase (No. 214 †) are represented two warriors, who cover their left side with their shields and hold in their uplifted right hand a lance, which they thrust at their enemies, of whom, however, the figure of only one is partly preserved. The armour of the two warriors and that of the opponent is perfectly identical with that of the six warriors described before, except the head-dress, which, instead of bronze helmets, consists here seemingly of a low helmet of boarskin, with the bristles outside. In fact, these helmets vividly remind us of the low helm of oxskin which Ulysses put on his head when he and Diomed went in the night as spies to the Trojan camp.‡ I may here remark that the word κυνέη means dogskin, and that consequently the low helmets must originally have been made of dogskin. But at the epoch of

---

* For example, *Il.* I. 450 :—

τοῖσιν δὲ Χρύσης μεγάλ᾽ εὔχετο χεῖρας ἀνασχών.

"Loud prayed for them Chryses lifting up his hands."

† See Vignette to Chapter VI.

‡ *Il.* X. 257–259.

. . . ἀμφὶ δέ οἱ κυνέην κεφαλῆφιν ἔθηκεν
ταυρείην, ἄφαλόν τε καὶ ἄλλοφον, ἥτε καταῖτυξ
κέκληται, ῥύεται δὲ κάρη θαλερῶν αἰζηῶν.

"On his brows he placed
A helmet, wrought of bull's hide, without crest
Or cone, and commonly cataityx calle l,
Such as defends the head of blooming youths."—I. CH. WRIGHT.

Homer the original conception of the word had long disappeared, and he not only uses κυνέη for a low helm, but
also for a large bronze helmet.   Behind the warrior to the
left is seen part of the coat of mail and the shield of another
man, and behind the other warrior is seen a shield; thus
it seems that many warriors were here represented fighting
together.   Below the first handle is represented a flying
bird.   On the two cow-heads, in which the handles terminate, only the place of the horns is marked, because the
artist knew that, if he made them, they would at once break
when the vase was to be used.   The clay of this vase, which
has been made on the potter's wheel, is unusually bad and
mixed with coarse sand; the fabric also is extremely rude;
inside it is painted red.

There were further found in the Cyclopean house other
vases of excellent fabric, and ornamented with rows of
circles, containing numerous signs which at first sight
appear to be written characters, but from the continual
repetition of the same signs one soon sees the mistake.
There were also found in the Cyclopean house two copper
vessels, one of which is a tripod of very large size.

I now find here in the Acropolis numerous fragments
of hand-made pottery, but not in distinct layers as at Tiryns.
It is evident that the layer of prehistoric hand-made pottery (for there must have been such a layer) has been
disturbed; and I think it probable that it was disturbed
when the huge wall was built, which sustains the circular
double parallel enclosure of the Agora in the lower part
of the Acropolis, because this wall is at all events later than
the hand-made pottery.   What I find of this pottery has
usually an ornamentation of black horizontal bands or
spiral lines on a light green dead ground; but fragments of
monochromatic lustrous black vases also occur.

I have explained on pp. 3 and 4 that the name " Cyclopean walls" is founded on an error, being derived from the
mythic legend that the Cyclopes were distinguished archi-

tects, but that the name having come into use, we cannot help employing it for the different kinds of walls of huge blocks which I have specified. But in Tiryns as well as here in Mycenæ, where I am surrounded by the grandest Cyclopean walls in the world, I am, for brevity's sake and in order to avoid misunderstandings, bound to use the name "Cyclopean" even for the smallest walls of houses or water conduits which show the same kind of masonry. But it must be distinctly understood that I should of course not think of calling them so if I found them in places where there are no huge walls of that kind, for the name "Cyclopean" can only be applied to the gigantic.

No. 213 *a, b.* A very frequent type of Mycenean painted Pottery. Half-size

NOTE.—The pattern on the two fragments here shown, evidently representing a sea animal, a sort of cockle, is the most common pattern at Mycenæ ; but it never occurs either in the five royal tombs, or in the dromos before the Treasury, which circumstance leads me to conclude that it came into use at Mycenæ both after the epoch of the tombs and after the covering up of the dromos of the Treasury. The pottery with this pattern has nearly always a light yellow dead ground, only in a few instances a light red dead ground, and the pattern itself is always of a black (or dark red) colour. Now it is a remarkable fact that this pattern, which has never been found yet elsewhere, is to be seen, of exactly the same form, on nearly all the terra-cotta goblets, and on some of the terra-cotta vases from the sepulchre of Ialysus, which are now in the British Museum. At the same time I remind the reader that these Ialysus goblets have exactly the same shape as all the terra-cotta goblets of Mycenæ, and that this form has never yet been found elsewhere, except in the first and most ancient of the four prehistoric cities at Hissarlik. But then again it deserves particular notice that this pattern never and in no instance occurs on the Mycenean goblets, and solely on the Mycenean vases.

No. 214. Other Fragments of the Vase (No. 213). (5 m.) Size 1 : 6.

CHAPTER VI.

THE SECOND GREAT TREASURY ; ACROPOLIS ; AND CYCLO-
PEAN REMAINS IN THE NEIGHBOURHOOD OF MYCENÆ.

Further excavations of Mrs. Schliemann's Treasury — The *dromos*,
doorway, and threshold — Objects found there — Hera-idols —
Cyclopean water-conduits and cisterns in the Acropolis — Bronze
rings — Pottery with marks like letters — Earrings like those found
at Troy — Hand-made painted pottery — New forms of Hera-idols —
Terra-cotta tripods and cradles, probably votive offerings — A comb,
stilettos of opal, beads and buttons — A bronze sword — Iron tongs
of late date — State of the *débris* left at the Lions' Gate — The
excavations visited by the Emperor of Brazil — Ascent of Mount
Eubœa — The Cyclopean enclosure on its summit ; was probably a
very ancient sanctuary — Other Cyclopean remains near Mycenæ —
State of the excavations.

Mycenæ, October 30, 1876.

SINCE the 30th of September I have continued the excavations with the utmost vigour, employing constantly 125
labourers and 5 horse-carts.   In the Treasury the difficulties
were far greater than I had anticipated, particularly as the
delegate of the Greek Government opposed the removal of
the foundations of the Hellenic house just above the lower
part of the " dromos," which I have mentioned before.
Thus we have been unable to clear the latter of the *débris*,
9 ft. deep, which still covers its pavement, and have only

succeeded in clearing out the entrance passage, which is
13 ft. long and 8 ft. broad, and the central part of the Treasury; but we have left a border of huge stones and rubbish,
7 ft. to 9 ft. high, and 10 ft. to 15 ft. broad.

The two semi-columns to the right and left of the
entrance were fluted; one of them (4 ft. 3 in. high and
1 ft. 4 in. broad) was found in the passage near the door.
At 9½ ft. before the latter the "dromos" is shut up by a
wall of square blocks of calcareous stones, 5 ft. high. The
door of the Treasury has the enormous height of 18 ft.
5 in., and is 8 ft. 4 in. broad. On the threshold, which consists of a very hard breccia, and is 2 ft. 5 in. broad, we found
a very thin round leaf of gold. The floor of the Treasury
is the levelled rock covered with a coating of sand and
chalk, traces of which are visible in many places; it slopes
towards the centre, which is 1 ft. lower than the threshold.

There was found in the
Treasury a large fragment of
a frieze of blue marble, carved
with a circle and two rows of
a wedge-like ornamentation
in the form of fish-spines;
it is 9 in. high, 10 in. broad,
and 2 in. thick (No. 215).

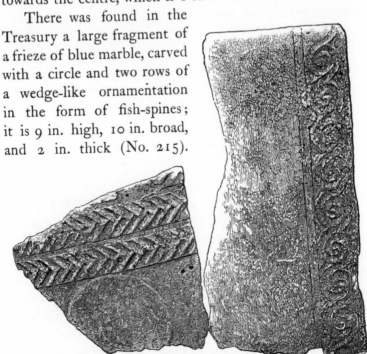

Nos. 215, 216.   Fragments of Friezes of blue and white marble, found in the Treasury near the
Lions' Gate   Size 1 : 4 about.

There was further found the fragment of a beautiful frieze of white marble, which is 1 ft. 4 in. long, 8 in. broad, and 3½ in. thick. The engraving here given (No. 216) represents the broad side of the frieze with an ornamentation of spirals between two small borders. We have already given the small face, on which we see, between two fillets on each side, an ornamentation of the same kind of spirals, which are, however, deeper cut and better preserved.* There were further found five unornamented blades of copper or bronze, 5½ to 6½ in. long, and a Hera-idol of the usual form, with two horns.

Treasure may be hidden in the large border of stones and *débris* which I have been forced to leave behind, but I scarcely believe it. Considering that very ancient fragments of pottery with geometrical patterns were found exclusively in the "dromos," and, on the other hand, a variety of potsherds of different ages in the Treasury itself, I am convinced that only the "dromos" and the entrance were covered up in remote antiquity, that the Treasury remained empty, and that the fragments of vases now found in it were contained in the thick layer of rubbish which covered the upper vault when, fifty-six years ago, Veli Pasha tried to force an entrance by this way.

In the Acropolis I brought to light, at a few yards from the second gate, a very curious Cyclopean water-conduit leading into one of the long narrow corridors. I therefore suppose that at least one, and perhaps two, of these are nothing else than cisterns. There is another Cyclopean water-conduit and another cistern immediately south of them; and the latter seems to be connected with the twelve recesses, in which I also recognize nothing but six small cisterns. These water-conduits, like that which runs into the two cisterns below the Cyclopean house, have doubtless brought the water from the copious spring

---

* See No. 153, p. 98.

"Perseia," whose name seems to be derived from Perseus, the founder of Mycenæ.

In clearing out the masses of *débris*, 13 ft. to 20 ft. deep, which obstructed the passage of the gate, I found three bronze rings. Two of these (Nos. 217 and 219), which were found close to the surface, may be of the Hellenic time, but it is impossible to say this with certainty. The former (No. 217), as shown by the hollow, has had a stone, which is now missing. The third ring is a seal-ring, and the intaglio is too archaic not to be derived from a period preceding the conquest of the city (468 B.C.). On it we see a young woman in a sitting posture, with extended arms; her head, which is turned

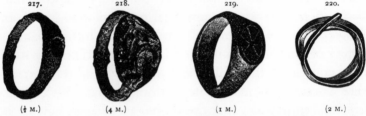

217.   218.   219.   220.

(⅔ M.)   (4 M.)   (1 M.)   (2 M.)

Nos. 217–220. Bronze Rings (two with intaglio engravings), and a twisted Gold Wire. Actual size.

aside, has luxuriant hair; to the right, a little further down, is a male figure, with a broad chest and extended arms.

There were also found many Hera-idols in the form of a cow or a horned female, and among the former a fragment showing on a light yellow dead ground a number of dark red signs, which may be letters, like those shown on the coloured plate B, fig. h; also large quantities of melted lead; further a very primitive golden earring (see No. 220), consisting of a quadrangular golden wire turned twice round. Mr. Chas. T. Newton concludes from the sharp angles of this and all the other quadrangular gold wires which I shall hereafter describe, that they have been a strip or riband cut out of a plate. But it is altogether inexplicable to me how the primitive goldsmith can have performed this operation, particularly as his knives must

necessarily have been of bronze. The same form of
earrings occurs also in the second of the four prehistoric
cities at Troy,* with the sole difference that the wire there
is round.

There were also found here, in a hollow of the rock, a
great many fragments of hand-made vases, coloured either
of a plain black or red, both inside and outside, or, on the
outside only, of a light green, with black spiral ornamentation. At only 6 ft. behind the Cyclopean wall, on the
east side of the passage, I have brought to light the remnants of an evidently much more ancient wall of huge
blocks.

In the large Cyclopean house, which tradition seems to
have indicated as the palace of the Atridæ, immediately
to the south of the circular Agora, were found Hera-
idols of new forms: for example, a perfectly flat cow
with only one big hind-leg and two fore-legs;† a female
idol, with a very compressed bird's face, and with a
Phrygian cap, instead of the usual "polos;" and a headless idol, with two protruding breasts, but with two long
cow-horns. There was likewise found a terra-cotta cow-
horn, 3½ in. long, which shows that there must have
been much larger idols than those hitherto found. I
further collected there a number of small terra-cotta
tripods in the form of arm-chairs and cradles, in one or
two instances even cradles containing children: all are gay-
coloured and may have served as offerings. Among the
other objects found there I may mention two perforated
parallelopipeds of variegated colours, 4 in. long, the use
of which I cannot explain;—a comb, which, according
to Professor Landerer, consists of a very hard white clay
paste;—several pointed sticks (stilettos) for female needle-
work,‡ which the same scholar recognises to consist of

* See 'Atlas des Antiquités Troyennes, Pl. 98, No. 2073.
† See No. 161, p. 106.   ‡ Nos. 131–136, p. 79.

opal;—six small perforated round flat transparent beads
of white stone, belonging to a necklace; and a large
button of alabaster, which seems to have been
on the handle of a sword. There was also found
the bronze sword (No. 221). A pair of tongs of
iron was found near the Lions' Gate close to the
surface, and may be of the Macedonian period.

To my very greatest annoyance and dis-
pleasure, but by the most urgent demand of the
Greek Archæological Society in Athens, I have
been forced to leave in the Acropolis, on either
side of the Lions' Gate, a large block of *débris*
untouched *in situ*, because this Institution has
not yet sent, as it intended to do, an engineer
to consolidate the sculpture of the two lions with
cramp-irons, and to repair the Cyclopean walls to
the right and left of it. But they still intend
to do this work sooner or later, and they believe
that the two masses of *débris* will facilitate the
raising of the blocks and their insertion in the
walls. I hope that this work will be done
promptly, so that the two blocks of *débris* may
not have long to wait for their removal, for they
give the excavations a miserable aspect, and
particularly the mass of *débris* to the right on
entering, because this latter consists of loose
ashes, and, should it be left for a few years more

No. 221.
Bronze Sword.
Size 1 : 6.

as it is, it will be washed away by the rains and spread
over my excavations. I call particular attention to this,
because every visitor will naturally attribute the leaving
behind of these two blocks of *débris* to my negligence.

Yesterday and to-day my excavations have had the
honour of being visited by his Majesty Dom Pedro II.,
Emperor of Brazil. Coming from Corinth, his Majesty rode
direct up to the Acropolis, and remained for two hours in my
excavations, which he attentively examined and re-examined.

The immense double parallel circle of slanting slabs, within which are the three lines of tombstones, and particularly the four sculptured ones, seemed to be of paramount interest to him, and he requested me to send him photographs of them to Cairo. The great Lions' Gate, through which the king of men (ἄναξ ἀνδρῶν) passed when he left for the most glorious expedition of the heroic age, the wonderful threshold of this gate, the large Cyclopean house, the three Cyclopean water-conduits, the immense Cyclopean circuit walls and all the other monuments of prehistoric times, seemed also to be of very great interest to his Majesty, who went thence to the Treasury which we have excavated, and afterwards to the Treasury of Atreus, where dinner was served. This meal, in the midst of the mysterious, dome-like underground building nearly forty centuries old, seemed to please his Majesty exceedingly. He afterwards examined with the deepest interest, in the village of Charvati, the large collection of prehistoric Mycenean antiquities produced by my excavations, and he particularly admired the enormous mass of differently-shaped Hera-idols, the intaglios, the marvellous Mycenean pottery, and the archaic sculptures. His Majesty also examined attentively, in and around Charvati, the ancient quarry whence all the stones for the Cyclopean walls, the Treasuries, and other buildings, have been extracted, and went thence to Argos and Nauplia. His Majesty called here again to-day, to see once more the Mycenean museum and the excavations, and returned hence by Corinth and Calamaki to Athens.

After the departure of his Majesty, Mrs. Schliemann and I ascended, not without the very greatest difficulty, the very steep northern peak of Mount Euboea, now called Hagios Elias, which is situated immediately north of the Acropolis, and is crowned by an open chapel of the prophet Elias (see Plate II.). The summit forms a very small triangle, the eastern side of which is 35 ft., the two other sides,

which converge due west, each 100 ft. long.   It is full of
rugged and pointed rocks, between which it is difficult even
to move, and it can therefore never have been inhabited by
men, the more so as there is no water.   The only even and
level place on the summit is in the south-east corner; it is
but 10 ft. broad and 23 ft. long, and is occupied by a very
small open shrine, dedicated to the prophet Elias.   But in
spite of its small dimensions, the summit is surrounded by
Cyclopean walls, which are on an average 4 ft. 2 in. thick,
and from 3 ft. to 6½ ft. high; but the masses of stones which
lie beside them can leave no doubt that they were once
much higher.

The entrance, which is on the eastern side, leads to
a short passage.   In the large stone which forms the
threshold of the door is still visible the hole in which the
lower hinge turned.   At a distance varying from 16 ft. to
53 ft. lower are, on all the three sides by which the summit
is accessible, Cyclopean walls, varying from 133 ft. to 266 ft.
in length, and 5 ft. thick, which are still now on an
average 10 ft. high, and appear to have once been much
higher.   From between the stones of all these walls I have
been able to collect a large number of fragments of hand-
made light green vases with black ornaments, which I consider as old as the walls of Tiryns and Mycenæ, because
in the former place I found them *in situ* on and near the
virgin soil, in the latter *in situ* only on the natural rock in
the recesses of the gate-passage, and in the tombs.   I conclude from this that the Cyclopean fortifications on Mount
Eubœa (Hagios Elias) must be contemporaneous with the
walls of both cities, and may perhaps claim even a still
higher antiquity.

The question now naturally arises, for what purpose all
these fortifications have been built.   The mountain being so
high and steep, and the summit so exceedingly small and
encumbered by protruding rocks, it can never have served
as a fortress.   Therefore the only explanation I venture to

give of the origin of these Cyclopean walls is that there
must have existed on the summit a small temple of great
sanctity and immense importance, and by a curious coincidence we may even find in the present cultus on the
summit the name of the deity who was worshipped there
in antiquity.   In times of great drought the inhabitants of
the surrounding villages are in the habit of going thither
on a pilgrimage in large crowds, the priests leading, to
invoke the prophet Elias to give rain.   And it appears
likely that the very site of the present open shrine of the
prophet Elias was in ancient times occupied by a sanctuary
of the Sun-god, who had a celebrated cultus there, and who
has given way to the prophet Elias, with hardly any change
in the orthography or pronunciation of the name, the Sun-
god having been originally called Ἥλιος, pronounced Eëlios.
This is a wonderful coincidence, because, as the name of
the prophet is purely Hebrew (אֵלִיָּה or אֵלִיָּהוּ, meaning
" Jehovah is God ") it can have no affinity with the
Homeric name of the Sun-god, Ἥλιος, which is probably
derived from the primitive name of the moon's husband
(perhaps Σείριος) and is at all events purely Greek.

Only half an hour's walk in a westerly direction from
the Lions' Gate, and close to the village of Phichtia, are
the ruins of a small Cyclopean building, in the same style
of architecture as the walls to the right and left of that
gate, and probably belonging to the same epoch.   This
also appears to have been a temple.   We likewise see,
at an hour's distance in a north-westerly direction from the
Lions' Gate, in a secluded valley, on the border of a deep
glen, the well-preserved ruins of a quadrangular Cyclopean
tower, of which every side measures 40 ft. in length; the
walls are 10 ft. to 11 ft. high.   At the south-westerly
corner is the door, which leads into a small corridor and
two chambers.   On the outer walls are seen two gutters.
The architecture is also very similar to that of the walls
close to the Lions' Gate.   Most likely this tower served

the Myceneans for dominating the narrow pass by which
the road leads from Argos to Corinth.

The present state of the excavations is represented by
the engraved Plate VII. First we see, to the left of the
spectator, the inner side of the great Cyclopean circuit wall,
which is terminated in the background by the Lions' Gate,
of which, however, there is only visible the reverse side
of the great triangular slab, on the exterior side of
which is the famous bas-relief of the two lions. The
Cyclopean wall seen in the background to the right was
part of an interior enclosure.

Further down, just behind the last man, is a Cyclopean
wall, of which, however, only the small portion close to the
Lions' Gate, with the chamber of the ancient door-keeper,
can claim the age of the circuit walls; the remainder is
much later, but anterior to the capture of the city by the
Argives (468 B.C.). Before this wall is the labyrinth of
corridors, two of which, at all events, are cisterns. To the
left, close to the circuit wall, is the small Cyclopean house
so often referred to, containing only one chamber.

In the foreground, below the feet of the workmen who
stand upon it, can be seen the great double parallel circular
row of slanting slabs, inclined inwards, which were covered
with cross slabs, and served as benches of the Agora and as
its enclosure. In the same line with this double circular
row of slabs are the twelve small tomb-like water-reservoirs
which we see in the direction of the Lions' Gate, and between
which is the entrance to the Agora, 7 feet broad. Thence
the circle of slabs slopes to the left of the spectator, from
the rock to the Cyclopean wall (12 feet high), which
has been built with no other intention than to sustain it,
and to raise it almost to the level of its continuation on
the rock; but as will be seen, nearly all the slabs in this
part have tumbled down, and only a few have remained *in
situ*. The wall which supports the parallel double row
can be well seen, slanting down at an angle of 15° from

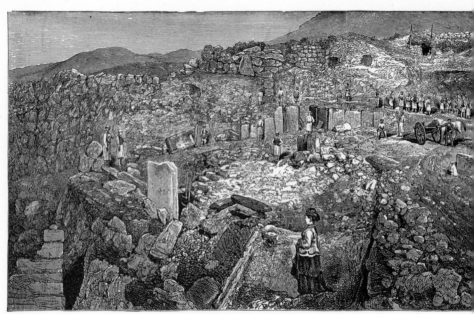

PANORAMIC VIEW OF DR. SCHLIEMANN'S EXCAVATIONS IN THE ACROPOLIS OF MYCENÆ, WITH THE CIRCULAR

PLATE VII.

FOREGROUND, WITHIN WHICH CAN BE SEEN FOUR OF THE TOMBSTONES; AS DESCRIBED IN CHAPTER VI.

the perpendicular, to the left of the spectator. The four sculptured _stêlæ_ are hidden behind the large standing slab just in front; of the unsculptured tombstones, two can be seen to the right, on the side of the entrance to the Agora, and two more on the side of the two horses. Therefore the ancient Agora of Mycenæ comprises the whole space which we see enclosed by the great circle of slabs.

In the middle is seen, in the background to the left, part of the steep slope of Mount Eubœa, on whose summit is the open chapel of the prophet Elias. In front, more to the right, is the great interior Cyclopean wall, crowned by the ruins of a tower, which gives to the Acropolis a particularly grand aspect. It forms part of a second enclosure. To the right there is a good view of the Mount of the Acropolis, on the slope of which remnants of inner enclosures can be seen in many places. All the walls which are seen lower down are those of Cyclopean houses, except the large supporting wall of the double parallel row of slabs, of which a small part may be seen in the lower left-hand corner. Below, to the right, are the ruins of the vast Cyclopean house, to which I have repeatedly referred, and which, though we cannot of course form a definite opinion, may well represent to an imagination enlightened by the vivid descriptions of Homer and the tragedians, the Royal Palace of Agamemnon and his forefathers.

NOTE.—I call the reader's particular attention to the Sectional Plan, B B, which shows the depths of the Five Royal Sepulchres, which are described fully in the two following chapters, beneath the surface of the soil, as it was before my excavations.

No. 222.   Fragment of a wooden Box (νάρθηξ).   (5 M.)   Size 6 : 7.

CHAPTER VII.

THE FIRST, SECOND, AND THIRD TOMBS IN THE ACROPOLIS.

Discovery of the *Tomb* indicated by the three sculptured *stêlæ* — Curious gold-covered buttons, objects of ivory, baked clay, gold, glass, bronze, &c. — Pottery, both wheel and hand-made — *Second Tomb* below the unsculptured *stêlæ* — Discovery of three human bodies, which had been partially burnt where they lay — Fifteen diadems of thin gold plate found on the bodies — Also crosses of golden laurel-leaves — Other curious objects, proving a knowledge of the art of glass-working and colouring — Knives of obsidian — A silver vase with a bronze mouth plated with gold, and other objects — Terracotta vases — The horned Hera-idols found in the tomb, a proof of that symbolic worship in the earliest times at Mycenæ — Its duration to the last age of the city — Primitive painted wheel-made vases of terra-cotta — Further discovery of sepulchral slabs — Various objects found with them — The *Third Tomb* — Several skeletons of men, not burnt, and objects found with them — A curious double-bladed bronze dagger — Narrow escape from a falling rock — Internal walls of the tomb — Three skeletons of women in it, evidently burnt where they lay — Laden with jewels of gold — Layers of round plates of gold with ornamentation of *repoussé* work under and over the bodies — Description of their many types — The other jewels described — Other chased and embossed beads — Golden griffins — Legend of the griffins of Indian origin — Heart-shaped and lion-draped gold ornaments — Curious brooches formed of palm-trees, stags, and lions — Women with pigeons — Golden cuttle-fish, butterflies, swans, *hippocampi*, eagles, sphinxes, trees, and birds — The splendid gold crown on the head of one of the bodies — Signs upon it — The second gold crown — Five more diadems of gold — Crosses of double leaves of gold — Golden stars — A gold brooch, and other ornaments — Necklaces and bracelets — Two pairs of golden scales — Golden plates — A child's mask of gold — Other ornaments — Balls, &c. of rock crystal, silver, and bronze, probably the handles of sceptres — Lentoid gems of agate, sardonyx, &c., with intaglios — A lentoid gem of amethyst engraved with a cow suckling her calf, as on the old coins of Corcyra — Gold wheels — A gold comb with bone teeth, &c. — Amber beads — Other ornaments — Pieces of gold-leaf strewn below and about the bodies — A gold goblet — A curious gold box, and gold vases with lids fastened on by wires — A silver vase and golden sceptre-handle — Boxes of copper plate filled with wood, perhaps pillows for the dead bodies — Other objects found in the third sepulchre — Hand-made and very ancient wheel-made pottery.

Mycenæ, December 6, 1876.

THE four sculptured tombstones having been removed to the village of Charvati, in order to be sent to Athens, I excavated on the site of the three with the bas-reliefs representing the warriors and the hunting scene,* and found a quadrangular tomb, 21 ft. 5 in. long and 10 ft. 4 in. broad, cut out in the slope of the rock. The earth in this tomb consisted of the detritus of house remains mixed with natural soil, which latter had been brought here from

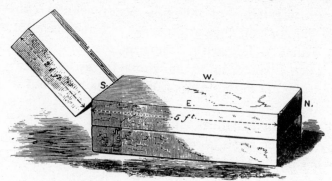

No. 223. Plan of Tombstones in the first Tomb.

another place. At a depth of 3 ft. 3 in. below the place where the tombstones had stood I found a curious sort of

---

* See Chapters III. and IV., pp. 80–85, 88–90.

monument, consisting of two long and narrow slabs
5 ft. long, 7 in. thick, and 12 in. broad, lying the one
upon the other, and at their south end a smaller slab
2½ ft. long in an oblique position, as if to serve for a
pillow to the corpse laid down on the upper slab. (See
No. 223.)   The latter stone had a border, and belongs
evidently to another monument, of which the other two
slabs may likewise have formed part.   Most probably there
was once on this tomb a large monument, ornamented
with the three sculptured tombstones which now marked
its site.

In digging lower down I found from time to time a very
small quantity of black ashes, and in this very frequently
some curious objects ; such as a bone button covered
with a golden plate, with a beautiful intaglio ornamentation,
or an imitation of a ram's horn cut out of ivory, having one
flat side with two holes, by which the object must have
been attached to something else, or other ornaments of
bone or small plates of gold.   I collected in this way twelve
gold buttons covered with gold plates ornamented with
intaglio work, one of which is as large as a five-franc piece.
The ornamentation of the gold plates consists either of
spiral lines or that curious cross 卐 with the marks of four
nails, which so frequently occurs on the whorls in Ilium,
and which I believe to be the symbol of the holy fire.*   All
the buttons are in the form of our shirt-buttons, but larger,
and similar to those shown in a later part of this work.
I collected there, besides the buttons, two objects of ivory
in the form of ram's-horns, like No. 225 ; and four pieces
of ivory in the form of a crescent, one side being convex,
the other flat, in which are four holes for fixing it to
something else (see No. 224) ; six long and narrow pieces
of ivory, like 227, having for ornamentation five vertical
incisions, and in the reverse side two deep vertical cuts for

* See 'Troy and its Remains,' pp. 103-106.

attaching them on another object. Very probably all these
objects have served as ornaments on horse-trappings.
There was found besides the ivory needle, No. 229;
further, six buttons of hard white stone with a circular
hole in the centre, into which is stuck a small blue stone
(No. 226). The round hole in the centre as well as the
presence of the small stones in it are inexplicable to me.
There were also found a small button of the same sort, the
gold-plated head of a bronze nail, eight long thin pieces
and four large disks of thin gold plate, two small tube-like

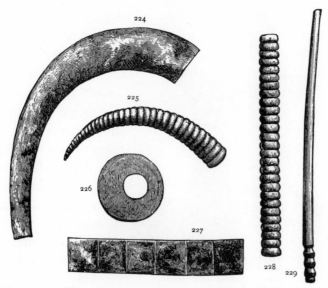

Nos. 224–229. Objects of ivory, bone, or metallic composition. Sepulchre I. Size 7 : 9.

pieces of a glassy substance, containing in the interior a
small tube of real blue glass, of which I shall have occasion
to speak hereafter. I also found there the green object
(No. 228), which has small horizontal flutings all round :
according to Professor Landerer it consists of an artificial
substance containing oxide of copper, which has been
pressed into its present form. The earth was intermixed
with numerous fragments of very ancient wheel-made
pottery, with a variegated painted ornamentation, and others

of hand-made monochromatic lustrous black or red or light green pottery with black spiral ornamentation; but to my astonishment I found also from time to time some fragments of painted vases made on the potter's wheel, of those sorts which are found even in the upper prehistoric strata, and which most decidedly belong to a much later period.

Among the most interesting of the hand-made pottery are the large lustrous black goblets, with a hollow foot and horizontal flutings in the middle (No. 230), which are frequent in the first prehistoric city of Troy; also the light green or yellow ones, with a most fantastical black ornamentation ; and the larger vases of a light red dead colour, with dark red circles, or with two protruding female breasts surrounded by circles of small black strokes.

No. 230.   Foot of a black hand-made Goblet.
Sepulchre I.   Size 6 : 7.

Having dug down to a depth of 10½ ft., I was stopped by heavy rain, which turned the soft earth in the tomb to mud, and I therefore took out the two unsculptured tombstones of the second line, which stood due east of the three sculptured ones, and at a distance of 20 ft. from them. One of these tombstones was 5 ft., the other 5 ft. 4 in., long. In excavating around them I found another tomb cut in the rock, 11 ft. 8 in. broad, and in length 21 ft. 3 in. on one side, and 19 ft. 8 in. on the other. It was entirely filled with unmixed natural earth,

which had been brought from another place. At from
2 to 2½ ft. below the two tombstones I found the fragments
of two other tombstones, also unsculptured, which appeared
to be older.

At a depth of 15 ft. below the level of the rock, or of
25 ft. below the former surface of the ground, as I found
it when I began the excavations, I reached a layer of
pebbles, below which I found, at a distance of three feet
from each other, the remains of three human bodies, all
with the head turned to the east and the feet to the west.
They were only separated from the surface of the levelled
rock by another layer of small stones on which they were
lying, and they had evidently been burned simultaneously in
the very same place where they lay. The masses of ashes of
the clothes which had covered them, and of the wood which
had partially or entirely consumed their flesh, as well as the
colour of the lower layer of stones and the marks of the
fire and the smoke on the stone wall, which at the bottom
of the sepulchre lined all the four sides—can leave no
doubt whatever on this point ; nay more, there were the
most unmistakable marks of three distinct funeral piles.
The wall, which at the bottom of the tomb lined its four
sides, consisted of pretty large stones joined without any
binding material ; it was 5 ft. high and 1 ft. 8 in. thick.
The small stones with which the bottom of the sepulchre
was strewn can, in my opinion, have had no other object
than to procure ventilation to the funeral pyres. These
could not have been large, and had evidently been intended
to consume merely the clothes and partly or entirely the
flesh of the deceased ; but *no more*, because the bones and
even the skulls had been preserved ; but these latter had
suffered so much from the moisture, that none of them
could be taken out entire.

On every one of the three bodies I found five diadems
of thin gold-plate, like those to be presently described,*

---

* See Nos. 282–284, pp. 186, 188.

each 19½ in. long, and 4 in. broad in the middle, from
which it gradually diminishes to a point at both ends. The
pointed ends have been broken off, but, as several of the
other diadems have such points, there can be no doubt that
all had been fashioned in the same way. All the diadems
were piped with copper wires in order to give them more
solidity, and a great many fragments of those copper wires
were found. All the fifteen diadems show the very same ornamentation of *repoussé* work, consisting of a border of two
lines on either side, between which we see a row of treble
concentric circles, which increase or diminish in size according to the breadth of the diadem, the largest circle being
in the middle. Between these treble circles is on either
side a row of smaller double concentric circles, which likewise increase or diminish in size in proportion to the breadth
of the diadems. As well in the larger treble as in the
smaller double circles, the central or innermost circle is
always hammered so as to protrude, which gives to the
diadems a splendid aspect. The diadems had at one end a
pin (ἔμβολον), and at the other a tube (αὐλίσκος) by means
of which they were fixed round the head; of course in
such a way that the largest treble circle was just in the
middle of the forehead.

I further found with two of the bodies ten very thin
golden crosses (five with each body), formed of laurel leaves
(No. 231); with the third body there were only four of
them. Each of these crosses is 7½ in. long; the breadth
of the leaves is 1⅔ in. The leaves of all the fourteen crosses
have also been piped with thin copper wire, to give them
more firmness. The ornamentation of the leaves is likewise
of *repoussé* work. It presents all round the leaves a small
border formed by a line, on which lies an uninterrupted
row of double concentric ovals in a slanting position, which
are probably also meant to represent leaves. In this way
the whole leaf is encircled by a broad band of such double
ovals or leaves, and the space left is filled up with three
double concentric circles.

I also found with the bodies many curious objects ; for example, small cylinders with a small tube throughout their length, as well as square pieces composed of four such cylinders, of which however only those at the two extremities have perforations. All these things have a greyish-white colour, and consist of a very soft matter, which falls into dust when pressed but softly with the hand. In the interior of each cylinder there is a hard, blue transparent tube, which Professor Landerer has analysed and found to

No. 231.   A cross of golden laurel leaves.   Sepulchre II.   Size 4 : 5, about.

consist of cobalt glass. Within the blue tube again is a small thin white tube, which shines like silver, and Professor Landerer has found it to consist of a glassy substance containing lead (*bleihaltig*). According to Professor Landerer, this discovery proves that the ancient Myceneans knew the colouring of glass as well as the art of encompassing a tube of glass with a second and a third one.* He assures me that the analysis of Egyptian glass has given the same

---

* Called in German the ' Umfangsmethode.'

result, and he supposes that the cobalt-glasses were derived from Egypt. He further mentions that all present blue-coloured glasses are of such cobalt-glass. All these cylinders and square pieces of four cylinders must have served as ornaments of the corpses.

The fabrication of glass was evidently in its very beginning at the time the tombs were constructed; but it seems to have made no progress here, for, except a few white glass pearls and some small ornaments of a glass paste, nothing was found of this article even in the upper strata, and it appears certain that at the capture of Mycenæ by the Argives (468 B.C.) even the small glass bottles, often found elsewhere, were still entirely unknown.

I further found a number of small knives of obsidian, many fragments of a large silver vase with a mouth of copper, which is thickly plated with gold and splendidly ornamented with intaglio work; unfortunately it has suffered too much from the funeral fire to be photographed. It appears that the Mycenean goldsmiths found it much easier to plate on copper than on silver; hence they made the mouth of this silver vase of copper. I also found a long and a short rusted bronze knife; a silver cup (φιάλη) with one handle, much damaged by the fire; four long perforated necklace-beads (two of agate and two of a glassy composition); a bronze vase handle; two horned Hera-idols of terra-cotta, of the usual form; and finally, many fragments of beautiful hand-made and of very ancient wheel-made pottery, among which was part of a vase with two tubular holes on either side for suspension with a string, like the vases in the lowest prehistoric city of Ilium.* There are also fragments of terra-cotta tripods, of which I found such an enormous quantity at Troy,† but which are

* See 'Troy and its Remains,' p. 310, No. 222, where "rings" should rather have been "tubes" or "tubular rings."
† *Ibid.* p. 285, No. 199.

less frequent at Mycenæ, nearly all the vases having a flat bottom. In this tomb was also found the fragment of a vase, ornamented with a sign which is nothing else than a ⊓⊔, the four arms of which have merely been converted into a spiral form.

The most important objects found in this tomb are no doubt the two two-horned Hera-idols previously mentioned, because they prove to us that the goddess was already worshipped, in this shape, in that remote antiquity to which the sepulchre belongs. As the very same type of the idol is found in all the strata of prehistoric ruins, and even in the *débris* of the houses which just preceded the later Hellenic city, it appears certain that it was still in use at the time of the capture of Mycenæ by the Argives (468 B.C.), and consequently it remained here unchanged for more than a thousand years. It is true that in all the prehistoric strata of *débris* above the tombs there are also found female idols of a different shape, which we cannot but assign to Hera; but, as their number is only very small as compared to the mass of horned idols, we may take it for granted that the horned idol was the most ancient, and that therefore the Myceneans clung with tenacity to that form.

The most remarkable wheel-made terra-cottas found in this tomb represent the lower parts of birds, in black colour on a light yellow dead ground. I also found two fragments of a hand-made vase belonging to the upper part of the bulge, with two female breasts; a large fragment of a most ancient wheel-made vase, presenting on a light yellow dead ground a beautiful and fantastic ornamentation of plants, circles or wave-like lines, painted in a very dark red colour (see Nos. 232, 233). These two fragments give a good illustration of Mr. Chas. T. Newton's remarks on the 9th June in the Royal Institution of London: "The floral ornaments of the Mycenean vases have a certain vague freedom and straggling lawless luxuriance, which

seems to imply the facility of hand which long practice
gives. The animal forms are ungainly and constrained in
action, and the anatomy is for the most part entirely
ignored or most feebly rendered. The floral and animal
patterns seem to be the result of impressions from nature
sufficiently vivid to awaken the mimetic faculty in an
uncultivated mind, but which the untrained hand was
unable to render in art."

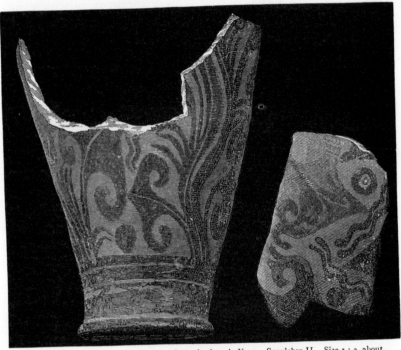

Nos. 232, 233.   Fragments of a very ancient wheel-made Vase.   Sepulchre II.   Size 1 : 3, about.

I also found here five fragments of very ancient
wheel-made vases, having an ornamentation, in similar
colours, of network, waving lines, plants, lines of points,
&c.; and finally some fragments of very ancient wheel-
made vases. Six of these fragments, which evidently
belong to the same vase, have, on a light red dead ground,
an ornamentation of crosses with four points. One has
in its pointed bottom a perforation, and may have served

as a sort of funnel. Another has the most curious ornamentation of all; it shews above what appears to be intended
for the head of a serpent; to the right is a circle surrounded by points, and in its centre a crescent and six
points; to the left of this is another circle, filled with and
surrounded by points.

Encouraged by the success obtained in the second tomb,
I took out the two large unsculptured tombstones of the
third line, which stood almost due south of the former.
One of them is 6 ft. 4 in. long, and 4 ft. broad; the other
is 4 ft. 10 in. long and 4 ft. 4 in. broad. They were extremely well fastened by square blocks, so that they could
not be got out without great efforts. These tombstones
stood precisely 13 ft. 4 in. below the surface, as I found it
when I began the excavations. Two feet below them, and
thus 15 ft. 4 in. below the former surface, I found two
large slabs in the form of sepulchral monuments, lying
horizontally. At a depth of 5 ft. lower I brought to light
three more slabs, the one lying, the other two standing, as
follows :—

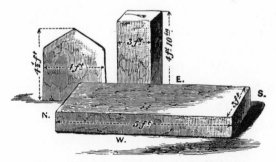

No. 234.   Plan of Tombstones above the Third Tomb.

The soil consisted of black earth, intermixed with
fragments of hand-made and very ancient wheel-made
pottery, and masses of small knives of obsidian. Besides a
small number of Hera-idols, I found there a solid piece of
ivory, one inch high and broad, in the form of a beehive,
having in the lower flat side a tubular hole for suspension

with a thread; while on the convex or globular side is an engraved cross, embellished with five gold pins with flat heads, each of which has a small hole in the centre of its head (see No. 235); also a piece of wood, 4 in. long and 2 in. broad, with beautifully carved spiral lines (No. 222),* which seems to belong to a box (νάρθηξ); also two well-polished pieces of wood with sharp points, but otherwise almost in the form of long thin cones.

No. 235.
Piece of ornamented ivory. (5 M.) Size 3 : 4.

In digging deeper I found that, at a distance of 33 ft. from the east side of the circular double parallel row of large slabs which encloses the Agora, the rock suddenly slopes, for a space of 30 ft. in length and width, at an angle of 30 degrees, the perpendicular height of the slope being 16½ ft. Further to the west the rock forms a platform 30 ft. long and broad, with two sepulchres, of which I shall first describe the smaller one, because the aforesaid two tombstones stood at a height of 16½ ft. above its mouth. This sepulchre, which in the Plan B I call the Third Tomb, is 16 ft. 8 in. long, and 10 ft. 2 in. broad, and it is cut into the rock, on the west side 2 ft. 4 in., on the south side 3 ft. 4 in., on the east side 7 ft., and on the north 5 ft. deep.† These different depths find their explanations in the slope and in the unevenness of the rock, because the bottom of the tomb is of course perfectly horizontal. At about 9 ft. above the mouth of this tomb I discovered close to it, on the slope of the rock, at a depth of 21 ft. below the former surface, a number of skeletons of men, which had evidently not been on the funeral pyre, but were so much destroyed by the moisture that none of the skulls could be taken out entire. The only objects I found with them were knives of obsidian and five very pretty hand-

* See Vignette to this chapter.   † See Plan B B.

made vases, two of which are of plain light yellow, the three others of a light green colour, with a rude black ornamentation (see Nos. 236, 237).

Immediately to the north of the tomb in question, and thus in the centre of the Agora, I brought to light the before-mentioned rock which protrudes from the plateau, and has, in my opinion, served as the platform or pulpit (βῆμα) for the orators. It had been split and was overhanging the great hollow in which are the two tombs just referred to. Below this rock, at a depth of 22 ft. below the surface, many Hera-idols, whorls, and other

Nos. 236, 237. Hand-made Vases of Terra-cotta. Depth 20 ft. Half-size.

objects were found; also a very curious sort of bronze dagger (No. 238), consisting of two separate two-edged blades, which had been soldered together in the middle, so that the four edges are separated from each other by a quarter of an inch; both blades are 10 in. long, the whole dagger being 13 inches long. The handle has evidently been inlaid with wood or bone, fastened by three small nails of bronze, which are preserved. As I considered one of the overhanging rocks particularly dangerous, I did all I could to keep my workmen back from it; however, as, in order to stimulate the workmen to be very attentive, I am in the habit of giving them a drink-penny for all objects, even the most trifling, which have any interest for science, and as so many small objects were found just below the dangerous rock, two of my workmen always returned to the spot. But seeing that the rock had a crack which widened, I literally dragged the two men from their perilous position, when all at once the rock fell with a thundering crash, and we were all three knocked down by its splinters, but none of us was injured.

No. 238.
A large bronze dagger, with two blades soldered together in the middle.
(6½M.) Size 7 : 20.

The four walls of the tomb which now occupies us were lined with pieces of schist of irregular size, which were joined with clay, and formed a slanting wall 5 ft. high and 2 ft. 3 in. broad.

I found in this sepulchre the mortal remains of three persons who, to judge by the smallness of the bones and particularly of the teeth, and by the masses of female ornaments found here, must have been women. As the teeth of one of these bodies, though all preserved, were evidently much used and were very irregular, they appear to belong to a very old woman. All had the head turned to the east and the feet to the west. As in the former tomb, the bodies lay at a distance of 3 ft. from each other ; they were covered with a layer of pebbles and reposed on another layer of similar stones, on which the funeral piles had been raised ; this last stratum lay on the bottom of the tomb, which, as is shown on Plan B B, was 29 ft. 8 in. deep below the former surface of the mount.

Precisely as in the former tomb, all the three bodies had been burnt simultaneously, but separately and at equal distances from each other, nay, in the very place where they now lay. This was proved by the evident marks of the fire on the pebbles below and around every one of the bodies, as well as by the marks of the fire and the smoke on the walls to the right and left, and by the masses of wood ashes which lay on and around the bodies. The bodies were literally laden with jewels, all of which bore evident signs of the fire and smoke to which they had been exposed on the funeral piles.

The ornaments of which the greatest number was found were the large, thick, round plates of gold, with a very pretty decoration of *repoussé* work, of which I collected 701. I found them as well below as above and around the bodies, and there can consequently be no doubt that part of them were strewn all over the bottom of the sepulchre before the funeral pyres were dressed, and that the rest were laid on the bodies before the fire was kindled. In the following engravings * I give all the different types of these wonderful plates. It is difficult to say how the Mycenean goldsmiths executed the *repoussé* work. Professor Landerer thinks they laid the gold-plate on a block of lead, and hammered and pressed the ornamentation into it. No. 239 contains broad round waving bands much resembling those on the fourth sculptured tombstone.† The curious ornamentation in the centre, which so often recurs here, seems to me to be derived from the 卐, the more so as the points which are thought to be the marks of the nails, are seldom missing; the artist has only added two more arms and curved all of them. No. 240 represents an octopus or cuttle-fish (sepia), whose eight arms have been converted into spirals, the head with the two eyes being distinctly visible. No. 241 represents a flower; No. 242 a splendid spiral ornamentation; No. 243, a beautiful butterfly; this

---

* All these are engraved in their actual size.
† See No. 142, p. 91.

No. 239.   Plate of Gold.   Sepulchre III.

type is exceedingly frequent.   Whether, as in the later
Greek art, the butterfly is here the symbol of immortality, as

No. 240.   Plate of Gold : a Cuttle-fish.   Sepulchre III.

No. 241.   Plate of Gold : a Flower.   Sepulchre III.

Mr. Chas. T. Newton reminds me, I do not dare to decide.
No. 244 presents a curious ornamentation of spirals in the

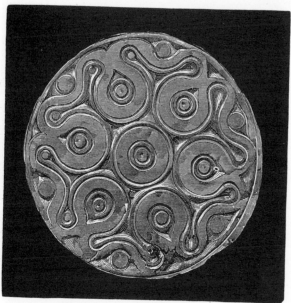

No. 242.   A Plate of Gold.   Sepulchre III.

No. 243. Plate of Gold : a Butterfly. Sepulchre III.

form of six serpents, round a central circle. In No. 245 we at once recognise again the ornamentation of the

No. 244. Plate of Gold. Sepulchre III.

No. 245. A Plate of Gold. Sepulchre III.

sepulchral *stêlê* (No. 142), as in No. 239, which this one very much resembles. No. 246 has a most curious pattern,

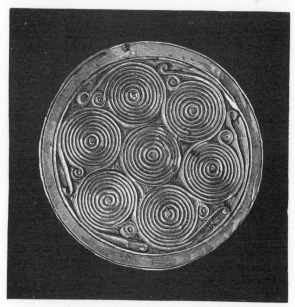

No. 246. A Plate of Gold. Sepulchre III.

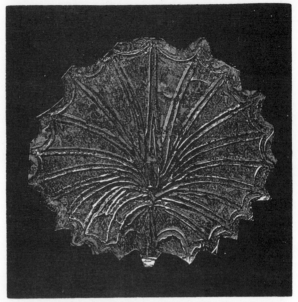

No. 247. A leaf in Gold Plate. Sepulchre III. Actual size.

which shows within a broad circular border six spirals,
all very cleverly finished off, each of them surrounding

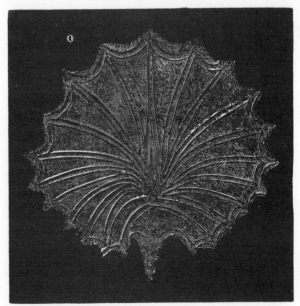

No. 248. A leaf-pattern in Gold Plate. Sepulchre III.

No. 249. A leaf-pattern in Gold Plate. Sepulchre III.

seven concentric circles, and all united around an ornament
likewise of seven concentric circles, which the artist seems

No. 250. A leaf-pattern in Gold Plate. Sepulchre III.

No. 251. A Star in Gold Plate. Sepulchre III.

to have vainly tried to unite at the upper part. Each of
the spirals separately very much resembles the hair-springs

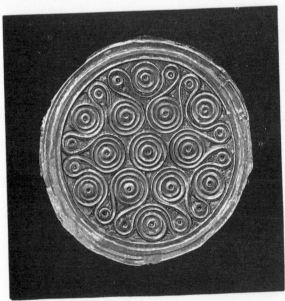

No. 252. A Plate of Gold. Sepulchre III.

of our watches, at least at the first glance, but on closer
examination we find that all the interior lines form separate
circles.   Nos. 247–250 represent beautiful leaves, all of
a kindred pattern.   No. 251 represents a beautiful star-
flower; No. 252 shows within a border of three circles a
splendid ornamentation of spirals and concentric circles,
such as we have not seen yet on the Mycenean antiquities.

I suppose that all these golden leaves are miniature
copies of shields, for though there were shields with a
central boss,* yet the majority of them were smooth
(ἐΐση)†: further most shields were round (εὔκυκλος),‡
and many of them, if not all, were works of art and beautifully ornamented.§   We further find around the Homeric
shields a border (ἄντυξ), which may have been sometimes
single, but which certainly was usually treble,‖ and such a
border we also find represented on several of these golden
plates.

In proceeding to describe the masses of other jewels
which had covered the bodies on the pyres and which still
lay partly on them and partly around them, I begin with
three perforated massive ornaments of gold, belonging to
necklaces, of which the first (No. 253) appears to represent,
in intaglio, Hercules killing the Nemean lion.   The hero is
represented here with long hair (καρηκομόων) and with a
long beard; his dress appears to reach only from the
waist to the middle of the loins, and the rest of the body
seems to be naked.   Having stepped forward with his left

---

* See *Iliad*, XXII. 111, ἀσπὶς ὀμφαλόεσσα; comp. 'Troy and its
Remains,' p. 324.

† See *Iliad*, III. 357; VII. 250; and in many other passages.

‡ See *Iliad*, XIII. 715; XIV. 428; and in other passages.

§ See for example *Il.* XI. 32 :—

ἂν δ' ἕλετ' ἀμφιβρότην, πολυδαίδαλον ἀσπίδα θοῦριν.
"Then he took the man-covering, artistically made, powerful shield."

See also all the wonders which Hephæstus wrought on the shield
of Achilles, *Il.* XVIII. 468–608.

‖ See, for example, *Il.* XX. 275, and XVIII. 480.

foot, he leans the whole weight of his body on it to deal
a deadly blow at the lion with a sword which he holds
in his uplifted right hand, whilst with his left he seizes the
lion's throat.   The animal stands before him on his hind-
legs, and has pounced with his fore-feet on the left leg of the
hero, whom he is going to bite in the breast when he
receives the deadly blow.   The body of the lion appears
to me to be faithful to nature, but not the head, which
resembles more a bear's head ; the mane is engraved with
true art.   I call particular attention to the large round
knob at the end of the handle of the sword, because many
such, all of alabaster or wood with golden nails, and frequently plated with gold, were found in the tombs suc-
cessively discovered.

Nos. 253, 254, 255.   Perforated Ornaments of Gold, with engravings in intaglio.   Sepulchre III.
Actual size.

The intaglio on the following smaller ornament (No. 254)
represents two warriors fighting a deadly duel.   The one to
the left of the spectator is a tall, powerful beardless young
man with an uncovered head, whose loins only are covered,
the rest of the body being naked.   He leans with all the
weight of his body on his advanced left leg, and with his
uplifted right hand he has just plunged his double-edged
sword into the throat of his antagonist, who falls mortally
wounded.   This latter is represented with a long beard.
His head is covered with a helmet, over which we see a
half-circle, which appears to be fastened into the fore-part of
the helmet and to represent the long curved horn which
we see protruding from the fore-part of the helmets of the
five warriors (No. 213).*   The horn seems here to be

---

* See p. 133.

nothing else than a λόφος, into which the crest was sunk, for this appears also to be visible.   But should this conjecture not be correct, then we can only explain the half-circle above the warrior's helmet by supposing that the middle part of the crest was fastened on the top of the φάλος of the helmet, so that there were properly two crests waving. On the wounded man's body we see a round shield with a circle of small points, probably meant to represent the glitter of the brass.   The shield being divided into an upper and a lower compartment, it may be that the artist intended to represent two shields, of which the lower one belonged to the wounded man, who had just let it fall, and that the upper shield belonged to the victor, whose left hand still holds it.   The anatomy of the two warriors is represented clearly, though rudely, and we wonder how this was at all possible without the aid of magnifying glasses.   I ask whether we do not see here in the young, powerful, handsome man, Achilles, the most beautiful man in the Greek army; and in his antagonist, " Hector of the dancing helmet-crest; " * for, just as we see represented on this bead, Hector was slain by Achilles by a stab in the throat.   It is true that the fatal stab was given, according to Homer,† with a lance, but the artist may have substituted a sword for want of space.

The third ornament (No. 255) represents, in good intaglio, a lion kneeling with his fore-feet on an uneven rocky slope, and turning his head round to the right; though, like the two other ornaments, this intaglio is very archaic and rude, it is, like them, tolerably executed, and the anatomy of the animal is carefully observed.   Mr. Achilles Postolaccas calls my attention to the fact that this lion in its style perfectly resembles the fore-part of the lion which we see on the gold staters of Sardis in Lydia, which Borrel attributes to Crœsus (560 B.C.).

---

* κορυθαίολος Ἕκτωρ.   Comp. ' Troy and its Remains,' p. 281.
† *Il.* XXII. 326.

Of the other golden ornaments here shown, No. 256 represents a butterfly of gold, which has, no doubt, served as an ornament on the dress; but, as it has no perforation, it is not clear to me how it may have been fastened; probably it has been glued or pasted on the drapery. Further, ten golden grasshoppers* with chains, of which Nos. 259 and 260 represent two; they appear to have been used as ornaments of the breast or hair. I collected also eleven very curious large globular ornaments,

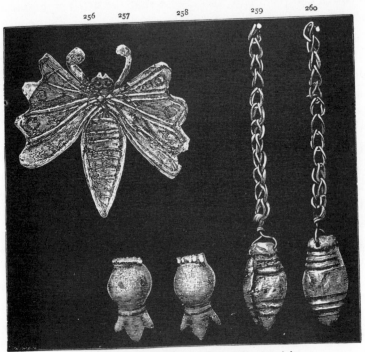

Nos. 256–260.   Golden Ornaments.   Sepulchre III.   Actual size.

of which Nos. 257 and 258 give the engravings of two; all have a tubular hole at the top, and are evidently from neck-laces. These ornaments, as well as the crickets, are of *repoussé*

---

* More properly the tree cricket (τέττιξ, Lat. *cicada*, It. *cigaia*, Fr. *cigale*), of which the Athenians wore golden images in their hair, to denote their autochthonic origin. Hence it was probably the common badge of the cognate Achæan and old Ionian races.

work, and consist of two halves, which were soldered together.

I further collected there three griffins of gold, of which I represent one (No. 261); the upper part of their bodies is that of an eagle, the lower that of a lion; the wing is orna- mented with spirals. Each of these objects has three perforations, which can leave no doubt that they have been sewn on the clothes as orna- ments. The griffins are mythic animals belonging to India, whence they came over to the West. We

No. 261.   Golden Ornament.
A Griffin.   Sepulchre III.
Actual size.

find the griffin on the most ancient fictile vases of a rude Egyptianising style, in company with sphinxes and winged lions. This fantastical animal has become the central point of a curious legendary cycle, for we find it already mentioned in Hesiod and Herodotus as watcher of the gold in the far north of Europe.* Pliny describes the *gryphi* as *ferarum volucre genus*, which *mira cupidi- tate* dig up the gold *ex cuniculis* and watch it, like- wise in the north of Europe, that is, in the land of the Scythians.† Damis Olear‡ maintains that the griffins have been derived from India, and gives the following description of them: "The gold which the griffins dig up consists of stones incrusted with golden drops like fiery points, which they beat off by the power of their hard beak. These animals are found in India, where they are sacred to the

---

Herodotus, III. 13, 14.
Milton alludes to this legend (*Par. Lost,* Bk. II.):—

> "As when a gryphon through the wilderness
> With winged course o'er hill or moory dale
> Pursues the Arimaspian, who by stealth
> Had from his wakeful custody purloined
> The guarded gold."

† *H. N.* VII. 2 ; XXXIII. 4, 21.
‡ *Apud* Philostrat. *Vit. Apoll. Tyan.* III. 48, p. 134.

sun, whence the Indian painters represent Helios riding on
teams of four griffins. The griffin has the size and strength
of the lion, but is superior to the latter by its wings, and
vanquishes even elephants and large serpents. But he
cannot overpower the tiger, who excels by his rapid
motion." Böttiger* explains these monsters as simple
productions of the Indian carpet-manufacture, because
from a remote antiquity the Indians delight in com-
pounding their sacred animals. It appears certain that the
griffin came in the retinue of Dionysus from India to
Greece, and that it therefore became here the symbol of
wisdom and enlightenment.

I further found with the three bodies of the third tomb
three ornaments in the shape of hearts, of which I give the
engraving of one (No.
262). As they have no
perforations, they must
have been glued on to
the drapery. There
were also found four
golden ornaments (see
No. 263) representing

Nos. 262, 263. Golden Ornaments. Heart and Lion.
Sepulchre III. Actual size.

crouching lions, with four or five perforations in the
margin for sewing them on the clothes or drapery.
Though rather roughly made, the body of the animal is
true to nature, and particularly the head. The passion of
the Mycenean artist for spirals is shown in the form of the
lion's tail. As Mr. A. S. Murray, of the British Museum,
justly observed to me, the spiral is no proof whatever of
oriental influence, because it is a form which every curling
wire would naturally suggest, and its general existence and
independent use is attested by the spiral ornamentations of
the ancient Mexicans, Peruvians, and Egyptians.

I further found on the three bodies of the third

---

* ' Vasengemälde.'

sepulchre twelve ornaments of gold, each representing
two stags lying down, with long three-branched horns,
leaning with the necks against each other and turning
the head in opposite directions, but so that the horns of
both touch each other and seem intended to form a
sort of a crown. The two stags repose on the top of a
date-palm tree with three fronds, of which the two to the
right and left extend below the bodies of the animals,
whilst the third stands upright. Two of these ornaments,
with double stags, were soldered together, and in the hollow
thus formed at the lower end was stuck a thick silver pin,
with circular horizontal flutings, which represented the
stem of the palm-tree, and which was fastened by a pin.
The hole through which this pin was stuck is seen at the

Nos. 264, 265.   Golden Ornaments.   Sepulchre III.   Actual size.

bottom of No. 264, and part of the silver pin in No. 265,
where we also recognise the horizontal flutings, which seem
to have been intended to imitate the rough bark of the
palm-tree. Thus we see before us a beautiful brooch,
presenting on either side two stags lying on a palm-tree.
But, the brooch being rather heavy, the silver pin was
perforated, as we see at the lower end of No. 265, to be
fastened with a thread or otherwise. Two of these ornaments had besides two perforations. Reckoning two such

ornaments as one brooch, there were found in this sepulchre in all six brooches with a pair of stags on either side.

There were also found two golden
ornaments (see No. 266), representing a similar date-tree with
three larger fronds, on which
two lion-cubs sit opposite each
other and are holding their
muzzles together; the tails of
the four cubs form spirals, just
as the ornaments with the double
stags. These two ornaments with
the cubs were also stuck together,

No. 266.   Golden Ornament.
Sepulchre III.   Actual size.

either by soldering or by pins, through the two perforations which we see in each of them; and in the hollow
below was fixed a silver brooch, and thus this ornament,
like the former, served as a breast-pin (πόρπη).

I further found with the three bodies of the third tomb
two golden ornaments, representing two women, each

Nos. 267, 268.   Golden Ornaments.   Women with Doves.   Sepulchre III.   Actual size.

having a pigeon on her head. One of them (No. 268)
has also a pigeon attached to each arm. Both women
are of the same type and have a long pointed nose, which
protrudes in a straight line from the forehead, and large

eyes. The heads of both are crowned with a diadem.
Each has a hollow in the left cheek, which is alone visible;
both touch their breasts with the hands, and this must be
a symbol of fertility or abundance. I call attention to the
resemblance in the attitude of these women to that of the
numerous terra-cotta idols of Aphrodite from Cyprus, as
well as to the so-called statue of Niobe on the rock of
Sipylos, which also touch their breasts with both hands.
The four pigeons are represented with spread wings, as if they
were flying. The first woman (No. 267) has four perforations and her bird has two, by which this ornament was
sewn on the clothes or drapery. On the other hand, the
woman with the three pigeons has evidently been fixed to
something else with two small gold
pins, the broad heads of which we
see, the one between the knees of the
woman, the other on her belly.

I further found in the same tomb
golden ornaments like No. 269, but
I find it difficult to explain whether
the artist intended to represent a
horse, a hippocampus, or a dog.

No. 269.   Golden Ornament.
Sepulchre III.   Actual size.

Of golden ornaments in the form of cuttle-fish, or sepias,
I found not less than twenty-seven of the shape of

Nos. 270, 271. Two Golden Cuttle Fish. Sepulchre III.   Actual size.

those represented under Nos. 270 and 271. All of them
are double, that is to say, two sepias are always soldered
together, so that the ornament represents a sepia on either

side.   The Mycenean goldsmith, always eager to convert everything into spirals, has done so here with all the feet of the sepias, every one of which forms a beautiful spiral. Some of the sepias, like No. 270, have in addition four perforations for fixing them with thread.   How these ornaments may have been used is altogether a riddle to me.

No. 272.   A Flying Griffin of Gold.   Sepulchre III.   Actual size.

No. 272 represents a flying griffin of gold.   Like No. 261, it has the body of a lion, the head and wings of an eagle, and is ornamented with spirals.   As it has no perforations, it must have been fastened with glue on the drapery.

Of the highest interest are two little golden figures, one of which is given under No. 273, each having four per-

No. 273.   Golden Ornament. Sepulchre III. Actual size.

forations in exactly the same places; they appear, therefore, to have been attached to each other, so that the same figure appeared on either side.   They exactly resemble each other.   Regarding the type of the features nothing can be said with certainty, for it may as well be Hellenic as Asiatic. Nor is there any indication whether the figures represent men or women, though their rich female dress leads us to suppose the latter to be the case.   Both have the hands joined on the breast like Aphrodité, but below them we see an object in the form of a disk, which seems to be suspended from the neck.   On each side of the breast, as well as on the lower part of the gowns, we see a number of straps, which probably represent ribbons or gold lace; also two rows of twelve small circles in each, which are no doubt intended to represent gold buttons with intaglio work, like those of which such large quantities were found, as we shall see, in two of the tombs.

I further gathered in the same tomb eight golden ornaments in the form of butterflies, of which I represent one under No. 275. Some of them have two, others have

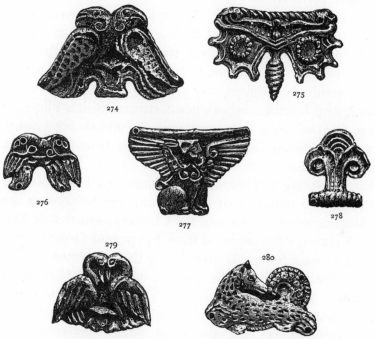

Nos. 274–280.　Golden Ornaments.　Sepulchre III.　Actual size.

four, perforations; and, as all are exactly of the same size and shape, I presume that these also have been fastened together in pairs with pins, so that there was a butterfly on each side. This supposition seems to be warranted by the reverse side, which is hollow. I think the same must have been the case with the other objects here engraved, of which duplicates were found, but not with No. 274, which represents two eagles. Very curious are the ornaments represented by No. 279, of which four were found;

two of them have two perforations each, the other two have none. All of them represent two swans standing opposite each other with the heads joined. There is something between the feet of the two swans which has the shape of a table, but I cannot say what it may be. There were found seven golden ornaments like No. 280, representing hippocampi; all have the head turned backward, and the tail is curved; all have perforations.

The golden ornament (No. 274) has also perforations for attachment to another object; it represents, as before mentioned, two eagles, which stand opposite each other with the heads turned round. There were found in the same tomb six sphinxes, like No. 277. They are winged lions, with beardless human heads, covered with a Phrygian cap, from which a long crest seems to stretch out; but it cannot be distinguished here whether the artist intended to represent a female or a male sphinx. I may here observe that, according to Hesiod, Apollodorus, and Euripides, the Sphinx is a daughter of Typhon and the Echidna or the Chimæra, or of Orthos and the Chimæra, and that it has, at all events, been imported from Egypt into Greece. But the Egyptian Sphinx is male, being the symbol of a king, while the sphinx in the Theban legend of Œdipus is female. The golden ornament (No. 278), of which four were found, seems to represent a tree; all of these have two perforations. Of the small golden jewels of this tomb, I may mention No. 276, representing two birds, the species of which cannot be distinguished. They stand against each other, their heads leaning over in opposite directions, the two being joined by spirals.

On the head of one of the three bodies was found the splendid crown of gold (στέμμα, No. 281), which is one of the most interesting and most precious objects that I collected at Mycenæ. It is 2 ft. 1 in. long, and profusely covered with shield-like ornaments. The work being *repoussé*, all the ornaments protrude and appear in low relief, giving to

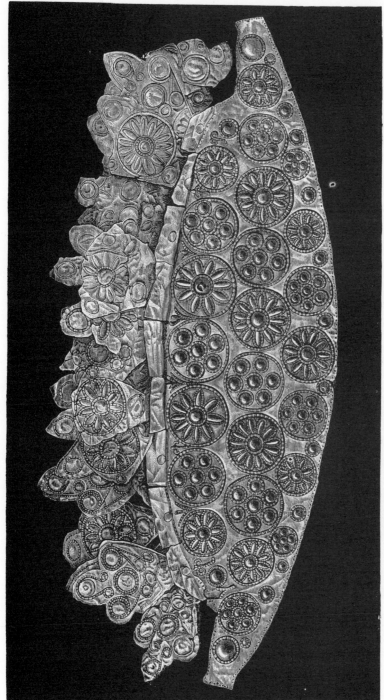

No. 281. The splendid Crown of Gold found on the head of one of the three persons interred in the Third Sepulchre. Size, rather more than 1 · 4

No. 282. Golden Diadem found on the head of
another body in the Third Sepulchre.
Size 1 : 5, about.

the crown an indescribably magnificent aspect, which is still further augmented by the thirty-six large leaves, ornamented in a like manner, which are attached to it. It deserves particular attention that the crown was bound round the head so that its broadest part was just in the middle of the forehead, and of course the leaves were standing upright around the upper part of the head, for had it been otherwise it would have shaded the eyes and the greater part of the face. Near each extremity can be seen two small holes, through which the crown was fastened by means of a thin golden wire. I call particular attention to the curious signs between the shield-like ornaments of the lowest row; five of these signs resemble beautiful flowers, the heads of which give an additional proof that the crown was worn with the leaves upwards, and so I found it on the head of one of the bodies. The four other signs resemble the κηρύκειον, or caduceus, the herald's staff of Hermes.

Around the head of another of the three bodies was found the magnificent golden diadem (No. 282), to which was still attached part of the skull; it is finely worked. It has a border, formed by parallel lines and a line of protruding points, which is broadest in the middle and gradually diminishes towards both ends. This border is ornamented with spiral signs, accompanied by small lines of deep or protruding points. The space between the two borders is filled up with a row of shield-like ornaments, the size of which varies according to the breadth of the diadem, containing a number of concentric circles around a central boss. The space between the circles is filled up, in the five larger ones, with a circular row of small leaves or of protruding points. We also see between the shield-like ornaments all along the border two rows of small bosses encircled by protruding points. At each end of the diadem is a perforation, which must have served to fasten it round the head by means of a thin wire of gold or copper. This diadem being of thick gold plate, it was not piped.

I further found with the three bodies five diadems of gold, of which I represent two under Nos. 283 and 284. Two of them (see No. 283) have an ornamentation similar to the foregoing, but less rich. Both are piped with copper wire, and have no border; and both consist of two halves, which seem not to have been soldered together, but merely joined by the piping wire. As neither of them has perforations in the extremities, there must have been attached to them thin wires of copper or gold, now broken off, by which they were fastened around the head. Both these diadems have suffered much from the funeral fire, which has blackened them so that the photographs could not take well. The diadem (No. 284), though not piped, has no border; it is also ornamented with shield-like circles representing beautiful flowers. We see an ornamentation in the form of a star at each end, and small shield-like bosses on both sides between the circles. At the right extremity is still preserved part of the gold wire

with which the diadem was fastened round the head. On
all these six diadems we recognise the fine black ashes of the

Nos. 283, 284.   Diadems of Gold.   Sepulchre III.   Size 2 : 9, about.

funeral pyre sticking to the gold. I may here mention that
we find round shields with an ornamentation of crescents

and stars represented on Macedonian coins ; but these can, of course, have no relation whatever to the Mycenean diadems, which may be twelve centuries older.   Although similar diadems with an ornamentation of rosettes have never been found before, yet there can be no doubt that they were in extensive use in a remote antiquity, for the British Museum contains six idols of Aphrodité from Cyprus, two of terra-cotta and four of marble—all of which have the head ornamented with similar diadems.   I see further

No. 285.   A Cross in Gold Plate.   Sepulchre III.   Actual size.

in the Assyrian collection of the same museum four figurettes of ivory representing Hercules, whose head is likewise ornamented with such diadems.

There are two other diadems with a still simpler shield-like ornamentation, and having in the middle two vertical rows of spirals.   Both these diadems consist of halves, which were seemingly joined only by the copper wire with which they are piped.   The thin wires at the extremities are here also broken off.

I found further with the three bodies of the third tomb
six crosses formed of double golden leaves, of which I
give engravings of four. The richest ornamentation is on

Nos. 286, 287, 288. Ornaments of Gold. Sepulchre III. Size 3 : 4, about

those represented by No. 285 ; the leaves resemble laurel
leaves, ornamented with beautiful flowers in *repoussé* work ;
and there is an ornamentation of spirals at both ends of

each leaf. In the centre of each of these crosses is fixed
a cross of small unornamented gold-plate. The cross
(No. 286) shows a similar pattern, and I suppose it has
been fixed in the centre of the star-like golden ornament
(No. 288); but, not being quite certain in this respect, I

Nos 289, 290. Golden Crosses. Sepulchre III. Size 4 : 5.

give separate engravings of both. No. 287 represents a
small golden ornament with three flowers. Very curious
is the small golden cross (No. 289), whose leaves show a
magnificent ornamentation of circles and spirals, and in

the centre of which is attached another cross of small
richly-ornamented gold leaves. The large gold cross (No.
290) shows a shield-like ornamentation, and also at the
end of each leaf three small circles containing two inner
ones.

In several places we see in the leaves of this latter cross
very small holes, which seem to prove that another

No. 291. A Cross of Gold. Sepulchre III. Size 4 : 7, about.

ornament was attached in the centre, probably a cross, as
we see in No. 285, or a star, such as No. 288. I also
found in this tomb the two large and beautiful golden
stars, of which I represent one (No. 291). They consist
of two differently-shaped crosses, with a magnificent ornamentation in *repoussé* work; both crosses are fastened
together with a golden pin with a large round flat head,

which is still preserved on the one shown in the engraving. In the centre of the other star there is only the impression which the pinhead, now lost, has made on the gold plate. It is perfectly impossible for me to say how these crosses served as ornaments of the dead, for I found none of them *in situ*.

On one of the bodies I found a gold brooch (πόρπη), with a very thick silver pin, 8 in. long (see No. 292),

No. 292.   A Golden Brooch (πόρπη).   Sepulchre III.   Actual size.

which, having seemingly been in contact with saline matter, has been turned into chloride of silver, and has, therefore, broken in two. Thus only the upper part of the pin is seen in the engraving. In the brooch we see a woman with extended arms, turning her face to the left of the spectator; her features are decidedly Greek. She has a long nose, which protrudes straight from the forehead, and large eyes; her hair only reaches down to the neck, which is ornamented with a necklace; her large breasts are well shown On her head we see a spiral ornamentation, from the middle of which rises a beautiful palm-tree, and from this there hang down to the right and left long tresses with tassels in the shape of flowers.

No. 293.   Golden Ornament from the Third Sepulchre.   Size five-sixths.

I also found in this tomb the two very curious golden ornaments (see No. 293), which are too large and heavy to have been worn as pendants of earrings and have probably been used as breast ornaments. Each consists of two pieces of *repoussé* work, which are soldered together, and thus these objects present the same ornamentation on either side.

No. 294.
A Golden Cross.
Sepulchre III.
Actual size.

There was also found a small golden cross, represented under No. 294, having an ornamentation of spirals on either side. It deserves particular mention that the last-named ornaments (Nos. 291–294), as well as some of the smaller ornaments of this sepulchre,* though of gold, have a reddish bronze-like colour, so that, if I had found them alone, I should decidedly not have claimed for them a very remote antiquity; but the conditions under which they lay in the sepulchre make it impossible to suppose that the objects found there were of different ages.

There were also found on each of the three bodies two golden ornaments (six in all) almost in the form of ear-rings, of which two are represented in the engravings Nos. 295 and 296. But as the two ends of each of these objects are in the form of spirals turned round four or five times, they can, of course, not have been used for the ears; besides they would be by far too heavy for that use, because they are of solid gold. The only use which, in my opinion, can have been made of them is to hold together the locks, and I think they perfectly explain the passage in Homer:†—

> " Those locks, that with the Graces' hair might vie,
> Those tresses bright, with gold and silver bound,
> Were dabbled all with blood."
>
> LORD DERBY.

I also collected on the three bodies eleven very curious golden ornaments, of which I give three engravings (Nos. 297, 298, and 299). All of them have in the middle a narrow tube, by which they appear to have been strung on a cord, for they can, in my opinion, only have been used for necklaces. They were made in the following way: to both ends of a small tube, which, as we see in the engra-vings, is ornamented with circular incisions, was soldered a thin golden wire, which was on either side turned eleven times round, and these spirals were soldered together, the outside turn of each also being soldered to the tube. Of

---

* Like Nos. 262, 264, 265, 266, 272, 273, 274, 275, 276, 277, 279, 280, 303, 305, 306, and 316.

† *Iliad*, XVII. 51 and 52 :—

αἵματί οἱ δεύοντο κόμαι χαρίτεσσιν ὁμοῖαι,
πλοχμοί θ', οἳ χρυσῷ τε καὶ ἀργύρῳ ἐσφήκωντο.

the same pattern were found six bracelets like No. 300, each of which consists of twelve spirals made of the same fine gold wire; they were fastened round the arm by the

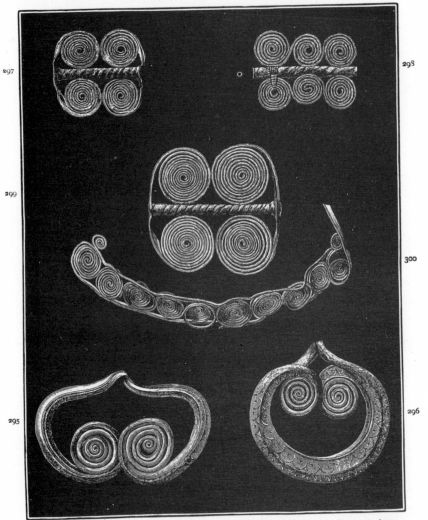

Nos. 295-300. Golden Hair-holders, Bracelets, and Ornaments of Necklaces. Size 5 : 6, about.

small golden staff at the right, and by the spiral at the left extremity, which latter served as a clasp.

There were further found two pairs of golden scales,

which I represent in the engraving (Nos. 301 and 302),
but I have been able to photograph the beam of only

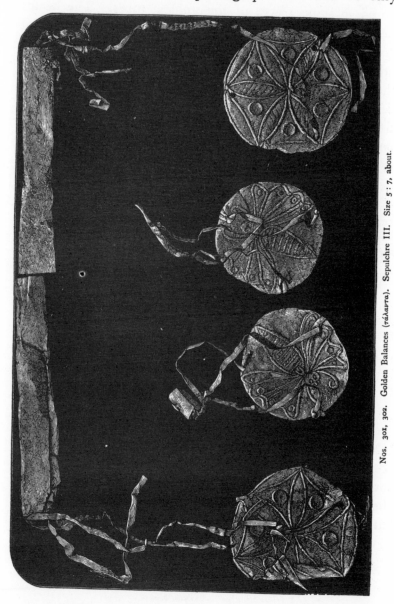

Nos. 301, 302. Golden Balances (τάλαντα). Sepulchre III. Size 5 : 7, about.

one pair, the other beam being too much compressed and
out of shape. Both beams consist of tubes of thin gold-

plate, through which was undoubtedly stuck a wooden stick to give them more solidity ; *débris* of charred wood were even found in some pieces of the golden tubes. The beams were attached to the scales by long and very thin straps of gold. Two of the scales are ornamented with flowers, the others with beautifully-represented butterflies. Of course these scales can never have been used; they were evidently made expressly to accompany the bodies of the three princesses into the grave, and they have, therefore, undoubtedly a symbolic signification. I may here call attention to the scales in the wall-paintings of the Egyptian sepulchres, in which are weighed the good and bad deeds of the deceased. At all events these scales vividly recal to our remembrance the beautiful passage of Homer,* where Jove takes golden scales and weighs the "lots of doom" of Hector and Achilles.

> "But when the fourth time in their rapid course
> The founts were reached, the Eternal father hung
> His golden scales aloft, and placed in each
> The lots of doom, for great Achilles one,
> For Hector one, and held them by the midst :
> Down sank the scale, weighted with Hector's death,
> Down to the shades, and Phœbus left his side."
>
> LORD DERBY.

There were further found with the three bodies the golden ornaments here represented. The golden plate (No. 303) must have been glued on something else, because otherwise its use is inexplicable. It has a beautiful ornamentation of *repoussé* work, such as we have not seen before in Mycenæ. The child's mask (No. 304) consists of very thin gold plate; the places for the eyes are

* *Il.* XXII. 209–213 :—

ἀλλ', ὅτε δὴ τὸ τέταρτον ἐπὶ κρουνοὺς ἀφίκοντο,
καὶ τότε δὴ χρύσεια πατὴρ ἐτίταινε τάλαντα·
ἐν δ' ἐτίθει δύο κῆρε τανηλεγέος θανάτοιο,
τὴν μὲν Ἀχιλλῆος, τὴν δ' Ἕκτορος ἱπποδάμοιο·
ἕλκε δὲ μέσσα λαβών· ῥέπε δ' Ἕκτορος αἴσιμον ἦμαρ,
ᾤχετο δ' εἰς Ἀΐδαο· λίπεν δέ ἑ Φοῖβος Ἀπόλλων.

cut out, and even in the present crumpled condition of
the mask the nose is slightly protruding.   It appears,
therefore, very probable that, together with the bodies of
the three women, a child was burnt and buried in this
tomb, and this would perfectly agree with the tradition cited
by Pausanias.*

I also found thirteen splendidly-ornamented objects of
gold plate, of which one is represented under No. 305 ;

Nos. 303–306. Golden Ornaments. Sepulchre III. Half-size.

their style of ornamentation has never been seen by me
here before.   At the upper extremity we see a perforation,
which makes it probable that these objects have served as
pendants of earrings   The gold plate (No. 306) must also
have been cemented on some other object, for it shows no

---

* II. 16, § 6.   See the passage fully quoted in Chapter III. p. 59.

perforations. It represents in defective *repoussé* work two men, of whom the one, who is winged and has horse's-feet and appears to play the flute, stands with his right foot on the head of the other, whose arms are extended and whose feet are wide apart. Both men have two horns on the head, and those of the lower figure are particularly conspicuous. To the right of the two men, and thus to the left of the spectator, is a very strange ornament, which at first sight appears to consist of written characters, but, on closer examination, we find that it is mere ornamentation.

There was further found here the perforated ball of beautifully-polished rock crystal (No. 307), which has

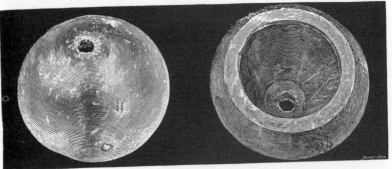

Nos. 307, 308.   Objects of Rock Crystal.   Sepulchre III.   Actual size.

evidently formed part of the handle of a sceptre or some weapon, for we see in the perforation a long piece of metal which appears to be gold, but which is probably only gold-plated bronze or silver.

The object, No. 308, is also of well-polished rock crystal; it has a large mouth, and a perforation on the opposite side; the interior has a lively ornamentation painted in red and white. The use of this object is altogether a riddle to me.

There were also found two objects of bronze, of which the one appears to be a fragment and the other the handle of some weapon.

I also picked up there the two objects, Nos. 309 and 310, which appear to be sceptres. The silver staff of each has been plated with gold, as we see on that part of it which sticks in the beautifully-turned knobs of rock crystal. The crystal ball of No. 309 is ornamented with small vertical furrows and quite perforated, and there are evident signs that another object, probably of gold, has been attached to its lower end; and such a piece of gold was found lying separately and is added in the engraving (*a*), the more so as its upper end had evidently been broken off; it is ornamented on both sides with *repoussé* work representing lions.

I call the reader's attention to the size of these presumed sceptres, which is here only about one-third of the actual size. I beg further to observe that the enormous gold plated silver rods were doubtless stuck

Nos. 309, 310.
Sceptres of silver plated with gold, with
handles of rock-crystal.
Sepulchre III. Size 1 : 3, about.
a. A ball of gold found separately, but
belonging to the handle.

in wooden staves covered with gold plate. For the abundance here of such staves with gold covers we can have no better testimony than the numerous tubes of gold plate found in these tombs, many of them still containing charred remnants of the wood which they once covered; a few even contained remnants of the wood pretty well preserved.

Further I found fifteen perforated beads of brown agate, like No. 311, which evidently belong to a necklace;

also a number of beads like No. 312: further the magnificent lentoid gem of sardonyx (No. 313), on which are represented two men, the one sitting, the other standing. The latter seems to seize the former with his right hand by the hair, while he thrusts with his left a long sword into his breast.

Very characteristic is the immense shield which we see on the standing man's back, and which resembles two shields joined at the border; it is not unlike the shield which we see on the fallen warrior, p. 174, No. 254.

No. 314 is a whorl-like ornament of black agate, with a spiral ornamentation on its lower side; it has no perforation.

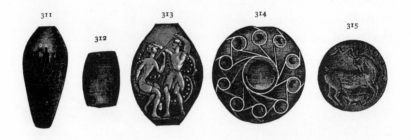

No. 311. Perforated bead of brown agate.—No. 312. Agate bead.—No. 313. Lentoid
gem of sardonyx, cut in intaglio.—No. 314. Ornament of black agate.—
No. 315. Lentoid gem of amethyst. All from Sepulchre III.
Actual Size.

Very curious is the lentoid gem of amethyst, No. 315, which is of a transparent violet-blue colour, with an intaglio, representing an animal turning round its head to look at its calf, which is sucking the milk from its udders. The body and legs of the animal, and even its head and horns, are decidedly those of a stag; but I may remind the reader that the most ancient didrachms of Corcyra represent in a similar style a cow turning her head and looking at her calf, which sucks the milk from her udders.

I also found there six golden ornaments in the form of wheels, of one of which I give the engraving (No. 316).

Like the wheels of bronze which we have passed in review, these six wheels have only four spokes, forming a cross around the closed axle, which is merely indicated; but the spokes are here curved, so as to form four semicircles. All of them are ornamented with

No. 316.   A Golden Wheel.   Sepulchre III.   Actual size.

horizontal incisions; the felloes are very broad, and have a spiral ornament all round.

I also found in this sepulchre a lady's comb of gold, with teeth of bone; but the latter are so much damaged that I cannot give an engraving of them; further, a large silver seal-ring, which, having been in contact with saline matter, has become chloride of silver, so that the engraving on it has disappeared. Also, twelve tubes of gold plate, which had evidently once been filled with wood to give them solidity; in some of the tubes there were still remains of charred wood. The use of these tubes is difficult to explain; they may have belonged either to sceptres or to distaffs. Further, a large quantity of small or larger gold beads of necklaces, and an enormous quantity of amber beads, likewise from necklaces. These beads have grown dark-brown, probably owing to their great antiquity, so that we at first mistook them for resin, but the analysis of Professor Landerer has shown that they consist of the purest amber. It will, of course, for ever remain a secret to us whether this amber is derived from the coast of the Baltic or from

Italy, where it is found in several places, but particularly on the east coast of Sicily; but it is highly probable that it was brought to Greece by the Phœnicians, its name in Greek being *electrum* (ἤλεκτρον), and *elek* signifying resin in Arabic, and probably also in Phœnician. Amber was well known to Homer, who mentions it three times in the Odyssey, as fitted, in lieu of precious stones, in gold ornaments.*

Amongst other objects found with the three bodies of the third tomb, were a square leaf ornament, two golden breast-pins, a golden flower on a silver stalk, many very small golden ornaments, a large number of beads of a transparent red stone from a necklace, a gold-plated brooch of bronze; seven ornaments of gold representing lions, of which, however, only two are with heads; also, a golden ornament representing an ox attacked by two lions. I collected there a large quantity of small pieces of very thin beaten gold, with which the whole tomb, below and above the bodies, was strewn.

With the three bodies of the third sepulchre were also found the gold goblet (No. 317) and the gold box (No. 318). The goblet has only one handle, and its outside is divided, by a band in relief of three stripes, into an upper and a lower compartment, and both are ornamented with *repoussé* work of fish, which are very faithful to

---

* *Odyss.* XV. 460 :—

χρύσεον ὅρμον ἔχων, μετὰ δ' ἠλέκτροισιν ἔερτο.

" Bringing a golden necklace set with amber."

And XVIII. 296 :—

ὅρμον δ' Εὐρυμάχῳ πολυδαίδαλον αὐτίκ' ἔνεικεν

χρύσεον, ἠλέκτροισιν ἐερμένον, ἠέλιον ὥς.

" He brought immediately to Eurymachus an artistic golden necklace, set with amber like the sun."

In both cases the *plural* agrees exactly with the sense of *amber-beads* set in a gold mounting.

The third passage, *Odyss.* IV. 73—

χρυσοῦ τ' ἠλέκτρου τε καὶ ἀργύρου ἠδ' ἐλέφαντος—

occurs in the description of the palace of Menelaus; and here the *yellow* gold and *amber* seem placed in poetic parallelism with the *white* silver and *ivory*.

nature. Very curious is the gold box (No. 318), with
a well-fitting lid, which was fastened on it with two gold
wires, by means of four perforations, one wire being on
either side of the lid, and one on either side of the rim
of the box. A similar contrivance is found in the box

Nos. 317, 318. A Goblet and a Box of Gold. Sepulchre III. Size 3 : 8, about.

which Arêtê, wife of King Alcinoüs, fills with presents for
Ulysses, for she recommends to him :—

"Look now thyself to the lid and tie quickly a knot on it, lest any
one should rob thee on the way, when thou reposest again in sweet
slumber, going in the black ship."*

Homer says in the verses immediately following :—

"But as soon as the much-enduring, divine Ulysses heard this, he
forthwith fitted on the lid, and quickly put upon it a manifold knot,
which venerable Circe had once prudently taught him." †

Odyss. VIII. 443-445 :—

Αὐτὸς νῦν ἴδε πῶμα, θοῶς δ' ἐπὶ δεσμὸν ἴηλον,
μήτις τοι καθ' ὁδὸν δηλήσεται, ὁππότ' ἂν αὖτε
εὕδησθα γλυκὺν ὕπνον, ἰὼν ἐν νηΐ μελαίνῃ.

† *Ib.* 446-448 :—

Αὐτὰρ ἐπεὶ τόγ' ἄκουσε πολύτλᾳς δῖος Ὀδυσσεύς,
αὐτίκ' ἐπήρτυε πῶμα, θοῶς δ' ἐπὶ δεσμὸν ἴηλεν
ποικίλον, ὅν ποτέ μιν δέδαε φρεσὶ πότνια Κίρκη.

In *Od.* II. 354, Telemachus, preparing for his voyage to Sparta, bids
his nurse Euryclea to fill twelve amphoræ with wine and fit them all
with lids, but these would need to be very close-fitting for liquids (cf.
p. 256) :

Δώδεκα δ' ἔμπλησον, καὶ πώμασιν ἄρσον ἅπαντας.

These passages can leave no doubt that chests and boxes with a similar contrivance were in general use in the time of Homer. They were also in general use at Troy, for I collected there hundreds of terra-cotta vases, and also a box, which shows the same principle.* Similar terra-cotta vases are also to be seen in the small collection of prehistoric pottery in the French school at Athens. They were found in a prehistoric city on the island of Thera, below a layer of pumice-stone and volcanic ashes, 60 ft. deep, thrown out by that great central volcano, which, in the opinion of competent geologists, must have sunk into the sea and disappeared about 1700–1800 B.C.

No. 319.
Golden Vase, with lid attached by a golden wire.
Sepulchre III. Size 7 : 10.

Chests and boxes fashioned in the same way, namely, with perforations in the rim and in the lid through which they were fastened by means of a string, must have been in general use in Mycenæ, because all the gold vessels with lids found here show exactly the same contrivance. The box before us has no ornamentation.

The beautiful globular gold vase (No. 319) has a handle on each side and one on the lid, in which latter can be seen the golden wire by which it was attached to the vase through

---

* See my ' Troy and its Remains,' p. 286, No. 200, p. 310, Nos. 222 and 223, and Plate XVII. Nos. 243 and 244.

the perforation in the rim. The only ornaments of this vase are the two rope-like bands in relief, with which its upper part is encircled. I also found with the three bodies of the third sepulchre the three gold vessels here engraved, all of which have holes in the rim and in the lid, for tying them together with a gold wire. No. 320 has a small handle on either side, and a large one on the lid; it is decorated with curved lines in relief. The handsome box (No. 321) has only a small handle on the lid, and no ornamentation. The beautiful vase (No. 322) has a handle on each side, and a very large one on the lid. It has no ornamentation. There can be seen protruding

Nos. 320, 321, 322. Three Golden Vessels. Sepulchre III. Size 2 : 3, about.

from it the long golden wire, by which the lid was bound to the rim of the vessel. All these and the former golden vases and boxes are of *repoussé* work. I likewise found in this tomb a plain silver vase with one handle.

There were found on the eastern side of this sepulchre four boxes of copper-plate (see No. 323) all filled with wood, which is pretty well preserved, only the upper part of it being partly charred by the funeral fire. Each of these boxes is 10 in. long, 5 in. high, and 4½ in. wide. The side plates of the boxes are soldered together, and nowhere are nails visible except in the rim of the upper side, which is open, where we see twenty long copper nails

beaten in from the outside and projecting far on the
inside; and the question naturally arises why they are
there. I cannot explain their presence in any other way
than by supposing that there has been on this side a
thick wooden plate, which was fastened by the twenty nails,
and which has been burned in the funeral fire. I conjecture that these copper cases, filled with wood, served
probably as head-pillows for the dead, and perhaps also for
the living, because they are, at all events, not harder, and

No. 323.   A Box of Copper Plate, filled with wood.   Sepulchre III.   Size 3 : 10, about.

even a little softer, than the pillows of alabaster or marble
found in the Egyptian tombs, of which several are in the
British Museum. I at first supposed that the wood in the
boxes might be sandal-wood, which might have served
to perfume the sepulchre whilst the funeral pile was burning,
but I have given up this idea, considering that there would
have been no use in preserving the odoriferous wood in
the boxes and shutting it up in them with long nails;
besides that, for such a purpose more of it would have
burned. But again, it may be that the sandal-wood has
been imported from India in these small boxes. In the

present deteriorated state of the wood it is utterly impossible to recognise the species of tree that it belongs to.

No. 324. Vessel of Terra-cotta. Sepulchre III. Size 7 : 10.

All these boxes were lying near the heads of the dead, but
none under any of them.

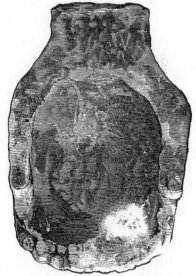

There were also found
with the three bodies of
the third sepulchre the
small hand-made vessel of
terra - cotta (No. 324),
which shows, on a light
yellow dead colour, the
following ornamentation of
a dark red colour: three
circular bands and a spiral
line interlacing eight circles,
each of which contains a
palm-leaf; every two circles
are further intersected by
two large round spots.

No. 325 is of alabaster,
but looks as if it were of

No. 325. An object of Alabaster. Sepulchre III.
Size 7 : 10.

shell; it represents two hands joined together in juxta-
position and forming a hollow; all the fingers are dis-

tinctly visible. The use of this object is difficult to explain, it being too heavy to have served as a spoon or trowel.

In the same tomb I found a second piece of splendidly polished rock-crystal; its form is more than a hemisphere; it has a perforation in the middle of the bottom, and another on each side. Its interior has paintings of a lively red colour. Its use is altogether inexplicable to me; were it not for the paintings I should believe it to be the handle of a sceptre; but as it is, it can never have served as such.

There were found in the same sepulchre an entire but quite plain silver vase, with one handle; a broken silver vessel with a spiral ornamentation, and a broken plain silver goblet; also a silver vase ornamented with a horizontal row of twelve golden stars of *repoussé* work, but unfortunately so much broken that it cannot be photographed. I may further mention a large bronze knife with a wooden handle.

I also found in this third tomb the copper-plated mouthpiece of a large vase, which consists, according to Professor Landerer, of a composition of silver and lead; the mouthpiece has probably only been plated with copper in order to plate this latter again with gold. Further, an alabaster cup, a fragmentary bronze vase, two very large copper vases with two handles, a large copper caldron (λέβης), with two handles, and two others with three handles. All these objects are similar to those found in the fourth tomb, of which the engravings will be given in the next chapter.

There were also found here a large mass of fragments of hand-made or very ancient wheel-made terra-cotta vases; and lastly, a long well-polished stone of nearly oval form, which, in the opinion of Mr. Eustratiades, may have served as a weight to draw to a door.

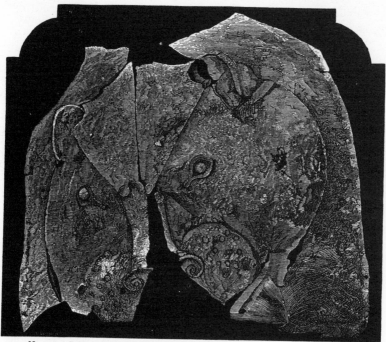

No. 326.   Golden Mask in the form of a Lion's Head.   Sepulchre IV.   Size ₁⁵ₒ, about.

CHAPTER VIII.

The Fourth Tomb in the Acropolis of Mycenæ.

Further search within the Agora, without the guide of tombstones —
Discovery of an altar of Cyclopean masonry, over the centre of the
great *Fourth Tomb*, containing the bodies of five men, burnt where
they lay, laden with jewels, and covered with a layer of white clay —
Objects found — Copper caldrons, one containing 100 gold-plated
buttons with intaglio work—Homeric mention of caldrons—A silver
cow's head with gold horns and a gold sun on its forehead : it represents Hera—Cow-heads with axes—Swords and lances of bronze—
Gold-plated wooden sword-sheaths and hilts with gold pins—Three
masks of gold covering the faces of the bodies—A fourth mask, representing a lion's head—Two seal-rings and a bracelet, with ornaments
—The state of art corresponds with that described in Homer—
Golden breastplates on two of the bodies — Golden crown by the
head of another — Golden ornament of the greaves — Borax used
then, as now, for soldering gold—More than one δέπας ἀμφικύπελλον,
and other vessels of gold and silver — The large gold goblet, with
doves on the two handles, like Nestor's cup in the *Iliad* — Two-

handled terra-cotta vases, hand-made, like those at Troy — Ornaments of alabaster — Gold shoulder-belts (τελαμῶνες) — Other objects
found in the tomb, of rock crystal, amber, alabaster — Golden
diadems, some seemingly for children; also a child's belt and
frontlet, or " belle Hélène," and other ornaments of gold — Double
edged battle-axes—their use by the Greeks as a symbol, especially
at Tenedos — A funeral fork of copper — Vase-lids of bone
— Vessel of silver and lead in shape of an animal — Buttons of
wood, plated with gold, splendidly ornamented — Their patterns and
workmanship —Hundreds of gold flowers, plain buttons, and other
ornaments of gold — Larger gold buttons splendidly ornamented —
Leaves of gold strewn under, over, and around the bodies — Wooden
comb with gold handle — Gold models of temples — Many golden
cuttle-fish — Gold knobs for sword-hilts, highly ornamented—Arrow-
heads of obsidian — Boars' teeth — Large copper vessels — Custom
of placing such vessels in tombs — A copper tripod — Uses of
tripods in Homer — Bronze swords, lances, and knives — Some
swords with parts of their wooden sheaths, alabaster handle-knobs,
golden studs, &c. — Remnants of linen sheaths — Oyster-shells and
unopened oysters — Broken pottery, indicative of a still existing
funeral custom — The bones of the deceased — Alabaster vases —
Hand-made and very ancient wheel-made pottery — Fragments of
a characteristic form of goblet, both of terra-cotta and of gold —
Another type of goblets — Two whetstones — A handle of unique
work, gold encrusted with rock crystal, " θαῦμα ἰδέσθαι.'

Mycenæ, December 6, 1876.

ENCOURAGED by my success, I resolved upon excavating
the whole remaining space within the great parallel circle
of slabs by which the Agora is enclosed, and my attention
was particularly directed to the spot immediately west of
the sepulchre last excavated, although the site was marked
by no tombstone. But, at marked variance with the colour
of the soil elsewhere, I found here only black earth, which,
at a depth of 15 ft., was already intermixed with nothing
else than hand-made and most ancient wheel-made pottery,
showing that the site had not been disturbed since a
remote antiquity; and this increased my hopes of making
an interesting discovery.

At a depth of 20 ft. below the former surface of the
mount I struck an almost circular mass of Cyclopean

masonry, with a large round opening in the form of a well; it was 4 ft. high and measured 7 ft. from north to south, and 5¼ ft. from east to west.* I at once recognised in this curious monument a primitive altar for funeral rites, and was strengthened in this belief by two slabs, in the form of tombstones, 2 ft. 9 in. long, and 1 ft. 6 in. broad, and a short column, which lay in a horizontal position below the altar, and which, in my opinion, must have once been erected on the spot to mark the site of a sepulchre. Fragments of beautiful hand-made or very archaic wheel-made pottery and knives of obsidian continued to be the only objects of human industry I met with.

At last, at a depth of 26½ ft., and at a distance of only 4 ft. 7 in. from the tomb last described, I found a sepulchre, 24 ft. long, and 18½ ft. broad, which had been cut into the rock to the depth of 6 ft. on its west side, 10 ft. on the north side, 8 ft. on the south side, and on the east side 6½ ft. deep, its bottom being 33 ft. below the former surface of the mount.†

It deserves particular notice that the funeral altar marked precisely the centre of this tomb, and thus there can be no doubt that it had been erected in honour of those whose mortal remains reposed therein. All round the four sides of the bottom of this tomb was, on a foundation of large common stones, a slanting wall, 7 ft. 8 in. high, of large pieces of schist, of irregular form, which had been joined with clay. This wall projected 4 ft., and thus considerably diminished the size of the sepulchre. As in all the other tombs, the bottom was covered with a layer of pebbles, on which, at about equal distances from each other, lay the bodies of five men; three of them were lying with the head to the east, and the feet to the west;

---

* See Plan F for a ground plan, and view of this altar, and a section of the ground, the altar itself, and the fourth sepulchre.

† See Plans B, BB, C, and Plate VI.

the other two were lying with the head to the north and the feet to the south. The bodies had evidently been burned on the very spot on which each lay; this was shown, as well by the abundance of ashes on and around each corpse, as by the marks of the fire on the pebbles and on the wall of schist. The cremation of all the bodies on the layer of pebbles on the very bottom of this, as well as of all the other tombs, has been officially authenticated by the three government clerks, whom the Director-General of Antiquities at Athens, Professor Panagiotes Eustratiades, has sent here to assist me in guarding the treasures, as well as by the Professor of Archæology, Phendikles, who remained here two weeks with me, and by the thousands of people who flock hither from all parts of the Argolid to see these wonders; and, therefore, any one who doubts the exactness of my statements as to the cremation is requested to apply to the said Director-General or to the Ministry of Public Instruction at Athens.

The five bodies of this FOURTH TOMB were literally smothered in jewels, all of which—as in the other tombs—show unequivocal marks of the funeral fires.

Here, as well as in the first and third tombs, I have noticed that, for a reason unknown to me, the burned bodies, with their golden ornaments, had been covered, after the cremation, with a layer (3 in. to 4 in. thick) of the same white clay which has been employed to join the pieces of schist of the slanting internal wall. On this layer of clay was put the second layer of pebbles. Down to about one foot above the upper layer of pebbles, the work of excavation is not difficult, for we have merely to direct our labourers to dig here or there. But from that point we have to do the work ourselves; the task is exceedingly difficult and painful to us, particularly in the present rainy weather, for we cannot dig otherwise than on our knees, and by cutting the earth and stones carefully away with our knives, so as not to injure or lose any of the gold ornaments.

Beginning the excavation of the lower strata of this tomb from the south side, I at once struck on five large copper vessels (λέβητες, 'caldrons'), in one of which were exactly one hundred very large and smaller buttons of wood, covered with plates of gold, with a splendid intaglio work of spirals and other ornamentation. Three of the copper vessels measure 14 to 20 in. in diameter each, and have two upright handles; the fourth is of the same form, but has three handles; the fifth is a can, 1 ft. 9 in. high, with two handles, of which the one is nailed to the mouth-piece and the upper part of the body of the vessel, and the other to its lower part. These five copper vessels stood all upright, close to the southern interior wall.

We find copper vessels (λέβητες) continually referred to in the Iliad, together with tripods, as prizes in the games or as presents.* But they are generally referred to in the Odyssey as basins, in which the hands were washed at the sacrifice or before dinner.† They were also used for the foot-bath.‡ It deserves particular attention that three of the five copper vessels, and particularly the large can, show unequivocal marks of long use on the fire. It deserves particular attention that there is *no soldering* in any one of the large copper vessels found in this or any other of the Mycenean tombs; these large vessels consist merely of copper plates, solidly joined together with innumerable small pins. All the handles are likewise attached with broadheaded nails.

Close to the copper vessel with the gold buttons, I found a cow's head of silver, with two long golden horns, which I represent in the engravings Nos. 327 and 328.

---

* See for example *Il.* IX. 123, 265, XXIII. 259 and 267, XXIV. 233; *Odyss.* XIII. 13.
† See *Od.* I. 137, III. 440.   ‡ *Od.* XIX. 386, 469.

No. 327.   The Cow's Head of silver, with horns of gold.   Sepulchre IV.
Size 7 : 20, about.

(NOTE. — The slight difference of *size* between this and No. 328 is merely accidental, the engravings being by different hands.)

No. 328.   Another view of the Cow's Head of silver, with horns of gold.   Sepulchre IV.

It has a splendidly ornamented golden sun, of $2\frac{1}{5}$ in. in diameter, on its forehead; in the middle of the head is a round hole, which may have served for flowers. I here remind the reader that the Egyptian Apis is represented with a sun between its horns.

The Mycenean goldsmith evidently did not understand the art of plating silver with gold, for, whenever he had to do it, he first plated the silver with copper, and then plated the copper with gold. He has done so with this silver cow-head, whose mouth, eyes and ears he had to plate, and, therefore, he first plated them with copper and then plated the copper with gold. On the mouth the gold plating is very well preserved, but from the eyes and ears it has almost entirely disappeared. There can be no doubt that this cow-head was intended to represent the goddess Hera, the patron deity of Mycenæ.

There were also found here thirty-five cowheads of very thin gold plate, like Nos. 329 and 330, which have a double axe between the horns. Six of these heads are quite well preserved; the other twenty-nine are all more or less

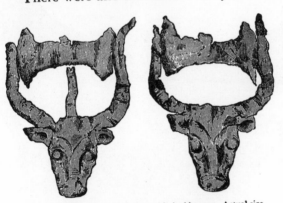

Nos. 329, 330. Two Golden Cowheads with double axes. Actual size.

mutilated. I also collected a great quantity of fragments of similar cowheads.

I shall discuss hereafter the symbol of the double axe, which occurs repeatedly in these tombs. I would here call particular attention to the three cowheads with long horns, two of which are of gold, and one seemingly of silver, which figure among the offerings in the wall paintings of an

Egyptian tomb in Thebes, conserved in the British Museum; the two of gold are brought by Asiatics on golden vases, whilst the silver cowhead is offered by Egyptians. I further call attention to Mr. G. A. Hoskins's ' Travels in Æthiopia,' p. 330, where a copy is given of a wall painting of a tomb in Thebes, representing a grand procession, in which, among other presents, are rings and four cowheads with long horns, seemingly all of gold.

In further excavating from east to west I struck a heap of more than twenty bronze swords and many lances. Most of the former had had wooden sheaths and handles inlaid with wood, of which numerous remnants could be seen. Lying all along and in the heap of swords I found a large quantity of round plates of gold with beautiful intaglio work, and remnants of flat round pieces of wood, which had once, in unbroken series, adorned both sides of the sword-sheaths. The largest plate was at the broad end of the sheath, the smallest at the opposite extremity. The wooden handles of the swords had likewise been ornamented with large round plates, covered with rich intaglio work. The remaining space has been studded with gold pins, and gold nails can be seen in the large alabaster or wooden hilt-knobs of the swords. On and around the swords and the remnants of the sheaths could be seen a great quantity of fine gold-dust, which can leave no doubt that the handles and sheaths had also been gilded.

Some of the lance-shafts seemed to be well preserved, but they crumbled away when exposed to the air. Unfortunately the skulls of the five bodies were in such a state of decomposition that none of them could be saved; the two bodies with the head to the north had the face covered with large masks of gold-plate in rude *repoussé* work, one of which, unfortunately, has been so much injured in the funeral fire and by the heavy weight of the stones and *débris*, and, besides, the ashes stick so firmly to it, that it was impossible to get a good photograph of it. However, by looking at it for some minutes, one gets a tolerable idea of the features. It represents a large oval youthful face with a high forehead, a long Grecian nose, and a small mouth with thin lips ; the eyes are shut, and the hairs of both eyelashes and eyebrows are well marked.

Quite a different physiognomy is represented by the second mask (No. 331), which shews a round face, with

No. 331.   Mask of Gold, found on the face of a body.   Sepulchre IV.   Size 1 : 3, about.

full cheeks and a small forehead, with which the nose does not range in a straight line, as on the other mask ; the mouth is but small, and has thick lips; the eyes are shut, and the eyelashes, as well as the eyebrows, which are joined, are tolerably represented.

A third mask of much thicker gold-plate was found covering the face of one of the three bodies which lay with the head to the east.

This mask, of which I give the engraving (No. 332),
exhibits again a totally different physiognomy: the wrinkles
to the right and left above the mouth, and the expression
of the very large mouth with thin lips, can leave no doubt

No. 332.   Gold Mask.   Sepulcnre IV.   Size 3 : 8, about.

that we have here the portrait of a man of more advanced
age. The forehead is very large and so are the eyes, which
are open and have neither lashes nor brows marked:
the nose has been much pressed by the stones and is

out of shape. In this mask is preserved part of the skull of the man whose face it covered.

The physiognomies represented by these three masks are so widely different from each other, and so altogether different from the ideal types of the statues of gods and heroes, that there cannot be the slightest doubt that every one of them represents the likeness of the deceased whose face it covered. Had it not been so, all the masks would have represented the same ideal type.

A fourth heavy golden mask was found at the head of another of the three bodies which had their heads turned to the east. This object was bent double, and looked so little like a mask that I took it for a helmet, and described it as such in my letter published in the *Times* of the 27th December last; but, having unbent it, I see that it has nothing of the shape of a cap and can only have been intended for a mask to cover the face of the body: it had probably been accidentally removed in the process of cremation. At first sight its engraving (No. 326, p. 211) resembles more a jacket than anything else; but, on closer examination, we find that it represents a lion's head, whose ears and eyes are distinctly seen. Being of the purest gold, it is so soft that several pieces have been broken away, as, for example, one from the vertex of the head, another from the nose, a third from the jaws, and a fourth from the mane, to the left of the spectator; but they are preserved, and can easily be added by an able goldsmith. But still, even in its present defective condition, the nose and the large upper jaws of the lion are distinctly seen. To the right of the spectator we see in the rim two small round perforations, and there are similar perforations in the missing piece of the left side. They must certainly have been used to fasten the mask on another object. I call particular attention to the disproportionately small and but very rudely represented eyes and ears of the lion's head.

Neither in Homer nor in any of the later classics

do we find any allusion to the custom of burying the dead with masks representing their portrait, or with any masks at all. Masks of wood, which however represent but an ideal type and no portrait, are sometimes found in Egyptian tombs.* In a tomb near Kertch there was also found the mask of a woman, which may represent a portrait.† A bronze mask was found at Nola.‡

A   B
Nos. 333, A, B. Two Gold Signet Rings. Sepulchre IV. Actual size.

I further found, with the three bodies whose heads were laid towards the east, the two large golden signet rings (Nos. 334 ·and 335) and the large golden bracelet (No.

Nos. 334, 335. Intaglios on the Signet Rings. Sepulchre IV. Actual size.

336). Nos. 333 A and B show the inverse side of the rings. The surfaces of both signets are slightly convex; the one (No. 334) represents in very archaic intaglio a hunter with his charioteer in a chariot drawn by two

---

* See Caylus, ' Recueil d'Antiquités,' I. 41, pl. XI.

† 'Antiquités du Bosphore Cimmérien,' Planche I. ; where also mention is made of a gold mask found at Olbia.

‡ Tischbein, ' Recueil de Gravures,' II. 1 ; where also mention is made of an iron mask from a sepulchre at Santa Agata dei Goti.

stallions, whose eight feet are in the air and in a line parallel with the ground, to indicate the great speed with which they are dashing forward. Their bushy tails are uplifted, and are very natural, as are also their bodies, except the heads, which are more like camels' than horses' heads. There are no straps visible to attach the horses to the chariot, which is of a different shape from the chariots which we see on the Mycenean sculptures, for here the sides are cut out in the form of a crescent and are consolidated by three projecting beadings, which probably go round the chariot, at least on three sides. But the wheel is exactly like those on the sculptures, for it has only four spokes, which form a cross round the axle.

The two men are naked, and wear merely a belt round the loins; their uncovered heads show thick but not long hair; both wear earrings; their faces are much protruding, and are very archaic, particularly that of the charioteer, of whose body we see the full front view, though his head is turned to the right: his shoulders are too broad and angular, and are disproportionate to the rest of the body. The hunter, who appears to be much younger than his companion, leans over the chariot, holding in his left hand a bow; with his right he has drawn the cord, and is just in the act of shooting an arrow at a stag with long horns, which is running before the chariot, and seems to turn its head back, full of anguish. It deserves particular attention that the stag is represented in the air, and that its hind-feet are on the same level with the men in the chariot, while its fore-feet are much higher still. Otherwise the body of the stag is made true to nature. The object just before the horses' feet is meant to represent the flat ground, though it looks rather like a tree on account of the curve of the ring. The object above the stag and above the archer is a mere ornament, and is perhaps intended to represent the clouds; Mr. Newton thinks it represents mountains.

Still more interesting is the battle-scene on the other

signet-ring (No. 335); where we see four warriors, of
whom the one has evidently vanquished the other three.
One of the latter, who is wounded, sits on the ground to
the right of the victor, supporting himself with his hands.
He has only a short helmet (κυνέη) on his head, and is
otherwise completely naked. His beard is well shown, and
the Mycenean engraver has taken great pains to represent
the anatomy of the body; though he is sitting and with
his feet stretched sideways to the spectator, yet we see
the full upper part of his body in front without any perspective diminution.

The second vanquished warrior seems also to be
wounded, for he is kneeling on one knee before the victor,
whilst his other foot is stretched on the ground ; but still he
is fighting against his antagonist, whose breast he has seized
with his left hand, endeavouring to stab him with the long
sword which he holds in his right hand. I call particular
attention to the large knob at the end of the sword-handle.

The wounded man is not quite naked, because we
distinctly see on him a pair of trousers, which, however,
reach only down to the middle of the thighs. His head
would, no doubt, have been quite well proportioned had
not the artist forgotten to remove a small particle of gold ;
by this a small white line is produced in the photograph,
which makes it appear as if there were only a helmet and
no head. If we imagine this small white line removed, we
at once recognise the true proportions of the head, with its
small helmet, which has an upper part (φάλος), but no
λόφος or crest. Though this man is also kneeling sideways
to the spectator, still we see his whole body in front without
any perspective diminution.

The third warrior seems to have taken to flight; we
see only his head and his feet, the rest of his body
being hidden by an enormous shield, of a peculiar form,
which, if the man were standing upright, would cover his
whole body from head to foot. We see a border all

around this shield, and there appears to be also some
ornament on it, which, however, is difficult to distinguish.
It is only owing to the curve of the ring that he is not
shown standing upright. This shield represents to us, no
doubt, one of the large Homeric shields, which were so
enormous that the poet compares them to towers : *

> " Ajax approached ; before him, *as a tower*,
>   His mighty shield he bore, seven-fold, brass-bound,
>   The work of Tychius, best artificer
>   That wrought in leather ; he in Hyla dwelt."
>
> LORD DERBY.

This warrior's head is covered with a helmet, having a
broad border and a large φάλος and attached to it the
λόφος, from which a long and well-represented crest
(ἵππουρις) is waving. He appears to have stopped in his
flight, and, having turned his head, he is trying to thrust
his long lance at the victor. This latter is of gigantic
proportions, and has on his head a helmet similar to that
of the other man with the tower-like shield ; only the
crest is different, consisting here of three straps which
may represent ostrich feathers. He appears to wear a
broad belt, because four long straps are hanging down
from his loins : his body is the best proportioned of all.
He seizes with his left hand the vanquished man before him,
whilst with his uplifted right hand he deals him a deadly
blow with a broad two-edged sword, on the handle of which
we again see one of those very large knobs, of which we
find here so many of alabaster or wood. The posture of
the victor is perfectly faithful to nature ; he is stepping with
his left foot forward and leaning on it the whole weight of
his body, in order to strike a more powerful blow. Above
the four warriors is an ornament in which Mr. Newton

---

* See *Il.* VII. 219 :—

> Αἴας δ' ἐγγύθεν ἦλθε, φέρων σάκος ἠΰτε πύργον,
> χάλκεον, ἑπταβόειον, ὅ οἱ Τυχίος κάμε τεύχων,
> σκυτοτόμων ὄχ' ἄριστος, Ὕλῃ ἔνι οἰκία ναίων.

also XI. 485 : XVII. 128.

may be right in seeing a rude representation of mountains. I may here add that both signet-rings are but very small, and could only fit on ladies' fingers.

When I brought to light these wonderful signets, I involuntarily exclaimed: "The author of the 'Iliad' and the 'Odyssey' cannot but have been born and educated amidst a civilisation which was able to produce such works as these. Only a poet who had objects of art like these continually before his eyes could compose those divine poems." Mr. Gladstone has already proved beyond any doubt in his celebrated 'Homeric Synchronism' that Homer was

No. 336.   A Bracelet of Gold.   Sepulchre IV.   Actual size.

an Achæan, and I am constantly bringing to light in the depths of Mycenæ thousands of additional proofs that he is perfectly right.

Highly interesting is also the very heavy, massive, golden bracelet, which I represent under No. 336. In remarkable contrast with the size of the signet-rings, it is so enormously large that it would fit on the loins of an ordinary man. It is ornamented with vertical strokes between two margins formed by two circular bands; and further with a beautiful flower of gold, which is not soldered directly on the bracelet, but is fastened with a silver pin to a plate of the same metal, and this latter is soldered on the ring. The silver plate, part of which is broken off all round, appears to have represented four flowers, and there are signs of its having been plated with copper, which has no doubt been plated with gold; because, as I have before stated, the Mycenean goldsmiths did not know the art of plating silver with gold.

The two bodies which are turned with the head to the east, whose faces were covered with gold masks, had also the breasts covered with large golden breast-plates. The one is of massive gold, but without any ornamentation; the other is of a much thinner gold plate, and decorated with a *repoussé* work of two borders of small circles, within which are five rows of shield-like ornaments with concentric circles. This latter breast-cover has, at each of its extremities, a hole for fastening it to the body. Close to the head of another body, I found the beautiful golden crown (στέμμα, No. 337), but it must be distinctly understood that it is represented here head downward, because to that side which is shown here as the lower, were attached, with very small pins, of which six can be seen, a number of leaves, a few of which still remain; and if, therefore, the crown had been put round the head as it is shown here, the leaves would have hung over the eyes, which can never have been the case.* Thus, this crown had on its upper side the leaves, and on its lower a small border with small oblique strokes, the intervening space being filled up in the middle with three rosettes, intersected by vertical rows of very small shield-like circles, and at both ends with similar circles or with larger ones. At each extremity, there is a very small perforation, through which the crown was fastened by means of a thin gold wire. This crown resembles the one already shown (see No. 281), but its ornamentation is much less sumptuous.

---

* This explanation is rendered necessary by the way in which the photograph was taken. To invert the position would require complete recomposition of the light and shadows; and this has been done by our artist in the case of No. 281, on account of the importance of the object.

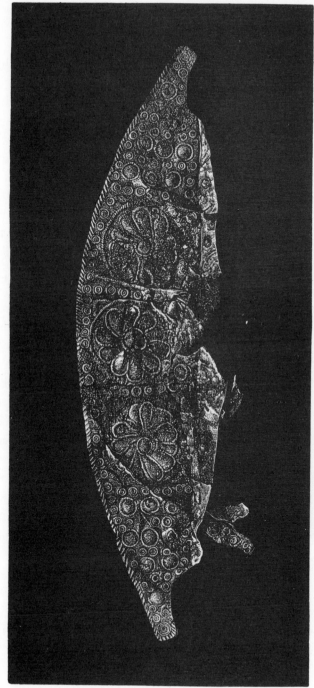

No. 337.   A splendid Crown of Gold found close to the head of one of the bodies in the fourth Sepulchre.   Size 1 : 4 about.

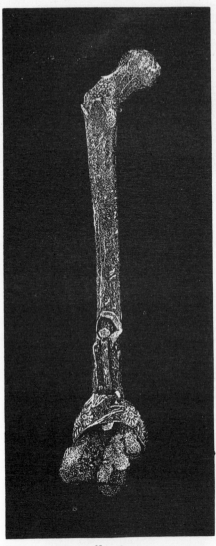

No. 338.
A Human Thigh-bone, with a gold ornament of the greaves still attached to it.
Sepulchre IV.   Size 1 : 4, about.

No. 338 represents the thigh-bone of one of the bodies of this sepulchre, around which was still attached the golden band, which served both for fastening and ornamenting the greave (κνημίς). The band consists of two parts, the lower horizontal and the upper vertical; the former being attached by a fine gold wire, the latter by means of the ring which we see at its extremity and which must have been fastened to a button fixed to the short trousers, of which we have seen a specimen on the ring (No. 335). We have already seen* that the greaves were attached above the knee, and the existence of this greave-holder on the thigh-bone can leave no doubt that such was the general custom. The lower band is decorated all round with an imitation of leaves, and in front with two rosettes. On the upper

---

* See No. 213, p. 133.

band we see soldered a smaller and thicker one, with the unmistakeable intention to give it more substance.

While speaking of soldering, I may mention that Professor Landerer informs me that the Mycenean goldsmiths soldered gold with the help of borax (borate of soda), which is still used at the present day for the same purpose. He adds that he was lucky enough to discover this salt on the border of an ancient false medal from Ægina; that it was called in antiquity χρυσόκολλα ("gold cement"), and that it was imported from Persia and India under the name of *Baurac-Pounxa-Tinkal.* In the Middle Ages, it was imported by the Venetians from Persia to Venice, where it was purified and exported under the denomination of *Borax Venetus.*

There were further found with the five bodies of this sepulchre nine vessels of gold; the first (No. 339) being a

No. 339. A Golden Goblet with two handles (δέπας ἀμφικύπελλον). Sepulchre IV.
Size 5 : 8 about.

large massive golden goblet with two handles, and, therefore, an Homeric δέπας ἀμφικύπελλον ; it has no ornamenta-

tion. The two golden goblets, one of which is shown
(No. 340), are, as Professor A. Rousopoulos observed to

No. 340. Golden Goblet with one handle. Sepulchre IV. Size 5 : 6, about.

me, of the pattern called in Greek αὐλακωτά ("furrowed"),
each of them being encircled by nine parallel furrows;
each has only one handle.
Another gold vessel (No.
341) found in this sepul-
chre, is a beautiful œnochoë,
with a large handle, and
decorated in *repoussé* work,
with three parallel horizontal rows of spirals, united
with each other and form-
ing an interwoven orna-
mentation, which fills the
whole body of the flagon
with a net-work, and which,
as Dr. Schlie remarked to
me regarding the perfectly
similar spiral net-work on
the sepulchral *stêlê* (No.
140)* is in principle the

No. 341.
A Golden Wine-Flagon (οἰνοχόη). Sepulchre IV.
Size 7 : 10.

* See p. 81.

same as the filling up with frets or spirals combined horizontally and vertically.   The foot of the *œnochoë*

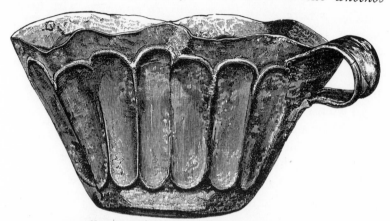

No. 342.   A Golden Cup.   Sepulchre IV.   Size 4 : 5.

is ornamented with small slanting strokes.   I also found a gold goblet with one handle (No. 342), the body

No. 343.   A plain massive Cup of Gold.   Sepulchre IV.   Size 2 : 5, about.

of which is encircled with a broad band of a plain ornamentation in *repoussé* work, resembling blades of knives.

Further, a plain massive golden goblet of a new shape (No. 343) having one handle, which, like all the other handles, is fastened to the vessel with gold nails with broad convex heads, which can be seen on the inner side of the rim. If we take away the handle, this goblet resembles our present water-glasses, but its cup is larger and its foot smaller.

I would here call very particular attention to the fact that this golden goblet more or less exactly represents the form of all the goblets of terra-cotta found at Mycenae (see No. 83, p. 70, and Nos. 84 and 88 on p. 71). It further deserves special notice that, as before stated, the British Museum contains, of perfectly the same shape, fourteen terra-cotta

No. 344. A large massive Gold Goblet with two handles (δέπας ἀμφικύπελλον), weighing 4 lbs. troy. Sepulchre IV. Half-size.

goblets found in the tomb of Ialysus. It is also worthy of particular notice that exactly the same form of goblet was found by me at Troy (Hissarlik), in a depth of 50 feet, in the most ancient of the four prehistoric cities.[*]

---

* See my 'Atlas des Antiquités Troyennes,' Plate 105, No. 2311.

But the most remarkable of the vessels deposited in this sepulchre is an enormous massive golden goblet with two handles—δέπας ἀμφικύπελλον—weighing four pounds troy (No. 344).* It is one of the most splendid jewels of the Mycenean treasure; but, unfortunately, it has been crumpled up by the ponderous weight of the stones and *débris*, and its body has been compressed upon the foot, so that the spectator cannot fully realise from the engraving the magnificence of this royal cup. Any gold-smith might easily restore it to its former shape, but I think it would be far better to leave it as it is, because it has thus a far higher value to science; and, as a general rule, I may remark that the less ancient jewels of gold are touched and handled, the better, because their great value lies in the tarnish of antiquity—the "*patina*"—which no human hand can imitate, and which, when once lost, can never be restored.

The body of this costly goblet is encircled by a row of fourteen splendid rosettes, between an upper band of three lines, and a lower one of two; the foot, by a band of large protruding globular points. Not only the flat sides of the handles, but even their edges, are ornamented. Here also may be seen the heads of the golden pins with which the handles are attached to the rim and body.

No. 345 (p. 236) represents a plain, large, massive golden goblet, with one handle, of which the side turned to the spectator is much crumpled and compressed; it has no other ornament than a thick, protruding band, by which the body is encircled.

The splendid massive golden goblet (No. 346, p. 237) is also defaced, having been pressed over to the left side of the spectator. It has two horizontal handles, each formed by thick plates, which are joined by a small cylinder. The

---

* The photograph was unfortunately taken in such a position as to show only one of the two handles.

lower plate of each of these handles is attached to the large round foot by a long broad thick gold band, whose upper part is embellished with a long opening, the upper end of which is pointed, the lower being round. The lower part of the band is, for a like purpose, cut out into three straps, which join again on the foot of the goblet, where the band is fastened with two golden pins, with broad flat round heads, which can be seen in the engraving. On each upper plate of the two handles is soldered a beautiful little golden

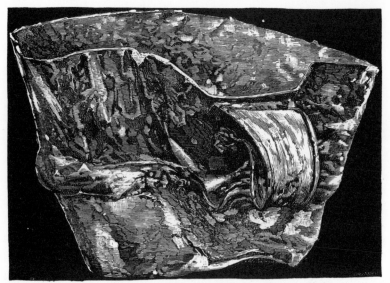

No 345. Gold Cup with one handle. Sepulchre IV. Size 11 : 12, about.

pigeon, apparently of cast-work, with the beak turned towards the goblet, so that the two pigeons are looking at each other. This goblet vividly reminds us of Nestor's cup.*

---

* *Il.* XI. 632–635 :—

πὰρ δὲ δέπας περικαλλές, ὃ οἴκοθεν ἦγ' ὁ γεραιός,
χρυσείοις ἥλοισι πεπαρμένον · οὔατα δ'αὐτοῦ
τέσσαρ ἔσαν, δοιαὶ δὲ πελειάδες ἀμφὶς ἕκαστον
χρύσειαι νεμέθοντο · δύω δ' ὑπὸ πυθμένες ἦσαν.

"She placed beside them a splendid goblet, which the old man had brought with him from home ; it was studded with golden pins ; it had four handles, on each of which pecked two golden pigeons ; the goblet had two bottoms."

Homer's description of this Nestorian goblet fully answers to the vase before us, except that the former is much larger and has four handles, each with two pigeons, instead of only two handles, each with but one pigeon, as our engraving shows. The Nestorian goblet had two bottoms, and so has our goblet, because it is impossible to understand by "two bottoms" anything else than the bottom of the goblet and the bottom of its foot. The usual explanation of the Nestorian goblet, as having an

No. 346.   A Golden Goblet (δέπας ἀμφικύπελλον) with two doves on the handles.   Sepulchre IV.
Size 3 : 8.

upper and a lower cup (the form also attributed to all the Homeric δέπα ἀμφικύπελλα), is altogether erroneous. A goblet of such a shape would have only one bottom common to its two cups, and it could not, therefore, answer the requirements of the Homeric description.   Further, as such a double goblet could at all events be filled only on one side at a time, there would be no *raison d'être* for the two cups in opposite directions.   Besides, whenever a goblet with wine is presented by one person to another, Homer clearly always means it to be understood that it

is a δέπας ἀμφικύπελλον, namely, that it is double-handled,
and that, being presented with the one handle, it is received
by the other. I may mention, besides, that no goblet with
an upper and a lower cup has ever yet been found, while
I found twenty differently-shaped goblets with two handles
at Troy, and a large number of double-handled goblets at
Mycenæ, all of which can be nothing else than δέπα
ἀμφικύπελλα.

Athenæus* lays great weight on the explanation of
the Nestorian goblet, as given by a certain Apelles, who
maintained that it was nothing else than a goblet with
a foot, on two sides of which latter were soldered two
bands (of metal), which had a common base, and stood
vertically not far from each other. These bands reached to
above the mouth of the goblet, and were bent over and
joined again in one sole piece, which was soldered to the rim.
Apelles maintained that by the four handles of the Nestorian goblet, Homer could mean nothing else than these
handles, which were properly but two, but were called four,
in consequence of being divided. Thus, as there were only
two pigeons at the juncture of each of those two metal
bands, the Nestorian goblet had in all only four pigeons.
This explanation of Apelles very nearly answers to the
shape of the goblet before us.

I would also suggest that the shape of the Nestorian
goblet may be imagined as perfectly similar to the goblet
before us, because this really has four handles; namely,
the two horizontal ones, on which the pigeons lie, and the
two lower ones which are produced by the thick vertical
straps, which join them at the foot. If so, the only
difference would be that Nestor's goblet had one more
pigeon on each of these double handles. But the question
is what that goblet was made of. Probably it was of wood
and studded with gold nails; because, if it had been of gold

---

* 'Deipnosophistæ,' XI. 77.

or some other metal, it is difficult to suppose that it could have been studded with gold nails.

I further picked up in this tomb the beautiful large golden goblet represented by No. 347. It has a broad

No. 347.   A large Gold Cup.   Sepulchre IV.   Size 4 : 5.

handle, which is attached to the rim and body by three pins with large flat heads. The outside of the goblet is divided by vertical lines into seven compartments, in each of which is represented, in magnificent *repoussé* work, a flower which fills the whole space between the rim and the bottom. I found in this tomb still another large golden goblet with splendid *repoussé* ornamentation, but, by a mistake quite inexplicable, it has not been photographed.

With the five bodies of the fourth tomb was further

found the beautiful heavy massive silver goblet (No. 348) which is exceedingly well preserved, and has only one

No. 348.   Large Silver Goblet, richly plated with gold.   Sepulchre IV.   Size 4 : 7.

handle, in the form of the golden handle of the cup No. 346.   This handle is fastened to the rim and body of

No. 349.   Hand-made Vase of Terra-cotta.   Sepulchre IV.   About half-size.

the goblet by four gold nails having large round flat heads. The piece of metal, which we see on the body of the vessel, was accidentally soldered to it by the fire of the funeral pile, and does not belong to it. The whole body was plated with copper, and this plating was again plated with gold, and the gold was covered with a splendid ornamentation of intaglio work, which seems to be very well preserved, but only very little of it can be seen, on account of the dirt with which the goblet is covered. Mr. A. Postolaccas reminds me that the spiral band, of which a small part is visible in the engraving, is also found on the medals of Tarentum, and represents there the waves of the sea.

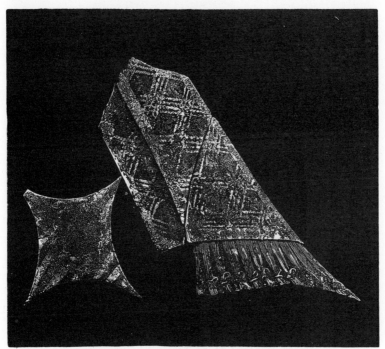

Nos. 350, 351.　Objects of Egyptian Porcelain, of unknown use.　Sepulchre IV.　Size 2 : 5.

There were further found in the same tomb three hand-made terra-cotta vases with two handles, one of which is represented (No. 349) ; this form is very common in Troy, but it is very often set on three small feet.*

---

* See ' Troy and its Remains,' p. 87, No. 53, and p. 169, No. 192.

I also found the two objects (Nos. 350 and 351) which Mr. Newton holds to be of Egyptian porcelain; their use is altogether unknown to me. The smaller piece has an ornamentation of white and black parallel lines; the other has, on a dead green ground, parallel bands of four white lines, which cross each other so as to form a number of small squares. The lower part of No. 351 has an impressed ornamentation, representing tassels painted black, in each of which we see a noose perfectly similar in form to the object

No. 352. Model of a sort of scarf tied in a noose. Egyptian porcelain. Sepulchre IV. Size 2 : 3, about.

represented in No. 352, which is also of Egyptian porcelain. The perforations show this object to have been an ornament nailed on something else. These scarfs also have, on a light-green dead ground, an ornamentation, now nearly obliterated, of parallel bands of two white lines, which cross each other at right angles and form small squares. At the lower end of the front piece of both are represented tassels in very low relief, which are painted black. Both these objects can be nothing else than ornaments, but the question is how they have been used as such.*

No. 353. A Silver Flagon (οἰνοχόη). Sepulchre IV. Nearly half-size.

The silver flagon, or *œnochoë* (No. 353), has a long vertical handle and a beautiful form, but no ornamentation, at least none that is visible; but there may be some in *repoussé* below the dirt with which the vessel is covered. There were further found three shoulder-belts (τελαμῶνες) of gold, of which I represent one. Of the other two, the one is a broad but thin band, without any ornamentation, and it appears to have been expressly made for the funeral,

---

* With regard to these ornaments, see further Appendix C.

for it is not solid enough to have been used by living men ; its length is 4½ ft., its breadth is 2 in. to 2⅓ in.

The golden shoulder-belt here shown (No. 354) is much thicker and more solid ; it is 4 ft. 1½ in. long and 1⅞ in. broad, and has on either side a small border produced by the turning down of the gold plate, and is ornamented with an uninterrupted row of rosettes. At one extremity are two apertures in the form of keyholes, which served to fasten the clasp which was attached to the other

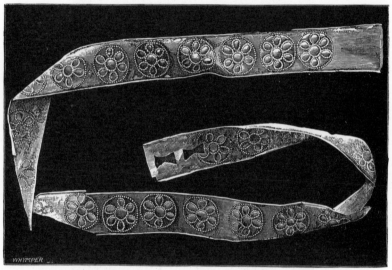

No. 354.   Gold Model of a shoulder belt (τελαμών).   Sepulchre IV.   Size 3 : 16, about.

extremity, as is shown by two small cuts and a small hole. The third golden shoulder-belt presents exactly the same model and ornamentation, as well as the same keyhole-like apertures at one end, and cuts where the clasps were fastened at the other extremity ; only this one has suffered much from the fire, and therefore the ornamentation is less distinct.   There were further found in the same tomb fourteen objects of very pure rock crystal, but their use is unknown ; also a thin disc of alabaster, which must have been the bottom of a vase.

At the left side of the head of the middle body of the
three which lay with the heads turned to the east, I found
a heap of more than 400 large and small beads of amber,
of which I represent eight (No. 355). About the same
number of similar amber beads were found with one of the
bodies the head of which lay to the north. All these amber
beads had, no doubt, been strung on thread in the form of
necklaces, and their presence in the tombs among such

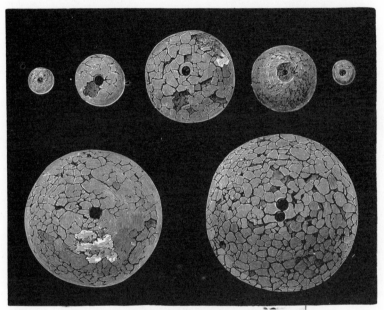

No. 355.   Amber Necklace-beads.   Sepulchre IV.   Actual size.

large treasures of golden ornaments seems to prove that
amber was very precious and was considered as a magnificent ornament in the time of the early Mycenean kings.

Among the finest objects found in this tomb were a vase
and three handles of alabaster, which are put together in
the engraving (No. 356). Each of the handles has two or
three perforations by which they were attached to the vase,
on which similar perforations are found. But, judging by
the smallness of the perforations, which are only large

enough for slight pins, the fragility of the elaborate handles, and the heaviness of the vase itself, we become convinced that it can never have been used for anything else than an ornament, and that it can never even have been lifted up by the handles.

There were further found four golden diadems, two

No. 356. A large three-handled Vase of Alabaster. Re-composed from the Fragments
Sepulchre IV. Half-size.

large and two small ones, similar to those already repre-sented.* The larger one is 1 ft. 8½ in. long and 4 in. broad in the middle. Between two borders of zigzag lines it has an ornamentation of shield-like double circles in *repoussé* work, the space between them being on either

---

* See Nos. 282, 283, 284, pp. 186, 188.

side filled up by small circles of the same pattern, whilst both extremities are covered with a beautiful spiral ornamentation. At the one end is a pin (ἔμβολον) and at the other a small tube (αὐλίσκος), by which the diadem was fastened round the 'head. The smaller diadems are only 1 ft. 5½ in. long, and 2⅘ in. broad in the middle, and appear to have adorned a child's forehead. Their ornamentation in *repoussé* work is most varied and curious. Between two borders, each of two lines, we see in the middle a circle surrounded by thirteen small ones, on either side of which follow two vertical bands filled with small horizontal strokes; next a vertical row of three circles, and again two vertical bands filled with horizontal strokes; after that a vertical band of spirals, and two concentric circles, surrounded by smaller ones of the same shape; then again a vertical band filled with horizontal strokes; and, lastly, two vertical bands of concentric circles, between which a horizontal band with oblique strokes goes to the extremity. Only one end, with a perforation, is preserved. The other end, probably, was similarly fashioned, and the diadem was fastened with a fine gold wire round the child's head. No body of a child was found, but the number of small ornaments which would only fit a child lead me to think that there has been one, or even more than one, in this sepulchre. None of these diadems were piped.

There were further found two golden diadems which, like the former, are of thin gold plate, but neither of them is piped. Both are so small that they could only fit round the heads of children; one is 1 ft. 4½ in., the other 1 ft. ⅓ in., long. The former is ornamented, between two borders of points, with five shield-like circles in the middle, of which three represent rosettes, the other two a wheel in motion. The remaining space to the right and left is filled up with small shield-like circles, together with two larger ones representing again a wheel in motion, and with spirals. The other diadem has, between two borders of concentric circles, in the middle a shield-like circle

Nos. 357, 358.
A Belt and "belle Hélène" of gold.
Sepulchre IV.   Size ⅓ (one-third size).

representing a wheel in motion, and to the right and left a similar circle representing rosettes. Above the second circle from the middle one, to the right of the spectator, is represented a bird. The remaining space is filled up with a beautiful and very symmetrical ornamentation of spirals, with two shield-like circles representing wheels in motion, and again with spirals or concentric circles. Both these diadems have at each end a fine wire for fastening them round the head.

Nos. 357 and 358 represent from the same sepulchre a small beautifully - ornamented golden belt and a golden "belle Hélène," that is, a fillet or frontlet. Both are of strong plate, but so short that they also seem to have been used as ornaments for a child. The belt is ornamented with seven shield-like circles, representing wheels in motion; it has at either end a perforation for fastening it with fine wires.

The "belle Hélène" is ornamented with rosettes and crosses of *repoussé* work; it has two perforations

in the rim, a little way from either end, from one of which
is still hanging the fragment of a very fine chain (*a*),
and a similar one has, no doubt, been suspended to the
other perforation.* Both the chains must have been much
longer, and ornaments must have been attached to them,
as to the Trojan diadems,† which Mr. Gladstone is right
in identifying with the Homeric "πλεκταὶ ἀναδέσμαι."
Attached to each extremity of this frontlet is a fine golden
wire for fastening it round the head. I also picked up in
this tomb a small golden belt-ornament, a golden greave-
ornament, two golden ribbons, and two golden leaves, all
with an ornamentation in *repoussé* work, such as we have
repeatedly passed in review, and therefore I do not give
the engravings of them here.

There were further found with the five bodies of the
fourth sepulchre the following objects of gold: the
richly-ornamented ribbon (No. 359), having at either extremity five perforations for nailing or sewing it to some
other object. The decoration forms two compartments,
one of which is divided by a multitude of vertical lines
into a number of smaller and larger fields. Three of these
show a waving line, having on either side small strokes which
give it the appearance of a feather. In the other compartment, between two borders, each composed of three or
four horizontal lines, are two rows of beautiful spirals and
two straps ornamented with small oblique strokes. The
two objects, Nos. 360 and 361, are heavy massive golden
pins, which may equally well have served as breast-pins or
as hair-pins, because Homer's countrymen, the Achæans,
wore very long hair, and were therefore called καρηκο-
μώοντες Ἀχαιοί by the poet. The heads of both these
brooches have almost the shape of helmets, and each of

---

* The Cut has to be viewed with the outer edge of the page
downwards.

† See ' Troy and its Remains,' p. 335, Plate XIX.

them has a vertical perforation, which may have been used for putting in an additional ornament, or perhaps a flower. Both these brooches appear to be much worn. Much thinner is the third golden pin (No. 362), which

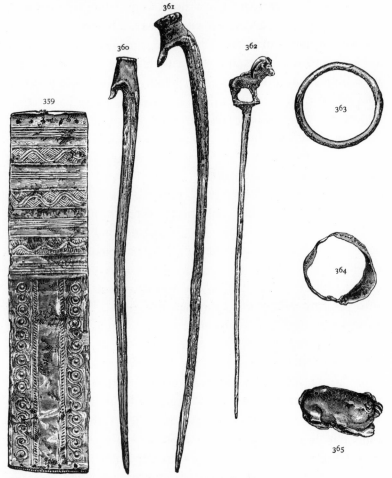

Nos. 359–365   Various ornaments of Gold.   Sepulchre IV.   Actual size.

is ornamented with an admirably-represented ram with long horns.

The rings (Nos. 363 and 364) are also of gold; the former, which is massive and has no ornamentation, seems to have been a finger-ring; the latter is a small ornamented

ribbon, which was turned round and fastened in the form
of a ring, and may have been used as an earring, similar to
which there were found two.

No. 365 is a lion's cub; it is of massive gold, very
heavy, and I share Mr. Newton's opinion that it is cast and
tooled.

The golden cylinder (No. 366) belonged no doubt,
to the wooden handle of a sword or sceptre, because we see
all along its middle part the row of pin-holes, and even

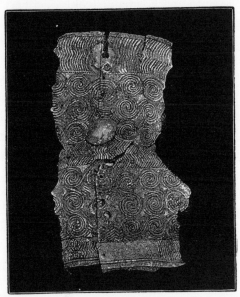

No. 366.   Highly decorated Golden Cylinder, probably the handle of a sword or sceptre.
Sepulchre IV.   Size 4 : 5.

four flat heads of pins, and in the centre the head of a
very large pin, by which it was attached.   It is ornamented
at both ends with a broad border of wave-lines, and the
whole remaining space is filled with interwoven spirals, all
in magnificent intaglio work.

There was also found an ornament consisting of three
double leaves of gold, which are soldered together in the
middle, representing a magnificent star, ornamented all
over with shield-like concentric circles of *repoussé* work.

The primitive artist has not forgotten to ornament the borders with small strokes, no doubt with the intention of making the leaves still more conspicuous. There were found two other stars, each of two double leaves of gold, which are soldered together in the middle, and, as the perforation shows, were fastened by a pin on some other object. The leaves of both stars are ornamented with a *repoussé* work of shield-like concentric circles, interspersed with pear-like designs ; the borders of the leaves are also ornamented with small strokes. In what manner all these stars have been used as ornaments, it is difficult to say.

I further found with the five bodies of this tomb two small rings (see No. 367), which have an impressed ornamentation of small circles. There were further found two small double-headed battle-axes, of thin gold plate (No. 368). Of the handle of the one shown, only part remains ; that of the other is almost entirely gone. Double-headed battle-axes of precisely the same form are seen on all the medals of the island of Tenedos ; we see them also on some of the gold ornaments from Mycenæ, on a lentoid gem from the great Heræum, which will be passed in review in the subsequent pages, and between the horns of the two small cow-heads on gold-leaf found in this sepulchre.* Mr. Postolaccas calls my attention to the passage in Plutarch :† "But the Tenedians have taken the axe from the crabs, which are with them abundant about the so-called Asterion, because it appears that the crabs alone have the figure of the axe in their shell." The same friend reminds me, besides, that the double battle-axe is the symbol of the Labrandian Jove, who was worshipped in Labranda, and it is represented on the medals of the ancient kings of Caria, as on those of Maussollus‡ (353 B.C.), Idrieus (344 B.C.),

---

* See Nos. 329–330, p. 218.
† *De Pythiæ Oraculis ; Op. Moral.* ed. Didot, vol. i. p. 488.
‡ This name is always Μαύσσολλος on the coins.

Pixodarus (336 B.C.) and Othomtopatos (334 B.C.) I also find in Plutarch* that the axe, πέλεκυς, was called in the Lydian language λάβρυς.

Nos. 367-370. Golden Ornaments. Sepulchre IV. Size 2 : 3.

Professor A. Rhousopoulos writes to me on this subject: " I suppose the double-edged axe on the coins of " Tenedos to be a sacrificial or a warlike symbol. I believe " this from analogy with other coins of a superior class.

---

* *Quæst. Græc.* p. 45.

" There was a proverb in ancient Greece, Τενέδιος πέλεκυς,
" 'Tenedian axe,' for those who resolve questions in a
" harsh or in a rather short way.   The Tenedian Apollo
" held in his hand the double axe, namely, that which is
" represented on the coins of Tenedos; but the interpreta-
" tion of this symbol in antiquity was twofold.   Some
" regarded it as the symbol of Tennes, others (and so
' Aristotle) maintained that a certain king of Tenedos
" made a law, that he who surprised an adulterer and adul-
" teress had to kill both with an axe.   Now, it happened
" that his own son was surprised as an adulterer, and the
" father decreed that the boy should be punished according
" to the common law.   In consequence of this event, the
" double axe was put on the medals of Tenedos, in memory
" of the prince's tragic fate."   However, as to the signification of this symbol in the remote antiquity to which the
Mycenean tombs belong, I do not venture to express an
opinion.

The magnificent golden object (No. 369) resembles very
much the usual ornaments for fastening the greaves round
the thigh, just above the knee; but it cannot have served
as such, the gold plate being by far too thick for that
purpose; besides, this ornament is perfectly straight, and
has evidently never been bent.   It must, therefore, be
something else.   As we see the object before us, it resembles a man such as children draw; the ring above the head
may represent a crown.   The splendid ornament in *repoussé*
work on the body we have seen, though less beautiful, in
the border of the sepulchral *stélé* (No. 24).*   The legs
show, between two narrow borders, rows of small signs
resembling the letter *koppa*, which we see on all the
Corinthian medals.

There were further found three golden objects, of
which I represent one under No. 370.   I do not venture

---

* See the Vignette to Chapter III., p. 52.

to give an explanation of them; they cannot have served as brooches, the pin at the foot being too short and fragile for that use. All three have a border all round, and in the middle a rosette formed by points.

There were further found the two objects of copper here represented. For what purpose the first (No. 371) may have been used, it is difficult to say; it has a quadrangular hole, which cannot, however, have served to put

Nos. 371, 372. Objects of Copper. Sepulchre IV. Size 1 : 3, about.

in a handle, because the copper-plate is not thick enough. The second object is a large fork, with three curved prongs, and a tube into which the wooden handle was stuck; this fork has evidently served to rake the fire of the funeral piles.

There were also found in this tomb the objects shown in the following cut. Nos. 373 and 374 are of bone and have the same shape. Both have on one side a carved ornamentation of spirals, a border, and two or three con-

centric circles, and two perforations ; in the centre there
seems to have been a knob, which is broken off.   On the
reverse side, in the border, are three protruding cones in
the form of feet.   I represent in the engraving the upper
end of one of these objects, and the reverse side of the
other.   The use of them would be almost impossible to

Nos. 373-375.   Two Bone Lids of Jars and a piece of an Alabaster Vase.   Sepulchre IV.   Size 5 : 6.

explain had I not found similar ones, but of terra-cotta, and
with four feet of conical shape, in Troy, and one of them
still *in situ*, as a lid on the mouth of a large can or jar.
The two perforations served to fasten the lid with a string
to the jars.*   Four such vase-lids of bone were found in
this tomb.

---

* See 'Atlas des Antiquités Troyennes,' Plate 21, Nos. 583 and
584.   This explains how the nurse Euryclea fastened on the lids of the
amphoræ for Telemachus.   (Hom. *Odyss.* ii. 354) :—

Δώδεκα δ᾽ ἔμπλησον, καὶ πώμασιν ἄρσον ἅπαντας.

No. 375 represents a fragment of an alabaster vase, on which a beautiful ornamentation is carved, displaying, between two parallel stripes, a row of spirals, and, below, a row of vertical flutings.

In a copper vessel in the south-eastern corner of this sepulchre was found the animal represented under No. 376, which Professor Landerer has found to consist of a

No. 376. A Stag, of an alloy of silver and lead. Sepulchre IV. Size 3 : 7, about.

mixture of two-thirds silver and one-third lead. It is hollow, and seems to have served as a vase, the mouth-piece, in the form of a funnel, being on the back. The whole body of the animal is very coarse and heavy, particularly the feet, which resemble the feet of a buffalo, but the head resembles a cow's-head. As, however, the head is crowned with two stag-horns, of which one is preserved, there can be no doubt that the artist intended to represent a stag. He may be excused for having made the animal so coarse, because had he given exactly the form of a stag, the vase he intended to make would have been too

Nos. 377-381. Buttons of Wood, covered with plates of gold, highly ornamented.   Sepulchre IV.
Actual size.

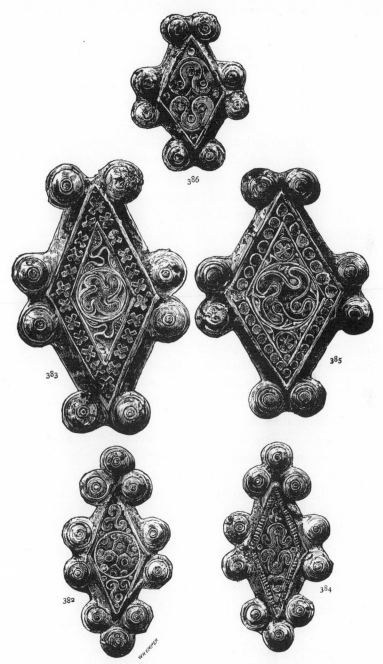

Nos. 382-386. Buttons of Wood, covered with plates of gold, highly ornamented.   Sepulchre IV.
Actual size.

fragile.   Vases of terra-cotta in the form of animals were frequent at Troy.*

There were further found with the five bodies of the fourth sepulchre twelve buttons of wood, in the form of crosses, plated with gold, which present a most magnificent ornamentation of intaglio and *repoussé* work (see Nos. 377–386).†   The largest of them (No. 377) is a little more than 3½ in. in length and is 2⅛ in. broad.   The most curious thing is, that all the wooden buttons present exactly the same beautiful ornamentation as the gold plate which covers them, as can be seen on the aforesaid large button in the place where part of the gold plate is missing.   The question, therefore, naturally arises, in what manner this effect can have been produced.   On mature reflection, we arrive at the conviction that it cannot possibly have been done in any other way than the following.   The pieces of wood were first shaped, and on them was carefully and artistically carved in low-relief all the ornamentation which we now see on the gold plate in *repoussé* work.   After that, the wooden buttons were covered with the gold plate, which, having been well attached on the reverse side, was hammered on the buttons, and in this manner the low-relief ornamentation of the wood was reproduced in the gold plate.   When this had been done, the intaglio work was made in the gold plate, which being very thin, all the cuts were at once impressed as deeply into the wood as into the gold.   I think this is the only way to explain this wonderful work.

The form of all these cross buttons is that of a *lozenge ;* nine of them being ornamented at each acute, as well as at each obtuse angle, with two protruding globular pieces, each of which has four concentric circles in intaglio. Only two of the cross buttons (Nos. 382 and 384) have

---

* See 'Troy and its Remains,' pp. 160, 208, 209, 214, 352.

† The two remaining buttons have similar patterns.

on each acute angle three such protruding globular pieces,
and one (No. 380) has three of them at all four corners.
The button (No. 378) has, in its interior lozenge, a broad
border, adorned with thirty-two beautiful little crosses, each
of which has a point in the centre, and within this border, two spirals in the form of an Omega, which stand
opposite each other, and are crowned with branches,
apparently, of a date tree ; to the right and left are small
rosettes.   On the large button (No. 377), the border of
the interior lozenge is filled all round with small circles
in intaglio, and within we see in the middle a double circle,
filled with a spiral ornamentation, likewise in intaglio, and
on each side of the circle a spiral, in the form of an Omega,
and some smaller spirals and signs, all in *repoussé* work.
No. 379 has simply a border of two lines, within which is
a circle with a spiral ornamentation, and in each acute
angle a spiral in the form of an Omega.   On this button
only the last-named spiral is *repoussé*, the rest is intaglio.
Still more simple is the ornamentation of No. 381, in
which the border consists also of two lines, and the
internal space is filled by two signs in form of Omegas,
and by four small flowers, which latter alone appear to be
repoussé, the rest intaglio work.   The button (No. 380)
has no border ; the whole space is filled by concentric
circles in intaglio, with only two or three small ornaments in *repoussé*.

On the other hand, on the button (No. 382) all the
ornamentation is produced by *repoussé* work ; even to the
border line of the interior lozenge, within which we see
a circle filled with small ones, and above and below it a
curious sign, which is very frequent on the Trojan whorls.
On the large button (No. 383) we again see a border filled
with twenty-eight crosses, and in the interior lozenge, in
the middle, a double circle, a 卍 with curved arms, in each
of which, as well as in the centre, is a point to mark the
nails by which the two pieces of wood for the production

of the sacred fire were fastened. The two acute angles are here again filled up with the same sign which we noticed on the preceding figure. The border with the crosses is of *repoussé* work ; the circle, with the 卐, of intaglio.

In the figure No. 384, the border of the interior lozenge is ornamented with horizontal strokes ; in the interior we see, in the middle, two spirals like Omegas, standing opposite each other, and in each acute angle a small ornament, perhaps a flower ; the latter and the border are here the only work in *repoussé*, the remainder being intaglio. The button (No. 386) has an identical ornamentation of two spirals which stand opposite each other, and resemble Omegas. Finally, the large button (No. 385) has a broad border filled with twenty-eight small circles in *repoussé* work, and of the same work is also the small encircled cross in each acute angle, whilst the large circle with the 卐 in the centre is of intaglio work. On the reverse side, the wood of all these twelve cross-like buttons is carved much like our shirt-studs, with the sole difference that the lower side is here of an oval form. Thus, there can be no doubt that all of them were used as ornaments on the clothes, but, of course, they can never have served as real buttons. All these buttons show unmistakeable marks of the funeral fire, but as the wood has been preserved, there can be no doubt that the fire was not intended to reduce the bodies to ashes, or to destroy the ornaments with which they were laden.

There were further found with the five bodies of the fourth tomb 110 small golden flowers, in the shape of the four represented under Nos. 387–390, and 68 gold buttons without any ornamentation like Nos. 391 and 392 ; 134 round pieces of gold plate with a border, like Nos. 395 and 396 ; and 98 large shield-like pieces of gold plate in *repoussé* work, with two rope-like borders, like No. 402 (p. 264). Not one of these 410 round pieces of gold plate shows any sign of having been fastened on wooden buttons, and we conclude from this that they must have been merely attached with glue to the clothes and drapery of the deceased.

In the same place were found 118 gold buttons with intaglio work of seventeen different types of ornamentation which are represented in the specimens shown under Nos. 393–401 and Nos. 403–413. All of them consist of gold plate, fastened either on wood buttons like our shirt-studs,

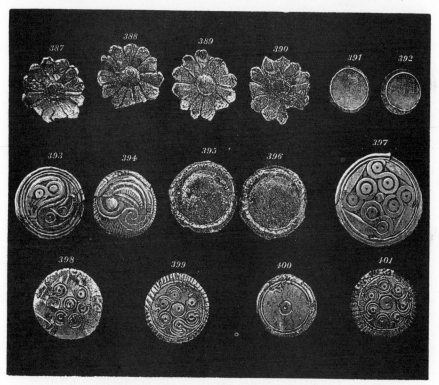

Nos. 387–401. Plates of Gold. Sepulchre IV. Actual size.

or merely on flat round pieces of wood; but of a large part of them the wooden button has disappeared, and only the gold plate remains. I need not describe the ornamentation of every one of these buttons, because the reader sees what they represent. I would here only call attention to the beautiful intaglio on the button, No. 397, which

represents four long broad knives, whose handles are pro-
longed into spirals.

Nos. 402–413.   Gold Buttons.   Sepulchre IV.   Actual size.

I further found there 130 large gold buttons with
splendid intaglio work, some like Nos. 414–420, which represent beautiful stars, flowers, or crosses, and others like
No. 421, which has a beautiful spiral ornamentation.   As
with the smaller buttons, many of these 130 buttons have
still retained their wooden button, shaped like a shirt-stud;
while many others have only flat pieces of wood, and of a
great many others the wood has disappeared and the gold
plate alone remains.

Finally I found eight gold buttons of very large size,
with beautiful intaglio work, of two of which I give the
engravings (Nos. 422 and 422a).   The former represents

Nos. 414–422*a*.   Gold Buttons.   Sepulchre IV.   Actual size.

a sun, in the centre of which is a beautiful 卐 trans-
formed into spirals, without, however, losing the marks of
nails with which it was fastened. The other represents also
a sun with his rays, in the interior of which is the spiral
ornamentation which we have so often passed in review.

All these eight very large buttons have merely flat pieces
of wood; and, as I sometimes find rows of buttons so
shaped, and which gradually diminish in size, lying along the
swords, I feel certain that they were glued in uninterrupted
rows to the wooden sheaths of these weapons, the largest
button being fixed where the sword was broadest and the
rest gradually diminishing in size according to the breadth
of the sword-sheath.* It also deserves particular attention
that, wherever the gold buttons have retained their pieces
of wood, whether flat or shirt-stud-like, these wooden
moulds have, without any exception, exactly the same
intaglio ornamentation which we see on the gold plating;
and there can, therefore, be no doubt whatever that all the
intaglio work was made on the gold plate after it had been
fastened on the wooden buttons, on which the intaglio
made on the gold plate was reproduced by the pressure
of the artist's hand.

The whole immense sepulchre was strewn with small
gold leaves, of which I collected about 200 grammes, or
more than half a pound troy. I found them in masses
even below the bodies, and I have, therefore, no doubt
that they were spread in the tomb before the funeral piles
were dressed there. I also collected from this sepulchre
two silver goblets, two silver bowls, ten silver vases, which
latter are all broken, and finally three large silver vessels
and a small one, which are plated with copper, and are
very flat. I presume, therefore, that they have been used
as basins or as a kind of saucers for large silver vases. I
further found a wooden comb, with a large curved golden

See the engraving, No. 460, on p. 303.

handle, which has evidently served for the forehead, to hold back the hair.

Perhaps the most curious objects of all are five small edifices of gold in *repoussé* work, of which I represent one

No. 423.   Model of a Temple, in Gold.   Sepulchre IV.   Actual size.

(No. 423).   They are too small for dwelling-houses, and I suppose, therefore, that they were intended to represent small temples or sanctuaries.   In this belief I am strengthened, alike by the four horns on the top, by the pigeons with uplifted wings which are sitting at either side, and by the column with a capital, which is represented in every one of the three door-like niches.   I call the reader's particular attention to the similarity of these columns to the column represented between the two lions above the Lions' Gate.   It is also deserving of special notice that the slanting lines to the right and left of the columns give to these niches a striking resemblance with the tombs and their slanting walls.   Below the three niches we see distinctly indicated four courses of masonry of large wrought stones.   Of capital interest is the tower-like upper part of the building, which appears to represent a wooden structure, and in the middle of which are three curious signs resembling letters. I would remind the reader of the coins of Paphos, on which is represented a temple of Aphrodité, with a pigeon sitting on each gable-end.

I also collected from the tomb not less than fifty-three golden cuttle-fish (sepias), of which I represent one

(No. 424). All these fifty - three sepias are perfectly alike, and have a curious ornamentation in relief representing spirals; all their arms are likewise curved into spiral forms. It is difficult to say how these sepias may

No. 424.   A Cuttle-fish in Gold.   Sepulchre IV.
Actual size.

have been used as ornaments; probably they were fastened on clothes and drapery; all appear to have been cast in the same mould, otherwise their *perfect* resemblance is inexplicable.

There were further found two objects of thick gold

Nos. 425, 426.   The two halves of a whorl-shaped object ot thick Gold Plate.   Sepulchre IV.
Actual size.

plate in the form of tops, each consisting of two halves; their use is altogether inexplicable to me.

No. 427. Gold Cover of the Knob of a Sword-handle. Sepulchre IV. Actual size.

I further found there ten golden plates, with beautiful intaglio ornamentation, intended to cover the wooden or alabaster knobs of sword-handles, of which I represent eight (Nos. 427–434). On No. 427 is represented a

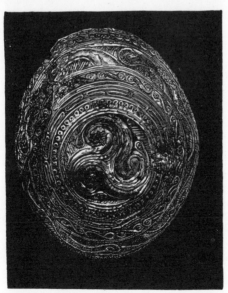

No. 428. Gold Cover of the Knob of a Sword-handle. Sepulchre IV. Actual size.

lion; No. 428 is profusely covered with a magnificent intaglio ornamentation, and there is no space as large as a quarter of an inch vacant. In the centre we see a double circle containing the beautiful spiral which often occurs at Mycenæ, but here represented with sextuple lines.

No. 429.
Gold Cover of a Sword-handle.
Sepulchre IV. Actual size.

Around this circle is another; the space between the two being filled up with miniature circles. Then follows a circle of a beautiful spiral ornamentation; after that, a circle filled with small separate spirals; then a border of three lines, and another circle with curious spirals; then again a circular band of three lines, and after that a broad circle of spirals. The golden object (No. 429) evidently belongs to the upper part of the hilt. The golden plate (No. 430) has evidently also covered the knob of a sword-handle, and we see in it the round holes of the gold

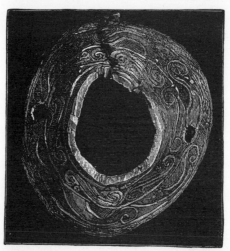

No. 430.   Gold Cover of the Knob of a Sword-handle.   Sepulchre IV.   Actual size.

nails with which it was fastened; it is ornamented with intaglio work representing beautiful spirals.

Not less sumptuous are the golden covers of sword-handle knobs (Nos. 431, 432), the former being ornamented in intaglio work with a number of concentric circles and spirals; the latter also in intaglio work, with a border of small beautiful spirals and several concentric circles, the innermost of which has a border of spirals in the shape of fish, the internal space being filled with ornaments in the form of horse-shoes.   In a similar way the two golden

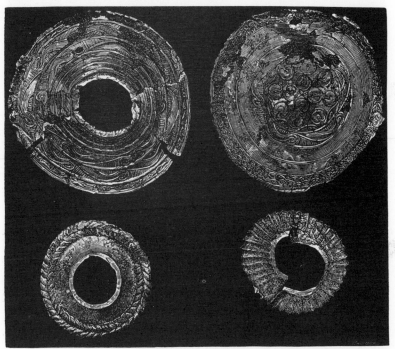

Nos. 431–434.   Gold Covers of the Knobs of Sword-handles.   Sepulchre IV.   Actual size.

objects, Nos. 433 and 434, have served as covers of sword-handle knobs; the former being ornamented with a double band in the form of ropes, the latter with vertical flutings.

There were further found in this tomb, in a heap together, thirty-five arrow-heads of obsidian, which were probably mounted on wooden shafts and contained in a wooden quiver which has disappeared.   I represent under

No. 435 the fifteen different types of these arrow-heads. Nothing could give a better idea of the great antiquity of these tombs than these stone arrow-heads, for the Iliad seems to know only arrow-heads of bronze.*   Probably

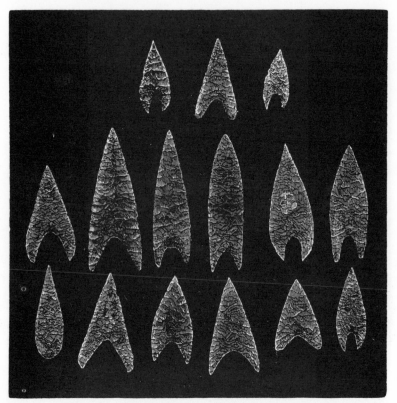

No. 435.   Arrow-heads of Obsidian.   Sepulchre IV.   Size 7 : 8, about.

there had also been bows deposited in the tomb ; but, being of wood, like the quivers and arrow-shafts, they would have decayed.

There were further found here sixty boars'-teeth ; of all which the reverse side is cut perfectly flat, and has two borings, which must have served to fasten them on another

* See, for example, *Iliad* XIII. 650 and 662.

object, perhaps on horse-trappings. But we see in the Iliad* that they were also used on helmets, either as a protection or as an ornament.

I found there also a large quantity of flat quadrangular pieces cut out of boars' teeth. They are from 1 to 2 inches long and from ½ in. to ¾ in. broad; and they have two perforations, one at each extremity, by which they were attached to other objects, most probably to horse-trappings.† I also found a piece of bone, flat and almost circular, with a round hole in the centre, and with six small perforations; its use is unknown to us.

I also found there two large copper handles with unequivocal marks that they had once been plated with gold, and thus it is probable that they belong to a large silver vase.

Besides the five large copper vessels found (as I have already said) at the southern end of the sepulchre, I found

---

* X. 261–265.

> . . . ἀμφὶ δέ οἱ κυνέην κεφαλῆφιν ἔθηκεν,
> ῥινοῦ ποιητήν · πολέσιν δ' ἔντοσθεν ἱμᾶσιν
> ἐντέτατο στερεῶς · ἔκτοσθε δὲ λευκοὶ ὀδόντες
> ἀργιόδοντος ὑὸς θαμέες ἔχον ἔνθα καὶ ἔνθα
> εὖ καὶ ἐπισταμένως.

> "And on his brows a leathern headpiece placed
> Well wrought within, with numerous straps secured,
> And on the outside, with wild boar's gleaming tusks
> Profusely garnished, scattered here and there
> By skilful hand." LORD DERBY.

† These ornaments of horse-trappings vividly remind us of the famous passage in the Iliad IV., 141 :

> ὡς δ' ὅτε τις τ' ἐλέφαντα γυνὴ φοίνικι μιήνῃ
> Μῃονὶς ἠὲ Κάειρα παρήϊον ἔμμεναι ἵππων ·
> κεῖται δ' ἐν θαλάμῳ, πολέες τέ μιν ἠρήσαντο
> ἱππῆες φορέειν · βασιλῆϊ δὲ κεῖται ἄγαλμα,
> ἀμφότερον, κόσμος θ' ἵππῳ, ἐλατῆρί τε κῦδος ·

> "As when some Carian or Mæonian maid
> With crimson dye the ivory stains, designed
> To be the cheek-piece of a warrior's steed,
> By many a valiant horseman coveted,
> As in the house it lies, a monarch's boast,
> The horse adorning, and the horseman's pride."
> LORD DERBY.

five more at the eastern side, behind the heads of the bodies ; further, ten on the west side, at their feet, and twelve at the northern extremity, towards which the heads of two of the bodies were turned.   Thus, the sepulchre contained in all thirty-two copper vessels, some of which, however, were too fragmentary to be preserved.   The chief types of these copper vessels are shown in the following engravings.

No. 436 represents a large can, 1 ft. 8 in. deep, and 1 ft. 4 in. in diameter ; it has two handles, of which the

one, which is upright, unites the rim to the body, and the other, which is horizontal, is on the lower part of the can.   Both handles are fastened with large pins to the vessel.   Of this type seven specimens were found in this tomb.

No. 437 shows one more can of the very same form, but only its upper part can be seen, because it sticks fast in another large copper vessel, and seems to have been welded to it

No. 436.
A large Copper Vessel.   Sepulchre IV.   Size 1 : 8.

by the funeral fire.   Of the form of the lower vessel seven specimens were found; it has two handles standing vertically, each of which is attached to the rim by four large pins.

No. 438 represents a large and deep vessel, with three vertical handles, which are likewise fastened to the rim with thick nails ; of this form also four were found, besides two specimens of a similar form of vessel, but with only two

No. 437.   Two large Copper Vessels stuck together.   Sepulchre IV.   Size 1 : 8, about.

No. 438.   Large Copper Vessel with three handles.   Sepulchre IV.   Size 1 : 8.

handles. No. 439 represents a large vessel with two vertical handles, of which eight or nine specimens were found.

Other forms, of which engravings are not given, are the following. First, a basin, or deep pan, with only one handle in the form of a tube, into which a wooden handle had been fixed; it is 2 ft. in diameter.

Next, a very large kettle with three vertical handles; it measures 2 ft. 6 in. in diameter, and, as is clear from the perforations in the rim of the bottom, the latter has been fastened with pins. This vessel is so large that it can only have served for heating water for the bath, and it would,

No. 439.   A large two-handled Vessel of Copper.   Sepulchre IV.   Size 1 : 4.

therefore, have been called λέβης λοετροχόος; but the poet mentions only such large vessels for heating the water for the bath with *three feet*, and calls them, therefore, τρίπους λοετροχόος.* There was also a beautifully-fashioned copper basin of oval form; it has probably had two handles in the two places where the rim is broken away. Of the last described three vessels no other specimens were found.

Most of these copper kettles, basins or cans, bear the most unmistakeable signs of having been for a long time

---

* *Il.* XVIII. 346; *Odyss.* VIII. 435.

used on the fire; whilst a few have the appearance of having never been on the fire.

The custom of placing a large number of copper kettles or large copper vases in the tombs belongs to a great antiquity. The museum of the Warwakeion at Athens possesses seven funeral urns of copper, with lids turning on hinges, which contained the ashes of the deceased. This small number shows how rarely copper vessels were used in Greece, even for this purpose; but that additional copper kettles should have been placed in a tomb merely in honour of the dead, is a thing unheard of in Greek tombs. But that such was the custom in a very remote antiquity is proved by these Mycenean sepulchres, and by the tomb of Corneto, as well as by the newly discovered tomb at Palestrina, of which I shall have occasion to speak hereafter. Copper vessels, as ornaments of the tombs, were found in the cemetery of Hallstatt, in Austria,* which belongs, however, to a much later period than the Mycenean tombs.

Of capital interest is the copper tripod (No. 440). It has three handles, of which two are horizontal and one vertical; to the right of the spectator is a small mouth. The tripod was used in the Homeric times for various purposes. In the Odyssey,† as well as in the Iliad,‡ we find it used for presents of honour. In the Iliad,§ it is given as a prize in the games, and it also occurs as an ornament of the rooms, || and, further, for the heating of water and for cooking.¶ To indicate its use for these latter purposes, Homer ** gives also the epithet ἐμπυριβήτης to the tripod.

There was further found in this tomb a mass of small

---

* See Edward Freiherr von Sacken, ' Das Grabfeld von Hallstatt. '
† XIII. 13; and XV. 84.　　‡ VIII. 290; and IX. 122.
§ XI. 700; XXIII. 264, 485, 513, 718.　　|| *Il.* XVIII. 373.
¶ *Odyss.* VIII. 434; *Il.* XVIII. 344.
** *Il.* XXIII. 702; XXII. 164 it is called τριπος instead of the usual form τρίπους.

thin round pieces of copper plate, having all around the rim perforations, which show that they have been used as ornaments, probably on horse-trappings; also, a copper vase-handle, plated with gold.

I collected in this tomb, forty-six bronze swords more or less fragmentary, also four lances and three long knives, of which I shall describe the most remarkable. One of the lances is represented under No. 441; like all the My-

No. 440. A Copper Tripod. Sepulchre IV. Size 1 : 4.

cenean lances, it has a tube, in which the wooden lance-shaft was fixed, but, as an exception, there is here a ring on either side, by which the lance-head was attached to the shaft by means of a cord, to prevent its being lost. As I have already stated, all Homeric lances seem to have had a similar tube, in which the shaft was fixed; on the outside of the tube of the lance we see the broad flat head of the nail with which the shaft was fastened.

Among the swords, ten were short and one-edged, of which I represent two under No. 442 and 442*a*; they consist each of one solid piece of bronze, and measure, when entire, from 2 ft. to 2 ft. 3 in. in length. The handle is too thick to have been covered with wood, and must have been used as it is: the end of it forms a ring, by which the sword was suspended to the shoulder-belt (τελαμών) or to the girdle (ζωστήρ or ζώνη). As these short one-edged swords are, properly speaking, nothing else than long knives, they evidently represent the original meaning of the Homeric word, φάσγανον,* which is derived, by a euphonic transposition of the letters, from the same root as that of σφάγη and σφάζω (*slaughter*), and thus this weapon must primitively have been used chiefly for slaughtering animals, and, perhaps, also for killing in close fight; but the name gradually lost its original signification, and in Homer it is perfectly synonymous with ξίφος and ἄορ.

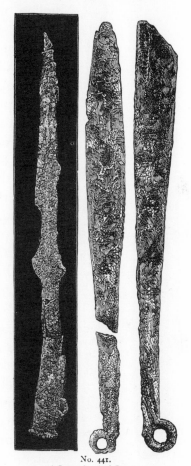

No. 441.
A Lance-head of Bronze.
Sepulchre IV.   Size 1 : 5, about.

Nos. 442, 442*a*.
Small one-edged Bronze Swords.
Sepulchre IV.   Size 3 : 16, about.

There was also found a double-edged weapon with a long tube (αὐλός); but this latter being very narrow, it is

---

* Φάσγανον for σφάγανον, from the root σφαγ. There was also a verb φασγάνω "to kill with the sword:" Hesych. *Lex. s. v.*

Nos. 443, 444
Fragment of a two-edged
Bronze Sword, and another
weapon, probably a Dagger.
Sepulchre IV.   Half-size.

hardly possible that it can be a lance, and I think it is a long dagger-knife, the handle of which has been made hollow, merely to make the weapon less heavy. No. 443 is a fragment of the blade of a two-edged bronze sword, whose ridge is serrated on both sides, either for the sake of ornamentation, or for the purpose of making the wounds inflicted with the sword more dangerous. Another weapon (No. 444) is formed by soldering two or three long narrow thick plates of bronze; and in the interior of the lower part, which is round, we see a great many small bronze pins, whose presence is just as inexplicable as the use of the weapon itself. From the point where the lower crevice ends, it is quadrangular; but its thickness gradually diminishes towards the end, which forms a small but sharp horizontal edge. There are sixteen marks of small nails or pins in the left border of the lower crevice, which lead me to venture the opinion that the lower round part must have been fixed in a handle of wood or bone, and that the weapon may have been used as a dagger. I may here mention that the Trojan Treasure contained two weapons similar in form but of one solid piece of metal.*

There is also a lance-head, with a tube for the shaft, but without rings such as those of the lance, No. 441; also a very peculiar fragment of the blade of a double-edged

---

* See 'Troy and its Remains,' p. 332, Nos. 267 and 268.

sword, on which the high protruding middle part or ridge is very conspicuous; further, the fragment of a blade of a short two-edged sword, on which we still see remnants of the wooden sheath. At its lower end there are, on either side, three large round flat golden pin-heads, by which it was fastened to the handle. I also mention the fragments of three very long two-edged sword-blades, of which two have retained remnants of their wooden sheaths. The first is 2 ft., the second 2½ ft., the third 1 ft. 9 in. long; but when entire, every one of them has probably been more than 3 ft. in length. All show, at either side of their lower end, the flat heads of the pins by which they were attached to the handles. On all three we see the protruding ridge. I must still notice two sword-blades and an alabaster sword-handle knob adorned with two large flat golden nail-heads (Nos. 445, *a*, *b*, *c*). Perfectly similar alabaster knobs, but without golden nails, were found by me at Troy, but I did not know then that they belonged to sword-handles, and I fancied they had served as handles

Nos. 445, *a*, *b*, *c*.
Two-edged Bronze Swords and
an Alabaster Sword-Knob.
Sepulchre IV.
Size, 1 : 6, about.

to house doors, or on walking-sticks.* The two-edged sword-blade (No. 445*a*), at the top of which are still attached remnants of the wooden sheath, measures 2 ft. 7 in.

---

* See 'Troy and its Remains,' p. 265.

in length.   On either side of its lower end we see the four bronze nails with flat heads, by which it was fastened to the handle.   The lower end of the sword-blade, No. 445c, is

adorned with three flat golden pin-heads on each side.

I further mention a long knife, with part of its bone handle, the extremity of which has evidently had a curve; also, the blade of a short two-edged sword, showing at the lower end, on each side, four large flat golden pin-heads (No. 446). A gold plate extends all along the middle part of the blade on both sides, and remnants of the wooden sheath are visible in the middle as well as at the end. I need only mention the fragments of four two-edged sword-blades. The middle part of the one is serrated all along. The lower extremity of another is, on either side, plated with gold and adorned with three large flat golden pin-heads; the gold-plated part is very distinct. No. 447 represents one of several alabaster sword-handle knobs, each ornamented with two golden pins or nails. Nos. 448 and 449 are sword-blades, of which the longer one (No 448) is very well preserved, and is 2 ft. 10 in. long. No. 449 has retained part of its

No. 446.
Two-edged Bronze Sword.
Sepulchre IV. Half-size.*

handle, which is plated with gold and attached by gold pins; all along the surface of the blade we see vertical lines of intaglio work, which give to the weapon a beautiful aspect.

* For an engraving of this sword, after cleaning, see Appendix D.

Another fragment of a large beautiful bronze sword has the blade plated with gold in its entire length, the handle being also thickly plated with gold and adorned with magnificent intaglio work. But it has suffered so much in the funeral fire, and it is so dirty from the smoke and ashes, that the ornamentation cannot be discerned in the photograph, and, therefore, I cannot give an engraving of it. Mr. Newton justly remarks regarding the Mycenean swords: "The ridge or thread on some of the swords is raised so high down the centre of the blade as to suggest the idea that this weapon was used like a rapier, only for thrusting."

I here call particular attention to the extreme narrowness of nearly all the Mycenean swords, and to the enormous length of most of them, which seems in a great many cases to have exceeded 3 feet; in fact, they are, in general, not broader than our rapiers. So far as I know, swords of this shape have never been found before.

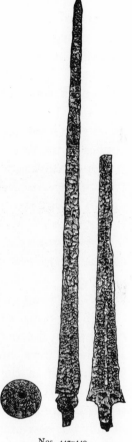

Nos. 447–449.
Two-edged Bronze Swords and an
Alabaster Sword-Knob.
Sepulchre IV. Size 1 : 8, about.

With some of the swords I found traces of well-woven linen, small particles of which were still attached to the sword-blades ; and there can consequently be no doubt that many swords had sheaths of linen.

I further collected in this tomb a large quantity of oyster-shells and many entire oysters, which had never been opened, from which I conclude that, as in the funeral customs of ancient Egypt, food was laid in the tombs

of the deceased. There was found in this sepulchre, as well
as in all the other tombs, a large quantity of broken
pottery, on seeing which, Mr. Panagiotes Eustratiades,
Director-General of Antiquities, reminded me of the habit
still existing in Greece, of breaking vases filled with water
on the tombs of departed friends. Mr. Eustratiades also
mentioned to me that copper kettles and vases were the
great ornaments of the houses, not only in antiquity, but
throughout all the Middle Ages until the Greek revolution. This is, so far, very well ; but, except these
Mycenean sepulchres, the cemetery of Hallstatt, and the
tombs of Corneto and Palestrina, we have not yet found
an example to prove that they served to ornament the
abodes of the dead.

One handle of a hand-made vase found in this tomb
particularly attracted my attention by its six perforations,
one of which was large enough for a thick string to pass
through, and it may, therefore, have served for suspension ;
but the other five would be too small even for a fine
thread, and they can, therefore, never have served for
suspension, and I suppose they were merely used to put
flowers in, as an ornament.

Of the bones of the five bodies of this tomb, as well as
of those of the bodies in the other sepulchres, I collected
all which were not too much decayed, and they will
be exhibited in the National Museum at Athens together
with the treasures. Of course the contents of each
sepulchre are to be kept separate. I give here an engraving
of only the best-preserved jaw (No. 450), with thirteen well-
preserved teeth ; three only are missing.

There were further found two broken alabaster vases,
and a pedestal of alabaster to stand vases on, besides a
very large quantity of fragments of hand-made or very
ancient wheel-made pottery. To the former category
belongs a vase, which has been wrought to a lustrous
surface by hand-polishing. It has had two handles, but

only one is preserved. Another vase is a beautiful specimen of the most ancient Mycenean wheel-made pottery. It has four handles, and on a light yellow dead ground an ornamentation of dark-red colour representing spirals, circular bands, and circles, filled with a network of lines.

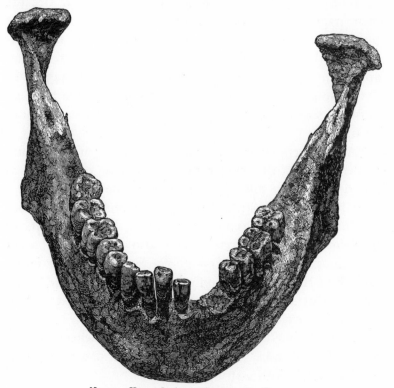

No. 450. Human Jawbone. Sepulchre IV. Size 3 : 4.

In this tomb, as well as in the four others, were found many fragments of that kind of terra-cotta goblet which maintained its form here for more than 1,000 years without any modification; only its colour and mode of fabrication varied, for, while in the sepulchres we find it of a light green colour with a beautiful black spiral ornamentation, we find it afterwards of a plain light green colour. but still hand-made. In later times we find it

either of a uniform lustrous plain dark red colour or of a
a light yellow dead colour with numerous dark red and
black bands, as shown in previous illustrations.*   In still
later times we find it with no other colour than the light
yellow or white of the clay itself.†   Goblets of this
latter sort must have been in use here for a great number
of centuries and until the capture of the city, because
their fragments are found in enormous quantities, and of
their feet I could have collected thousands of specimens.   We have also a number of specimens of this
goblet in gold, such as that shown under No. 343.‡   In
Troy I found this very same form of goblet in the first and
most ancient of the prehistoric cities, at a depth of about
50 ft.§

As a specimen of the only other type of terra-cotta
goblet I refer the reader to one already mentioned as
found in the first tomb.‖   It represents the lower part of a
large hand-made lustrous black goblet, with a hollow foot
and horizontal flutings in the middle.   But fragments of
this sort of goblets were found also in the four other
sepulchres.   This form of goblet is very rarely found
outside of the tombs, and only here and there in the lowest
strata.   But I found it in the ruins of the most ancient
prehistoric city at Troy.

In this fourth tomb were found two whetstones of
fine hard sandstone.   Both have at the top a perforation
for suspension with a string.

I have further to mention among the objects discovered in this tomb the beautiful golden cylinder (No.
451), and the splendid golden handle terminating in a
dragon's head (No. 452).   Both these objects undoubtedly
belong to each other, and most probably composed the

---

* See Nos. 84, 88, p. 71.
† No. 83, p. 70.   ‡ See p. 233.
§ See my 'Atlas des Antiquités Troyennes,' Pl. 105, No. 2311.
‖ See No. 230, p. 154.

handle of a sceptre, an augur's staff, or something of similar importance, for both offer the unique example among the Mycenean antiquities of gold incrusted with a sort of mosaic of rock-crystal. To examine first the golden cylinder (No. 451); it consists of four-leaved flowers united at the points of the leaves. Each of the latter shows in all its length a flat oval hollow incrusted with a piece of rock-crystal, which exactly fits into it.

Nos. 451, 452.   A Golden Tube ; and a Golden Dragon with scales of rock crystal, both being probably pieces of a sceptre-handle.   Sepulchre IV.   Size 3 : 4.

Between every two flowers is a square space with curved sides, which is also filled up with well-fitting pieces of rock-crystal. Of these latter only one can be seen in the engraving before us in the middle of the right side of the cylinder, as it is represented; the other pieces, which are mostly preserved, will be put in again as soon as the Archæological Society shall be able to exhibit the Mycenean collection.

The appearance of the cylinder, when all the transparent crystal pieces were in their places, must have been of marvellous beauty. The golden handle with the dragon's head (No. 452), which belongs to the cylinder, is hollow, and still contains *débris* of the wood with which it was filled. The head of the dragon, with its large eyes, of which one only appears in the engraving, as well as its open jaws, can be distinctly seen. The scales of the dragon have been skilfully imitated by means of small beautifully-cut pieces of rock-crystal, which fit so well into the small symmetrical hollows prepared for them in the gold, that only one of them has as yet fallen out. This is the more astonishing as the handle represents the most unmistakable marks of the fire to which it has been exposed on the funeral pile. If Homer had seen this extraordinary handle when it was entire, he would undoubtedly have ascribed it to the skilful hand of Hephæstus, and would have uttered his sense of its beauty in the words θαῦμα ἰδέσθαι, "a wonder to look upon."

NOTE ON THE ROYAL PALACE.

I omitted to mention, in Chapter V., that in my opinion the ruins extant to the south of the Agora, in which we see no windows, can be only the *substructions* of the Royal Palace. I would further suggest that all these substructions reached only to the level of the great Cyclopean circuit wall, and that upon them was built the palace proper, of wood. This opinion seems to be corroborated by the tremendous quantities of yellow wood-ashes with which the interior of those substructions was filled up, as well as by the impossibility of admitting that the Royal Palace should have had no windows, and should have been built in the deep hollow, so as to be shut out by the great Cyclopean wall from any view of the lower city and the plain.

No. 474. Massive Golden Mask of the body at the south end of the First Sepulchre. Size 1 : 3, about. (For description, see page 312.)

CHAPTER IX.

The Fifth Sepulchre, and the First Again.

At length again a guard and watchfire on the Acropolis of Mycenæ — Exploration of the *Fifth Tomb* — Its sepulchral *stêlæ* — The tomb described ; containing only one body — Golden diadem and other objects found in the tomb—Hand-made vases of terra-cotta ; one with female breasts, like the prehistoric vases at Santorin and Troy— Wheel-made pottery—Excavation of the *First Tomb* completed— Its position and construction—Three bodies in it : the middle one has been disturbed and rifled of its ornaments—Large size of the bodies—Golden mask and state of the first—Wonderful preservation of the third—Its ponderous gold mask, face, and teeth—Description of the body—its remarkable compression—Golden breast-plate, and leaves of gold on the forehead, eyes, and breast—Excitement caused by the discovery — Measures taken to preserve and remove the body—Its shoulder-belt and bronze sword with crystal ornament, and disks of gold for the sheath : all special funeral ornaments, and not for ordinary use—Description of the golden breast-covers

of this and the first body — Highly-decorated bronze swords and
other objects found with the third body—Ornamented golden leaves,
a wooden comb, and bronze swords, with the second body — A
large heap of broken bronze swords, with knives and lances—Other
weapons, chiefly in fragments — Amber and gold beads, and various
objects of gold and silver — An alabaster vase — Wonderful plates
of gold — The two massive golden masks of the first tomb—The
skilled work argues a long-trained school of artists—Several large
goblets of gold and silver — Objects in this sepulchre — A silver
vase, with copper and gold plating—A drinking-cup of alabaster—
Plates of gold, in form of double eagles, &c.—Fragments of silver
vases ; one with a gold mouth-piece and handle—A splendidly ornamented plate of gold, covering a cylinder of charred wood—Hundreds
of gold button-plates, large and small, with various ornamentation—
The new types shown — Gold plates, ribbons, and ornaments for
greaves — Tubes and buttons of bone ; their probable use — An
ivory plate, and a curious object of glazed Egyptian porcelain —
Hand-made and wheel-made pottery — Seven large copper vessels,
caldrons and cans—A quadrangular wooden box, with most interesting reliefs.

Mycenæ, 6th December, 1876.

FOR the first time since its capture by the Argives in
468 B.C., and so for the first time during 2,344 years,
the Acropolis of Mycenæ has a garrison, whose watch-
fires seen by night throughout the whole Plain of Argos
carry back the mind to the watch kept for Agamemnon's
return from Troy, and the signal which warned Clytemnestra and her paramour of his approach.‡ But this time the
object of the occupation by soldiery is of a more peaceful
character, for it is merely intended to inspire awe among
the country-people, and to prevent them from making
clandestine excavations in the tombs, or approaching them
while we are working in them.

Already while engaged in the excavation of the large,
Fourth Tomb, the results of which I have described, I
explored the *Fifth and last Sepulchre*, which is immediately
to the north-west of it (see Plan B and the Ichnography,

---

* See the opening scene of the *Agamemnon* of Æschylus.

Plate VI.), and which had been marked by the large *stêlé* with the bas-relief of frets or key-patterns resembling two serpents, and by an unsculptured tombstone, both of which were 11 ft. 8 in. below the surface of the mount, as it was when I began the excavation. At a depth of 10 ft. below the two sepulchral *stêlæ*, or of 21 ft. 8 in. below the former surface, I found two unsculptured *stêlæ*, evidently much older; and, only 3 ft. 4 in. below these, I found a tomb 11 ft. 6 in. long and 9 ft. 8 in. broad, which had been cut out in the calcareous rock to a depth of only 2 ft., so that its bottom is 27 ft. below the former surface of the mount. Unlike the other tombs, the four inner sides of this sepulchre were not lined with walls, but merely with large pieces of schist, which were placed in a slanting position against the low border of the tomb, and had not been joined with clay.

As usual, the bottom of the tomb was strewn with a layer of pebbles, on which I found the mortal remains of only one person, with the head turned towards the east, which, like all the other bodies, had been burned on the precise spot where it lay. This was proved by the calcined pebbles below and around the corpse, as well as by the undisturbed masses of ashes with which it was covered, and finally by the marks of the funeral fire on the walls of rock. Around the skull of the body, which was unfortunately too fragile to be saved, was a golden diadem, similar to those already represented, with an ornamentation in *repoussé* work, showing in the middle three shield-like circles, with flowers or a wheel in rotation; the remaining space being filled up with beautiful spirals.

On the right side of the body I found a lance-head with a ring on either side, like that already shown;† also, two small bronze swords and two long knives of the same metal. On its left was found the gold drinking-cup now repre-

---

* See No. 441, p. 279.

sented (No. 453). It has only one handle, and its ornamentation in *repoussé* work exhibits four horizontal bands,
joined two and two, and ornamented with slanting strokes
which converge in the form of wedges, so that the ornamentation of every two bands conjointly resembles fish-
spines ; and in order to enhance still more the beauty of
these bands, the wedges of each two bands point in opposite

No. 453. A richly ornamented Cup of Gold. Sepulchre V. Size 9 : 10, about.

directions. The whole upper part is ornamented with a
continuous row of pointed arches, the joined sides of
which are adorned with nine horizontal strokes. The
handle is fastened with four nails to the rim and the body
of the goblet. With the swords were found small rags of
beautifully-woven linen, which, doubtless, belonged to the
sheaths of these weapons.

In the same tomb was found a fragmented light green
vase, 6½ in. high, of Egyptian porcelain, ornamented with
two rows of protruding bosses, three in each row ; also

fragments of a light red vase of terra-cotta, ornamented with black spiral lines, and with two female breasts surrounded by circles of black strokes. Professor Landerer, who has examined and analysed a fragment of the former vase, writes me that the porcelain is very calcareous, and would be called in mineralogy "Thonmergel-schiefer" (clay-marl-slate); that the borders, examined with a magnifying glass in the sun, exhibit a gold-like and silvery glaze, produced by a lead varnish with which the vase was covered and which was afterwards burned in.

With regard to this vase with the female breasts, similar vases were found on the islands of Thera (Santorin) and Therassia, in the ruins of the prehistoric cities which, as before stated, were covered by an eruption of that great central volcano which is believed by competent geologists to have sunk and disappeared about 1,700 to 1,800 B.C. They are also very frequent in the ruins of Troy, where, however, most of them have also a navel and an owl-face.*

There were further found in this tomb, besides a mass of fragments of hand-made pottery, fragments of beautiful wheel-made pottery, ornamented with plants turned into spirals; and other fragments, which present on a light yellow dead colour a magnificent ornamentation of dark red spirals.

The mud in the *First Sepulchre*, whose site had been marked by the three *stêlæ* with low reliefs, having dried up in the fine weather, I continued the excavation there, and struck at last the bottom of the tomb, which is cut out in the rock, 17½ ft. deep on the north side, and 17 ft. deep on the south-east side. But from these points the slope is so abrupt that, although the upper breadth of the sepulchre does not exceed 10 ft. 10 in., yet the greater part of its west side needed only to be cut 11 ft. deep into

---

* See 'Troy and its Remains,' p. 35, No. 13; p. 106, No. 70; p. 307, No. 219.

the rock to make a level bottom. This west side is close
to the Cyclopean wall, with the parallel double row of large
calcareous slabs, which forms the enclosure and benches
of the Agora, and rises vertically over the sepulchre. (See
Plans B and C.) For all these reasons it appeared to me,
on first excavating this tomb, that the wall passed through
its north-west angle. But, by propping up with planks and
beams the earth and stones which cling to the wall and
overhang the north-west corner of the tomb, I have now
cleared the latter in its entire length, and visitors will perceive that the wall does not pass through the tomb but
merely touches its brink in the north-west corner.

The length of the tomb is 21 ft. 6 in., its breadth at
the bottom is 11 ft. 6 in., and thus 8 in. more than at the
top. The four inner sides were lined with a Cyclopean
wall, 3 ft. high and 2 ft. broad; and this had superposed
on it a slanting wall of schist plates joined with clay,
which reached to a height of 6½ ft., and projected on all
sides a foot more than the Cyclopean wall, and thus in
all 3 feet on the bottom of the tomb. The latter was
covered with the usual layer of pebbles, which were, however, more irregularly strewn than in the other tombs,
there being places without any pebbles; which circumstance made me at first believe that there was no layer
of pebbles at all in this tomb. But on careful examination,
I found such a layer, and below the bodies I found it just
as regular as in any other tomb, which circumstance appears
to give an additional proof that those layers of pebbles
were merely intended to procure ventilation for the pyres.

The three bodies which the sepulchre contained lay at
a distance of about 3 ft. from each other, and had been
burnt in the very same place where I found them. This
was evident from the marks of the fire on the pebbles and
on the rock below and also around the bodies, and to the
right and left of them on the walls, as well as from the
undisturbed state of the ashes. Only with the body which

lay in the midst the case was different. The ashes had evidently been disturbed; the clay with which the two other bodies and their ornaments were covered, and the layer of pebbles which covered the clay, had been removed from this body. As, besides, it was found almost without any gold ornaments, it is evident that it had been rifled. This opinion is also confirmed by the twelve golden buttons, the small golden plates, and the numerous small objects of bone, which had been found together with small quantities of black ashes at different depths below the three sculptured tombstones which adorned this sepulchre. It is further confirmed by the fragments of the usual Mycenean pottery of later times, which in this tomb were mixed up with the very ancient hand-made or wheel-made vases. Most likely some one sank a shaft to examine the tomb, struck the body in question, plundered it recklessly, and for fear of being detected, carried off his booty in such a hurry that he only thought of saving the large massive gold ornaments, such as the mask, the large breast-cover, the diadems and the bronze swords, and, in remounting to the surface, dropped many of the smaller objects, such as the twelve golden buttons, etc., which I found at intervals in digging down. There can be no doubt that this larceny occurred *before* the capture of Mycenæ by the Argives (468 B.C.); for, if it had been committed while the later Greek city stood on the top of the prehistoric ruins, I should also have found fragments of Greek pottery in the tomb; but of these I saw no vestige.

The three bodies of this tomb lay with their heads to the east and their feet to the west; all three were of large proportions, and appeared to have been forcibly squeezed into the small space of only 5 ft. 6 in. which was left for them between the inner walls. The bones of the legs, which are almost uninjured, are unusually large. Although the head of the first man, from the south side, was covered with a massive golden mask, his skull crumbled away on being exposed to the air, and only a few bones could be saved besides those of the legs. The same was the case with the second body, which had been plundered in antiquity.

But of the third body, which lay at the north end of the tomb, the round face, with all its flesh, had been wonderfully preserved under its ponderous golden mask; there was no vestige of hair, but both eyes were perfectly visible, also the mouth, which, owing to the enormous weight that had pressed upon it, was wide open, and showed thirty-two beautiful teeth. From these, all the physicians who came to see the body were led to believe that the man must have died at the early age of thirty-five. The nose was entirely gone. The body having been too long for the space between the two inner walls of the tomb, the head had been pressed in such a way on the breast, that the upper part of the shoulders was nearly in a horizontal line with the vertex of the head. Notwithstanding the large golden breast-plate, so little had been preserved of the breast, that the inner side of the spine was visible in many places. In its squeezed and mutilated state, the body measured only 2 ft. 4½ in. from the top of the head to the beginning of the loins; the breadth of the shoulders did not exceed 1 ft. 1¼ in., and the breadth of the chest 1 ft. 3 in.; but the large thigh-bones could leave no doubt regarding the real proportions of the body. Such had been the pressure of the *débris* and stones, that the body had been reduced to a thickness of 1 in. to 1½ in. The colour of the body resembled very much that of an Egyptian mummy. The forehead was ornamented with a plain round leaf of gold, and a still larger one was lying on the right eye; I further observed a large and a small gold leaf on the breast below the large golden breast-cover, and a large one just above the right thigh.

The news that the tolerably well preserved body of a man of the mythic heroic age had been found, covered with golden ornaments, spread like wildfire through the Argolid, and people came by thousands from Argos, Nauplia, and the villages to see the wonder. But, nobody

No. 454. The upper part of a Body found in the First Tomb.
From an Oil Painting made directly after its discovery.

being able to give advice how to preserve the body, I sent for a painter to get at least an oil-painting made, for I was afraid that the body would crumble to pieces. Thus I am enabled to give a faithful likeness of the body, as it looked after all the golden ornaments had been removed. But to

my great joy, it held out for two days, when a druggist
from Argos, Spiridon Nicolaou by name, rendered it hard
and solid by pouring on it alcohol, in which he had dissolved gum-sandarac. As there appeared to be no pebbles
below it it was thought that it would be possible to lift it
on an iron plate; but this was a mistake, because it was
soon discovered that there was the usual layer of pebbles
below the body, and all of these having been more or less
pressed into the soft rock by the enormous weight which
had been lying for ages upon them, all attempts made to
squeeze in the iron plate below the pebble-stones, so as to
be able to lift them together with the body, utterly failed.
There remained, therefore, no other alternative than to
cut a small trench into the rock all round the body, and
make thence a horizontal incision, so as to cut out a slab,
two inches thick, to lift it with the pebble-stones and the
body, to put it upon a strong plank, to make around the
latter a strong box, and to send this to the village of
Charvati, whence it will be forwarded to Athens as soon
as the Archæological Society shall have got a suitable
locality for the Mycenean antiquities. With the miserable
instruments alone available here it was no easy task to
detach the large slab horizontally from the rock, but it was
still much more difficult to bring it in the wooden box
from the deep sepulchre to the surface, and to transport
it on men's shoulders for more than a mile to Charvati.
But the capital interest which this body of the remote
heroic age has for science, and the buoyant hope of
preserving it, made all the labour appear light.*

The now nearly mummified body was decorated with a
golden shoulder-belt (τελαμών), 4 ft. long and 1¾ in. broad,

---

* I think it my duty to state here that the Archæological Society in
Athens has alone incurred all the trouble and expense of *drugging* the
body so as to render it hard and solid, and raising it from the sepulchre
and carrying it to the village of Charvati, and that I have had no
trouble or expense from this operation.

which, for some cause or other, was not in its place, for it now lay across the loins of the body, and extended in a straight line far to the right of it.   In its midst is suspended, and firmly attached, the fragment of a double-edged bronze sword (see No. 455), and to this latter was accidentally

No. 455.   A Golden Shoulder-belt (τελαμών), with a fragment of the two-edged Sword.
Sepulchre I.   Size 1 : 4.

attached a beautifully-polished perforated object of rock crystal, in form of a jar (πίθος), with two silver handles. It is pierced in its entire length by a silver pin.   This little object has unfortunately been detached in removing the treasure from Charvati to Athens, and thus I represent it separately (No. 456). Together with the shoulder-belt and the little crystal jar was found the small object of

No. 456.
A small Jar of rock crystal.
Sepulchre I. Actual size.

rock-crystal (No. 457), which has the shape of a funnel. In the extremity of the shoulder-belt, to the left of the spectator, are two perforations; at the other end there has probably been a clasp, because there are no perforations; on the fragment of the sword we see one of those small shield-like or button-like golden disks, with an ornamentation of *repoussé* work, which have decorated the sheaths of the swords in uninterrupted rows, their size being always determined by the breadth of the

No. 457.
A funnel-shaped
object, of rock cry-
stal. Sepulchre I.
Actual size.

sheaths. The disk before us is divided by three concentric circles into three circular compartments, of which the outer and the central one represent a number of ornaments resembling horse-shoes. A glance at this shoulder-belt will convince every one that it is by far too thin and fragile to have been worn by living men. Besides, I feel certain that no living warrior has ever gone to battle with swords in sheaths of wood ornamented on either side with rows of gold plates, which are merely glued on the wood. Thus, we may consider it beyond all doubt that a great part of all the golden ornaments have been expressly prepared for funeral use. There was also found an alabaster stand for a vase.

The massive golden breast-plate of this same body is perfectly plain, and it is therefore unnecessary to engrave it. It is $15\frac{3}{5}$ in. long and $9\frac{1}{2}$ in. broad; it has no ornamentation, but two protruding breasts can be distinctly seen; they are not, however, in the middle, as they ought to be, but more to the right of the spectator. While speaking of breast-covers, I may as well give here the

breast-cover of the body at the southern end of this first
tomb (No. 458). It is 1 ft. 9 in. long and 1 ft. 2⅗ in.

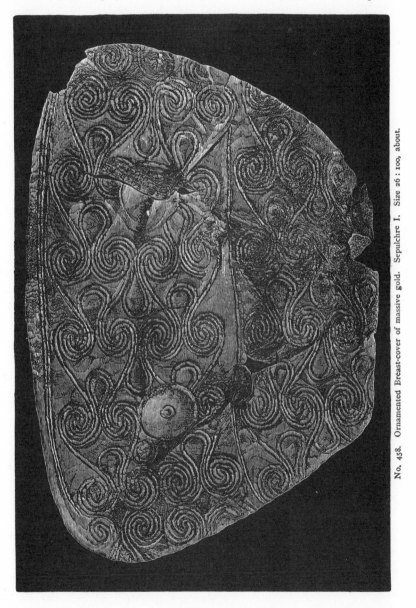

No. 458. Ornamented Breast-cover of massive gold. Sepulchre I. Size 26 : 100, about.

broad. Here the two breasts are well represented by
two protruding shield-like bosses, and the whole re-

maining space is richly ornamented with beautiful spirals in *repoussé* work.

The best preserved parts of the same body, at the southern end of the tomb, are two large bones and a small bone. On the latter, which is probably an arm-bone, is still attached a broad golden ribbon, with a splendid ornamentation of *repoussé* work (No. 459).

No. 459.
Small Bone, with the fragment of a splendidly ornamented Gold Ribbon. Sepulchre I. Size 3 : 8.

I return to the body at the northern extremity. To its right lay the two bronze swords represented under No. 460, and close to them all the other objects just as we see them in this engraving. The handle of the upper sword is of bronze, but thickly plated with gold, which is all over covered with a magnificent intaglio work of the most varied description. On the upper part of the handle, where the blade issues from it, is fastened a broad curved gold plate with splendid intaglio work, similar to that represented below (No. 462),* of which we only here recognise the exact use. No doubt this sword has had a wooden sheath, which must have been ornamented with the long gold plate, with a ring and much resembling the shape of a man, which we see to the right of it. This gold plate is similar to that represented under No. 369.† The sheath must have been further adorned with the golden button, with engraved concentric circles, which we see close to the blade. Much still richer has evidently been the ornamentation of the other bronze sword,

---

* See p. 305.   † See p. 253.

for its wooden sheath must evidently have been adorned, in its entire length, on both sides, with a series of those large golden buttons with a magnificent intaglio work of spirals which we see below and on the right side of the sword. The sheath has evidently been also adorned with the tubular golden plate, ornamented with spirals in intaglio work, which we still see around the sword.

The handle of this sword must have been of wood, because it has entirely disappeared, and it must necessarily have been adorned with the two quadrangular golden plates which we see lying, still closely joined together, in the very place where the knob of the handle ought to have been; only on the small side, which is turned towards the spectator, the two plates are slightly disjoined. They are perfectly similar in size and shape to that shown a little later under No. 472 ;** See p. 311. both have exactly the same ornamentation in *repoussé* work of interwoven spirals; and, as on No. 472, we see

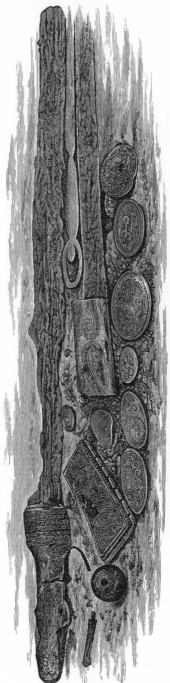

No. 460.   Two Bronze Swords with golden handles ; golden buttons belonging to the destroyed wooden sheaths ; two gold plates, &c. ; found lying beside a body in Sepulchre I.   Size 1 : 3, about.

in their long sides the marks of a number of small pins, which must have served to attach both plates to a piece of wood which stuck between them, and of which some traces remain.   This piece of wood must have been very

thin, for otherwise the two plates could not after its disappearance have fallen together so exactly as to appear still joined.   Certainly they must have served as ornaments of the sword-handle, but how this was done is altogether inexplicable to me.   I find it impossible to suppose that the sword-handle terminated in a thin piece of wood, so as to be fastened between the two plates; besides, this is contradicted by their raised borders.   With the two plates was found a bead of amber, the presence of which here must be only accidental, for of course it can have nothing in common with the swords.   To one of these swords was doubtless attached the golden tassel represented under No. 461, which I found near them. Probably all these weapons had been suspended on a belt of embroidered work which has disappeared.

No. 461.
A Gold Sword-tassel.
Sepulchre I.   Size 5 : 8.

At a distance of hardly more than one foot to the right of the body I found eleven bronze swords, of which nine had suffered more or less from moisture; but the other two were pretty well preserved.   One of them has the enormous length of 3 ft. 2 in., the other of 2 ft. 10 in.   With the swords I found the two golden plates represented under No. 462, both of which have belonged to sword-handles; that to the left having been on the upper part of the handle, to which it was attached with no less than twelve gold pins, of which five with large globular heads are still visible. This object is so thickly covered with ashes of the funeral fire that but little of its spiral ornamentation in intaglio can be discerned. The other golden plate has been used as the cover of the wooden sword-handle, and it is perfectly similar to those which we passed in review in describing the discoveries in the fourth tomb (see Nos. 430, 431).

I further found with the swords three tubes of gold

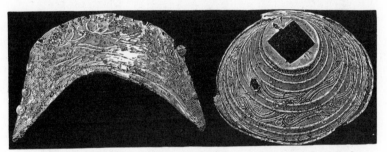

No. 462.   Golden Covers of Sword-handles, with intaglio ornamentation.   Sepulchre I.
Size 4 : 9.

plate, one 12½ in. long, another 10½ in. long, both containing remnants of wood, and the third 5⅗ in. long. There were also 124 large round gold buttons, plain or with splendid intaglio work, two of which are two inches in diameter, and four of the size of five-franc pieces; the other 118 are smaller. Further, six large splendidly-ornamented golden buttons in the form of crosses, three of which are 3 in. long and 2¼ in. broad. All these buttons consist either of flat pieces of wood covered with gold plates, and in this case they have invariably been pasted or soldered as embellishments on sword-sheaths or other objects, or they are real wood buttons resembling our present shirt-studs and covered with gold plates, and in this case they must have been used on clothes. The magnificently engraved ornamentation of both these kinds of buttons can leave no doubt as to the importance attached to them. I may add that in this tomb not only all the cruciform gold buttons, but also all the very large round gold buttons, have on their lower side a flat piece of wood.

Nos. 463–466.   Bronze Battle-axe and Swords.   Sepulchre I.   Size 1 : 4, about.

With the body which lay in the middle of the tomb were found some round leaves of gold with an impressed ornamentation, and the remnants of a wooden comb. With the body at the south end of the sepulchre I found fifteen bronze swords, ten of which lay at his feet. Eight of them are of very large size, and tolerably well preserved.

A large heap of more or less broken bronze swords, which may have represented more than sixty entire ones, was found on the west side, between the last-mentioned body and the middle one ; also a few bronze knives and lances. Very remarkable is the battle-axe, No. 463, for I have never yet found this shape here, but I very frequently found it in Troy, and fourteen of them were contained in the Trojan treasure.* Compared with our present axes, this Mycenean and the Trojan battle-axes have no hole in which the wooden handle could be fixed, and thus they had evidently been fastened in or on the handle instead of the handle being fastened in them. Some of the swords show traces of having been gilded; several of them have golden pins at the handle. The other weapons shown under Nos. 464, 465, and 466, are short swords. At the lower end of No. 465 are remnants of gold-plating.

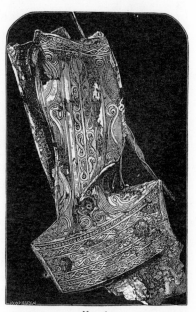

No. 467.
Sword-handle, plated with gold, richly ornamented. Sepulchre I. Half-size.

I also found, with the body at the south end of the tomb, the large handle with a fragment of a bronze sword represented under No. 467. This handle is covered with thick gold plate richly ornamented with intaglio work, which can be well distinguished, though the handle is very dirty from the smoke and ashes of the funeral pyre. The ornamentation is exactly the same on both sides. In

---

* See 'Troy and its Remains,' pp. 330, 331.

the hollow of the handle is still preserved part of the wood
with which it was once filled.

I also found with the body at the southern end a large
quantity of amber beads and five small plain cylinders of
gold plate (in one of which still sticks a piece of wood),
which have evidently covered a stick, perhaps a sceptre;
further seven large sword-handle knobs of alabaster and
one of wood, all ornamented with gold
nails; a small piece of gold in the form of a
bar of a watch-chain (see No. 468), which
cannot but have served as a sort of clasp
to a shoulder-belt (τελαμών); thirty-seven
round gold leaves of various sizes, twenty-
one fragments of gold leaves, two fragmentary silver vases, a pair of silver tongs
or tweezers (see No. 469), and a large vase
of alabaster, with a mouthpiece of bronze,
plated with gold. The perforations on three
sides in the upper part of the body can
leave no doubt that this vase has had three
handles, and the large round hole with four
small perforations in front show that it has
had a pipe. In this vase I found thirty-two

Nos. 468, 469.
A curious Object of
Gold, and Silver
Tongs. Sepulchre I.
Actual size.

small and three large round gold buttons
with rich intaglio patterns, as well as two
gold buttons in the shape of crosses, each
with two very small golden handles; further
a large gold button of conical shape, and a wedge-shaped
golden tube.

The following engravings represent three more of those
wonderful gold plates, two of which we have already passed
in review in explaining the objects engraved under No. 460.
There were found twelve of them in all, to the right and
left of the body at the northern extremity of the tomb.
No. 470 represents a lion chasing a stag; the four feet of
the former are in a horizontal line to show the great speed

with which he is running; he has just overtaken the stag, which sinks down before him, and his jaws are wide open to devour it. The head of the lion, as well as the mane, are pretty well represented. On the other hand, the repre-

No. 470. A Gold Plate, with Intaglio of a Lion chasing a Stag. Sepulchre I. Actual size.

sentation of the stag, which has no horns, is clumsy and indistinct; beyond it we see an animal with spines and a long fishtail, probably a sea monster. Above the lion are represented two long palm-fronds, and below it the crowns of two palm-trees and a palm-frond.

• No. 471. A Gold Plate, with Intaglio of a Lion catching a Stag. Sepulchre I. Actual size.

No. 471 represents nearly the same subject: we see again a lion running at full speed and catching a stag, which is represented with the body turned towards his pursuer and with his head in the opposite direction; he

stands on his hind-legs, into which the lion, with open
jaws, is just biting. The fore-feet of the stag are uplifted,
and his lower feet protrude at a right angle from the knee.
Just before the uplifted loins of the stag we see the wide-
open jaws of a large cow-head with two long horns of the
crescent form and two enormous eyes, to which I call
particular attention. Between the two large horns we see
two smaller ones, the space between which is filled with
small objects in the form of figs; similar objects are seen
between the small and the large horns. Though the artist
has given us a front view of the cow-head, yet he represents
its jaws in profile. To the right of the cow-head we see
five long palm-fronds, below which, in the corner to the
right of the spectator, is an object which I cannot recognise; it resembles a bird's foot.

The whole scene certainly appears to be symbolic.

I think there can be no reasonable doubt that the cow-
head represents Hera Boöpis,* the patron deity of Mycenæ,
and that when, in later times, this goddess received a female
head, her enormous cow's eyes alone survived of her former
cow-shape ; because her sole characteristic epithet βοῶπις,
consecrated as it was by the use of ages, was thenceforward
indiscriminately used for both goddesses and mortal women
to designate large eyes. Thus, for example, Clymene, one
of Helen's female servants, is called by Homer ox-eyed †
(βοῶπις). Hera's representation here, with a double pair
of horns and the fruits between the four horns, can, I think,
have no other purpose than to glorify her. I further
believe that the lion represents the house of the Pelopids,
and perhaps Agamemnon himself, and that the stag represents a sacrifice offered by the lion (the house of the
Pelopids or Agamemnon himself) to the patron deity of

---

* Homer's βοῶπις πότνια Ἥρη, "our lady Hera with the head of a
cow;" hence "cow-faced;" and then, with large eyes like a cow, or
"ox-eyed." (See Note at the end of Chapter I.)

† Il. III. 144.

the town, and the open jaws of the cow-head may have the meaning that she benignantly receives the sacrifice.

The remaining plate (No. 472) represents the same spiral ornamentation which we have so frequently passed in review.

To the reverse side of these wonderful golden plates there sticks a good deal of a blackish matter, perhaps a sort of cement, which must have served to attach them to flat pieces of wood, on each side of which must have been one plate. This opinion seems also to be confirmed by the marks of nails which we see in the rims of the plates,

No. 472. Gold Plate, with a spiral ornamentation in Intaglio. Sepulchre I. Actual size.

for the nails can, of course, only have been used to fasten them to a softer substance.

No. 473 represents the massive golden mask of the same body at the north end of the first tomb ;* unfortunately, the lower part of the forehead has been so much pressed upon the eyes and the nose, that the face is disfigured, and the features cannot be well distinguished. Highly characteristic is the large round head, the enormous forehead, and the small mouth with the thin lips.

In a perfect state of preservation, on the other hand. is the massive golden mask of the body at the south end of

---

* See Vignette to Chapter X., p. 333.

the tomb (No. 474).* Its features are altogether Hellenic and I call particular attention to the long thin nose, running in a direct line with the forehead, which is but small. The eyes, which are shut, are large, and well represented by the eyelids ; very characteristic is also the large mouth with its well-proportioned lips. The beard also is well represented, and particularly the moustaches, whose extremities are turned upwards to a point, in the form of crescents.† This circumstance seems to leave no doubt that the ancient Myceneans used oil or a sort of pomatum in dressing their hair. Both masks are of *repoussé* work, and certainly nobody will for a moment doubt that they were intended to represent the portraits of the deceased, whose faces they have covered for ages.

The question now naturally arises :—have they been made in the lifetime, or after the death, of the persons ? Probably after their death : but then we wonder again how the masks can have been made so quickly ; because here, as in all hot climates, the dead are buried within twenty-four hours after their decease ; and this must have been the custom here at all times. If Homer leaves the bodies of Patroclus and Hector for ten or twelve days unburied, it was owing to peculiar circumstances ; and if they remained well preserved, it was that Thetis dropped ambrosia into the veins of the former, and Apollo into those of the latter. However that may have been with the bodies before us, we are amazed at the skill of the ancient Mycenean gold-smiths, who could model the portraits of men in massive gold plate, and consequently could do as much as any modern goldsmith would be able to perform.

But this skill of the early Mycenean goldsmiths shows a great practice in similar work, and it can leave no doubt that they were preceded by a school of artists

---

* See Vignette to this Chapter, p. 289.
† " There is nothing new under the sun."

which had flourished for ages before such work could be produced.

There was further found to the right of the body at the north end of the sepulchre the very large gold drinking-cup, with one handle, represented under No. 475. It is 6 in. in diameter, and as much in height; it has a beautiful ornamentation in *repoussé* work, divided by a rope-like horizontal band into two compartments. The upper one represents a row of arches, founded as it were

No. 475.   Large Gold Cup.   Sepulchre I.   Size 3 : 7, about.

on high pilasters of square cut stones, and much resembling a Roman aqueduct; the lower compartment contains a wedge-like ornamentation.

In the same tomb I found another very large golden cup, which likewise has only one large broad handle (No. 476). It is $5\frac{3}{5}$ in. in diameter, and is likewise divided by a horizontal band into two compartments, both of which are decorated in *repoussé* work with two parallel horizontal rows of beautiful spirals. In these occur a large number of that curious cross, which is so frequently met with in the ruins of Troy, and which is thought to be the symbol of the holy fire, the Arani of the Brahmans.*

Another large and splendid thick gold goblet found here is represented under No. 477. It is ornamented in *repoussé* work with three lions, which are represented as running with great velocity. This goblet represents again the type of all the terra-cotta goblets at Mycenæ, with but one exception. (See Nos. 83, 84, 88.) The handles of

No. 476. Large Gold Cup. Sepulchre I. Half-size, about.

all these golden goblets are fastened to the rim and body of the vessels by gold pins with large flat heads.

There were further found two golden goblets, one of which is likewise of thick gold plate, but it is nevertheless much crumpled; it has a beautiful massive handle, of a shape which we have repeatedly passed in review in the fourth tomb. The other gold goblet has an ornamentation in *repoussé* work of two double parallel rope-like bands; the upper compartment representing a horizontal

---

* See 'Troy and its Remains,' Plate XXIV. Nos. 348, 350, 351.

zigzag line, united by vertical bands of horizontal strokes to the upper double rope-like band. The ornamentation has a remarkable resemblance to the form of the ogive-like passages in Mycenæ and Tiryns. In this latter goblet sticks a very thin and much crumpled smaller golden drinking-cup.

There were also found four silver goblets; one of them

No. 477.   A Golden Goblet.   Sepulchre I.   Size 7 : 10, about.

has a handle, but no ornamentation; the second is orna-mented in *repoussé* work with bands of double lines, which terminate at the top in bows. The other two goblets are very large, but broken and defaced; the one, whose sole ornamentation is a raised horizontal band, is still filled with ashes of the funeral pyre. The second of these is ornamented with a number of furrow-like horizontal bands, and in it sticks a smaller silver cup. To the bottom of this goblet is still attached one of the pebbles with which the bottom of the tomb is strewn.

There was also found in this first sepulchre, close to

No. 478.   The top and lower part of a large Silver Vase, from the First Sepulchre.
Size 4 : 10, about.

the body in question, a large silver vase, 2 ft. 6 in. deep and 1 ft. 8 in. in diameter in the body; but, unfortunately, it had been in contact with a saline substance, which had converted the silver into chloride, in consequence of which the vase is broken into many pieces. No. 478 represents the upper and the lower part of it, put together. Its whole body was ornamented with a *repoussé* work of interwoven spirals; the lower part with horizontal parallel flutings; but it must be distinctly understood that we see in the engraving only the *inner* side of the lower part. The mouth, as well as the band marked with strokes on the upper part of the body, are plated with copper, and the copper had been plated with gold. The bottom is entirely of copper, probably in order to give more solidity to the vessel; very likely the rim of this copper bottom had also been plated with gold. Of this vase, therefore, it may be said that the early artist endeavoured to the utmost to combine solidity with splendour.

No. 479.
A large Goblet of Alabaster.　Sepulchre I.
Size 3 : 8, about.

There was also found the large drinking-cup of alabaster represented under No. 479; it is 10¼ in. high, and its form is not unlike our present glasses.

There were further found five plates of gold in the form of double eagles, of which I represent two under No. 480; all of them are of *repoussé* work, and have exactly the same size and shape. The figures of the eagles are true

to nature, except for a spiral line which protrudes from
their neck; just below this spiral we see a long serpent
across the bodies of the two eagles: both the serpent and
the spiral may have a symbolic meaning.   The eagles are
leaning against each other with their whole body, and even
with their claws, but are turning their heads in opposite

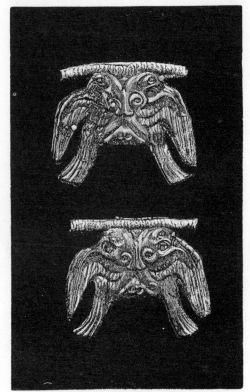

No. 480.   Double Eagles in Gold Plate.   Sepulchre I.   Actual size.

directions; above the heads we see a long tube, which can
only have served to draw the ornaments on a string for a
necklace.

There were also found five large shield-like disks, and
a small one, of thin gold plate, with an ornamentation in
repoussé work, representing in the centre a star, and around

it, within a border of two double circles of points, an
ornamentation of spirals (see No. 481). Further, two
whorl-shaped, hollow objects of gold, which fit together,
but whose use is unknown to us. Perfectly similar objects
have been represented under Nos. 425 and 426.* Further,
a fragmentary silver vase, with the beautiful golden mouth-
piece (No. 482) and the golden handle (No. 483); both

No. 481.   Gold Plate, with a pattern in *repoussé* work.   Sepulchre I.   Actual size.

having an ornamentation of *repoussé* work. In the mouth-
piece we see the six perforations by which it was fastened
with pins to the neck of the silver vase, of which we see a
fragment still attached to the handle. There were further
found two fragmentary plain silver vases, of one of which
the lower half is preserved: also a fragmentary silver
vase, with a copper bottom and mouthpiece, which latter

---

* See p. 268.

may have probably been plated with gold. Also, a large fragmentary silver vase, with a *repoussé* work of spirals;

No. 482.   Golden Mouthpiece of a Vase.   Sepulchre I.   Size 5 : 7, about.

and two large disks of copper, plated with silver, which probably belong to silver vases.

No. 483.
Golden Vase-handle.
Sepulchre I.   Actual size.

From the same tomb came the small cylinder of gold plate (No. 484), which is profusely covered with intaglio work, and still contains a piece of charred wood, to which the cylinder was attached below with three gold pins; one of these can still be seen to the right of the spectator. If we look from the top of the cylinder downward, we see that its upper part is divided by horizontal bands of three or four lines into four compartments, of which the upper one has an ornamentation of small concentric circles* the second of vertical strokes, the third again of concentric circles, and the fourth of vertical strokes; on both sides of this fourth compartment were golden pins, of which the one to the right is still in its place. The space below is divided by vertical bands into three compartments, of which those to the right and left are filled with an ornamentation of spirals, and the middle one with a tree-like band, from the top of which project, to the right and left, branch-like spirals forming circles, in which we again see small spirals: the remaining space is filled up with spirals and closely joined wedge-like ornaments. Thus we see on this cylinder not the tenth part of an inch unornamented.

No. 484.
A Cylinder of Gold Plate
Sepulchre I. Actual size.

Inclusive of the gold buttons already mentioned, there were found in this first tomb in all 340 such buttons, from most of which the wooden mould has disappeared, so that only the gold plates remain. Of these, eighty-four are plain and without any ornamentation; namely, thirty-five very large ones, being 2 in. in diameter, thirty-six of a less size, measuring 1½ in. in diameter, and thirteen small ones, measuring 1 inch or less. The remaining 256 gold buttons are ornamented with intaglio work. The total number consists of thirteen very large ones of 2 in. in diameter, thirty-nine of about 1½ in. and 194 of 1 in. or less, and eight large and two smaller ones, in form of crosses; making in all ten cross-shaped buttons, all of which have retained their wooden moulds. As before-mentioned, two of the cross-like buttons have each two small gold handles. Not to

---

* Owing to the ashes and smoke with which the cylinder is covered, the upper row of circles did not appear in the photograph.

fatigue the reader, I give no engravings of the plain buttons, and even of the richly ornamented ones I represent in the accompanying plates only those whose ornamentation shows a variance from that of the types of the buttons of the Fourth Tomb. The reader may therefore take it for granted that, of the large buttons of this First Tomb, those represented under Nos. 485–491 are the only ones whose ornamentation exhibits new types.

On No. 485, we see around three concentric circles, and within a border of two circles, a star-like ornament with curved sides and obtuse points, each of the latter containing a small circle, the space between each curve and the border being filled up by a crescent and a small circle. In 486 we

Nos. 485, 486.   Ornamented Gold Buttons.   Sepulchre I.   Actual size.

see six concentric circles around a magnificent central ornamentation of spirals of a new form; in the border an uninterrupted row of a sign which resembles the letter *koppa*.

In No. 487, we see in the centre two spirals standing opposite each other, and surrounded by five concentric circles, then by an ornamentation of four signs in the form of a cornucopia, and by four circles, which form the border. In the following button (No. 488) we see in the middle a figure approaching the oval form, within which are spirals impossible to describe, the remaining space being filled up by a small border and a large number of curved lines and two signs resembling hand-saws, with handles of a spiral form. In No. 490, we see around the central circle two borders, of which the outer one is filled with a circular row of double circles, the inner one with a circular row of signs resembling a sling with a stone in it. The ornamentation of No. 491 is very beautiful, but I find it impossible

Nos. 487–491. Ornamented Gold Buttons. Sepulchre I. Actual size.

to describe. As to the gold buttons of the second size, the only new pattern I found is No. 489; it represents in the centre a beautiful spiral in the shape of a coiled-up serpent, whose head is distinctly visible; around it are three concentric circles, and a border filled up with an ornamentation resembling a row of figs.

Nos. 492–506. Ornamented Gold Buttons. Sepulchre I. Actual size.

Of the small buttons, I represent the new types under Nos. 492–499 and 501–512. I have added a couple of those whose patterns the reader has seen before, because of superior beauty. In No. 492 we see, within a small border of two circles, a flower-like ornament, with three inner and three outer circles; in No. 493, within a border with round or square signs, a spiral in the form of a serpent; in No. 494, two concentric denticulated circles; in No. 495, a spiral ornament, which very frequently occurs both here and at Troy; in No. 496, we see two concentric circles of small triangles; in No. 497, we again see a flower. No. 498 is a massive gold button, and represents a beautiful flower; it is perforated, and it may be that it never served as a button, but as a lid of a small golden can or bottle. In No. 499, we recognise the shape of a beautiful flower with two denticulated circles; No. 501 represents the very same ornament as No. 495; No. 502 and No. 503 represent flowers. The ornamentation of No. 504 is difficult to describe; if we turn the figure to the right it resembles the bust of a man; in No. 505, we see two spirals of a new shape; in No. 506 again a flower. No. 507 exhibits a treble 卍, with the arms converted into spirals, each of them terminating in a round point, which is joined by a stroke to the usual points, the marks of the four nails. No. 508 has no other ornament than four concentric circles; in No. 509, we see only a single 卍, with curved arms and the marks of the four nails; No. 510 exhibits an ornamentation resembling three knives with handles in the form of spirals; No. 511 is identical with No. 501; and finally No. 512 shows us a figure similar to that of No. 507, with the sole difference that it is here but single and there treble.

Of the ten large cross-like buttons I give the engraving, under No. 500, of the only new pattern. As with the cross-like buttons of the fourth tomb, the wooden moulds,

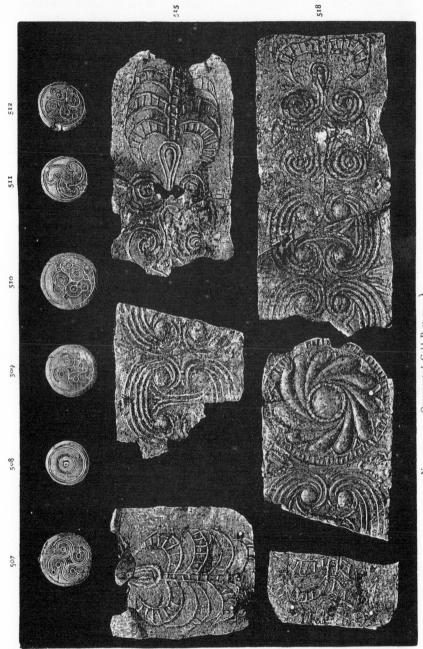

Nos. 507–512. Ornamented Gold Buttons. } Sepulchre I. Size 5 : 6.
  „ 513–518. Ornamented Gold Ribbons. }

beneath the gold plates of the ten buttons have exactly the same intaglio ornamentation which we see on the latter, and there can consequently be no doubt that the intaglio work was made when the gold plate was already fastened on the wooden buttons, and that the engraving made on the former was reproduced on the latter by the pressure of the artist's hand. The ornamentation of the cross-like button, No. 500, is as follows: it has at each acute angle of the lozenge three and at each obtuse angle two globular projections ornamented with concentric circles, and in the interior lozenge two spirals in the form of *omegas* standing opposite each other; the four angles being filled up by small circles.

Of the other cross-like buttons, not sufficiently different to require engraving, we have the following patterns. One has at each angle three globular projections, but the ornamentation consists solely of circles, which stand together, forming flowers. On another large button there are only two globular projections at each corner, and the lozenge has a broad border filled with an uninterrupted row of small circles; in the centre we see a double circle filled with spirals, of the form we have so frequently passed in review; the remaining space in each acute angle being filled up with an *omega*-like spiral and three small figures similar to those in No. 501. Identical with this is the ornamentation of another cross-like button, with the sole difference that its border is wider and that, instead of the sign in No. 500, it has only one small circle in each acute angle of the interior lozenge. I have no observations to make on the other cross-buttons, for their patterns are perfectly similar to those already represented.

In the same sepulchre I found the broad golden ribbons represented under Nos. 513–518, with a magnificent ornamentation in *repoussé* work.

There was also found a round gold plate, having in its centre a star, surrounded by three concentric circles, a circular row of small spiral ornaments, and a border of three circles.   Also another double gold plate, which has probably formed a cylinder.

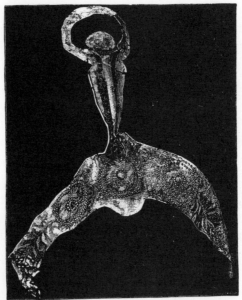

No. 519   Golden Ornament of the Greaves.   Sepulchre I.   Size 10 : 13.

Of objects of gold there were further found in this tomb two ornaments for greaves (κνημίδες), of which I represent one under No. 519.   It consists of an upper

Nos. 520-524.   Bone Tubes and Buttons.   Sepulchre I.   Actual size

golden band, terminating in a ring which must have served
to attach it to a button, and a lower golden band, broad
in the middle and gradually diminishing in breadth towards
the two extremities, which has served to fasten the greave
round the thigh. There is no ornamentation on the upper
band, where we see only a thicker tube-like gold plate,
which, being soldered to the rim of the ring, becomes
gradually smaller, and is fastened with
small pins to the lower end of the
upper band, which it is intended to
make more solid. The lower horizontal band is decorated with *repoussé*
work, showing in the middle three
ornaments, composed of treble concentric circles of protruding points,
and at each end a branch with leaves.

I have further to mention among
the objects found in this tomb the
three tubes of bone, Nos. 520, 521,
and 522, and the two bone buttons,
Nos. 523 and 524, the latter still
having a fragment of the bone-stick,
which must have served as a syringe-
handle in the three tubes, which have
undoubtedly been fastened together.
We therefore have here in all probability an ancient Mycenean clyster-
pipe.

No. 525.
Piece of Ivory : perhaps
Handle of a Dagger.
Sepulchre I. Actual size.

The object, No. 525, is a thick flat
piece of ivory, and may have served as
handle to an ornamental dagger. The upper rounded end
is slightly concave, and we see engraved on it a double
concentric circle with that beautiful type of spiral ornamentation which so often occurs here. Below it are four
treble concentric circles and a band of three horizontal
lines.

The object, No. 526, in the form of a horse-shoe, is, according to Professor Landerer, of Egyptian porcelain, which has been rubbed with a lead-glazing before being put into the oven; by this process it has got a glancing greenish colour. On the reverse side it is hollow, and must therefore have been fastened on something else. All the objects now described have evidently been much exposed to the funeral fire.

This tomb contained a vast quantity of fragments both of beautiful hand-made and wheel-made pottery. Among

No. 526. An object of Egyptian Porcelain. Sepulchre I. Actual size.

the former, particular attention is claimed by the goblets of the usual Mycenean type, but of a light greenish colour with black spiral ornaments; also, the much larger black goblets with a large hollow foot and deep horizontal furrows in the middle; further, the splendidly-fashioned small monochromatic lustrous red or black vases, whose fabrication is far superior to any painted wheel-made vases to be found here; further, the light green vases with black spirals, likewise hand-made; these vases are rather rudely

made, and their painted ornamentation is still ruder.
I found fragments of the last-named vases in all the
tombs, and also among the stones of the Cyclopean walls
on Mount Eubœa. Of the painted wheel-made vases
the most interesting are those with a dark red ornamentation on a light red or yellow dead ground, of which I
represent a specimen under No. 527.

Of large copper vessels I found in this tomb only seven,
all of which stood on the west side; one of them, a λέβης

No. 527. A wheel-made Vase of Terra-cotta.   Sepulchre I.   Size 1 : 3, about.

λοετροχόοs, or kettle for heating water for the bath, like the
one already represented (No. 438, p. 275.) It has three
vertical handles, and measures 22 in. in diameter. There is
another smaller one of the same form and also with three
vertical handles, and three of the same shape with only two
handles; also two enormous cans with two handles, of
which the one joins the rim to the body, while the other is
fastened below. As perfectly similar cans, found in the
fourth tomb, have been already represented, I abstain from

giving any more engravings of them. (See Nos. 436, 437, pp. 274, 275.)

I may further mention the copper bottom of a vessel; and, among other objects, a marble disk which may have served as the bottom to a vase of alabaster, and a large whetstone of very fine sandstone; also 16 flat quadrangular pieces of bone, having at each end two perforations; they are $1\frac{10}{12}$ in. long and $\frac{7}{12}$ in. broad, and must have served somehow as ornaments, probably on horse-trappings. Especially characteristic of this tomb was the large quantity of wood it contained. Besides a number of half-burnt pieces of wood of the funeral fires, I found there a piece of cypress-wood, 9 in. long and $4\frac{1}{2}$ in. broad, which had not been touched by the fire, though apparently it had been on the pyre. There was also collected in this tomb a very large quantity of cloven wooden instruments or handles, and three lids of wooden boxes, as well as remnants of sword-sheaths or domestic utensils.

Perhaps still more important and interesting than all the jewels found in this tomb was a small quadrangular wooden box (νάρθηξ), of which I picked up two sides, on each of which are carved in relief a lion and a dog. Small as these sculptures are, they are nevertheless of capital interest to science, because they prove to us that the art of carving in wood flourished in the mythic heroic age.

When first taken out of the grave all this wood was moist and soft like a sponge, but it is now dry, and I hope that with proper care it can be preserved. There were also found many larger and smaller pieces of cork, several of them with a curved border, from which I conclude that all must have belonged to shields; otherwise their use is quite inexplicable. Food seems also to have been deposited with the three bodies of this tomb, for I gathered in it a large quantity of oyster-shells, and among them several unopened oysters. A very large number of boars' teeth were also found.

No. 473. Massive Golden Mask of the body at the north end of the First Sepulchre. Size 1 : 5, about. *

CHAPTER X.

CONNECTION OF THE FIVE TOMBS WITH THE ROYAL HOUSE OF PELOPS; AND DATE OF THE AGORA.

Discussion of the identity of the five tombs with those mentioned by Pausanias as the tombs of Agamemnon and his companions — Opinions of scholars about the Trojan War — The ancients unanimous for its reality — The author's faith in the traditions led to his discovery of Troy and of the five Royal Tombs at Mycenæ — The civilisation of Mycenæ higher than that of Troy — The pottery of both very primitive — Alphabetic writing known at Troy, but not at Mycenæ — The different civilisations may have been contemporaneous — The appearances in the tombs prove the simultaneous

---

* Described on p. 311. I call particular attention to the fact that the engraving represents the mask in only one-fifth of its actual size.

death of those interred, certainly in each tomb, and probably in all
the five — Traditional veneration for the sepulchres — Monuments
repeatedly placed over them — No tombs between the two circular
rows of slanting slabs which formed the enclosure of the Agora and
its benches — Agora probably erected when the tombstones were
renewed, and the altar built over the fourth tomb, under the
influence of the enthusiasm created by the Rhapsodists — These
monuments buried in the course of time, but the memory of the
site was fresh by tradition long after the destruction of the new city
of Mycenæ — Testimony of Pausanias — The enormous treasures
prove the sepulchres to be *royal*, but royalty at Mycenæ ended with
the Dorian invasion — This must have been much earlier than the
received date, 1104 B.C. — An objection answered — Honours paid
to the remains of murdered princes even by their murderers —
Custom of burying the dead with their treasures — The sepulchral
treasure of Palestrina — The sepulchre of Nitocris at Babylon —
Case of Pyrrhus and the royal sepulchres at Ægeæ — The sepulchre
at Corneto.

HAVING in the preceding pages described the five great
sepulchres and the treasures contained in them, I now pro-
ceed to discuss the question, whether it is possible to
identify these sepulchres with the tombs which Pausanias,
following the tradition, attributes to Agamemnon, to
Cassandra, to Eurymedon, and to their companions.

The Trojan war has for a long time past been regarded
by many eminent scholars as a myth, of which, however,
they vainly endeavoured to find the origin in the Rig-
Vêdas. But in all antiquity the siege and conquest of
Ilium by the Greek army under Agamemnon was considered as an undoubted historical fact, and as such it is
accepted by the great authority of Thucydides.* The
tradition has even retained the memory of many details of
that war which had been omitted by Homer. For my
part, I have always firmly believed in the Trojan war; my
full faith in Homer and in the tradition has never been
shaken by modern criticism, and to this faith of mine I am
indebted for the discovery of Troy and its Treasure.

---

* Thucyd. I. 8–10.

However, the want of ornamentation on the Trojan jewels, the hand-made uncoloured pottery with impressed or engraved ornamentation, and, finally, the want of iron and glass, convinced me that the ruins of Troy belong to such a remote antiquity, as to precede by ages the ruins of Mycenæ, the date of which I thought I could fix by the result of the 34 shafts which I sank in the Acropolis in February 1874.   I therefore believed that Homer had only known the siege and destruction of Troy from an ancient tradition commemorated by preceding poets, and that, for favours received, he introduced his contemporaries as actors in his great tragedy.   But I never doubted that a king of Mycenæ, by name Agamemnon, his charioteer Euryme-don, a Princess Cassandra, and their followers had been treacherously murdered either by Ægisthus at a banquet, " like an ox at the manger," as Homer * says, or in the bath by Clytemnestra, as the later tragic poets represent ; † and I firmly believed in the statement of Pausanias,‡ that the murdered persons had been interred in the Acropolis, differing in this respect, as I have said before, from Leake, Dodwell, O. Müller, E. Curtius, Prokesch, and other travellers in the Peloponnesus, who had all misunder-stood the statement of Pausanias, and thought that he meant the murdered persons to have been buried in the lower town.

My firm faith in the traditions made me undertake my late excavations in the Acropolis, and led to the discovery of the five tombs, with their immense treasures.   Although I found in these tombs a very high civilisation, from a tech-nical point of view, yet, as in Ilium, I found there only hand-made or most ancient wheel-made pottery, and no iron. Further, writing was known in Troy, for I found there a number of short inscriptions, in very ancient Cypriote

---

* *Odyss.* IV. 530-535, and XI. 409-411.
† Æschylus, *Agamemnon*, 1438 ; Euripides, *Orestes*, 26.
‡ Paus. II. 16, § 6.

characters; and, so far as we can judge, in a language
which is essentially the same as Greek;* whereas we have
the certainty now that the alphabet was unknown in
Mycenæ. Had it been known, the Mycenean goldsmiths,
who were always endeavouring to invent some new
ornamentation, would have joyfully availed themselves
of the novelty to introduce the strange characters in
their decoration. Besides, in the remote antiquity, to
which the Homeric rhapsodies and the tradition of the
Mycenean tombs refer, there was as yet no commercial
intercourse. Nobody travelled, except on warlike or pira-
tical expeditions. Thus there may have been a very
high civilisation at Mycenæ, while at the very same time
the arts were only in their first dawn in Troy, and
writing with Cypriote characters may have been ·in use in
Troy more than 1000 years before any alphabet was known
in Greece.

I have not the slightest objection to admit that the
tradition which assigns the tombs in the Acropolis to
Agamemnon and his companions, who on their return from
Ilium were treacherously murdered by Clytemnestra or
her paramour Ægisthus, may be perfectly correct and
faithful. I am bound to admit this so much the more, as
we have the certainty that, to say the least, all the bodies
in each tomb had been buried simultaneously. The
calcined pebbles below each of them, the marks of the fire
to the right and left on the internal walls of the tombs,
the undisturbed state of the ashes and the charred wood
on and around the bodies, give us the most unmistakable
proofs of this fact. Owing to the enormous depths of these
sepulchres, and the close proximity of the bodies to each
other, it is quite impossible that three or even five funeral
piles could have been dressed at different intervals of time
in the same tomb.

* See 'Troy and its Remains,' pp. 363–372.

The identity of the mode of burial, the perfect similarity of all the tombs, their very close proximity, the impossibility of admitting that three or even five royal personages of immeasurable wealth, who had died a natural death at long intervals of time, should have been huddled together in the same tomb, and, finally, the great resemblance of all the ornaments, which show exactly the same style of art and the same epoch—all these facts are so many proofs that all the twelve men, three women, and perhaps two or three children, had been murdered simultaneously and burned at the same time.

The veracity of the tradition seems further to be confirmed by the deep veneration which the Myceneans and in fact the inhabitants of the whole Argolid, have always shown for these five sepulchres. The funeral pyres were not yet extinguished when they were covered with a layer of clay, and then with a layer of pebbles, on which the earth was thrown at once. To this circumstance chiefly are we indebted for the preservation of so large a quantity of wood and the comparatively good preservation of the bodies ; for in no instance were the bones consumed by the fire, and on several bodies, which were covered with golden masks and thick breast-plates, even much of the flesh had remained. The site of each tomb was marked by tombstones, and when these had been covered by the dust of ages and had disappeared, fresh tombstones were erected on the new level, but precisely over the spot where the ancient memorials lay buried. Only on the large fourth sepulchre with the five bodies, instead of new tombstones, a sacrificial altar of almost circular form was built.

As before explained, the first tomb had, according to all appearance, been originally decorated with a large monument, from which came the three tombstones with the bas-reliefs, and these sculptured tombstones must have been taken out and erected on the new level.

Before proceeding to what I have further to say of

the Agora, I must here add to the discussion opened in Chapter V. the testimony of Homer himself to the form and use of the Agora in the heroic age. In that beautiful passage in which he depicts the trial of a suit, as represented on the Shield of Achilles, he expressly describes the Agora as *a sacred circle*, with the elders *sitting round it on polished stones*, or—as we may now venture to translate—*on smoothed slabs*, like those in the Acropolis of Mycenæ :—*

> " But the townsmen, all assembled
>   In the forum, thronging stood;
> For a strife of twain had risen,
>   Suing on a fine of blood.
> All was paid, the first protested,
>   Pleading well to move the crowd ;
> Nought was had, upheld the second :
>   Each to obey an umpire vowed :
> And the hearers, as they sided
>   This or that way, cheered aloud :
> And the heralds ordered silence ;
>   And, *on chairs of polished stone,*
> *Ranged in venerable circle*
>   Sate the Elders.   One by one
> Each the clear-toned herald's sceptre
>   Took, and standing forth alone
> Spake his mind.   Two golden talents
>   Lay before them, to requite
> Only him, among the Judges,
>   Straightliest who should judge the right."

---

* *Iliad*, XVIII. 497-508 :—

λαοὶ δ' εἰν ἀγορῇ ἔσαν ἀθρόοι· ἔνθα δὲ νεῖκος
ὡρώρει· δύο δ' ἄνδρες ἐνείκεον εἵνεκα ποινῆς
ἀνδρὸς ἀποφθιμένου. Ὁ μὲν εὔχετο πάντ' ἀποδοῦναι,
δήμῳ πιφαύσκων, ὁ δ' ἀναίνετο μηδὲν ἑλέσθαι·
ἄμφω δ' ἱέσθην ἐπὶ ἵστορι πεῖραρ ἑλέσθαι.
λαοὶ δ' ἀμφοτέροισιν ἐπήπυον, ἀμφὶς ἀρωγοί·
κήρυκες δ' ἄρα λαὸν ἐρήτυον. Οἱ δὲ γέροντες
εἵατ' ἐπὶ ξεττοῖσι λίθοις ἱερῷ ἐνὶ κύκλῳ,
σκῆπτρα δὲ κηρύκων ἐν χέρσ' ἔχον ἠεροφώνων·
τοῖσιν ἔπειτ' ἤϊσσον, ἀμοιβηδὶς δὲ δίκαζον.
κεῖτο δ' ἄρ' ἐν μεσσοισι δύω χρυσοῖο τάλαντα
τῷ δόμεν ὃς μετὰ τοῖσι δίκην ἰθύντατα εἴποι.

The translation is by Mr. Gladstone, in the *Contemporary Review* for February, 1874.

What reader can follow this vivid picture, in the light furnished by my discovery of the Agora at Mycenæ, without feeling that the poet had often witnessed such a scene, perhaps on this very spot?

Homer makes the Trojan Agora, the assembly of *all the people*, old and young, with the *elders*, meet in the citadel of Ilium, at the gates of Priam.*

In several passages of the Odyssey he describes the Agora of the Phæacians, which was also in the citadel, near the port. Hither the people were led by Alcinous, to hear the wonderful adventures of Ulysses, and they also " coming, *seated themselves near ' on polished stones* (or *smoothed slabs*) ; and the *spaces of the Agora and the seats* were quickly filled by the thronging people." †

To complete the parallel, this Phæacian Agora (that is, its circular enclosure) was " fitted together with stones dragged to their places and sunk in the ground," like the slabs of the Agora at Mycenæ ; and it surrounded " a beautiful Posideüm," which we must naturally suppose to have been a small open sanctuary in the centre of the Agora.‡

I may add, as a proof of the great importance of the Agora in the civic life of the Heroic age, that its absence

---

* *Il.* II. 788–9 ; VII. 345–6 ; where ἀγορά is the *assembly*, from which *the place of meeting* took its name ; ἀγορά, from the verb ἀγείρω, " assemble."

† *Odyss.* VIII. 4–7, and 16, 17 :—

τοῖσιν δ᾽ ἡγεμόνευ᾽ ἱερὸν μένος Ἀλκινόοιο
φαιήκων ἀγορήνδ᾽, ἥ σφιν παρὰ νηυσὶ τέτυκτο.
ἐλθόντες δὲ κάθιζον ἐπὶ ξεστοῖσι λίθοισιν
πλησίον ·   .   .   .   .   .
καρπαλίμως δ᾽ ἔμπληντο βροτῶν ἀγοραί ;ε καὶ ἕδραι
ἀγρομένων.

‡ *Odyss.* VI. 266–7 :—

ἔνθα δέ τέ σφ᾽ ἀγορή, καλὸν Ποσιδήϊον ἀμφίς,
ῥυτοῖσιν λάεσσι κατωρυχέεσσ᾽ ἀραρυῖα.

among the Cyclopes is cited by Homer to characterize their barbarous state.*

I at first thought that every one of the large slabs of the circular double parallel row, which forms the enclosure of the Agora and its benches was a tombstone, and marked a grave; but this could not be the case. There are no real tombs either between the two parallel rows or on either side of them. The twelve quadrangular tomb-like recesses which form part of the enclosure of the Agora on the north side, have turned out to be nothing else than small reservoirs or cisterns. They were filled with household remains and bones of animals. At all events the Agora appears to have been erected in honour of those who were buried in the five sepulchres, but evidently at a later period, though undoubtedly centuries before the capture of Mycenæ by the Argives. I infer this from the irregula' and careless architecture of the Cyclopean wall whicl supports the double parallel row in the lower part of the Acropolis, and from the number of slabs which it contains resembling those of that enclosure.

As a further proof, I may mention that between the stones of this wall, as well as between the two double circular rows of slabs which form the enclosure and benches of the Agora, and in the tomb-shaped cisterns, I find only fragments of the usual Mycenean pottery, and no trace of that ancient hand-made and wheel-made pottery which is found in the royal tombs. I think it therefore highly probable that the erection of the Agora coincides with the renewal of the tombstones on the 1st, 2nd; 3rd, and 5th tombs, and the erection of the sacrificial altar on the 4th tomb; and that this renewal was occasioned by the immense enthusiasm which the Rhapsodists, who went from house to house chanting the Homeric hymns, roused

---

* *Odyss.* IX. 112:—τοῖσιν δ' οὔτ' ἀγοραὶ βουληφόροι οὐδὲ θεμίστες, "But they have neither *assemblies for council* nor laws"—each ruling apart in his own family.

among the people for the heroes of the Iliad and the
Odyssey. Very likely the glorious acts of the king of men,
Agamemnon, and his companions, were frequently chanted
here in the Agora on their very sepulchres. I may here
observe that while the whole Acropolis is covered with
remnants of Cyclopean house-walls, I found no trace
whatever of any prehistoric building within the sacred
precincts of the circular Agora.

But, nevertheless, the accumulation of *débris* continued, and in the course of time the new tombstones, as
well as the Agora itself, were buried and disappeared, while
the site of the tombs remained always fresh in the memory
of the inhabitants. I think, however, we may consider it
as perfectly certain that the Agora continued to serve for
the National Assembly until the capture of Mycenæ by
the Argives (468 B.C.), because not only were the Myceneans attached to those sacred precincts by the most
glorious and most affectionate reminiscences, but also
-because the Agora was the most imposing and most beautiful situation in the whole city, whence the Assembly
overlooked not only the whole lower city, but also the
whole plain, with Argos, Tiryns, Nauplia, as well as the
splendid Gulf of Nauplia. It is therefore equally certain
that until 468 B.C. the Agora was kept clean, and that the
accumulation in it only began after the Myceneans had
been forced to emigrate. I think I have proved by the
passages in Euripides * that this poet must necessarily have
visited Mycenæ; for he was fully acquainted with the
peculiar architecture of its Cyclopean walls, he perfectly
knew the Agora in the Acropolis, and he was well aware
that close to it was the building, laid bare by my spade,
to which tradition pointed as the ancient Royal Palace.

---

* *Iphig. Taur.* 845; *Iphig. Aul.* 152 and 1498–1499; *Hercul.
Furens,* 944; *Orest.* 1246–47; *Troad,* 1088; *Electra,* 710–712 and
1158. See Chapter II., pp. 37–38.

To the above testimony might also be added the passage where the messenger says to Orestes, " Even if thou camest within the walls (the Acropolis) thou wouldst not be able " (to kill Aegisthus)*; further, the passage where the messenger says of a person that he " seldom comes to the city (Mycenæ) and to the circle of the Agora."†

From the former of these passages we also infer that Euripides knew the Palace of Aegisthus to be in the Acropolis, and from the latter we have an additional proof that he knew the Agora to be of circular form. I think we might, as a further proof of Euripides' acquaintance with Mycenæ, also adduce the passage : " I see the people go and sit down on the height (no doubt the Acropolis) where, as tradition goes, Danaus first assembled the people on common seats when he was brought to trial for the offence against Aegyptus."‡ Mr. Newton thinks that the poet speaks here of Argos, and so it certainly appears by the names of Aegyptus and Danaus, of whose visit to Mycenæ there is no tradition; besides, the walls of the Acropolis of Argos were attributed to Danaus. But after reading all that precedes, I think the passage can only refer to the Acropolis of Mycenæ. However that may be, at all events the passage gives us an additional proof that the people were *sitting* in the Agora.

It is impossible to say how many years after its capture by the Argives (468 B.C.) Mycenæ was visited by Euripides, who was born in 480 and died in 402 B.C. But the particulars he gives us of the Agora, as well as his allusions to the royal palace, seem to leave no doubt that he saw these monuments, and that consequently they were not yet totally buried in the *débris* when he visited the Acropolis.

---

* *Elect.* 615 : τειχέων μὲν ἐλθὼν ἐντὸς οὐδὲν ἂν σθένοις.

† *Orest.* 919 : ὀλιγάκις ἄστυ κἀγορᾶς χραίνων κύκλον.

‡ *Orest.* 871–3 : ὁρῶ δ᾿ ὄχλον στείχοντα καὶ θάσσοντ᾿ ἄκραν
οὗ φασι πρῶτον Δάναον Αἰγύπτῳ δίκας
διδόντ᾿ ἀθροῖσαι λαὸν εἰς κοινὰς ἕδρας.

On the other hand, my excavations have proved that the Agora was already covered by a deep accumulation of *débris* when the later Greek city was built on its top, and for the various reasons I have adduced* there can be no doubt that the new settlement was founded about 400 B.C. But as all the *débris* which covered the Agora must necessarily have been washed down by the rain from the five upper natural or artificial terraces of the steep mount of the Acropolis, we are led to the conclusion that Euripides visited Mycenæ in his younger years, and thus shortly after the city's capture, for otherwise the enormous accumulation of *débris* in about 400 B.C. would be altogether inexplainable.

But though buried deep below the new city, the precise site of each tomb was perfectly remembered by the inhabitants of the Argolid. After an existence of about 200 years, the new city was, for some cause or other, again and finally abandoned. But still the tradition remained so fresh, that nearly 400 years after the destruction of the new town the exact place of each tomb was shown to Pausanias. Nay, the interest which the inhabitants of the Peloponnesus felt in the sepulchres was still so great sixteen or eighteen centuries after the tragic event, that, as Pausanias states, the Lacedæmonians of Amyclæ disputed with Mycenæ the honour of having Cassandra's tomb, which they thought they possessed in their own city. At all events, Pausanias† says that the Amycleans had in their village the sanctuary and the statue of Alexandra, whom they identified with Cassandra.

The five tombs of Mycenæ, or at least three of them, contained such enormous treasures, that they cannot but have belonged to members of the royal family. But the period of the kings of Mycenæ belongs to a very remote antiquity. Royalty ceased there at the Dorian invasion, the

---

* Chapter III., p. 63.   † Paus. III. 19, § 6.

date of which has always been fixed at 1104 B.C. Thucydides says that it took place eighty years after the war of Troy, which has been hitherto supposed to have ended in 1184 B.C. But, in agreement with all archæologists, I hold to the conclusion that, on the evidence of the monuments of Troy, the capture and the destruction of that city, and consequently also the Dorian invasion, must have occurred at a much earlier date.

It has been objected that the five sepulchres cannot possibly contain the bodies of Agamemnon, Eurymedon, Cassandra, and their followers, for the reason that they were killed by their enemies, Ægisthus and Clytemnestra, who had usurped the power, and who would neither have buried them nor have permitted them to be buried with immense treasures. But this objection falls to the ground before the testimony of Homer, that even he who killed his enemy burned him in his full armour, with all his weapons. Thus, for example, Andromache says to Hector : *

> . . . " Father I have none,
> Nor honoured mother ; for divine Achilles
> My father slew, and sacked Cilician Thebes,
> Fair-peopled city of the lofty gates.
> Yet stript he not Eëtion of his arms,
> Through the restraint of a religious awe,
> But burning him with all his panoply,
> Heaped high his tomb."   I. C. WRIGHT

That it was the custom in the heroic age to bury the dead with those objects which had been dear to them in life, is further proved by Homer, where the soul of Elpenor begs Ulysses to bury his body with his weapons,

---

* *Il.* VI. 413-419 :—

> . . . οὐδέ μοί ἐστι πατὴρ καὶ πότνια μήτηρ.
> ἤτοι γὰρ πατέρ' ἀμὸν ἀπέκτανε δῖος Ἀχιλλεύς,
> ἐκ δὲ πόλιν πέρσεν Κιλίκων εὐναιετάωσαν,
> Θήβην ὑψίπυλον· κατὰ δ' ἔκτανεν Ἠετίωνα
> οὐδέ μιν ἐξενάριξε · σεβάσσατο γὰρ τόγε θυμῷ ·
> ἀλλ' ἄρα μιν κατέκηε σὺν ἔντεσι δαιδαλέοισιν,
> ἠδ' ἐπὶ σῆμ' ἔχεεν.

and to erect a mound over him.* My esteemed friend
Professor Semiteles reminds me that Ajax, in the tragedy
of Sophocles, prays to be buried with his arms.†

It would therefore appear that, in burying the fifteen
royal personages with immense treasures, the murderers
merely acted according to an ancient custom, and consequently only fulfilled a sacred duty.

On the other hand, the usage of the age appears to
have left the murderers at full liberty regarding the form
of the sepulchres and the mode of the burial, which were
consequently as ignominious as possible. The graves were
merely deep irregular quadrangular holes, into which the
royal victims were huddled by three and even by five, and
on the bottom of which they were burnt, but each separately, so that their bones might not be mixed together.

I perfectly share Mr. Newton's opinion, that all the
five immense and magnificent Treasuries in the lower city
and in the suburb must necessarily be more ancient than
the five royal tombs in the Acropolis; and if we reflect that
princes, who used such magnificent underground palaces as
storehouses of their wealth, should have been huddled away
like impure animals into miserable holes, we find in this
ignominious burial alone a powerful argument in favour of
the veracity of the tradition which points to these sepulchres as those of the king of men, Agamemnon, and his
companions, who on their return from Ilium were treacherously murdered by Aegisthus and Clytemnestra.

Professor Paley reminds me that the excellent Greek

---

* *Odyss.* XI. 72-76 :—

μή μ' ἄκλαυτον, ἄθαπτον, ἰὼν ὄπιθεν καταλείπειν
νοσφισθείς, μή τοί τι θεῶν μήνιμα γένωμαι·
ἀλλά με κακκεῖαι σὺν τεύχεσιν, ἅσσα μοί ἐστιν,
σῆμα τέ μοι χεῦαι, πολιῆς ἐπὶ θινὶ θαλάσσης.

" Do not leave me behind, unwept for, unburied, when you go away, lest I should
become the cause of the wrath of the gods against thee ; but burn me with all the
arms which belong to me, and erect over me a mound on the shore of the hoary sea."

† Soph. *Ajax*, 555 :—

τὰ δ' ἄλλα τεύχη κοίν' ἐμοὶ τεθάψεται.
" My other weapons shall be buried together with me."

scholar, Miss A. Swanwick, the translator (among other works) of the *Oresteia* of Aeschylus, has already made the just remark, that the ancient tradition made Agamemnon to be buried in *silence* and *ignominy;* and the same friend calls my attention to the following passages in the tragic poets to show how all of them agree upon this. Thus we read in Aeschylus : " By our hands has he fallen and died, and we shall bury him not with the lamentations of his household."* But we see continually in Homer that the *lamentations* of *relations* and of all those who belonged to the household were regarded as quite essential to the honour as well as the peace of the dead. So, for instance, we read in the Iliad † : " So spoke (Briseïs) weeping, and the women (the other female slaves) broke out into lamentations, seemingly for Patroclus, but in reality every one of them was merely lamenting over her own misfortune."

We further read in Aeschylus : " O insolent mother, with the funeral of an enemy thou hast dared to bury your lord, a king without the tear of his citizens, a husband without his wife's " ‡ : and " O father, who hast not died in the manner of kings."§ Also in Sophocles : " Having ignominiously slain him like an enemy, she chopped and hacked his limbs." ‖ Likewise in Euripides : " Certainly like a criminal thou wilt be buried ignominiously by night, not in the daytime." ¶

---

* *Agam.* 1552–1554 : . . . πρὸς ἡμῶν
  κάππεσεν, κάτθανε, ἡμεῖς καὶ καταθάψομεν
  οὐχ ὑπὸ κλαυθμῶν τῶν ἐξ οἴκων.

† *Il.,* XIX. 301–302 :
  ὣς ἔφατο (Βρισηὶς) κλαίουσ' · ἐπὶ δὲ στενάχοντο γυναῖκες,
  Πάτροκλον πρόφασιν, σφῶν δ' αὐτῶν κήδε' ἑκάστη.

‡ *Choëph.* 430–3 : πάντολμε μᾶτερ, δαΐαις ἐν ἐκφοραῖς·
  ἄνευ πολιτᾶν ἄνακτ',
  ἄνευ δὲ πενθημάτων
  ἔτλης ἀνοίμωκτον ἄνδρα θάψαι.

§ *Ibid.* 479 : πάτερ, τρόποισιν οὐ τυραννικοῖς θανών.

‖ *Electra,* 444 : ὑφ' ἧς θανὼν ἄτιμος, ὥστε δυσμενής,
  ἐμασχαλίσθη.

¶ *Troad,* 446 : ἦ κακὸς κακῶς ταφήσει νυκτός, οὐκ ἐν ἡμέρα.

I may here observe that Sophocles seems never to have visited Mycenæ, for he fancied Agamemnon's sepulchre to have the form of a tumulus * : " On the mound of this grave I proclaim this to my father."

That in a remote antiquity it was the custom to bury kings with their treasures is proved by various classics. Thus, for instance, we are told by Diodorus Siculus† that Sardanapalus, the last king of Assyria, erected in one of his courts an immense pyre, on which he burnt himself together with all his treasures, his royal ornaments, his wives and his eunuchs.

We further read in Herodotus : ‡ " This same queen, Nitocris, committed the following fraud : Above the most frequented gate of the city (Babylon) she erected for herself a sepulchre, which projected from the upper part of the gate. And on this sepulchre she engraved an inscription of the following tenour : ‘ Whichever of the kings of Babylon who succeeds me may stand in need of money, let him open the sepulchre and take treasure as much as he likes. But let him open it in no other case than when he really needs money ; because that would not be good.' This sepulchre remained intact until the kingdom passed over to Darius. Darius was vexed that he could never use the gate, and that, though treasures were lying there, and though the treasures themselves invited him, he should not be allowed to take them. But this gate he could not use, because in passing through he would have had the corpse above his head. Now, on opening the tomb he found no treasures, but only the corpse, and an inscription which was as follows: ‘ If thou wert not insatiable and greedy for treasures, thou wouldst not have opened the tombs of the dead.' "

This account of Herodotus proves two things ; first, that it was the custom at Babylon to bury the royal dead with

---

* *Elect.* 894 : τύμβου δ' ἐπ' ὄχθῳ τῷδε κηρύσσω πατρί.
† II. 21–28.   ‡ I. 187.

treasures, and, secondly, that the people were prevented by a religious fear from plundering the abodes of the dead.

We further read in Diodorus : * "When Pyrrhus had pillaged Ægeæ, which was the residence of the Macedonian kings, he left there the Galatians. These having learned from some people that, according to an ancient custom, large treasures were buried in the royal tombs together with the deceased, they excavated all the sepulchres, and having rifled them, they divided the treasures among themselves, but the bones of the dead they threw away. Pyrrhus upbraided them on account of this sacrilegious act, but he did not punish them because he needed them in his wars." This proves again to us that it was an ancient custom in Macedonia to bury the dead of royal houses with treasures, and that the people were deterred by a religious fear from touching them, because, although it had been known for ages that the tombs contained treasures, yet nobody had dared to plunder them.

I may further remind the reader of the large treasure of elaborately ornamented gold and silver vases and other jewels, as well as of bronze vessels and vases, arms, etc., recently discovered in a tomb at Palestrina in Italy (the ancient Præneste), and attributed to the seventh century B.C.,—"that period at which the influence of the civilization and industry of the East dominated in Etruria and Latium, before those countries became subject to the force of Hellenic genius—the period when the two currents of Assyrian and Egyptian luxury and thought had become intermingled in their effect upon art, and spread by the Phœnician artisans and traders through the Western countries whither they carried their productions, ornamented according to the ideas they had imbibed, from the banks of the Euphrates on the one side, and the Nile on the other." †

I also call attention to the sepulchre of Corneto, the

---

* IV. 22, 23.

† From an account of the Tomb at Palestrina in the *Times*, February 17, 1877.

contents of which, as I have before stated, are in the Museum of Berlin. This tomb, which belongs to an epoch anterior to the influence of Greek culture in Italy, and therefore anterior to the seventh century B.C., contains not only the armour and weapons, but also the whole household furniture, copper kettles, drinking vessels, and so forth, of a rich warrior. I hardly think it necessary to remind the reader of the custom in ancient Egypt of burying the dead with treasures, for all the collections of Egyptian antiquities in the world are procured from Egyptian tombs.

My learned friend Dr. Karl Blind, in his excellent pamphlet, entitled ' Fire Burial,' cites the Odin Law in Scandinavia, which reads as follows:—" Odin ordained that the dead should be burnt, and that everything that had been theirs should be carried to the pyre. He said that every one should go up to Walhalla with as many riches as would be heaped upon his pyre, and that he should enjoy in Walhalla all those things also which he had hidden away in the earth. The ashes should be thrown into the sea, or be buried deep in the soil; but for illustrious men a mound should be raised as a token of remembrance."

Dr. Blind also gives in the same pamphlet the description of Beowulf's funeral, to prove that it was also the habit with the Anglo-Saxons to burn their dead with treasures :—

> " Geatland's men for him then made
> A pyre broad, most firmly built,
> With helms bedeckt, with war-shields hung,
> And armour bright, as he them bade.
> In the midst they laid, the sorrowing heroes,
> Their mighty ruler, their beloved lord."

Thus we have the proof that in a remote antiquity it was the custom in Babylon, Egypt, Italy, Macedonia, Scandinavia, and Germany, to bury the rich with their treasures, and my excavations have proved that this custom existed also at Mycenæ in the time of the Atridæ.

No. 528. A Golden Goblet (δέπας ἀμφικύπελλον), with dog's-head handles.
From the Tomb south of the Agora. Half-size.

CHAPTER XI.

TREASURE OF THE TOMB SOUTH OF THE AGORA.

Discovery and description of another tomb in the Acropolis outside the
Agora—Its Cyclopean masonry like that of the five sepulchres—The
golden trinkets of this tomb — Double-handled goblets — A plain
gold cup (φιάλη) — Spirals and rings of gold and silver wire, like
those of the Egyptian tombs — A golden seal-ring covered with
intaglio-work — Its full description — The face-covers of the female
figures prove the use of masks during life—A figure meant for a
Palladium — Six other rude figures· resembling the Tιojan idols:
their likeness to the " Corinthian helmet " of Athena — The work ot
this ring calls to mind Homer's description of the shield of Achilles
— A smaller golden signet-ring, with four *Palladia* and three Hera-
idols — A beautiful lion of massive gold — Gold necklace beads —
Bones of animals found in this tomb — The human remains probably removed when the water conduit was built, but the small
jewel-recess escaped being rifled — Three curious lentoid gems of
necklaces. one found on the site of Phœnicé, the others near the
ancient Heræum — The first represents Phœnician figures — De-

scription of the other two — The Cyclopean foundations of the ancient Heræum, probably as old as the walls of Tiryns and Mycenæ — It was destroyed by fire in 423 B.C., and its site deserted.
Telegrams to and from the King of Greece—Conclusion.

Athens, March 1, 1877.

My engineer, the Lieutenant Vasilios Drosinos, of Nauplia, having proceeded on the 20th of January to Mycenæ, in company with the painter D. Tountopoulos, who had to make for me an Ichnography of the five large sepulchres and the circular Agora by which they are surrounded, in verifying the plans he had made for me, recognised, due south of the Agora the form of a tomb, the site of which is marked with the letter P on the Plan B, and of which I give a most accurate separate plan.*   By the latter it will be seen that the construction of this tomb differs from that of the five sepulchres within the Agora, for on its north side the rock is cut vertically for a distance of 2 metres (6 ft. 8 in.) only, whilst on its east side it is cut for more than double the distance required for it; the vertical height of this rock being 1 m. 70 c. (5 ft. 8 in.) The eastern rock, which is cut vertically, is lined with a roughly built wall of stones joined without cement, and the same is the case with the northern rock, but here the Cyclopean wall continues in a straight line for 6 metres (20 feet), and thus for 13 ft. 4 in. farther west than the extent of the rock. On the west and south sides there is no rock at all, but merely the same kind of rude wall, which is so irregularly built that, whilst the north side of the tomb is 20 ft. and the eastern side 13 ft. 4 in. long, its southern side is 17 ft. 4 in. and its west side 12 ft. long. In the south-east corner of the tomb the Cyclopean masonry has been demolished for a distance of 1 m. 80 c. (6 feet), apparently by those who laid the water conduit,

---

* See Plan G.   Tomb south of the Agora.

which, built of uncut stones without cement, runs all along the eastern and northern sides of the tomb, and is doubtless much later than the latter.

As will be seen by Plan G, I had excavated this site to a depth of 6 m. 70 c. or 22 ft. 4 in., and had penetrated on one side 5 ft., on the other 5 ft. 4 in. deep within the walls of the tomb, in which I had left a layer of *débris* only 1 ft. 10 in. deep. But as the tomb is immediately east of the large Cyclopean house, of which I had excavated many rooms down to the rock without finding anything particular, I had considered the sepulchre as a dependency of the house, and had not cared to excavate the little *débris* which still covered its site.

But my most excellent engineer was more keen-sighted. Being struck by the appearance of the walls built in a much ruder way than those of the Cyclopean house, he at once recognised the identity of the masonry with that of the masonry in the large tombs, and as he saw the northern wall partly and the eastern entirely leaning against the rock, he had the firm conviction that it was a sepulchre. Therefore on his return to Nauplia he communicated his important discovery to a government clerk of the name of Stamatakes, who had been sent that very day by the Director-general, Mr. P. Eustratiades, to Nauplia, in order to choose a place in the Acropolis of Mycenæ on which to build a wooden hut for the watchmen. Mr. Drosinos indicated to him on my plans the precise site of the tomb, and gave him the most minute information in relation to it, so that the clerk found the place at once, and engaged a workman, at whose first or second blow of the pickaxe a golden vessel came to light, and in less than half an hour the following objects were gathered. First, four large golden goblets with two handles, of which I represent one as the vignette to this chapter (No. 528). All the four goblets have exactly the same form and are nearly of the same size. All of them represent the Homeric δέπας

ἀμφικύπελλον, because all have two handles.　These are
attached with golden nails to the body and rim, and all
of them terminate in a dog's head, which holds the rim in

No. 529.　Gold Rings, gold wire (round and quadrangular) in spirals, and one Silver Ring.
All of the double size.

his jaws and seems to drink from the cup.　Besides the
dogs' heads, these four goblets have no ornamentation
whatever, and their form is identical with that of the cup

No. 343,* with the sole difference that the latter has only one handle.

Together with the four goblets was found a large plain gold cup (φιάλη). It has only one handle, which is fastened to the rim and body with four gold pins with large flat heads. There were further found four spirals of thick quadrangular, and seven spirals of thick round gold wire, five plain gold rings, and a similar one of silver, of which a selection is represented under No. 529. I remind the reader that similar spirals and rings of thick gold wire occur in the wall paintings of the Egyptian tombs. They are supposed to have served as presents, or perhaps as a medium of exchange.

No. 530.   Gold Signet-ring, from the tomb to the south of the Agora.   Double size.

In this tomb was further found a gold seal-ring of the same form, but more than twice as large, as those which I discovered in the fourth sepulchre.† From the engraving of this new ring, which is represented in double size under No. 530, it will be seen that it is entirely covered with intaglio work. To the left of the spectator is represented a tree, whose stem certainly resembles that of a palm-tree; it has fifteen short branches on which we

---

* See p. 233.   † See Nos. 334, 335. p. 223.

see no leaves, but large clusters of a small fruit, each cluster resembling a pine apple; below the tree stands a small female, who is leaning over a little backwards and extends both her hands just below the lowest cluster of fruit, as if in the act of plucking it.　My esteemed friend the Professor of Botany, Mr. T. Orphanides, of Athens, says that of all trees in Greece this tree resembles most a pine, but that, as the little woman is going to pluck one of its fruits, the fruit must necessarily be eatable, and he thinks therefore that it must be a breadfruit-tree, because of all the fruits of India the breadfruit most resembles that of the tree before us.　But I do not remember having ever seen the breadfruit-tree in India.　I have only seen it in Central America.　My other esteemed friend, the Professor of Botany, von Heldreich, in Athens, thinks that the Mycenean artist intended to represent here simply a vine laden with bunches of grapes, and that, merely by his ineptitude, the vine has been represented as a thick tree; and this is also my opinion.

Two long tresses of hair are hanging from the little woman's head down on the back; her dress below the waist is divided by two horizontal bands into three compartments, probably to make us aware of its richness; from her arms there project two bands, which may be intended to represent the sleeves.

On the other side of the tree, and leaning with her right arm against it, is sitting a tall woman, with noble Grecian features.　Her eyes are large and her nose projects in a straight line with the forehead, just as we see it on the sculptures in the Parthenon; her head is covered with a turban running out into a point, from beneath which a tress of hair is hanging down on her back; just above this tress we see two ornaments on the turban.　I call particular attention to the curious sign just above her forehead, which is no doubt meant to represent her diadem; but I have not found a diadem of this kind in any of the

five tombs. The upper part of her dress is tightly fitted
to the body, but nevertheless the woman's two breasts protrude. The lower part of her dress is ornamented with
a large number of horizontal bands, and is in the form of
wide pantaloons which end at the ankles in crescents. Her
right hand rests on her waist, and she holds in her uplifted left hand three poppies, which she appears to offer
to a tall woman, splendidly dressed, who is standing before
her and extends her right hand towards the flowers.

The head of this tall standing woman is covered with a
sort of turban, which strikingly resembles the turbans now
worn in India, with the difference that here the turban
runs out into a point, from which a long ornament hangs
down on the back. A further difference is that from the
forepart of the turban there projects a sort of mask, on
which the two eyes and the nose are well represented, but
here this mask is lifted, and we see the woman's eyes from
below it; a third difference between this and an Indian
turban is that from its right side, on the left of the
spectator, hangs down a band which must also represent
an ornament; a fourth difference is the strange ornament
which we see just above the forehead, and which must be a
sort of diadem. The features of this woman are certainly
masculine and her hair is cut short, but the artist wished
her sex to be distinctly understood and gave her two large
protruding breasts. Just above her breasts we see two
horizontal bands, which may be intended to represent
necklaces; but we ought not to leave unnoticed the long
band which hangs from her right shoulder. Her lower
dress seems also to be in the shape of enormously wide
pantaloons, and from the loins downward we see on the
dress of each leg five large curved parallel bands, which
can have no other object than to represent the splendour
and costliness of her attire: these bands become more
curved the lower they are, and the lowest is exactly in the
form of a crescent. Below the extremity of the panta-

loons we see that the woman wears drawers, which are fastened with clasps. Above the forepart of this woman's turban is again represented an ornament, the nature of which cannot be discerned.

Just below her outstretched right arm we see another small female figure, probably a child, holding in each of its extended hands an object, the nature of which we are unable to discern, and which it seems to offer to the seated woman. The child's head is covered with a turban, and a long tress of hair, or some ornament, is hanging down its back. It wears a necklace, and its dress is divided by horizontal parallel bands into three or four compartments. The features of the child are very expressive.

Just above the extended hand of the tall standing woman we see two double axes on one handle, exactly like those on the Tenedian medals and those between the horns of the cows (Nos. 329, 330), but richly ornamented. The second double axe is seen projecting on both sides from behind the first one. The handle of these axes, which runs out into a sharp point, is artistically made.

Behind this tall standing woman stands another, whose dress I shall not describe, as it is perfectly identical with that of her companion, and above the forepart of her turban we see the same strange ornament, the nature of which cannot be recognised. Very visible is her Indian turban which also terminates in a point, and from which a long band-like ornament hangs down on her back. The mask, which projects from the forepart of her turban, closely covers the upper part of her face and her nose; it contains openings for the eyes, for her large left eye is glancing out from it. I call very particular attention to the vizors of both these women, because they give us the most unmistakable proof that masks were not only used for the dead but that they were also worn by the living. She holds in her uplifted right hand three objects, whose form certainly resembles that which we see on the forepart of the turban of the seated woman. In her left she holds two flowers with long stalks, which Professor Orphanides thinks to be lilies. From her left shoulder we see projecting two bands, and another from her left elbow. Like her tall companion, she is barefooted, but wears drawers, and on her right foot is distinctly visible the ornament with which the drawers are fastened.

Just above the strange objects which this second tall standing woman holds in her right hand, we see a curious figure holding a long staff, meant probably to represent a lance; her head is shown in profile; the rest of her body, which is given in full view, consists of two circles, of which the upper one represents the upper part of the body from the neck to the waist, and the lower one the lower part of the body as far as the loins; no legs are shown and only one arm is seen; from the back project two long bands. The two circles of which the body consists have a small border, and look altogether like shields; but that shields were not intended to be represented is shown by the two points indicating the breasts.

This rudely represented figure, in the presence of the splendidly dressed women, can in my opinion be nothing else than a *Palladium* of a very ancient and primitive type, which, like that of the cow-headed or horned Hera-idols, was, on account of the sanctity attached to it, subject to no caprice of fashion and remained for ages unchanged.

The border of the seal, between the *Palladium* and the feet of the second tall woman, is filled up by six objects of a strange form with heads and eyes, also with a kind of helmet. From the great resemblance of these six objects to the Trojan idols* we believe that they also are meant to represent *Palladia*. But Professor Rhousopoulos reminds me of the great similarity of these six figures to the κράνος κορινθιακόν, or Corinthian helmet of Pallas

---

* See 'Troy and its Remains,' p. 36.

Athena, as represented on the Corinthian coins of the fourth century B.C., and to the same helmet on the three bronze busts of that goddess, in natural size, of which one is in the British Museum, the second in the Ministry of Public Instruction at Athens, and the third in a private house in the Piræus. The forepart of the helmet is represented, on the Corinthian coins and on the bust of the goddess, as drawn up, because she only drew it over her face when she was fighting. On this forepart of the helmet we see the two eyes, the nose, and the mouth; consequently it represents a mask, and gives an additional proof that it was customary to wear masks.

The resemblance between the six figures and the κράνος κορινθιακόν is certainly striking; the latter was assuredly not invented in the fourth century B.C., but it has certainly been copied from a very ancient idol, and I have not the slightest doubt that the six figures represent this very same idol.

Finally, we see near the top two waving lines which cannot possibly represent anything else than the sea, which is represented in like manner on the coins of Tarentum. From the sea rises to the left the sun in full splendour, the rays being well represented, and to his left (to the right of the spectator) rises the crescent of the moon. On seeing this marvellous ring, Mrs. Schliemann and I involuntarily exclaimed, " This ring must have been seen by Homer before he described all the wonders which Hephæstus wrought on the shield of Achilles." *

Mr. Sayce writes me that in his opinion the seated woman is in the act of adoration; that the two tall figures are men

---

* *Il.* XVIII. 483–489:—

" There he wrought earth, sea, and heaven,
　　There he set th' unwearying sun,
And the waxing moon, and stars that
　　Crown the blue vault every one ;
Pleiads, Hyads, strong Orion,
　　Arctos, hight to boot the Wain.

He upon Orion waiting,
　　Only he of all the train
Shunning still the baths of ocean
Wheels and wheels his round again."

From Mr. Gladstone's translation of the " Shield of Achilles" in the *Contemporary Review*, Feb. 1874 ; vol. xxiii. p. 337, New Series.

dressed in the characteristic costume of early Babylonian priests, and that the sun and half-moon seen above are ordinary ancient Babylonian symbols. He declares further that the figures, their grouping and *ensemble*, are a repetition of what we see on Babylonian gems of the most remote period, and he decides that this ring must also belong to that epoch. In his opinion, this period (in so far as regards its influence upon foreign art) ends with the 13th century B. C., when Assyrian influence began to be predominant.

I call attention here to two Babylonian figures on pp. 318

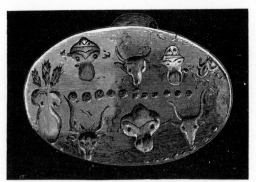

and 319 of Rawlinson's *Herodotus ;* they also wear turbans and robes like those of the figures upon our ring. It appears that at Babylon the engravers made use of magnifying glasses in cutting fine gems; at all events, they were

No. 531.   Second Gold Signet-ring.   Same tomb.   Double size.

already used in Nineveh (Rawlinson's *Herodotus*, I. 512).

Lying together with this was found another smaller golden signet-ring, which I likewise represent in double size (No. 531). We see on this signet not less than four *Palladia* and three Hera-idols in good intaglio work. The former perfectly resemble the Trojan idols of Pallas Athena ;* only there is a slight difference in the head, which is here a little less obtuse, and may be intended to be represented with a helmet. The *Palladium* in the lower row to the left is exactly like the Trojan idols; but it is a little effaced, and above it we see three ears of corn. Of the Hera-idols in the form of cow-heads with two horns, we see one in the upper and two in the lower row; the horns of the two latter are particularly

---

* See 'Troy and its Remains,' p. 36.

long, and between those of the head to the left of the spectator we see two smaller ones; therefore this cow-head has four
horns.   At the right end of the upper row is represented a
curious object which I cannot well distinguish; if we turn
the engraving to the right, it looks like a bird.   Between the
two rows are eleven signs, resembling eyes.

Together with the two signet rings was found the
beautiful massive golden lion, which is represented in
double size (No. 532).   It is fastened on a thick golden

No. 532.   Golden Lion, from the same tomb.   Double size.

wire, and is represented lying down, with the head facing
the spectator; and both the head and the rest of the body
are perfectly faithful to nature.   I share Mr. Newton's
opinion that the lion has been cast and tooled.

There were further found fourteen golden beads of a
necklace, of which I represent six (Nos. 533–538); they

Nos. 533–538.   Gold Beads of a Necklace from the same tomb.   Double size.

are ornamented all round with four rows of globular projecting points.

As will be seen by Plan G, all the above-described
jewels were found together in one spot, which was only
2 ft. long and 8 in. broad, and precisely 6 m. 90 c., or
23 ft., below the surface of the soil before the beginning
of my excavations, or only 8 in. below the surface of my

excavation, as I left it on the 6th of December last. It
further appears by Plan G, that the *débris* below the site
of the jewels was still 1 ft. 2 in. deep.

There were found bones in this tomb, which were at
first thought by us to be human bones, but my esteemed
friend Dr. Theodoros Aretæos, the celebrated Athenian
surgeon, who has examined them, declares them to be the
bones of animals. As before stated, the Cyclopean water-
conduit, represented in Plan G, was evidently built at a
later prehistoric period than that to which the tomb
belongs, and its builders, who necessarily had to excavate
the tomb down to the virgin rock, no doubt robbed it of
its contents and threw away the bones of the skeleton ;
but, luckily that small place near the wall (only 2 ft. long
and 8 in. broad), where the above jewels lay, was not dug

Nos. 539–541.   Three Lentoid Gems of Serpentine and Agate with intaglio-work, found on the site
of Phœnicé and of the Heræum.   Actual size.

up by them, and therefore the jewels have been saved for
science.*

Lastly, I represent three lentoid gems of necklaces
which I have bought in Chonika, a village situated in the
Plain of Argos, close to the site of the ancient city of
Phœnicé (Φοινίκη), and at a distance of one English mile
from the ancient Heræum. I call the attention of the
reader to the name Chonika, which is nothing but a
corruption of the name Φοινίκη.

The two peasants, who sold me the three lentoid gems,

---

* The spot where the jewels were found is marked by the letter (*a*),.
both on the plan and section (Plan G).

said that they had found the middle one in labouring on
the site of Phœnicé, and the other two close to the site
of the ancient Heræum.   I have no reason to doubt their
statement to be correct, because, as the name sufficiently
proves, Phœnicé was a Phœnician colony, and the middle
gem (No. 540) which is said to have been found there, most
decidedly represents two Phœnician figures, probably very
ancient types of idols.   Their heads are marked by a mere
horizontal hollow, and no face is shown; their necks are
very long, and their shoulders, which, like all the rest of
their bodies, are rectilinear, are enormously broad.   Very
characteristic are their long legs and their feet, which
rather resemble horse-hoofs than human feet; one man
holds in his right hand, and the other in his left, a zigzag,
probably intended to represent a symbol of fire and perhaps
lightning.   The very short left hand of the man to the
left of the spectator is uplifted, and seems to hold some
object, whilst the left hand of the other figure is very long
and nearly touches the ground.   Over the right shoulder
of the man to the left of the spectator is a strange sign,
perhaps a written character, and an arrow-like sign is close
to the neck of the other man; to both these signs I call
particular attention.   This lentoid gem is of dark red
agate, semi-globular, and has a horizontal perforation.

The lentoid gem to the left of this (No. 539), as seen
by the spectator, is of greenish serpentine.   It is convex on
both sides and has likewise a horizontal perforation.   It
represents, in beautiful intaglio, two horses standing on
their hind-legs opposite each other, their heads leaning
over in opposite directions.   The tail of the horse to the
left of the spectator is represented by a mere band; that
of the other is bushy; to the head of each horse is attached
an ornament, which probably belongs to the trappings.
Between the heads of the horses we see two human figures,
of which that to the left of the spectator has a Phrygian
cap on its head, and extends its hands towards the other

figure, whose head seems to be uncovered, and which is holding a round object in its only hand which is visible.

On the third lentoid gem (No. 541), which is an agate of variegated white and brown colour, also convex and horizontally perforated, we see a much more artistic intaglio work, representing a Hera-idol, in the form of a cow-head, with two long horns, in perfectly faithful imitation of nature. Between the two horns we see, head downward, an ornamented double-edged axe, with its handle, the extremity of which is ornamented with two rings or turned buttons. To the right and left of the cow-head we see a beautifully ornamented object, the nature of which we are unable to explain; it resembles a cornucopiæ.

I remind the reader that this lentoid gem, as well as the other with the two horses, was found close to the ancient Heræum, of which the foundations, consisting of various courses of Cyclopean masonry of enormous uncut blocks, still exist, and may be as old and even older than the walls of Mycenæ and Tiryns. But my explorations on the site, in February, 1874, have shown that the accumulation of *débris* there does not exceed 1½ to 3 ft. in depth, and consequently excavations there are impossible. The ancient Heræum was accidentally destroyed by fire in 423 B.C., and its site has remained deserted, the new Heræum being built on the slope, about 50 ft. below the ancient one.

Mr. A. H. Sayce writes to me:—"I am inclined to believe that the antiquities of Mycenæ are of a much earlier date than that which you have attributed to them. I should place the most ancient as far back as the epoch when Babylonian influence began to prevail in the western Mediterranean basin, after the conquests of the Chaldean king Naram Sin of Agana (whose successor was the victorious Elamite Khamuragas, who extended his power to the bor-

ders of the Mediterranean, 2000–1700 B.C.).   Further, I believe that the treasuries, the Gate of Lions, etc., are of prior
date to the tombs and the Cyclopean walls.   Assyrio-Babylonian civilization came into Greece not only through
Phœnicia, but through Asia Minor.   The drawings of M.
Perrot, and of several other explorers, are like links in the
chain which joins ancient Greek to Assyrian (or rather
Babylonian) art.   Perhaps in exploring Sardis an art and
types similar to those of Mycenæ will be found.   But the
great centre from which this art spread through Asia Minor
was Karkhemish, the rich capital of the Hittites, the ruins
of which have been discovered at Jerablus (near Birajik on
the Euphrates) by Messrs. Skene and George Smith.   By
making excavations, a second Nineveh might be found there,
with sculptures which would show the transition of Assyrian
art to the form which may be called the Greek, or that of
Asia Minor.   These are not mere conjectures, for pieces of
sculpture have already been discovered which present this
character.   The Hittite domination extended to Cilicia and
Lycaonia, as is proved by recently discovered carvings, and
especially by that found at Ibreez, bearing an inscription in
Hittite hieroglyphs.   This fact, which I have pointed out to
Mr. Gladstone, confirms the evidences which he has furnished
in favor of the identity of the Hittites and the Keteians
(Κήτειοι).

   "I see in the Mycenæan antiquities one point of decisive
importance: the art of carving on stone in Western Asia
and Europe came from Babylon, where stone was rare and
precious.   In archaic Babylon (prior to the sixteenth century
B.C.) civilization had made great progress; yet it was still in the
bronze age.   Iron was not used in Babylon, and was probably
unknown.   How then can we explain the relatively advanced
state of civilization in ancient Mycenæ, although iron was
unknown there, without supposing that this civilization had
its origin in that of archaic Babylon, or that it was connected with it in some way or other?   If it had been related

to the civilization of Assyria, of Egypt, or of the Babylon of a period *later* than the sixteenth century B. C., we should assuredly have found at Mycenæ some trace of a knowledge of iron."

Mr. A. H. Sayce further calls my attention to the learned article of J. P. Mahaffy, professor in Trinity College, Dublin. This article, published in the *Hermathena*, V., is entitled "On the Date of the Capture of Mycenæ by the Argives." I reproduce it here.

"No one seems to have found any difficulty in the statement of Diodorus, which Pausanias repeats, that the town of Mycenæ was destroyed by the people of Argos *after the Persian Wars*, though I fancy most scholars, when they first come to attend to it, are surprised that the ancient city of Mycenæ should have lasted so long in close neighbourhood to Argos, and made so little figure in Greek history. I suppose any doubt of this kind is allayed by the recollection that Herodotus mentions eighty Mycenæans as having joined the Greeks at Thermopylæ, and that he also enumerates both Tirynthians and Mycenæans among the cities or tribes of Greeks which were inscribed on the pedestal of the tripod at Delphi as joining in the repulse of the Persians. The actual pedestal at Constantinople confirms him, for we read in the list Μυκᾶνες, and thus the existence of Mycenæans up to the year 470 B. C. is beyond all doubt.

"I have, nevertheless, grave suspicions whether either historian has given us a true account of the matter, and therefore propose the following hypothesis, to invite discussion. If I have overlooked any decisive evidence, I hope it will be put forth in refutation of my conjecture. I will first quote all Pausanias' statements on the point, but will group them into two classes, irrespective of their order, for the sake of more convenient discussion :—

II. 15, 4.

"ἐγὼ δὲ αἰτίαν τε γράψω τοῦ οἰκισμοῦ, καὶ δι' ἥντινα

πρόφασιν Αργεῖοι Μυκηναίους ὕστερον ἀνέστησαν. 16, 5.
Μυκήνας δὲ Ἀργεῖοι καθεῖλον ὑπὸ ζηλοτυπίας. ἡσυχαζόντων
γὰρ τῶν 'Α. κατὰ τὴν ἐπιστρατείαν τοῦ Μήδου, Μυκηναῖοι
πέμπουσιν εἰς Θερμοπύλας ὀγδοήκοντα ἄνδρας οἱ Λακεδαι-
μονίοις μετέσχον τοῦ ἔργου [inaccurate]. τοῦτο ἤνεγκε
σφισιν ὄλεθρον παροξῦναν Ἀργείους.

"Then follows the famous passage about the ruins, and
about the tombs of Agamemnon and his party, which M.
Schliemann has brought into such fresh notoriety.

V. 23, 2.

"[In the list of cities inscribed on the monument of the
victory over the Persians, which Pausanias saw at Olympia,
and which appears not to have been an exact duplicate of
that at Delphi.]

"ἐκ δὲ χώρας τῆς Ἀργείας Τιρύνθιοι, Πλατ. δὲ μόνοι
Βοιωτῶν, καὶ Ἀργείων οἱ Μυκήνας ἔχοντες. 3. τούτων τῶν
πόλεων τοσαίδε ἦσαν ἐφ' ἡμῶν ἔρημοι. Μυκηναῖοι μὲν καὶ
Τιρύνθιοι τῶν Μηδικῶν ὕστερον ἐγένοντο ὑπὸ Ἀ. ἀνάστα-
τοι.

VII. 25, 5.

" Μυκηναίοις γὰρ τὸ μὲν τεῖχος ἁλῶναι κατὰ τὸ ἰσχυρὸν
οὐκ ἐδύνατο ὑπὸ Ἀ. (ἐτετείχιστο γὰρ κατὰ ταὐτὰ [this is not
accurate] τῷ ἐν Τίρυνθι ὑπὸ τῶν Κυκλώπων καλουμένων)
κατὰ ἀνάγκην δὲ ἐκλείπουσι Μ. τὴν πόλιν ἐπιλειπόντων
σφᾶς τῶν σιτίων, καὶ ἄλλοι μέν τινες ἐς Κλεωνὰς ἀποχωροῦ-
σιν ἐξ αὐτῶν, τοῦ δημοῦ δὲ πλέον μὲν ἢ ἥμισυ ἐς Μακεδο-
νίαν καταφεύγουσιν παρ' Ἀλέξανδρον, ᾧ Μαρδόνιος ὁ Γω-
βρύου τὴν ἀγγελίαν ἐπίστευσεν ἐς Ἀθηναίους ἀπαγγεῖλαι·
ὁ δὲ ἄλλος δῆμος ἀφίκοντο ἐς τὴν Κερύνειαν, καὶ ἐς τὰ ἔπειτα ἐγένετο ἐπιφανεστέρα διὰ τὴν συνοίκησιν τῶν Μυκ.

"Nothing seems more precise than this. Pausanias was
evidently quite sure of his facts, though one of them—the
participation of the Mycenæans in the battle of Thermopylæ—was certainly wrong according to Herodotus. They
went there, indeed, but retired with the other Greeks, who
left the Spartans and Thespians with Leonidas. Apart from
this, it seems, then, that the Argives were so jealous of the

fame of Mycenæ on account of this glorious battle (at which Mycenæans never fought), that they undertook the siege of the great Cyclopean fort, and having starved out the population of the place, which they could not storm, they drove them out of the land to Kleonæ, Kerynea, and to Macedonia. The same lot befell the Tirynthians for the same reason, though Pausanias adds no details about the siege of their equally wonderful fort, which excited his loudest admiration.

"Herodotus corroborates the participation of Mycenæ and Tiryns in the Persian War, and says they together furnished four hundred men to the army of the Greeks, which fought at Platæa. He is perfectly silent as to the consequences of this act.

" Let us now examine a very different passage.

VIII. 27, 1.

" συνῆλθον δὲ ὑπὲρ ἰσχύος ἐς αὐτὴν [sc. τὴν Μεγαλὴν πό-λιν] οἱ Ἀρκάδες, ἅτε καὶ Ἀργείους ἐπιστάμενοι τὰ μὲν ἐτι πα-λαιότερα μόνον οὐ κατὰ μίαν ἡμέραν ἑκάστην κινδυνεύοντας ὑπὸ Λακεδαιμονίων παραστῆναι τῷ πολέμῳ ἔπει δὲ ἀνθρώ-πων πλήθει τὸ Ἄργος ἐπηύξησαν, καταλύσαντες Τίρυνθα καὶ Ὑσιάς τε καὶ Ὀρνεὰς καὶ Μυκήνας καὶ Μιδείαν καὶ εἰ δή τι ἄλλο πόλισμα οὐκ ἀξιόλογον ἐν τῇ Ἀργολίδι ἦν, τά τε ἀπὸ Λακ. ἀδεέστερα τοῖς Ἀργ. ὑπάρχοντα, καὶ ἅμα ἐς τοὺς περι-οίκους ἰσχὺν γενομένην αὐτοῖς.

"This passage is corroborated by II. 25, 6 and 8, in which the destruction of Orneæ and of Tiryns are mentioned in the same way. Thus, in § 8, ἀνέστησαν δὲ καὶ Τιρυνθίους Ἀργ., συνοίκους προσλαβεῖν καὶ τὸ Α. ἐπαυξῆσαι θελήσαντες.

"This account appears not only inconsistent with the former, but contradictory to it. There, the inhabitants of Mycenæ are expelled, and added to the strength of other cities; here, the special reason of the dispute is to secure more citizens for Argos, and to increase and consolidate its power. Any one who considers the conditions of the ques-

tion for one moment will not hesitate to prefer this latter—
a sound political view—to the sentimental story about
Argive jealousy.   The συνοικισμός of the Argive territory
was like that of Thebes, of Athens, and of Megalopolis; and
there can be no doubt that the importance of Argos in
Greek history was wholly due to its early success in this
most difficult and unpopular revolution.

" But is it possible that it took place *after* the Persian
Wars?   I think not.   In the face of the patriotic conduct
of Tiryns and Mycenæ, and at the moment of Argos'
greatest national unpopularity, any such attempt to destroy
free Greek cities would have brought down the vengeance
of all Greece.   Moreover, early historians are silent about
it.   Herodotus and Thucydides never allude to it.   What
is still more remarkable, the contemporary Æschylus, though
composing plays which ought to have had their scene laid
at Mycenæ, never once mentions Mycenæ, and transfers the
palace of Agamemnon to Argos.*   If the more ancient
city, whose inhabitants had fought with him in the great
Persian struggle, had only lost its independence in his mature
age, is such a curious ignorance on his part conceivable?   I
think, then, that the συνοικισμός of the Argive territory
must have taken place long before, and that Pausanias was
misled by the monuments of the Persian War to transfer it
to an impossible period.

" If we look back into earlier history, and consider at
what time Argos was daily expecting an attack from Sparta,
and found it necessary to strengthen its power, I think the
most natural period will be not immediately after the Per-

---

* This mistake seems to have been noted by critics of an early
date, for both Sophocles and Euripides mention and distinguish the
two cities, though they seem to confuse the inhabitants.   I was unable,
when on the spot, to make out the picture suggested at the opening of
Sophocles' *Electra*, which seems, as it were, drawn on the spot, but is
more probably a fancy sketch.   But Mycenæ is very prominent in it.
Sophocles even wrote a play called Μυκηναται.

47

sian, but immediately after the Messenian Wars, that is, the
second Messenian War, which was concluded in Ol. 29.
According to our revised chronology, the development of
Phidon's power at Argos must be placed close to this time,
and it was probably the twenty-eighth Ol. which he celebrated with the Pisatans at Olympia to the exclusion of the
Eleans. Of course the Spartans were bound to interfere,
but the Messenian War must have greatly hampered their
vigour. When this war was over, and Sparta had acquired
new territory and prestige, the Argives must have expected
that they would be the first to suffer. Hence I attribute to
Phidon, and to his policy, the consolidation of all the
smaller towns in Argos, and perhaps this may have been the
secret of his greatness.

" But how then is the existence of Tiryns and Mycenæ
during the Persian War to be explained? I suppose that
these towns, though conquered, and their gods transferred
to Argos, nevertheless continued to exist as κῶμαι or villages, but inhabited by Argive citizens, and that accordingly
these descendants of the old inhabitants, who took the patriotic side, and had not forgotten their history, joined the Hellenic army under these obsolete names, which the nation
was glad to sanction as a slight to the neutral Argives.*
The very small number of men they were able to muster
(80 from Mycenæ at Thermopylæ, 400 from Mycenæ and
Argos together at Platæa) strongly corroborates this view;
for in that day the smallest Greek towns had a considerable armed population—Platæa, for example, had 600. It
is very likely that the Argives were nettled at this conduct,
and determined to efface these places altogether; and this
change, which was very unimportant, as the real συνοικισμός
had been long accomplished, attracted no notice at the time,
but gave rise afterwards to a distortion of history.

---

* Of course they need not have come directly from Mycenæ, but
may have been exiles, who came together under the name of their
old city.

" I will quote, in conclusion, what seems to me a parallel case.   Pausanias says (IV. 27, 10), that the Minyæ of Orchomenus were expelled by the Thebans *after the battle of Leuctra*.   We know very well that the power of Orchomenus was gone long before, but the increased strength of Thebes, and some offence on the part of the subject city during the struggle with Sparta, determined its complete extinction by the Thebans.   But this was no great siege or subjugation of a free city.   That had been done by the Thebans long before.   So I believe the capture of the great fort at Mycenæ probably occurred long before the Persian Wars.

" The explicit passage in Diodorus (xi. 65), which seems at first sight a conclusive corroboration of the ordinary view, only strengthens my conviction that it is wrong. Diodorus is precise about the date.   He says that in the 78th Ol. (468–4), while the Spartans were in great trouble on account of a destructive earthquake and rising of the Helots and Messenians, the Argives took the opportunity of attacking Mycenæ.   But they did so because Mycenæ *alone of the cities* in their territories would not submit to them.   This distinctly asserts that all the other towns, such as Tiryns and Midea, had been formerly subdued, and contradicts Pausanias.   Diodorus then enumerates the various claims of Mycenæ to old privileges about the Heraeon and the Nemean Games, and adds what Pausanias says about their joining the Greeks at Thermopylæ, alone among the Argive cities.   The share taken by Tiryns with Mycenæ at Platæa seems unknown to both authors.   But after long waiting for an opportunity, the Argives now collected a considerable force from Argos and the allied cities, and made war upon Mycenæ—upon Mycenæ, which was only able, jointly with Tiryns, to supply 400 men at Platæa, and which, when unaided, sent 60 men to Thermopylæ!   The Argives first defeated them in battle, and then besieged the fortress, which, after some time, through lack of defenders (which is indeed credible), they *stormed*.   Here again

Pausanias is contradicted.   Diodorus concludes with stating that they *enslaved* the Mycenæans, consecrating a tenth of the spoil, and levelled the town with the ground.

"I think my theory is perfectly consistent with the critical residue which may be extracted from this passage.   It is probably true that the Argives chose the opportunity of a Messenian war to make this conquest, but it was the second, not the third, Messenian war.   It is probably true—nay, I should say certainly true—that they levelled Mycenæ with the ground in the 78th Ol.; but this was not their first conquest of it.   If they enslaved the then inhabitants, this harsh measure was probably by way of punishment for the impertinence of a subject town in sending an independent contingent to a war in which the sovereign city had determined to maintain a strict neutrality.   That the facts related by Diodorus should have caused no general comment throughout Greece, or that no echo of it should have reached us, seems to me almost incredible.   There is a possible corroboration of Diodorus' statement that Mycenæ was the last conquered of the subject cities in the Homeric catalogue, where Tiryns is mentioned as already subject to Argos, while Mycenæ is the capital of Agamemnon.   But even when that catalogue was compiled, Argos had conquered all the seaboard of the Argolic peninsula, and Mycenæ lies at the extreme south of the territory (chiefly Corinthian and Sicyonic) which is assigned to Agamemnon.   Possibly the traditions were still too strong for the poet to make Mycenæ subject to Argos, but he plainly denies any hegemony of Mycenæ over the Argive plain."

Mr. A. H. Sayce further directs my attention to a passage of Homer, which, in my opinion, also seems to favor this hypothesis, and which seems categorically to contradict the stories which Pausanias and Diodorus have borrowed from Ephorus.*   This last has seemingly made an error as

---

* According to Sayce, who has carefully studied the fragments of Ephorus, these and certain other indications prove that Diodorus has

to the epoch of Pheidon.   The passage pointed out by Mr. Sayce is in the Iliad, IV., 50–56:

" Τὸν δ' ἠμείβετ' ἔπειτα βοῶπις πότνια Ἥρη·
Ἤτοι ἐμοὶ τρεῖς μὲν πολὺ φίλταταί εἰσι πόληες,
Ἄργος τε Σπάρτη τε καὶ εὐρυάγυια Μυκήνη·
τὰς διαπέρσαι, ὅτ' ἄν τοι ἀπέχθωνται περὶ κῆρι·
τάων οὔτοι ἐγὼ πρόσθ' ἵσταμαι οὐδὲ μεγαίρω.
Εἴπερ γὰρ φθονέω τε καὶ οὐκ εἰῶ διαπέρσαι,
οὐκ ανύω φθονέουσ', ἐπειὴ πολὺ φέρτερός ἐσσι."

> " To whom the stag-eyed Juno thus replied:
> ' Three cities are there dearest to my heart;
> Argos and Sparta and the ample streets
> Of rich Mycenæ; work on them thy will;
> Destroy them, if thine anger they incur;
> I will not interpose nor hinder thee;
> Mourn them I shall; reluctant see their fall,
> But not resist; for sovereign will is thine.' " *

In the opinion of Mr. Sayce, it is clear that Homer meant in this passage to refer to the destruction of at least one of the three cities which he names, and as Argos and Sparta were *not* destroyed, the city which *was* destroyed could have been no other than Mycenæ.   Mr. Sayce believes that it may be inferred from the word διαπέρσαι that the destruction of Mycenæ must have been complete.   If it was so, nothing can better prove the great antiquity of the event than this citation from Homer.

I must say that this hypothesis of Messrs. Sayce and Mahaffy, according to which Mycenæ must have been destroyed at a period of great antiquity, is but too strongly confirmed by the monuments.   I recall to the reader here what I said on this subject near the end of Chapter IV.:—
"On the west side the Cyclopean wall has been nearly de-

---

almost copied his relation literally from that of Ephorus, and that he has only reproduced a large part of what Ephorus wrote.

* Lord Derby's translation.

molished for a distance of 46 feet, and on its interior side a
wall of small stones joined with earth has been built to sustain its ruins.   It must remain mere guesswork when the
Cyclopean wall was destroyed and the small wall built, but
at all events this must have occurred long before the capture of Mycenæ by the Argives in 468 B. C., because the
small wall was buried deep in the prehistoric *débris*."

I also recall the fact that the following inscription

T o B E R o o ξ) E M

which we know positively to belong to the sixth century
B. C., is cut upon a fragment of that black Greek pottery
which seems to be of at least three centuries' later date than
the archaic Mycenian pottery, even the most modern, which
is found at Mycenæ just at the bottom of the bed of *débris*
of the Macedonian city.

Further, I call the special attention of archæologists to the
immense number of idols in the form of cows or of women
with cows' horns or heads, which I collected at Mycenæ
(see, for example, figs. 2–11, 111–119, 212, 327–330, 531).
These are beyond contradiction the most ancient types of
idols which have been found in Greece.   All of them are
discovered down as far as the surface of beds of archaic
débris ; it is therefore very certain that they were still in
use at the time of the taking of Mycenæ.   But it seems to
us quite impossible that here the tutelary divinity of Mycenæ should have been represented as late as the fifth century B. C., under the form of a cow or of an idol showing the
characteristic features of a cow.

It is evident that in the Homeric poems Hera is a woman, without any of the attributes of a cow ; the only trace
of them that she has preserved is in the epithet βοῶπις,
consecrated to her by the usage of centuries, but certainly

not signifying in Homer more than "the large-eyed" goddess.

It seems certain that at the time of Homer the habit of representing Hera under the form of a cow, or with the attributes of a cow, had fallen into disuse and been abandoned; and that, consequently, the catastrophe of the complete destruction of Mycenæ should be referred to an ante-Homeric epoch. In fact, considering the character of the monuments I have discovered, I see no objection whatever to referring it to the period of the invasion of the Heraclides. And indeed, the destruction of Mycenæ by the Heraclides would explain also the singular fact that Orestes never reigned at Mycenæ.

I cannot discover any trace of Egyptian influence in the art of Mycenæ; but the multitude of objects which certainly came from Egypt—like the immense golden cow-heads, the ostrich egg, the sphinx (see fig. 277), and the pieces of Egyptian porcelain—forces us to the conclusion that there must have been relations between the city and that country. The strongest testimony that such relations existed is the worship of the lunar divinity Hera under the form of a cow —a divinity whom I have proved (see the note on Hera Boöpis at the end of Chapter I.) to be identical with the Egyptian goddess Isis, who was similarly worshipped in Egypt in the form of a woman with the horns of a cow. Further, I may recall the fact that Isis was said to have been born at Argos (Diodorus Sic., I. xxiv. 25; Apollodorus, II. i. 3), and that Apis, grandson of the Argive river-god Inachos, and nephew of the cow-faced lunar goddess Io, was at first king of Argos; that from his name this town and the whole Peloponnesus was called Apia; that Apis at length made over to his brother his Grecian dominion, and became king of Egypt (Eusebius, Chron. I. 96, 127, 130, edit. Aucher; Augustine, de Civ. Dei, xviii. 5); that after his death he was worshipped in Egypt under the name of Serapis and the form of a bull. In the same way the Greek myth makes the Argive cow-faced goddess to migrate to Egypt, where she brings into the world Epaphos, which is only a second name for the bull Apis.   But, according to Diodorus Sic. (I. xxiv. 25), Apollodorus (II. i. 3) and Hygin (145), Io was identical with Isis.   All these Greek myths seem to prove, not that the worship of the cow-faced moon-goddess came into Argos *from* Egypt, but that, on the contrary, it was carried *into* Egypt from Mycenæ or Argos; and perhaps Egyptologists, by determining the period at which the worship of Isis began in Egypt, can give us an idea of the antiquity of the relations between that country and Mycenæ. In fact, the worship of the moon-goddess under the form of a cow *could* not have been brought from Egypt to Mycenæ, but necessarily *must* have been introduced from Mycenæ into Egypt, since Io was distinctly a Pelasgian goddess; she had a celebrated temple at Byzantium, and the legend even attributes the foundation of that city to her daughter Keroessa, also called " she who wears horns."   The worship of Io seems to have been brought from Asia by the Pelasgians; at all events they introduced it at a very remote epoch into Argolis.   I would note also that even in classic times the name of Io continued to be given to the moon in the religious mysteries of Argos, and that this name is purely Greek (see the note on Hera Boöpis at the end of Chapter I.).

In conclusion, let me call attention to the fact that in consequence of the discovery of a sixth tomb in the Agora of Mycenæ, after my departure, there has been an attempt to deny the identity of these tombs with those which the tradition reported by Pausanias points out as the burial-places of Agamemnon, Cassandra, Eurymedon, and their companions.   But one need only re-read the famous passage of Pausanias (II. xvi. 6) to see that it does not clearly give the number of the tombs.   It speaks distinctly of six; but one may admit that there were even more than six, and yet do no violence to Pausanias's text :—τάφος δὲ ἔστι μὲν Ἀτρέως, εἰσὶ δὲ καὶ ὅσους συν Ἀγαμέμνονι ἐπανήκοντας ἐξ Ἰλίου δειπνίσας κατεφόνευσεν Αἴγισθος.

My esteemed friend, the celebrated Orientalist, M. Émile Burnouf, honorary director of the French school at Athens, writes to me:

"I do not think it would be difficult to prove that the tombs at Mycenæ are certainly those of the Pelopides; their position in the Acropolis and the quantity of precious objects with which they were filled show clearly that they are the burial-places of royal and not of private personages. The circular enclosure, built on a higher level than its surroundings, at a time when these princes had fairly become tutelary heroes, proves the same thing; it may have served as an agora, as the texts indicate; but it was certainly also a burial enclosure where sacrifices were celebrated in honor of the dead buried below. You have found traces of these national ceremonies. I do not think that the skeletons found can be considered the remains of members of dynasties earlier than the Pelopides; these have no historic character, and belong altogether to the mythology of the Aryan races. It may be objected that a very considerable part of the legend of the Pelopides is itself mythological; but this is common to all the prehistoric dynasties of the Aryan peoples—dynasties whose real existence is nevertheless not contested by any scholar. Besides, this particular one actually touched the historic period; for it was brought to an end by the Dorian invasion, the date of which can be very closely approximated.

"You ask me also my opinion with regard to the objects found by you at Mycenæ. There are several categories of these, which it would be unwise to confuse and consider as one—for they bear marks of different origins. It is impossible to mistake the Assyrian or Assyrio-Babylonian character of the gold objects which your fine excavations have brought to light in such great numbers. These ornaments are identical with those which we see on the Assyrian carvings in the museums of London and Paris; they have no resemblances to Egyptian jewelry. Two among them are characteristic,

and may give rise to important discussions,—these are the
two golden signet rings which you have published as figures
530 and 531.   The seal of the first represents a religious cer-
emony, that of the plucking of the sacred plant: everything
is Assyrian; the sun, with the crescent moon and the waters
of heaven, the six days, the tree, the costume of the persons
represented.   The second is a kind of Asiatic hieroglyph,
such as is often met with on the cylinders and carved
stones of the countries along the Euphrates and the Tigris;
it relates, beyond doubt, to some event which happened during the first of the great months of the year—that is to say,
after the vernal equinox; the object at the left seems to indicate that it refers to some agricultural operation—reaping
or sowing.   However this may be, these two signets seem to
me to have come to Mycenæ from an Asiatic country—perhaps from the banks of the Euphrates or Tigris.

"I can tell you nothing in regard to the mass of fragments of pottery which you have taken from the excavations.
They have a great resemblance to those found on all the
shores of the Mediterranean.   Their origin is now attributed
to the commerce of the Phœnicians, or, more exactly, of the
Sidonians; but perhaps there is some exaggeration in this.
It is not probable that Sidon furnished all the pottery of the
Mediterranean; and the character of the clay used by its
manufacturers varied in different places; but the process of
manufacture is nearly the same, and the character of the ornamentation changes but little.   One is thus led to believe that
the potter's art first came to the Mediterranean from the
East, but that it was almost everywhere established in local
factories at a very early period.

"The idols and cows, found in such numbers by you in
the ruins of Mycenæ are, evidently, of local origin.   If these
rude statuettes had been Phœnician, and had represented
Astoreth, it would not have been Hera, but Aphrodite, who
would have been the principal goddess of Argolis; there
would have been not a Heræum, but an Aphrodisium.   More-

over, the *coiffure* of many of the Mycenæan idols charac-
terized Hera all through the succeeding centuries; and, as
you very rightly note, the form of the crescent in others indicates that ancient goddess of the moon, who bore the
name of Io, and who was, *au fond*, identical with Hera.
I should say the same of the terra-cotta cows; it is a mani-
fest error to identify them with the Egyptian bull.   The
museums of Europe contain a great number of specimens
of the Apis; they have very distinct forms and characteris-
tics which are not wanting in a single case;—such are especially the three large black spots on the crupper, the back,
and the hinder part of the body.   The Mycenæan cows are
more often yellow, striped with red.   It is true that they
have no udders; but neither have they the male organs.

"Apropos of this, permit me to correct an error which
has fairly become classic; the words βοῦς and *bos* of Greek
and Latin mythology are almost always translated *ox ;* but
they are generally feminine in the classic authors, and mean
cow—the *cows* of the sun-god, the *cows* stolen by Cacus—
abstractæque boves, abjuratæque rapinæ ; and we know
also the great supreme *cow* of the Indian hymns—*i. e.*, the
heavens considered as the source of cosmic life, and identical with the Hera of Greek tradition.   I would call your
attention to the fact that the ancient agricultural peoples of
Asia and Europe did not raise oxen, but cows; that they
yoked bulls to the plough; and that the ox was almost
never used among them.   Thus the absence of sex in the
Mycenæan terra-cottas leaves only the choice between bulls
and cows; while religious tradition, as well as the epithet
βοῶπις, constantly point out the *cow* as the symbol of Juno.
It is this goddess, therefore, who is meant by the terra-cotta
images.   And as you have found them in great numbers in
your excavations, this is a new proof of the importance
given in Argolis to that divinity.   These conclusions are
moreover in perfect agreement with the Homeric texts and
with the religious traditions of all Greek antiquity.   I may

add that they come to the support of the often-combated assertion, that the Trojan idols were meant to signify Athena Glaukopis. The Mycenæan cow and the Trojan owl are two facts of the same order, which occupy corresponding places in Greek mythology, and relate to the same epoch of linguistic development in the religious symbolism of antiquity."

M. Burnouf also informs me that he has sent to the *Révue des deux Mondes* an extended article on the excavations at Mycenæ.

--- --- ---

On the discovery of the Treasures of the Royal Sepulchres, I had the honour of addressing a telegram to His Majesty, the King of the Hellenes, which I insert here, with His Majesty's gracious reply :

"A SA MAJESTÉ LE ROI GEORGE DES HELLÈNES, ATHÈNES.

" Avec une extrême joie j'annonce à Votre Majesté que j'ai découvert les tombeaux que la tradition, dont Pausanias se fait l'écho, désignait comme les sépulcres d'Agamemnon, de Cassandra, d'Eurymédon et de leurs camarades, tous tués pendant le repas par Clytemnestre et son amant Egisthe. Ils étaient entourés d'un double cercle parallèle de plaques, qui ne peut avoir été érigé qu'en honneur des dits grands personnages. J'ai trouvé dans les sépulcres des trésors immenses en fait d'objets archaïques en or pur. Ces trésors suffisent à eux seuls à remplir un grand musée, qui sera le plus merveilleux du monde, et qui, pendant des siècles à venir, attirera en Grèce des milliers d'étrangers de tous les pays. Comme je travaille par pur amour pour la science, je n'ai naturellement aucune prétention à ces trésors, que je donne, avec un vif enthousiasme, intacts à la Grèce. Que Dieu veuille que ces trésors deviennent la pierre angulaire d'une immense richesse nationale !

" HENRY SCHLIEMANN.

"MYCÈNES, 16 (28) *Novembre* 1876."

His Majesty's Reply:—

"MONSIEUR LE DOCTEUR SCHLIEMANN, ARGOS.

"J'ai l'honneur de vous annoncer que Sa Majesté le Roi, ayant reçu votre dépêche, a daigné me charger de vous remercier de votre zèle et amour pour la science, et de vous féliciter de vos importantes découvertes, et Sa Majesté espère que vos efforts seront toujours couronnés d'aussi heureux succès.

"Le Secrétaire de S.M. Hellénique,
"A. CALINSKIS."

I cannot conclude without mentioning the names of my esteemed friends, Professor Euthymios Castorches, Professor Stephanos Coumanoudes, and Professor Kokkides, of Athens, and thanking them here publicly for all the kindness they have shown me during the time of my toilsome excavations at Mycenæ.

I also deem it my agreeable duty to thank here publicly my excellent engineer, the sagacious Lieutenant Vasilios Drosinos, for his scrupulous care and attention in making all the plans of Mycenæ, as well as for the great service he has rendered to archæology by promptly indicating to the government clerk the tomb which he had discovered in my excavations, so that its contents could be saved for science.

I further fulfil an agreeable duty in warmly recommending to all visitors to Athens the most excellent photographers, Messrs. Romaïdes Brothers, from whose wonderful photographs all the engravings of this work have been made;* in fact, I do not exaggerate if I assure the reader that their photographs can hardly ever be excelled.

It is also my pleasant duty to thank publicly the celebrated printers, Messrs. William Clowes and Sons, of London, who printed this book, as well as the most excellent engravers, Messrs. J. W. Whymper and J. D. Cooper, who made all the engravings, for the superior skill and the unremitting zeal and scrupulous attention with which they have executed their part in the work.

Lastly, I here express my warmest gratitude to the learned publisher of this work, my most esteemed friend, Mr. John Murray, as well as to my most excellent learned friend Mr. Philip Smith, for all the kind services they have rendered me and all the valuable assistance they have lent me in carrying out the present work.

---

* Except the body (No. 454, p. 297), and a few diagrams and new drawings of objects, besides the Plans.

APPENDIX A.

(See page 126.)

IN a careful re-reading of Pausanias and Herodotus, I have found a considerable number of passages proving that the Agora often served as a burial-place for persons of very great distinction. For example, the tomb of Orestes was in the Agora of Sparta, near the temple of the Fates; and near this, in the same Agora, were the tombs of Epimenides of Crete and Aphareus, son of Perieres. The tomb of Talthybios, Agamemnon's herald, was pointed out to Pausanias in the Agora of Ægium, in Achaia; and that of Oxylos in the Agora of Elis. In the Agora of Phigalia was the vast common burial-place (πολυάνδριον) of the chosen Oresthasians, to whom funeral sacrifices were offered. The tomb of Podares was in the Agora of Mantinæa. In that of Tegea Pausanias was shown the graves of Lycaon and his wife Mæra, and in that of Elæa, the tomb of Thersandros. It is very interesting to notice that the same honor was conferred upon Herodotus, for he was buried in the Agora of Thyrium (Θουρία), where his tomb was preserved for ages. The Agora of Sikyon contained the heroön of Adrastus; and that of Thebes the Mausoleum of Euphron.

APPENDIX B.

(See pages 133 and 134.)

MY lamented friend Dr. Moss, of Arctic celebrity, when serving as staff-surgeon on board H. M. S. *Research*, which for some months in the fall of 1878 lay in the Gulf of Besika, visited me daily in my excavations at Troy. He afterward served as staff-surgeon on board the *Atalanta*, and with that unfortunate vessel came to an untimely end.　Under date of November 5, 1879, he wrote to me from the *Atalanta*, " My dear Friend: I cannot leave England without asking you— with reference to the most curious object attached to the spears of the warriors depicted on the vase No. 213, p. 133, in your *Mycenæ*—whether the ancient warriors carried their *water-flasks* slung on their spears, for the strange object can mean nothing else, I think.　If so, we can understand why David took Saul's spear and *water-bottle* (I. Samuel, xxvi. 11 and 16).　I fear I may be suggesting what is perfectly well known."

APPENDIX C.

(See page 243.)

MYCENÆ must have had commercial relations with Egypt, especially as, according to Pausanias (IV. xxxv, 2), Nauplia was an Egyptian colony.

M. Hubert, professor in the gymnasium at Posen, Prussia, writes to me on this subject: " I find in the *Deutsche Revue*, edited by R. Fleischer (Berlin, Jaake publisher, second year, number for April 7, 1878, p. 42), the following passage at the end of an essay by Brugsch-Bey on the religious mysteries of the ancient Egyptians:—' It was customary for the Egyptians who had been initiated into the mysteries to carry a token or badge, which consisted of a ribbon tied in a running noose (as represented in the accompanying engraving).　In visiting Egyptian museums, it will be noticed that a great many of the statues represent- ing kings, priests, and other prominent personages, carry this mystic ribbon in the hand, to signify by this outward sign that they have been initiated into the mysteries.' The idea at once occurred to me that I had lately seen a similar ribbon elsewhere; and a search confirmed my recollection.　It was in your work on Mycenæ (figs. 351 and 352, objects of Egyptian porcelain).　In your engraving, it is true, the upper part of the noose is more curved, it being represented in the hieroglyph as entirely upright; still the forms of the two objects seem to present a close analogy.　The three holes in figure 352 may have served to fasten the noose with nails to the hand of a statue; but no hand was found in the fourth tomb.

"It seems to me doubtful, but not impossible, that some connection may be established between these knots and the alabaster object in figure 325, which comes from the third tomb, and represents two hands placed side by side, leaving a hollow between them. This hollow may have held two of these alabaster nooses, and it might be important to see if there are any traces of nails.

"You, in your book, and Mr. Gladstone in his preface, show that your discoveries establish in many directions numerous relations between Mycenæ and Egypt. You will have determined a decisive point, if you can prove that your alabaster nooses are really the mystic Egyptian badges."

APPENDIX D.

(See figure 446, page 282.)

THE sword represented in figure 446, having been carefully cleaned by my friend the assistant keeper, Mr. Athanasios Koumanoudes, it was found to be plated with gold on both sides, and to be ornamented on one side with an incised representation of a lions' hunt, on the other with the representation of a lion devouring an animal, probably a roe or stag, and chasing four others. I represent here both sides. Hardly anything more interesting can be imagined than the lions' hunt, which occupies five men armed with the same sort of shields as we have seen on the gem No. 313, or with quadrangular ones such as we saw on page 223, No. 335, and with long lances. There are three lions; two are running away. The third has become furious by the wound it received in the haunch, has turned against its aggressors, one of whom it has already killed; curiously enough the dead man is represented as having both his feet against the falling shield. The following man is holding his shield before him so that only his head is visible above it. The third man's shield is represented as hanging on his back, and so is the shield of the fifth man. The second, the third, and the fifth men are in the act of throwing their lances against the furious lions. Not so the fourth man, who seems to have no lance, and who is represented as kneeling with one foot and shooting an arrow from the drawn bow which he holds in his

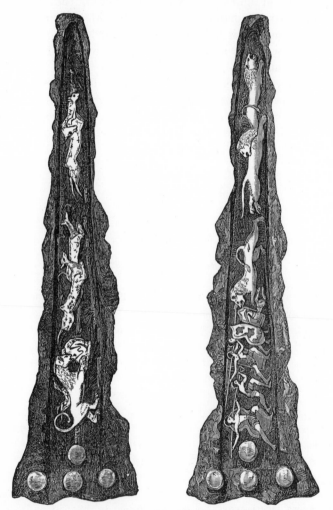

Two-edged Bronze Sword. Sepulchre IV. Half size. After cleaning.

hand. I call particular attention to the short breeches of the men, and to their curious decoration; also to the curious signs on one of the shields, as well as to the crosses with which the bodies of the roes or stags are ornamented.

ANALYSIS OF MYCENEAN METALS.

MR. P. EUSTRATIADES, the Director of the Antiquities of Greece, having kindly given me some specimens of the Mycenean metals, I thought I could not do better than submit them for analysis to the celebrated chemist and metallurgist, Dr. PERCY, in London, to whom I cannot adequately express my gratitude for his invaluable Report. I would especially direct the reader's attention to the evidence, which is suggested by the analysis, of the extensive use at Mycenæ of what is probably *native gold,*—to that use of *gold largely alloyed with silver* which, when carried somewhat further, produced the well-known *electrum,* of which I found several goblets in the ruins of prehistoric Troy,— and to the new light thrown on the question of the Homeric χαλκός (so largely discussed by Mr. Gladstone) by the proof that *both copper and bronze* were in use in the heroic age of Mycenæ, but that the weapons (and some of the vases) were of bronze, while the domestic utensils, such as kettles, were of copper. Thus the metal of a sword from one of the royal sepulchres contains a little more than 86 per cent. of copper and above 13 per cent. of tin, and that of a vase-handle contains nearly 90 per cent. of copper and above 10 of tin ; whereas that of a kettle contains 98·47 per cent. of copper, and a mere trace of tin. I would remind the reader that of the Trojan bronze battle-axes the one contained only 4 per cent., the second 8 per cent., and the third about 9 per cent., of tin.*

The course taken by Dr. Percy to effect the analysis is described in the following letter with which he has favoured me :—

DEAR DR. SCHLIEMANN,   London, August 10, 1877.

I have now the pleasure of communicating to you the results of the examination of the various specimens of metal which you placed in my hands for that purpose. A considerable time and very great care have been required to complete this work ; and I must ask you to be so good as to state that the analytical investigation, with two exceptions, has been wholly conducted by my able assistant, Mr. Richard Smith, in the Metal lurgical Laboratory of the Royal School of Mines, London. Mr. Smith, I can assure you, has laboured most earnestly and heartily in this investigation ; and whatever credit there may be is due to him. Some of the results are, I think, both novel and important, in a metallurgical as well as archæological point of view.

I remain, yours very truly,

JOHN PERCY, M.D., F.R.S.
Lecturer on Metallurgy at the Royal
School of Mines, London, &c.

Dr. SCHLIEMANN.

---

* See ' Troy and its Remains,' p. 361.

I.—ARGENTIFEROUS GOLD FOIL.   (No. 542.)

The whole of the specimen weighed 2·177 grains, and its thickness varied from 1-500th to 1-600th of an inch. It was one of those gold leaves which were found strewn in vast numbers about the bodies. It was much crumpled, of a reddish yellow colour, and both surfaces appeared as if they had been varnished or lacquered. A sketch of the specimen is annexed of the actual size. By heating, the metal becomes much paler in colour and assumes a greenish yellow tinge, a volatile substance, probably organic, being given off at the same time. The colour of the metal is not affected by digestion in warm alcohol, ether, or benzole ; but by boiling it in a strong aqueous solution of caustic potash, it loses its red tinge, and becomes paler, though not so pale as when heated.   1·168 grain of the metal, by cleaning with warm water, dilute hydrochloric acid, and finally gentle rubbing, lost 0·015 grain, which is equal to a loss of 1·28 per cent. The 1·153 grain of cleaned metal was submitted to analysis, with the following results :—

No. 542.
A piece of Argentiferous Gold Foil.
Sepulchre IV.   Actual size.

COMPOSITION PER CENT.

Gold	..	..	..	..	..	73·11
Silver	..	..	..	..	..	23·37
Copper	..	..	..	..	..	2·22
Lead	..	..	..	..	..	0·35
Iron	..	..	..	..	..	0·24

99·29

From the composition of the specimen it may be inferred that it was an artificial alloy, as the amount of copper and lead present is, so far as we know, much larger than has ever been found in " native gold " from any locality. The presence of the lead is probably owing to the fact of the silver used in preparing the alloy having been refined, though imperfectly, by means of lead. The large proportion of silver present may have been used to economise the gold. An alloy composed of 75 per cent. of gold and 25 per cent. of silver has a distinct gold-yellow colour ; but when the silver amounts to 33·33 per cent. the alloy is much paler in colour, and alloys containing more than about that proportion of silver would cease to be designated as gold ; the presence of copper would tend to counteract the paleness imparted by silver to gold.

The alteration in colour produced by heating the metal may possibly be due not only to the removal of a coating of organic matter from its surface, but also to the following action. It is well known that an alloy of silver and gold, which contains so much of the former metal as to resemble it in colour, may be made to acquire the colour of gold by superficially removing the silver. This may be effected by various processes, some of which, there is reason to believe, were known to the ancients. When such alloys of silver and gold as those above mentioned are heated to redness for a certain time, after having acquired superficially the colour of gold by any of the processes in question, they resume their original silvery colour. The large oval medal-like coins of the Japanese furnish an excellent illustration of this fact. Such a coin has been found in the Laboratory of the Royal School of Mines to consist of about two parts by weight of silver, and one part of gold. On heating such an alloy sufficiently, it becomes almost silver-white ; and on subsequently treating it with hot sulphuric acid the original golden colour is restored.

II.—SHEET GOLD. (No. 543.)

The total weight of the specimen was 1·702 grain, and its thickness was about 1-100th of an inch. Its specific gravity at 60° Fahr. was 18·867. Annexed is a sketch of the specimen, of the actual size. It was yellow, soft, ductile, and marked or indented on the surface, which appeared as though slightly tarnished. After cleaning with warm water, dilute hydrochloric acid, and gentle rubbing,

No. 543.
A piece of Sheet Gold. Sepulchre IV.
Actual size.

the metal weighed 1·698 grain, which is equal to a loss of 0·235 per cent. 1·4 grain of the cleaned metal was analysed with the following results :—

COMPOSITION PER CENT.

Gold	..	..	..	..	.. 89·36
Silver	..	..	..	..	.. 8·55
Copper	..	..	..	..	.. 0·57
Iron	..	..	..	..	.. 0·20

98·68

The absence of lead suggests that possibly the metal may have been native gold, or prepared with native gold, of which silver is always a constituent in varying proportions.

III.—PART OF A SILVER VASE.

A sketch of this, of the same size as the original, is annexed; it was distinctly curved, having formed part of a hollow thin vessel.

The total weight of the specimen was 44·36 grains. The metal was much corroded on both surfaces. The convex

544   545

Fragments of a Silver Vase. Sepulchre IV. Actual size.
No. 544. Convex Surface. No. 545. Concave Surface.

or outer surface was completely covered with a somewhat irregular crust while the concave or inner surface was only partly covered with a similar crust, and partly with a yellowish, tarnishlike film.

When broken across, the fractured surface of the crust on both sides of the metal was found to be in two distinct layers; that next the metal was black, dull, somewhat sectile, and easily broken; while the other, or outer layer, was light-grey, soft, sectile, and wax-like. In some places the metal was corroded completely through. The crust was removed by warm dilute ammonia-water and gentle rubbing; the residual metal was found to be very brittle, much pitted on the surface, dull white in fracture, granular, and containing minute irregular cavities; no appearance of fibre or crystalline structure was observed, even with the aid of the microscope. By annealing, the softness and malleability of the metal were restored in a marked degree. The thickness of the specimen, inclusive of the crust on one surface only, was 1-25th of an inch ; and where the crust was thickest it was 1-20th of an inch. The thickness of the metal, after the removal of the crust by dilute ammonia-water and rubbing, was 1-40th of an inch.

A portion of the specimen was selected for analysis to which the crust was attached on the convex or outer surface only, and which was comparatively free from crust on the opposite surface.; the quantity operated on was 15·786 grains. By repeated treatment with warm moderately strong ammonia-water, gentle rubbing, and washing with warm water, the crust was easily removed ; most of it being dissolved by the ammonia-water, which became pale blue, while the insoluble part was left as a brownish black powder, intermixed with some particles of metallic silver. The metal, after this treatment and drying, weighed 11·823 grains. The metal itself (*a*), the portion of the crust soluble in ammonia-water (*b*), and the residue insoluble in ammonia-water (*c*) were separately analysed, with the following results :-

COMPOSITION PER CENT.

(*a*) *Metal.*	Silver	71·60	
	Gold	0·22	
	Copper	2·42	
	Lead	0·33	
	Iron	0·09	
	Chlorine	traces	
			74·66
(*b*) *Crust.*			
Portion	Chloride of Silver	19·98	
soluble in	Protoxide of Copper }	0·56	
ammonia-water.	(Black Oxide) }		
	Chlorine	0·15	
	Copper	0·13	
	Sulphuric Acid	traces	
	Carbonic Acid }	1·15	
	Water }		
			21·97
(*c*) *Crust.*			
Portion	Gold	0·05	
insoluble in	Silver	1·36	
ammonia-water.	Protoxide of Copper }	0·09	
	(Black Oxide) }		
	Carbonate of Lime	1·36	
	Silica }		
	Peroxide of Iron }	0·30	
	Alumina }		3·16
			99·79

The composition per cent. of the metal, exclusive of the crust, as calculated from the above analysis, is given underneath ; but it certainly cannot be inferred that the original metal had the exact composition shown in that analysis, because some of the ingredients may not have been carried away during corrosion in the same relative proportions in which they were present in the original alloy.

COMPOSITION PER CENT.

Silver	95·59
Gold	0·30
Copper	3·23
Lead	0·44
Iron	0·12
	99·68

A portion of the crust when heated in a glass tube gave off water, and the glass was stained yellow.

A portion of the crust treated with dilute hydrochloric acid effervesced, the acid became pale blue, and was found to contain copper and lime.

The crust was examined under the microscope, but no trace of crystalline structure could be detected. A qualitative examination was made of a portion of the inner crust, from which it appeared that its composition was similar to that of the outer crust.

IV.—PORTION OF A BRONZE SWORD. (No. 546.)

The weight of the specimen, inclusive of the incrustation, was 585 grains ; it was about 1½ inch in length, and varied from about 5-8ths to 7-8ths of an inch in thickness. A sketch of a section of the specimen is annexed.

No. 546.
Piece of a Bronze Sword. Sepulchre IV. Dimensions stated in fractions of an inch.

The whole of the specimen was coated with an irregular layer or layers of matter, varying in chemical and physical characters and in thickness. In the centre, where the crust was removed, the solid metal varied from about 4-8ths to 5-8ths of an inch in thickness.

One side was chiefly incrusted with irregular patches of dull earthy non-crystalline matter, of varying shades of green and brown, which were found to consist of green carbonate and oxy-chloride of copper in different proportions ; a few minute pale green needle-like crystals were noticed on the other surface ; there were also observed irregular thin layers or patches of green (found to be green carbonate of copper, in some places containing more or less of oxychloride of copper) and blue crystals (found to be blue carbonate of copper) of varying tints and lustre. One end of the specimen was covered with a dark green crust with a velvety lustre, which was found to consist of minute transparent crystals of oxychloride of copper ; the opposite end, which was flat, and had the appearance of having been cut or rubbed, was chiefly coated with deep red non-crystalline red oxide of copper ; and a depression on the surface was lined with the dark green velvety crust ; on the edges, where the outer part of the crust had been broken off, was a dull white opaque layer of peroxide of tin, and on either side of it were layers of dark red compact red oxide of copper, having cavities here and there filled with ruby-red brilliant transparent crystals of the same substance. When the outer incrustation had been subsequently removed, these substances were found to extend more or less over the surface underneath.

The specimen was cut across in the centre when portions of the incrustation were detached ; by this means the structure of the specimen, and the nature of the substances forming the incrustation, could be well observed. The substances were generally found to occur in the following order, from within outwards.

I.—Solid metal.

II.—Particles of metal resembling filings, tarnished on the surface, and intermixed more or less with a dull greenish-grey substance, which was found to contain chlorine, copper, and tin.

III.—A pale green dull soft compact layer, which was found to consist chiefly of carbonate of copper, containing chlorine, probably in combination as oxychloride of copper, and a little peroxide of tin.

IV.—Red oxide of copper, varying in colour from brick-red to dark red, compact, dull and opaque, and in part crystalline.

V.—Peroxide of tin : examined under the microscope it was found to be veined with minute thin layers of red oxide of copper.

VI.—Red oxide of copper similar in character to No. IV.

VII.—Irregular patches of amorphous and crystalline substances of various shades of green, blue, and brown, as before described.

The above order of superposition was not always observed ; thus, in some places there was a layer of red oxide of copper in No. III.

When the incrustation had been removed by sawing the specimen across the middle, and filing, the metal was found to be very sound and free from cavities.   The fracture was yellowish copper red, and finely granular.

Portions of the solid metal perfectly free from incrustation were selected for analysis.

COMPOSITION PER CENT.

			I.		II.		Mean.
Copper	..	..	86·41	..	86·31	..	86·36
Tin ..	..	..	13·05	..	13·07	..	13·06
Lead	..	..	—	..	0·11	..	0·11
Iron ..	..	..	0·17	..	—	..	0·17
Nickel	..	..	0·15	..	—	..	0·15
Cobalt	..	..	traces	..	—	..	traces
							99·85

The specific gravity of the metal was 8·858 at 60° Fahr.

A portion of clean solid metal weighing 24·811 grains was employed for the experiment.

The substances forming the incrustation could not possibly be separated from each other with sufficient accuracy to allow of their being separately analysed.

V.—FRAGMENT OF A BRONZE VASE-HANDLE.

Sketches of this, of the actual size, are annexed (Nos. 547–549).   It is curved, and on the convex side there are three parallel indented lines, which doubtless were connected with ornamentation.   It was everywhere incrusted with the products of weathering action.   On the convex surface the prevailing colour was green, with here and there patches of grey and dark blue ; on the concave surface the incrustation was much thinner and more uniformly green. It is quite impossible to describe accurately in words these appearances. The portion analysed was freed by filing

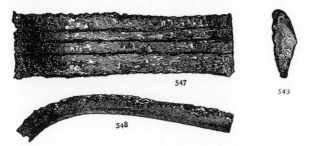

Nos. 547–549. Plan, side elevation, and end elevation, of a Bronze Handle of a Vase. Sepulchre IV. Actual size.

from incrusting matter. This analysis was made in the laboratory of the Royal School of Mines by Mr. W. F. Ward.

COMPOSITION PER CENT.

Copper	..	..	· ..	..	..	89·69
Tin	..	..	..	..	..	10·08
						99·77

This is the most usual composition of ancient bronze. The metal seems to have been exceptionally pure.

VI.—FRAGMENT OF A COPPER KETTLE.

FROM THE FOURTH SEPULCHRE.

This specimen was in a single piece, much crumpled, irregular in shape, and ragged at the edges ; it weighed about 800 grains, and varied from 1-25th to 1-30th of an inch in thickness. There were three rivets in the metal, the ends of which protruded on one side to the extent of about 1-8th of an inch ; and there was one rivet-hole without its rivet. After filing, the colour of the metal forming the rivet appeared to be the same as that of the sheet metal. There was no trace of the article which had been attached by means of those rivets. On one surface the specimen seems originally to have been pretty generally encrusted with blue and green matter, between which and the metal was, as usual, a thin coating of red oxide of copper ; on the other surface, or that showing the protruding ends of the rivets, the metal was coated first with the red oxide of copper and then with dark greenish brown matter, with here and there patches varying from light green to dark blue and dark green, especially round the ends of the rivets.

Portions of the sheet metal were heated to redness in a current of hydrogen, whereby they acquired a coppery colour and lustre. The water evolved in this process was found to contain both copper and chlorine, thus indicating the existence of oxychloride of copper in the incrusting matter, a portion of the subchloride of copper (cuprous chloride) having escaped decomposition by the hydrogen. A piece of the metal, free from incrustation, was boiled in a flask containing hydrochloric acid and perchloride of iron, and the vapour evolved was passed into a refrigerating vessel, when a liquid was obtained in which arsenic was found in considerable quantity. This process was used for the quantitative determination of the arsenic as ammoniacal arseniate of magnesia, and the result was confirmed by several repetitions. The metal taken for analysis was that which had been heated in hydrogen as stated above. The analysis was made in the laboratory of the Royal School of Mines by Mr. W. F. Ward.

COMPOSITION PER CENT.

Copper	98·47
Tin	0·09
Lead	0·16
Bismuth	traces
Silver	0·013
Iron	0·03
Nickel	0·19
Arsenic	0·83
	99·783

INDEX.

THE END.

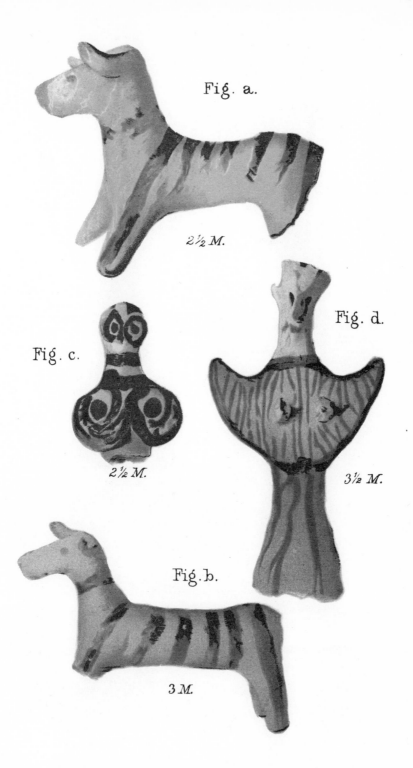

Fig. a.

2½ M.

Fig. c.

2½ M.

Fig. d.

Fig. b.

3½ M.

3 M.

TERRA-COTTA COWS AND IDOLS FOUND AT TIRYNS.
Size 3:4.

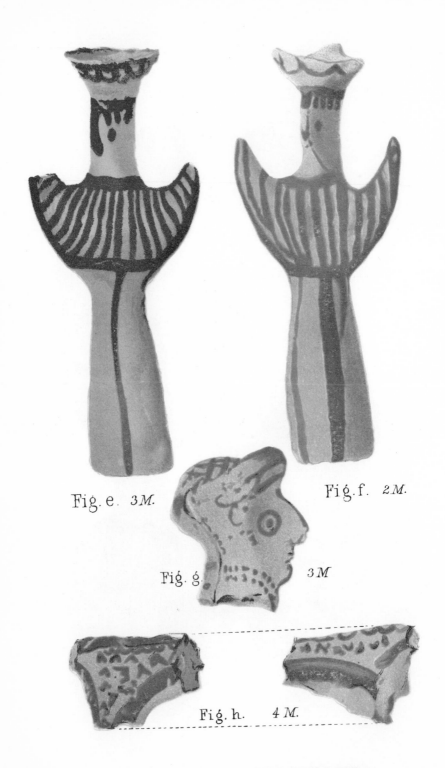

Fig. e. 3M.

Fig. f. 2M.

Fig. g. 3M

Fig. h. 4M.

TERRA-COTTA IDOLS FROM MYCENÆ.
Actual Size.

Plate C.

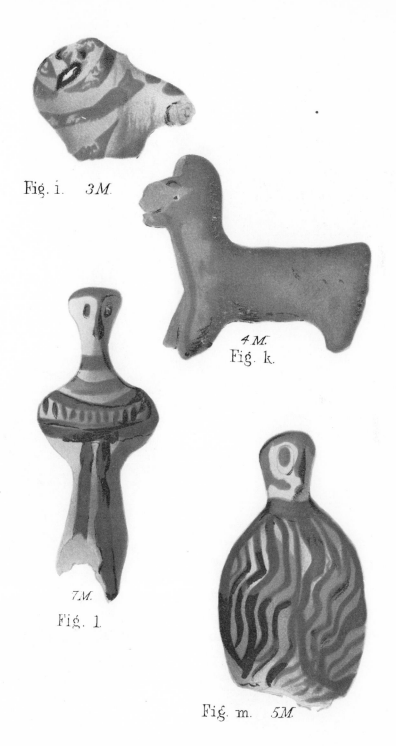

Fig. i. *3M.*

4 M.
Fig. k.

7.M.
Fig. l

Fig. m. *5M.*

TERRA-COTTA IDOLS, COW, &c. FROM MYCENÆ.
Actual Size.

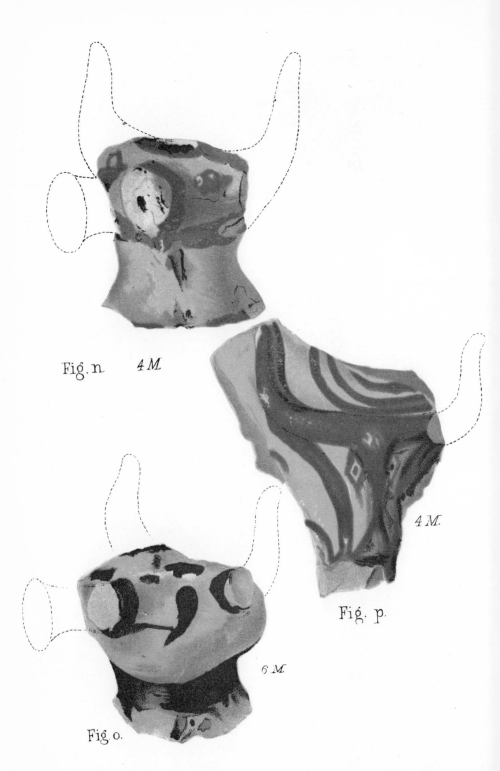

Fig. n.   4 M.

4 M.

Fig. p.

6 M.

Fig. o.

FRAGMENTS OF TERRA-COTTA COW-HEADED IDOLS, FROM MYCENÆ.
Actual Size.

PLATE VIII

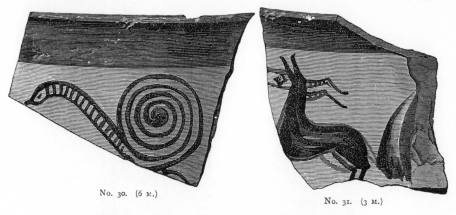

No. 30. (6 M.)

No. 31. (3 M.)

No. 32. (3 M.)

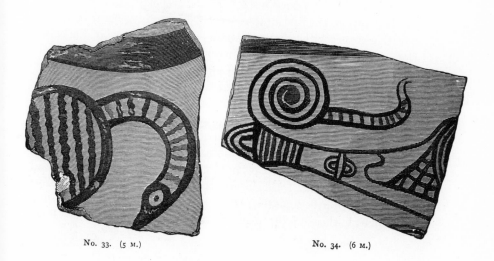

No. 33. (5 M.)

No. 34. (6 M.)

Nos. 30—34. FRAGMENTS OF PAINTED VASES FROM MYCENÆ.
Some actual size, and some reduced.

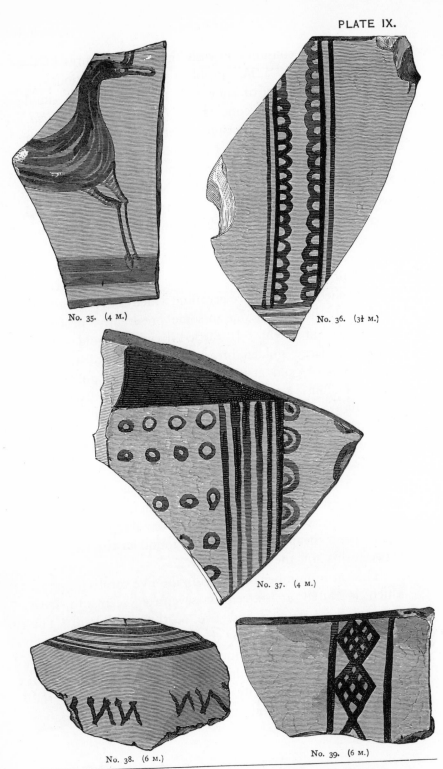

PLATE IX.

No. 35. (4 M.)

No. 36. (3¼ M.)

No. 37. (4 M.)

No. 38. (6 M.)

No. 39. (6 M.)

Nos. 35—39. FRAGMENTS OF PAINTED VASES FROM MYCENÆ.
Some actual size, and some reduced.

PLATE X.

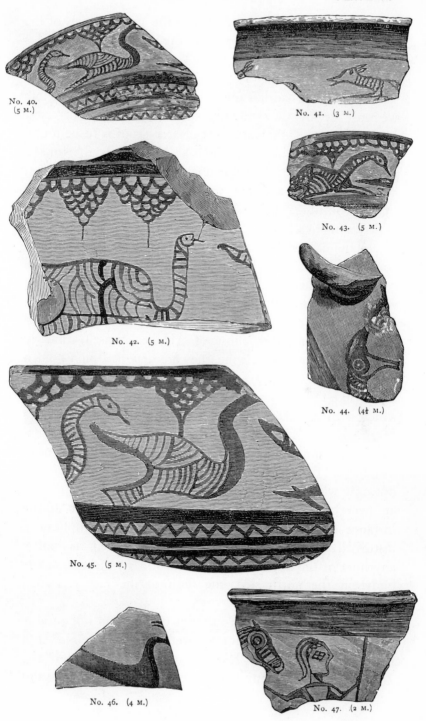

No. 40. (5 M.)

No. 41. (3 M.)

No. 42. (5 M.)

No. 43. (5 M.)

No. 44. (4¼ M.)

No. 45. (5 M.)

No. 46. (4 M.)

No. 47. (2 M.)

Nos. 40—47. Fragments of Painted Vases from Mycenæ.
Some actual size, and some reduced.

PLATE XI.

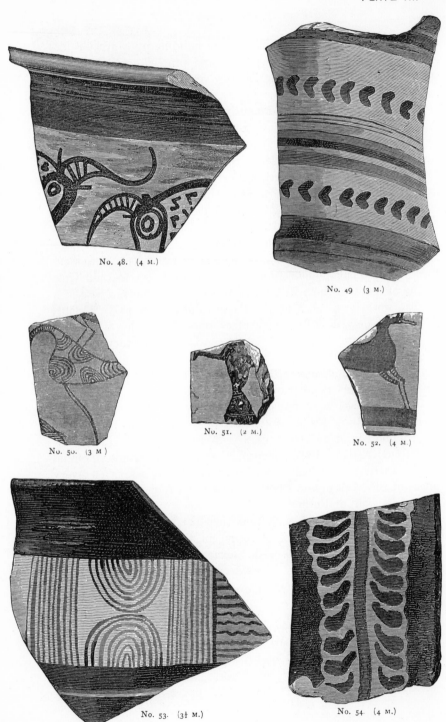

No. 48. (4 M.)

No. 49 (3 M.)

No. 50. (3 M.)

No. 51. (2 M.)

No. 52. (4 M.)

No. 53. (3½ M.)

No. 54. (4 M.)

Nos. 48—54. FRAGMENTS OF PAINTED VASES FROM MYCENÆ.
Some actual size, and some reduced.

PLATE XII.

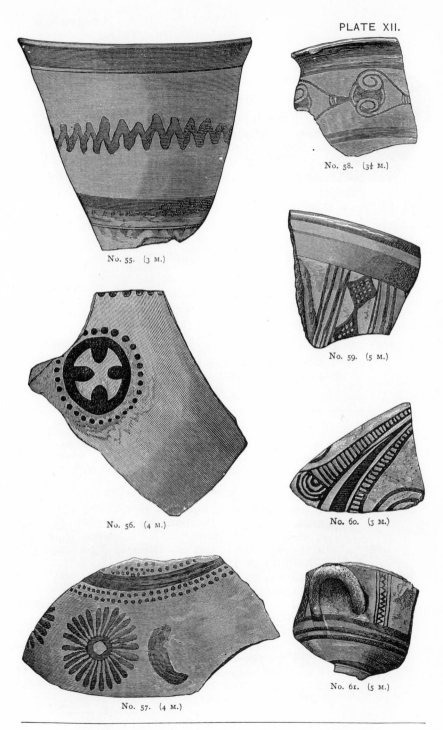

No. 55. (3 M.)

No. 58. (3½ M.)

No. 56. (4 M.)

No. 59. (5 M.)

No. 60. (5 M.)

No. 57. (4 M.)

No. 61. (5 M.)

Nos. 55—61.   Fragments of Painted Vases from Mycenæ.
Some actual size, and some reduced.

PLATE XIII.

No. 62. (4 M.)

No. 63. (5 M.)

No. 64. (6 M.)

No. 66. (5 M.)

No. 65. (4 M.)

No. 67. (5 M.)

NOS. 62—67. FRAGMENTS OF PAINTED VASES FROM MYCENÆ.
Some actual size, and some reduced.

PLATE XIV.

No. 68. (2 M.)

No. 69. (6 M.

No. 70. (5 M.)

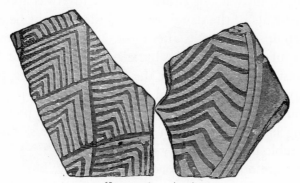

Nos. 71 and 72. (5 M.)

Nos. 68—72. Fragments of Painted Vases from Mycenæ.
Some actual size, and some reduced.

PLATE XV.

No. 73. (2 M.)

No. 74. (5 M.)

No. 75. (2 M.)

No. 76. (5 M.)

No 77. (5 M.)

No. 78. (5 M.)

Nos. 73—78. Fragments of Painted Vases from Mycenæ.
Some actual size, and some reduced.

PLATE XVI.

No. 90. (4¼ M.)

No. 91. (6 M.)

No. 92. (6 M.)

No. 93. (3¼ M.)

NOS. 90—93. TERRA-COTTA IDOLS. *Actual size.*

PLATE XVII.

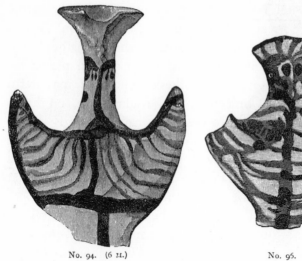

No. 94. (6 M.)   No. 95. (5 M.)

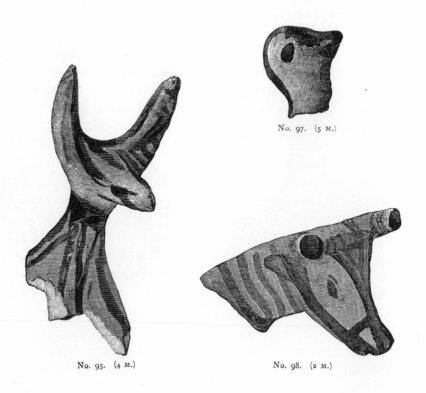

No. 97. (5 M.)

No. 95. (4 M.)   No. 98. (2 M.)

NOS. 94–98. TERRA-COTTA IDOLS. *Actual size.*

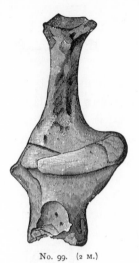

PLATE XVIII.

No. 99. (2 M.)

No. 100. (8 M.)

No. 101. (8 M.)

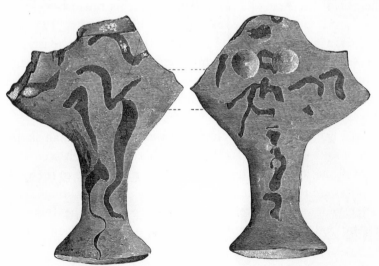

No. 102. (5¼ M.)

NOS. 99—102. TERRA-COTTA IDOLS. *Actual size.*

PLATE XIX.

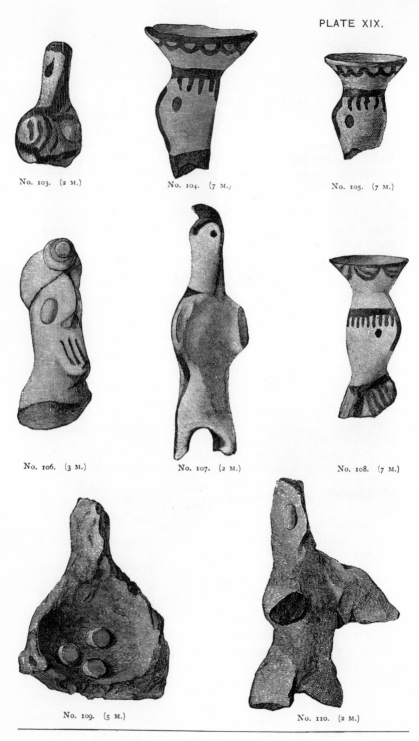

No. 103. (2 M.)

No. 104. (7 M.)

No. 105. (7 M.)

No. 106. (3 M.)

No. 107. (2 M.)

No. 108. (7 M.)

No. 109. (5 M.)

No. 110. (2 M.)

Nos. 103—110. Terra-Cotta Idols. *Actual size.*

PLATE XX.

No. 192. (5 M.)

No. 193. (5 M.)

No. 194. (5 M.)

No. 195. (5 M.)

No. 196. (6 M.)

No. 197. (3 M.)

NOS. 192—197. FRAGMENTS OF PAINTED POTTERY FROM THE APPROACH TO
THE TREASURY NEAR THE LIONS' GATE. *Half-size.*

PLATE XXI.

No. 198. (2 M.)

No. 202. (2 M.)

No. 199. (5 M.)

No. 203. (3 M.)

No. 200. (5 M.)

No. 201. (2 M.)

No. 204. (8 M.)

NOS. 198—204. FRAGMENTS OF PAINTED POTTERY FROM THE APPROACH TO
THE TREASURY NEAR THE LIONS' GATE. *Half-size.*

PLAN A.

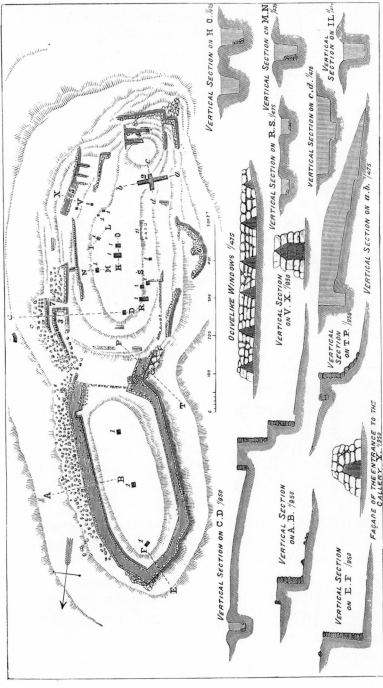

THE ACROPOLIS OF TIRYNS.

ₓ, 1.—Shafts sunk by Dr. Schliemann.
   2.—Trench dug by the same.
   3.—The Tower.

4.— Ruins of two parallel ogive-like Galleries.
5.— Ogive-like Gallery.

6.—Ogive-like Gallery.
7.—Gateway to the Acropolis.

Note.—(1) The letters A, B, &c., indicate the lines along which the appended Sections are taken.
        (2) To each Vertical Section is appended its exact proportional scale.

PLAN B.

THE CIRCULAR AGORA, WITH THE FIVE ROYAL SEPULCHRES, IN THE ACROPOLIS OF MYCENÆ.

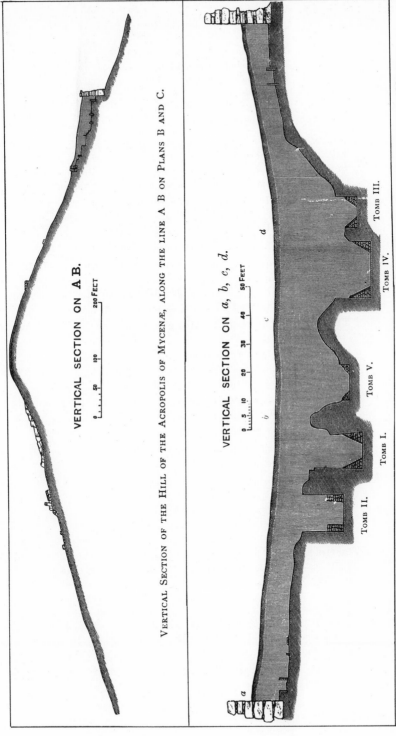

PLAN B B.

VERTICAL SECTION ON A B.

0   50   100   200 FEET

VERTICAL SECTION OF THE HILL OF THE ACROPOLIS OF MYCENÆ, ALONG THE LINE A B ON PLANS B AND C.

VERTICAL SECTION ON *a*, *b*, *c*, *d*.

0 5 10   20   30   40   50 FEET

TOMB III.

TOMB IV.

TOMB V.

TOMB I.

TOMB II.

VERTICAL SECTION SHOWING THE DEPTHS OF THE FIVE TOMBS BELOW THE LOWER TERRACE OF THE ACROPOLIS OF MYCENÆ.

Plan of the
ACROPOLIS OF MYCENAE
WITH THE EXCAVATIONS
made by
Dr HENRY SCHLIEMANN
by *Vasilios Drosinos*
Lieutenant of Engineers

Metres

English Feet

For line et section. A–B see Plan B.B.

THE LIONS & DOOR DETAILS IN 1:50 SEE PLAN X.

For Dr Schliemann's excavations enclosed
within figures I to IX see Plan B.

EXPLANATION OF PLANS B AND C.

Note.—PLAN B *shows the Excavations of Dr. Schliemann in the Acropolis, of which* PLAN C *gives c. General Plan.*

I. II. III. IV. V.—Cyclopean Walls of the Inner Enclosure, dividing the Agora and the adjacent Buildings from the rest of the Acropolis.

VI. VII. VIII. IX.— Part of the Cyclopean Circuit Wall which encloses the whole Citadel.

a, a, a.—Double Circle of Slabs, forming the enclosure and Bench of the Agora (A A A on Plan C).

b, b, b.—Wall supporting the same in the lower part of the Acropolis.

A, A, A.—Cyclopean Houses.

B, B, B.—Cyclopean Cisterns.

P.—Sepulchral Recess, where Gold Ornaments were found.

No. 6.—Ruins of a large Quadrangular Tower.

(*On* PLAN C *only.*)

M, N.—Traces of the ancient winding Street, which led to the Lions' Gate.

1, 1, 1.—Shafts sunk by Dr. Schliemann.

4—Cyclopean Buildings.

5.—Cisterns.

8.—Treasury outside of the Lions' Gate.

DOTTED SECTIONAL LINES.

A B.—Line of the Vertical Section of the Acropolis (see Plan B B, upper part).

a', b', c', d'.—Lines of the Vertical Section through the Tombs (see Plan B B, lower part).

Plan of the whole
CITY OF MYCENAE
by *Vasilios Drosinos*
Lieutenant of Engineers

Metres

English Feet

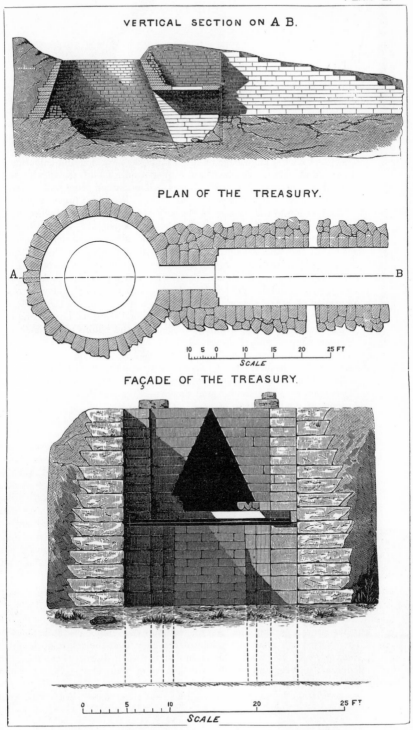

VERTICAL SECTION ON A B.

PLAN OF THE TREASURY.

A   B

10 5 0   10   15   20   25 FT.

SCALE

FAÇADE OF THE TREASURY.

0   5   10   20   25 FT.

SCALE

FAÇADE, PLAN, AND SECTION OF THE TREASURY NEAR THE LIONS' GATE.

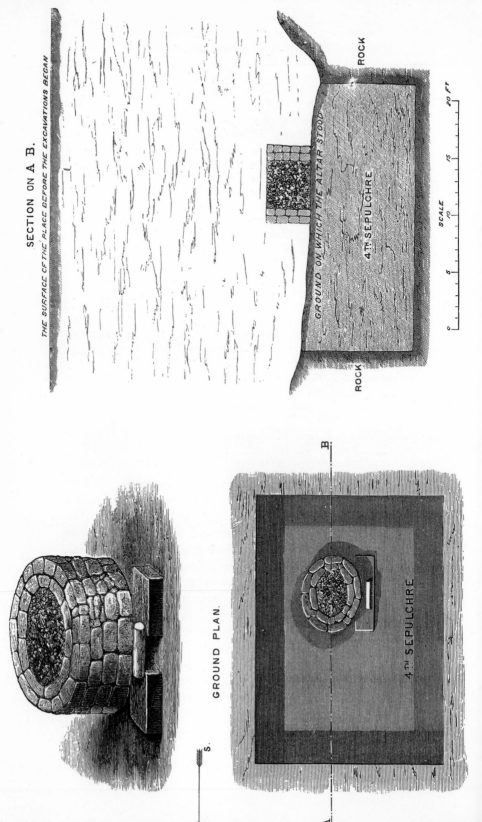

PLAN F.

SECTION ON A B.

THE SURFACE OF THE PLACE BEFORE THE EXCAVATIONS BEGAN

GROUND ON WHICH THE ALTAR STOOD

ROCK

ROCK

4.TH SEPULCHRE

SCALE

0   5   10   15   20 FT

GROUND PLAN.

N.

S.

4.TH SEPULCHRE

A.

B.

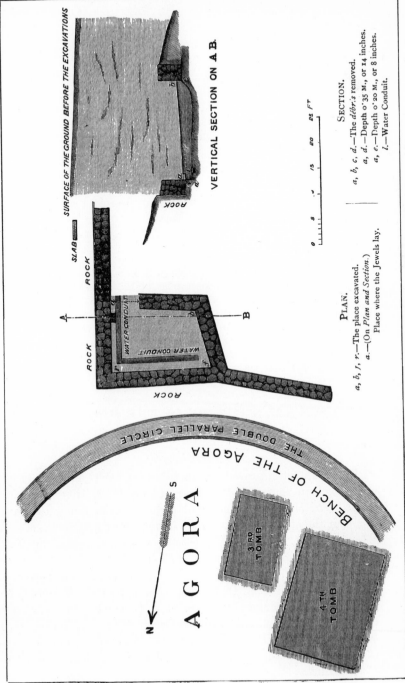

PLAN G.

SURFACE OF THE GROUND BEFORE THE EXCAVATIONS

SLAB

ROCK

ROCK

ROCK

WATER-CONDUIT

WATER CONDUIT

ROCK

A

B

VERTICAL SECTION ON A. B.

0 5 10 15 20 25 FT

BENCH OF THE PARALLEL CIRCLE

THE DOUBLE

AGORA

N

S

3 RD TOMB

4 TH TOMB

PLAN.

a, b, J, r.—The place excavated.
a.—(On *Plan and Section.*)
Place where the Jewels lay.

SECTION.

a, b, c, d.—The *débris* removed.
a, d.—Depth 0·35 M., or 14 inches.
a, e.—Depth 0·20 M., or 8 inches.
l.—Water Conduit.

PLAN AND SECTION OF THE TOMB SOUTH OF THE AGORA, IN THE ACROPOLIS OF MYCENÆ.